CONSTITUTIONAL AMENDMENT IN CANADA

The Constitution Act, 1982, contains the amending formula that outlines distinct procedures required to make changes to the Canadian Constitution. Recent debates over Senate reform, the status of the Supreme Court of Canada, and the rules governing royal succession have highlighted how important the amending formula is in maintaining the vitality and relevance of the governing system.

   Constitutional Amendment in Canada is the first volume to focus solely on the implications of the amending formula in Canada. Emmett Macfarlane has brought together a group of experts to address such topics as the difficulties of constitutional reform, the intersection of various levels of government and the judiciary, and the ability of the public to veto proposed changes. Filling a serious gap in the literature, *Constitutional Amendment in Canada* is an authoritative study of the historical and contemporary implications of the amending formula.

EMMETT MACFARLANE is an assistant professor of political science at the University of Waterloo. He is a regular contributor to *Maclean's*, the *Globe and Mail*, and the Institute for Research on Public Policy's *Policy Options*.

Constitutional Amendment in Canada

EDITED BY EMMETT MACFARLANE

UNIVERSITY OF TORONTO PRESS
Toronto Buffalo London

© University of Toronto Press 2016
Toronto Buffalo London
www.utppublishing.com

ISBN 978-1-4426-4049-8 (cloth)   ISBN 978-1-4426-2873-1 (paper)

Library and Archives Canada Cataloguing in Publication

Constitutional amendment in Canada / edited by Emmett Macfarlane.

Includes bibliographical references and index.
ISBN 978-1-4426-4049-8 (cloth). – ISBN 978-1-4426-2873-1 (paper)

1. Canada. Constitution Act, 1982.   2. Constitutional amendments –
Canada.   I. Macfarlane, Emmett, author, editor

KE4228 C65 2016   342.7103   C2016-902511-X
KF4483 A4 C65

This book has been published with the help of a grant from the
Federation for the Humanities and Social Sciences, through the
Awards to Scholarly Publications Program, using funds provided by
the Social Sciences and Humanities Research Council of Canada.

University of Toronto Press acknowledges the financial assistance to
its publishing program of the Canada Council for the Arts and the
Ontario Arts Council, an agency of the Government of Ontario.

Canada Council   Conseil des Arts
for the Arts   du Canada

ONTARIO ARTS COUNCIL
CONSEIL DES ARTS DE L'ONTARIO
an Ontario government agency
un organisme du gouvernement de l'Ontario

Funded by the   Financé par le
Government   gouvernement
of Canada   du Canada

Canadä

For Anna

Contents

Acknowledgments

In the spring of 2014, following the release of two Supreme Court of Canada reference opinions that involved the constitutional amending formula – Part V of the Constitution Act, 1982 – I decided to write a paper on the implications of this new jurisprudence for potential future changes to the Canadian Constitution. An idea for a conference panel on the topic emerged before that paper was written, and by the time the panel met at the July 2014 meeting of the International Political Science Association in Montreal, the idea for this book had crystallized.

As the introductory chapter to this volume notes, surprisingly little has been written about the amending formula – as distinct from the much broader topic of constitutional reform, or even compared to the great amount of ink spilled on the historical debates leading up to the formula's entrenchment in 1982. This book approaches the subject from an interdisciplinary perspective, bringing together political science and legal views to examine the law and politics of the amending formula. My hope is that it stands as the most comprehensive examination of the topic in Canada to date, with the added hope that it will spur even deeper scholarly examination of constitutional amendment in the future.

This project would not have been possible without the work and support of a great number of people. First and foremost, I would like to thank the contributors to this volume. Horror stories abound about the administrative headaches and snail-like pace of editing collections, but thanks to this wonderful group of contributors I could not have had a more rewarding experience.

I am also grateful to Dan Quinlan and the editorial team at the University of Toronto Press for so smoothly ushering this volume through the publishing process, and to the anonymous peer reviewers for their helpful feedback. My thanks to Barry Norris for his valuable copy-editing work. Material for my chapter on the Senate first appeared in the *McGill Law Journal*, and I am grateful for the use of that material and to the peer reviewers of that article.

A special word of thanks to my friends and colleagues at the University of Waterloo. I would especially like to thank Anna Esselment and Dan Henstra, who were subjected to frequent, unsolicited updates on the project's progress.

Finally, this book would not have been possible without the support of my family. My thanks to my parents and sister for their continued support, and to Anna, the best spouse I could ever hope to ask for.

CONSTITUTIONAL AMENDMENT IN CANADA

Introduction
Striking a Balance: The Players and Procedures of Canada's Constitutional Amending Formula

EMMETT MACFARLANE

Following years of effort to reform the Senate by ordinary statute, the federal Conservative government referred a series of questions to the Supreme Court of Canada in 2013. Having attempted to introduce term limits for senators and consultative elections as an element of the appointments process, the government finally sought an answer to the ongoing debate over whether a constitutional amendment was required. That same year, the constitutional status of the Court itself and the eligibility rules for its members became the subject of its own reference, following a legal challenge to the prime minister's appointment of a Federal Court judge to one of the "Quebec seats" on the Court. And changes to the rules for royal succession also raised the question of whether a formal constitutional amendment was required in that context.[1] Suddenly, the process by which the Canadian Constitution is changed was at the forefront of a number of major institutional debates. The first two of these issues resulted in ground-breaking reference opinions issued by the Supreme Court in 2014, the first time the Court has substantively addressed the constitutional amending formula, Part V of the Constitution Act, 1982 in its jurisprudence.[2]

In both opinions, the Court effectively blocked Parliament from implementing unilateral changes. In the *Supreme Court Act Reference*, the majority found that the eligibility requirements for Supreme Court appointees are part of the "composition of the Supreme Court," and thus changes to them require the unanimous consent of the provinces. In so doing, the Court effectively entrenched certain elements of the Supreme Court Act in the Constitution. In the *Senate Reform Reference*, the Court determined unanimously that both a proposed consultative elections process for senatorial appointments and term limits for senators require the consent of at least two-thirds of the provinces representing at least 50 per cent of the population under the general amending formula. In so doing, the Court minimized the scope of Parliament's authority to implement changes to the Senate unilaterally.

A constitution can be understood as the framework or "rules of the game" for the operation of a country's institutions and the exercise of state power. Determining who sets those rules and the processes by which they are changed is of paramount importance. The constitutional amending formula – which outlines distinct procedures for amending different aspects of the constitution – is central to ensuring the continued vitality and relevance of the broader system of government. A constitution should not be too easy to change because the binding principles enunciated within it represent the highest law in the land and, in certain respects, such as in the case of a bill of rights, the entrenchment of a society's deepest values. Yet neither should a constitution be too difficult to change when there is deep and broad consensus about needed reform, particularly to ensure the continued relevance of rules and institutions as a society and its governance evolve. In a federation such as Canada, the consent of the provinces to major changes affecting them is clearly an important factor.

Given the breadth of scholarly focus on the Constitution Act, 1982, it is surprising how little attention has been paid to the amending formula – the very part that "patriated" the Constitution from the final control of the United Kingdom; indeed, arguably, Canada did not become fully sovereign until 1982, when Part V of the Constitution Act gave it full control over future changes to its own Constitution. Yet relative to the other main components of the Act – specifically, the Charter of Rights and Freedoms and the Aboriginal and treaty rights embedded in section 35 – the amending formula has been seriously understudied. As David Smith notes, this is all the more striking because an amending formula was the primary impetus for the negotiations that led to 1982.[3]

Most commentary on post-1982 constitutional amendment in Canada has centred on the failed attempts at major constitutional reform, particularly the Meech Lake and Charlottetown accords.[4] These processes were so embedded in attempts to repair the perceived damage to the legitimacy of the Constitution among some in Quebec following that province's refusal to "sign on" to the 1982 agreement, and both comprised such varied and substantial reform, that the amending formula itself has been largely overlooked. Indeed, if there is a meaningful distinction between constitutional reform and constitutional amendment – where the former refers to "broad-based packages of amendments" and the latter specifically to the rules governing constitutional change[5] – the amending formula clearly has received far less scholarly attention. Only two book-length studies pertain directly to the amending formula: a 1996 federal government publication written by senior civil servant James Ross Hurley that examines the history and processes around amendment, and a 1996 legal text by Benoît Pelletier.[6]

The controversies in the 1980s and 1990s over constitutional reform highlight the importance of renewed attention to Part V, the amending formula of the Constitution Act, 1982. *Constitutional Amendment in Canada* thus aims to fill the gap in scholarly analysis of the political and legal implications of the amending formula, and addresses a number of important themes relevant to constitution-making, judicial power, intergovernmental relations, and democracy. As commentators have routinely observed, a central concern of the amending formula is to ensure both stability and flexibility.[7] Thus, a central feature of this book is its examination of Canada's experience with constitutional amendment to determine if the procedures in Part V set too high a threshold for successful change and if the political culture surrounding the Constitution renders it even more difficult to make amendments – something Richard Albert has described as "constructive unamendability."[8] In the comparative context, Albert argues that Canada's might be one of the most difficult constitutions to amend in the world.[9] The question of whether Canada suffers from constitutional stasis in this regard has important legal and political implications across a number of pressing institutional and governmental issues, including Senate reform, changes to the appointments process for the Supreme Court of Canada, potential reform of the Crown, the division of powers, and the addition of new rights to the Charter of Rights and Freedoms.

Another important component of this volume's analysis is its assessment of the Supreme Court's role in interpreting the scope of Part V, as a broad interpretation of its particular provisions could raise the threshold of consensus required for certain types of changes. In addition to the two reference opinions noted above, the Court has enunciated constitutional principles with implications for constitutional change in decisions such as the 1998 *Quebec Secession Reference*.[10] The judiciary's role in interpreting the amending formula means the Court itself wields tremendous power, as it ultimately sets the conditions for political actors to follow, determining not only which issues fall under the various amending procedures listed in Part V but also their scope. The Court's 2014 opinions have directly affected the balance between flexibility and rigidity with respect to constitutional change, as they suggest that Parliament is unable to effect certain institutional changes on its own – such as the eligibility requirements for Supreme Court justices – something not necessarily obvious in certain areas prior to those rulings.

Finally, the book explores the actors and politics surrounding the process of amending the Constitution. As Alan Cairns has noted, the amending formula Canada arrived at in 1982, with its procedures centred on legislative ratification, is representative of the old "governments' constitution," in which executive federalism and legislatures were privileged over the newer "citizens' constitution," which, as represented in the Charter of Rights and Freedoms, emphasizes grassroots participation.[11] Questions about who is permitted to participate in the process of constitutional amendment are thus fundamental.

Part V: The Players, the Procedures, and the Issues

Part V of the Constitution Act, 1982 includes at least five procedures – and possibly more, depending on how they are counted – for amending the Constitution.[12] The general procedure of section 38 – also known as the 7/50 rule – requires resolutions of the Senate and House of Commons and of the legislative assemblies of at least two-thirds of the provinces representing at least 50 per cent of the population. Provinces are free to opt out of amendments that affect their powers or rights. Section 40 mandates that the federal government provide compensation to provinces that opt out of an amendment that transfers powers from the province to Parliament relating to education or cultural matters. Section 41, the unanimity procedure, requires the approval of the Senate and House of Commons and all provincial legislatures over specific matters, such as the office of the Queen or the composition of the Supreme Court. Section 42 outlines specific matters that fall under the general amending procedure. Section 43 states that any amendments that apply to one or more provinces but not to all may be passed by resolutions of the Senate and House of Commons and the legislatures of those provinces to which the amendment applies. Section 44 permits Parliament alone to make changes relating to the executive government of Canada or the Senate and House of Commons. Section 45 permits each province to make changes relating to its own provincial constitution. Section 47 provides the Senate a suspensive veto in relation to sections 38, 41, 42, and 43, meaning that any resolution not adopted by the Senate can be overridden by the House of Commons after 180 days.

It seems inevitable that this complex set of amending procedures would require judicial interpretation to determine their scope and limits. Indeed, the fact that it took over thirty years for the Supreme Court to be confronted with doing so reflects the Canadian political class's avoidance of major constitutional change since the early 1990s.

Who Has a Say?

The complex procedures outlined in Part V reflect the decades-long struggle of the federal government and the provinces to reach an agreement, as Nadia Verrelli explores in Chapter 1. As noted above, the amending formula's design privileges the legislative bodies of the federal and provincial orders of government to the exclusion of a more populist mandate, such as ratification by referendum – although some might argue that the Charlottetown Accord process established a convention that Canadians be consulted via referendum on constitutional changes, this is contested – or of the explicit consent of Canada's Indigenous and francophone populations. There is a coherence to this design, ordered around "the federal principle," as Carissima Mathen explores in Chapter 3. Yet it remains a contested vision of federalism in important ways, particularly with respect to Quebec's demands for special status, but also in the difficulties in sorting out the dividing line or overall balance among Part V's various procedures.

The final version of the amending formula was negotiated in the aftermath of the Supreme Court's decision in the *Patriation Reference*,[13] in which the Court determined that then-prime minister Pierre Trudeau could legally seek the unilateral patriation of the Constitution from the UK Parliament, but that, by convention, major changes to the Constitution required a "substantial" degree of provincial consent. Peter Hogg writes that the patriation of the Constitution clarified the roles of the federal and provincial governments in the amending process, and that the "vague and unsatisfactory rules laid down by the Supreme Court of Canada in the *Patriation Reference* have accordingly been supplanted and have no current relevance."[14] Yet the Court's *Patriation* opinion led to what many critics regard as one of the biggest problems emanating from the final agreement in 1982 and the composition of Part V itself. As Smith writes,

agreement on a domestic amending formula, which for its method of calculation treats all provinces, including Quebec, as equal – came at the cost of disguising the essence of the Canadian federation. At one time the compact theory – that is, Confederation is the product of the uniting provinces, and any change to its terms requires the assent of the same provinces – was a levelling theory (for those who held it) that applied to all provinces, including Quebec. Over the last thirty years a division has arisen that sets Quebec apart from the other provinces ... The source of the change lay in the Supreme Court's opinion in the patriation reference ... Patriation invalidated existing assumptions about constitutional amendment. The new formula subsequently agreed upon by all first ministers, except Quebec's, could not logically revert to a unanimous rule analogous to the old compact theory.[15]

Samuel LeSelva similarly writes that both the *Patriation Reference* and the *Quebec Veto Reference*[16] "contain tragic elements, in that the court failed to grant to French Canadians the federal comity that underlies Confederation."[17] Thus, for some critics, Part V does not so much supplant the Court's unsatisfactory rules as it entrenches them. Nevertheless, there is a legitimate debate to be had about whether Canadian federalism, even with its myriad special provisions relating to Quebec's distinctive legal system and culture, is properly understood as requiring that province's right to a veto over constitutional change. Smith's articulation of the compact theory makes the principle of provincial equality clear, but also transforms it into a rule of unanimity for constitutional change – something provincial equality need not necessarily mean and, in the case of several important amendments implemented without any provincial consent before patriation, was not always a principle all major players in Confederation acknowledged.

This volume will not settle the historical debate. Indeed, its chapters focus less on the debate about what Part V might have been and more on the political and legal implications of the existing formula. Chapters 7 and 8, however, explore Quebec's ability to effect constitutional change with regard to its own unique status. Importantly, with respect to the question of a Quebec veto, recent jurisprudence on Part V might have consequences for the federal regional veto act,[18] passed in the immediate aftermath of the 1995 referendum on sovereignty. The Act prohibits government ministers from proposing constitutional resolutions unless consent is first obtained from Ontario, Quebec, British Columbia, and majorities in the prairie and Atlantic regions (in effect also giving Alberta its own veto). Rainer Knopff examines the regional veto act and the debate over its constitutionality in detail in Chapter 6.

Notably, in Chapter 9, Dennis Baker and Mark Jarvis question whether the Act might now be regarded as an entrenched element of the Constitution, following the Supreme Court's decision to embody at least part of the Supreme Court Act in the *Supreme Court Act Reference*. By contrast, in Chapter 11, I raise the question of whether the Court's logic in the *Senate Reform Reference* might mean that the regional veto law is unconstitutional.

Is It Too Difficult to Amend the Constitution?

Since the failure of the Charlottetown Accord, it is common to portray Canada as suffering from constitutional fatigue. Since then, fear of "opening the Constitution" has become a dominant narrative when issues of reform arise.[19] In part, this perceived difficulty applies specifically to broad, sweeping reforms, and some scholars suggest the solution could be simply to focus on amendments of a more specific nature.[20]

Notably, there have been a number of constitutional amendments since 1982, most of which were adopted under the bilateral procedure of section 43 (see Chapter 7, by Dwight Newman). These include adding section 16(1) to the Charter of Rights and Freedoms, which installed protections of equal status for the anglophone and francophone communities in New Brunswick, allowing a fixed-link bridge to replace the constitutionally required ferry services to Prince Edward Island, replacing church-based education in Newfoundland and Labrador, allowing Quebec to replace its denominational schools, and changing the name of Newfoundland to Newfoundland and Labrador. Parliament has also enacted unilateral amendments under section 44, including changing the formula for apportioning seats in the House of Commons and granting the newly created territory of Nunavut representation in the Senate (for more on section 44, see Chapter 5, by Warren Newman).

These amendments make it clear that very specific measures relevant only to certain provinces or aspects of federal institutions are possible under the relevant amending procedures of Part V. At a basic level, then, they demonstrate that Part V does not render the Constitution completely frozen in time. However, only one post-1982 amendment has involved the general amending procedure under section 38, and that was the result of a constitutionally mandated conference in 1983 that sought to better define the meaning of existing Aboriginal rights in section 35 (for more on section 35 and constitutional amendment, see

Chapter 4, by Christa Scholtz). The conference was largely unsuccessful at reaching consensus on this goal, but it did result in several more minor amendments recognizing modern land-claims agreements as "treaty rights" under section 35, that Aboriginal and treaty rights apply equally to male and female persons, and the principle that the federal and provincial governments will hold a constitutional conference and that Aboriginal representatives will take part in discussions before any constitutional amendments are implemented relating to Aboriginal and treaty rights or to section 25 of the Charter.

This record over the course of more than thirty years does not make it easy to draw any straightforward conclusion about whether Part V imposes too high a threshold for major constitutional amendments. Although there have been a fairly high number of amendments over that period, their relatively minor nature – coupled with the failure of Meech and Charlottetown, the only two attempts at major constitutional reform – suggest that the dividing line between the different procedures in Part V is especially important.

The Supreme Court has played a fundamental role both in the development of Part V, in large part due to the *Patriation Reference*, and also now, over three decades later, in shaping the meaning and application of several of the amending procedures (for a closer examination of the Court's jurisprudence relating to constitutional amendment, see Chapter 2, by Adam Dodek). The implications of the Court's opinions in the *Senate Reform* and *Supreme Court Act References* should not be overstated, but the analyses in this volume make it clear that the potential for constitutional stasis as it relates to significant reform in Canada is real. The book's contributors tackle this key issue in the context of the amending formula's specific procedures and a set of important contemporary issues, including the constitutional status of the Supreme Court, Senate reform, the Crown, and secession (see Chapters 10 to 13, by Erin Crandall, Emmett Macfarlane, Philippe Lagassé and Patrick Baud, and Kate Puddister, respectively).

Outline of the Book

This volume is divided into three parts, examining the players, the procedures, and important contemporary issues surrounding constitutional amendment in Canada. The first four chapters explore the fundamental question of who gets a say in the amending process. In Chapter 1, Nadia Verrelli investigates the historical debate leading up to patriation and the contested visions of federalism that encapsulate the negotiations leading to the Constitution Act, 1982. She notes that underlying questions of influence and inclusion (and exclusion), particularly as they relate to Quebec and to Canada's Indigenous peoples, continue to reverberate in the post-1982 context.

Another key player is the judiciary, particularly the Supreme Court itself. As noted above, the Court's *Patriation* and *Quebec Veto Reference* opinions played an important role in the process leading to the amending formula entrenched in 1982. As Adam Dodek makes clear in Chapter 2, judicial interpretations surrounding constitutional change continue to play a vital role, both in determining what counts as part of the Constitution for the purposes of amendment and in identifying which procedures are required to effect changes in particular contexts.

In Chapter 3, Carissima Mathen provides an account of the federal principle that lies at the heart of Part V. She notes that the centrality of the constituent units of the federation in the amending process means that provinces are essential actors whose consent to changes affecting them cannot be overridden by popular will or other interests, including the federal government's. Intergovernmental relations and the process of dialogue and negotiation are thus fundamental to the legitimacy of any changes that might be sought. Yet there is a risk, Mathen says, that the recent judicial approach to Part V might result in "reifying the federal principle at the expense of other values."

In Chapter 4, Christa Scholtz examines the place of Canada's Indigenous peoples in the constitutional amending process, which is complicated by the fact that, although Indigenous peoples are not mentioned in Part V itself, the Aboriginal rights in Part II commit the federal and provincial governments to the "principle" of consultation with "representatives of the aboriginal peoples of Canada" prior to any changes directly affecting them – specifically, those relating to section 91(24) of the Constitution Act, 1867, section 25 of the Charter of Rights and Freedoms, or Part II of the Constitution Act, 1982. Scholtz explores the different possible implications of this. First, she analyses the argument that Part V remains unconstrained by Part II's requirement, rendering the principle of consultation a political duty, but not a legal or constitutional requirement; second, she assesses the argument that Part II imposes a legal constraint on Part V rooted in the honour of the Crown.

The second part of the book examines the various procedures available to effect constitutional change. The chapters in this part share a theme: in different ways, they each ponder the flexibility or relative stasis of the constitutional amending process. In Chapter 5, Warren Newman examines constitutional amendment by legislation under the unilateral procedures in sections 44 and 45. He explores the context of unilateral amendments to the constitutional text, but also "legislation of a constitutional, quasi-constitutional, or organic character that does not alter the text of the Constitution, but that might be considered, in a broad, analytical sense, as a form of constitutional amendment or reform." There have been a number of such laws that, although they do not depart from or alter constitutional principles, serve to enhance those principles in important ways. Where formal amendments to the constitutional text must respect the broad principles of multilateralism enunciated in the Supreme Court's recent reference opinions, Newman notes there might be great potential in this latter legislative category of legislation.

In Chapter 6, Rainer Knopff examines the "clash" between the unanimity requirement of section 41 and unilateralism in section 44. He then examines the regional veto and fixed election date laws as examples of legislation that attempt to effect changes indirectly, as "workarounds" that do not formally bind political actors. With regard to the failed legal challenge to the fixed election date law, Knopff explores the potential implications of – and inconsistencies between – the perceived constitutionality of this law and the impugned proposals in the *Senate Reform Reference*.

Dwight Newman, in Chapter 7, analyses the bilateral amending procedure of section 43, which he contends has the potential to create room for much greater flexibility for future constitutional change than is often recognized. So long as changes affecting one or more provinces do not have direct legal implications for the country's other constituent units, there might be a significant avenue for the inclusion of further asymmetrical arrangements in the Constitution. Newman argues that this is the case despite reasoning in the Supreme Court's *Senate Reform Reference* that arguably constrains constitutional flexibility with respect to Part V's other procedures.

Emmanuelle Richez explores in detail in Chapter 8 provincial constitutions and changes to them under section 45. Her analysis makes it clear that the provinces have considerable capacity to effect changes relevant to their own institutions and democratic representation. Her case study of section 45's implications for Quebec, however, suggests that that province's ability to alter the Constitution to promote asymmetry, particularly in the area of identity-building, is fundamentally constrained.

The specific procedures outlined in Part V of the Constitution do not constitute an exhaustive path to constitutional change in Canada. In Chapter 9, Dennis Baker and Mark Jarvis examine the prospects for informal constitutional change, particularly through statutes and declaratory statements. In contrast to Warren Newman's chapter, which touches on a few examples of such statutes, Baker and Jarvis contend that the Supreme Court's recent jurisprudence imposes a likely "chilling effect" on the prospects for informal amendment. The Court, they conclude, might not be wrong to protect constitutional forms from their derogation, but if a chilling effect takes place for even minor alterations to processes and institutions, Canada is at real risk of constitutional stasis.

The third part of the book examines a number of contemporary issues in relation to recent developments around the amending formula. The Supreme Court itself is the subject of Chapter 10 in which Erin Crandall assesses the long history of the Court's constitutional status, a journey that appears to have come to a conclusion in the *Supreme Court Act Reference*. Yet, as Crandall explains, the Court's opinion raises many questions, as it is as yet unclear which features of the institution are effectively entrenched and which are not.

In Chapter 11, I examine and critique the *Senate Reform Reference*, arguing that the Supreme Court's approach – particularly its reliance on the "constitutional architecture" metaphor – has introduced considerable ambiguity about what changes are feasible. Further, the justices' rationale, particularly as it relates to the issue of senatorial term limits, is ultimately unsatisfying because it fails to identify properly the boundaries of Parliament's authority to make institutional changes under section 44. This, I suggest, does not slam the door on all future informal changes, but the considerable uncertainty that results from the Court's opinion might make future reform efforts less likely.

In Chapter 12, Philippe Lagassé and Patrick Baud examine amendments affecting the Crown, which is most obviously implicated by section 41's unanimity procedure, applying to changes affecting the offices of the Queen, the governor general, and lieutenant-governors. But several important aspects of the Crown might be changed under the general amending formula or even by Parliament itself under section 44, which provides for laws amending the Constitution in relation to the executive. Lagassé and Baud explore these issues in light of the *Senate Reform Reference* and past jurisprudence.

In Chapter 13, Kate Puddister examines the fundamental debate surrounding the constitutionality of secession in light of the *Quebec*

Secession Reference and the two 2014 references. The Supreme Court's emphasis on unwritten principles in the *Quebec Secession Reference* – the Court did not even touch on Part V itself – makes it unclear what type of amendment process might be required for secession, but Puddister suggests that many aspects of a potential provincial secession ultimately would require the unanimity procedure.

In the concluding chapter, I examine areas of clarity and disagreement that emanate from these contributions, with a focus on the themes of constitutional flexibility and stasis, judicial interpretation, and the inclusivity of the amending process. I then briefly examine the future of constitutional amendment in Canada.

Notes

1 Janyce McGregor, "Royal baby law challenge could end up at Supreme Court," *CBC News*, June 12, 2013; available online at http://www.cbc.ca/news/politics/royal-baby-law-challenge-could-end-up-at-supreme-court-1.1415337.
2 *Reference re Senate Reform*, 2014 SCC 32; *Reference re Supreme Court Act, ss. 5 and 6*, 2014 SCC 21.
3 David E. Smith, *Federalism and the Constitution of Canada* (Toronto: University of Toronto Press, 2010), 125.
4 See, for example, Jeremy Webber, *Reimagining Canada: Language, Culture, Community, and the Canadian Constitution* (Montreal; Kingston, ON: McGill-Queen's University Press, 1994); Peter Russell, *Constitutional Odyssey: Can Canadians Become a Sovereign People?* (Toronto: University of Toronto Press, 2004).
5 Guy Régimbald and Dwight Newman, *The Law of the Canadian Constitution* (Markham, ON: LexisNexis Canada, 2013), 20.
6 James Ross Hurley, *Amending Canada's Constitution: History, Processes, Problems and Prospects.* (Ottawa: Minister of Supply and Services Canada, 1996); Benoît Pelletier, *La Modification Constitutionnelle au Canada* (Scarborough, ON: Carswell, 1996).
7 Guy Favreau, "The Amendment of the Constitution of Canada," in *Canada's Constitution Act 1982 & Amendments: A Documentary History*, vol. I, edited by Anne F. Bayefsky (Toronto: McGraw-Hill Ryerson Limited, 1989), 44; Webber, *Reimagining Canada*, 82.
8 Richard Albert, "Constructive Unamendability in Canada and the United States," *Supreme Court Law Review* (2d) 67 (2014): 181–219.
9 Richard Albert, "The Difficulty of Constitutional Amendment in Canada," *Alberta Law Review* 53, no. 1 (2015): 85–114.

10 *Reference re Secession of Quebec*, [1998] 2 S.C.R. 217.
11 Alan Cairns, *Charter versus Federalism: The Dilemmas of Constitutional Reform* (Montreal; Kingston, ON: McGill-Queen's University Press, 1991), 93.
12 One might choose to count the options for opt out and compensation as different "sub-procedures" under section 38, for example.
13 *Reference Re Resolution to amend the Constitution*, [1981] 1 S.C.R. 753.
14 Peter W. Hogg, *Constitutional Law of Canada* (Scarborough, ON: Thomson Canada Limited, 2003), 64.
15 Smith, *Federalism and the Constitution of Canada*, 123.
16 *Reference Re Amendment to the Canadian Constitution*, [1982] 2 S.C.R. 793.
17 Samuel V. LeSelva, *The Moral Foundations of Canadian Federalism: Paradoxes, Achievements, and Tragedies of Nationhood* (Montreal; Kingston, ON: McGill-Queen's University Press, 1996), 10.
18 An Act respecting constitutional amendments, S.C. 1996, c. 1.
19 Peter Aucoin, Mark D. Jarvis, and Lori Turnbull, *Democratizing the Constitution: Reforming Responsible Government* (Toronto: Emond Montgomery, 2011), 226.
20 Ibid.

PART ONE

The Players

1 Searching for an Amending Formula: The 115-Year Journey

NADIA VERRELLI

With the passing of the Constitution Act, 1867 – originally known as the British North America Act, 1867 (the BNA Act) – Canada as we know it today began a long journey to full sovereignty. Notably missing from the Act, and preventing Canada's ascension to full sovereignty, was a general domestic amending formula. As Peter Russell notes, the Fathers of Confederation "did not see [this] as posing any practical problems ... the new constitution would take the form of an imperial statute [and so, it] would be formally amended by the British Parliament."[1] And it was. In fact, this lack of an overall domestic amending formula did not prevent the BNA Act from being amended, not only by the UK Parliament, but also by Imperial Orders in Council and the federal and provincial governments. Over the years, though, the lack of an overall domestic amending formula became, at best, an inconvenience, and at worst, a national embarrassment as it continued to indicate that Canada's nation-building project was incomplete.[2] However, this was not from lack of trying. Indeed, Canada's first ministers attempted to arrive at a general domestic amending formula on seven different occasions: 1926–7, 1935–6, 1950, 1961, 1964, 1968–71, and, finally, the successful effort, 1978–81. Although all seven efforts concerned "the search for a general domestic amending formula," the issues considered by the first ministers began multiplying. By the 1950s, the distribution of powers between the two orders of government had been added. By 1964, the lack of an overall amending formula had become an issue in the wider sense, with the Quiet Revolution and the nation-building project under way in Quebec.[3] And by the late 1960s, political leaders had begun discussing changes to the Senate and the Supreme Court of Canada, and entrenching a bill of rights and freedoms in addition to a general domestic amending formula and patriation of the Constitution. The items added to the agenda unfortunately delayed the patriation process, as it became increasingly difficult to meet all the various demands.

Nonetheless, in November 1981, on the seventh attempt, the first ministers, with the exception of Premier René Lévesque of Quebec, approved a constitutional package leading to the eventual patriation of the Constitution. With the enactment of the Constitution Act, 1982 on 17 April 1982, 115 years after Confederation, Canadians alone were able to amend all parts of the Constitution; the country was fully sovereign at last. Indeed, it was a time to celebrate. Or was it?

The long road to patriation inevitably raises two questions. First, why did it take so long for Canadian political leaders to agree upon a domestic amending formula? Second, is Canada's nation-building project complete with the 1982 patriation?

The search for a domestic amending formula quickly coincided with discussions about the type of federation Canada was and ought to be. The questions, implicit, explicit, or sometimes both, concerned were twofold. First, is Canada made up of equal provinces whereby their unanimity on a proposed patriation package and/or proposed amendment to the newly patriated Constitution is required, or would a majority of provinces (however defined) suffice? And, second, is Canada made up of two nations, whereby Quebec ought to agree to a proposed patriation package and ought to have either a constitutional veto or the ability to opt out with compensation in any proposed amending formula, so as to enable the province to protect its political identity and distinct interests? Although the latter vision was much more pronounced in the post-1960 period, hints of it were present in efforts to patriate the Constitution prior to the 1960s.

This discussion on Canada's character arguably influenced three factors present in all seven attempts. One was executive federalism, whereby political leaders negotiated among themselves behind closed doors, with little to no public participation or involvement of legislative assemblies. Prior to the 1978–81 effort, patriation of the Constitution and debates on Canada's federal character and identity were not issues that captured the public's imagination in any significant way. It should be noted, however, that throughout the 115-year journey, there were episodes of political leaders involving legislative assemblies and, to a certain extent, the public. The second factor was the compartmentalization of the Constitution, whereby different parts could be subjected to different amending formulas; considering the different interests articulated by the provinces and the federal government, it seemed the only way to appease the provinces. According to J. Peter Meekison, "[g]overnments had to be sensitive to the position and concerns of Quebec in Confederation. Neither could the vast population differences between the most populous province, Ontario, and the least populous, Prince Edward Island, be ignored."[4] The third factor was the exclusion of Indigenous peoples, as the debate on Canada's federation, which centred on equality of the provinces versus dualism left no room for a discussion of the role of Indigenous peoples in the future of Canada. As Peter Russell notes, "[f]or the Europeans who fashioned the Canadian Confederation, the Aboriginal peoples were subjects on whom sovereignty could be imposed, not peoples with whom one formed a political community."[5] As a result, the Indigenous peoples were not only excluded from the negotiations; they and their interests were initially ignored and only later, upon protests by Indigenous groups, were they revisited. And so, the political environment as well as the different interests at play affected not only the various constitutional negotiations – specifically, the different amending formulas proposed and considered by the first ministers – but also the viability of the proposed constitutional packages and the acceptance or rejection of the final agreement.

From the Balfour Declaration to the Fulton Formula

Questions of Canada's ability to amend its Constitution without the approval of the UK Parliament were not seriously considered by Canadian political leaders until after the First World War. Prior to that, there was some discussion in the media, but "these were isolated cases and were considered as claims of extremists if not real anti-imperialists."[6] In March 1920, however, William Lyon Mackenzie King, then leader of the opposition, raised the issue of a domestic amending formula in the House of Commons. Although he received support from Minister of Justice C.J. Doherty, who had been discussing the issue with several provincial attorneys-general, a uniform consensus on the matter did not exist. Premier Louis-Alexandre Taschereau of Quebec indicated his government would not agree to a formula or amendment that "would affect civil law, property and civil rights, education, language and religion, powers over taxation, or a fixed representation of Quebec in Parliament."[7] Similarly, Premier William Martin of Saskatchewan indicated he was not entirely enthusiastic about the idea of formally severing all ties with Britain. Between 1920 and 1925, political leaders continued to disagree on the type of formula, the degree of provincial involvement, and whether they wanted to severe ties formally with the Imperial government. It was in this environment of mixed desire and disagreement that the prime minister and the premiers of the then-nine provinces sat down in 1927 to discuss a general domestic amending formula.

With the 1926 Balfour Declaration, the UK Parliament, although it continued to amend the BNA Act upon the request of the Canadian Parliament, was prepared to hand over complete autonomy and sovereignty to Canada and the other five self-governing dominions of the British Empire. With this, Canadian political leaders were presented with the first real opportunity since Confederation to devise and agree upon a general domestic amending formula, which they attempted to capitalize on in a meeting held in Ottawa in November 1927.[8] Three assumptions underpinned this conference: first, the constitutional question was one that would be best dealt with by federal and provincial governments outside public scrutiny; second, different parts of the Constitution could be subjected to a different amending formula; and, third, the federal government "would not act on the question of Canada's constitutional sovereignty without full consultation with the provinces,"[9] which clearly indicated that the provinces were to be equal players in determining the parameters of Canadian constitutional sovereignty.

On the second day of the conference, dominion Minister of Justice Ernest Lapointe argued that, in light of the Balfour Declaration and the cumbersome procedure required to amend the Constitution, Parliament, after consulting with the provinces, should be able to make ordinary amendments with the consent of the majority of provinces, but that fundamental amendments involving questions of provincial rights, rights of minorities concerning race, language, creed, and religion, and denominational schools should require the unanimous consent of the provinces. The proposal generated support, but opposition was strong, and no general agreement was reached. According to Russell, "differences within Canada among its governing elites, not differences between Canada and Great Britain, prevented Canada from assuming the full autonomy proclaimed in the Balfour Declaration."[10]

Then, in 1929, a special "Canada clause" was proposed at the Conference on the Operation of Dominion Legislation and Merchant Shipping, but the provinces were not consulted on the wording. In a House of Commons debate in May 1930, the Official Opposition, led by Conservative R.B. Bennett, was adamant that the provinces be consulted, but no consensus was reached, and the clause's adoption was delayed. Later in the year, when the Conservatives formed the dominion government, Ontario premier George Ferguson, drawing on the theory that Confederation was a compact among the provinces, sent a memorandum to Prime Minister Bennett insisting on provincial consultation before any constitutional change could be adopted, a sentiment echoed by Quebec and other provinces.

In the end, Bennett did not proceed with adopting the proposed Canada clause. Instead, in April 1931, he convened a dominion-provincial conference to discuss the UK Parliament's pending Statute of Westminster, with the provinces wanting to ensure that the Statute would "not be construed as to permit the powers of the provinces to be curtailed, lessened, modified, or repealed."[11] The first ministers unanimously agreed to the wording of a special clause exempting Canada from the full autonomy promised in the Balfour Declaration, and when the UK Parliament passed the Statute in 1931, the clause (section 7) – "with a view to retaining the procedure of an act of Parliament of the United Kingdom as the only means of constitutional amendment" – was included.[12] This action arguably started a trend that would define the practice of Canada's asking the UK government to enact a patriation package only upon the federal government's obtaining the unanimous consent of the provinces; the only exception to this was in 1982.

Discussions of a general amending formula continued between 1930 and 1935, but they took place mainly among university scholars, with the participation of some political leaders, most of whom seemed concerned with safeguarding provincial powers in education, language, and religion. Then, in February 1935, the House of Commons established a special committee to study and propose the best method to amend the Constitution. The effects of the Great Depression and the climatic phenomenon known as the Dust Bowl in undermining agriculture on the prairies led to concerns, however, about an imbalance between federal fiscal resources and provincial legislative powers. The committee thus faced two key issues: "the need for a specific amendment to deal with economic problems confronting Canada," and "agreement on an amending formula."[13]

Between 18 February and 18 June 1935, the committee met eleven times, and heard from both dominion government officials and university professors. It also sought the opinions of provinces that had expressed their opposition to the committee's mandate, insisting that the matter of a general domestic amending formula ought to be discussed at a formal dominion-provincial meeting with all concerned parties present. On 19 June the committee accordingly recommended that a dominion-provincial conference be convened to discuss "amendments to the distribution of powers and a clarification on the powers of taxation."[14]

In December 1935, the newly elected Liberal government, under the leadership of W.L. Mackenzie King, convened a conference of the dominion and provincial governments to discuss the committee's report, as well as a memorandum that contained additional suggestions for an amending formula. After three days of meetings, the first ministers resolved – with the dissent of New Brunswick – that a new amending formula "satisfactory to the Dominion Parliament and to the provincial legislatures be devised."[15] At another conference, in early 1936, participants quickly agreed – again with the dissent of New Brunswick[16] – that the BNA Act be amended to include a general domestic amending formula. A subcommittee established to consider and propose an overall domestic formula met in February 1936, and adjourned in March with a tentative proposal:

- If the proposed amendment affected the dominion government's jurisdiction alone, then the Constitution could be amended by an Act of Parliament subject to the following exceptions: the offices of the governor general and lieutenant-governor; the constitution of the Privy Council; the constitution, membership, and powers of the Senate and the House of Commons (except for the representation of the provinces in both houses); and the Consolidated Revenue Fund.
- Amendments affecting the dominion government and one or more province could be put into effect by an Act of Parliament with the consent of the province(s) affected.
- Amendments concerning the powers of the dominion government and all the provinces required the consent of Parliament and a majority of the provinces making up 55 per cent of the population, with one caveat: if a proposed amendment affected sections 92(13) (property and civil rights in the province) or 92(16) (generally, all matters of merely local or private nature in the province) of the BNA Act, a province could opt out.
- Fundamental matters, including "the vesting of executive power in the Queen,"[17] the Senate, the House of Commons (specifically, the number of senators and provincial representation in both the Senate and the House), and section 133 (the use of French and English in

the House of Commons and the Quebec legislature, as well as in dominion and Quebec courts), required joint action by the federal Parliament and all the provincial legislatures.
• Exclusive provincial legislative powers, including sections 92(12) (solemnization of marriage), 92(14) (administration of justice), and 93 (education), also required joint action by the federal Parliament and all provincial legislatures.[18]

Although no general agreement was achieved, ending another effort in the search for a general domestic amending formula, this exercise remains important not only for the proposal to compartmentalize the Constitution, but also for its introduction of the "opting out" concept, which was intended to ease concerns of the Maritime provinces that changes agreed upon by the other six provinces would be forced on them.[19] Both features reappear in future proposals to amend the Constitution, which, in fact, did not stray far from the 1935 formula.

Between 1936 and 1950, discussion of a general domestic amending formula continued. In 1937, the dominion government established the Rowell-Sirois Committee. Although its mandate did not include a new amending formula, provinces appearing before the committee continued to press their views on the matter. For example, the governments of Nova Scotia, Manitoba, Saskatchewan, and British Columbia expressed their support for patriation, with Nova Scotia and Saskatchewan arguing for an amending process whereby different parts of the Constitution would be subjected to different amending formulas.[20] New Brunswick, Ontario, and Quebec, for their part, insisted that unanimity of the provinces on a new domestic amending formula should be required. All, however, agreed that the matter was not one for the Rowell-Sirois Committee to consider.

Also, during this period, key amendments to the BNA Act were put into effect – most notably, section 91(1), a 1949 amendment that enabled the dominion government to amend the Constitution unilaterally on matters affecting only its own jurisdiction – thereby specifically excluding provincial legislative powers, schools, the use of French and English, the requirement that Parliament convene at least once per year, and the requirement that the House of Commons continue for no more than five years, except in times of war, invasion, or insurrection. The new section not only signalled the Constitution's partial patriation; it also led directly to an attempt in 1950 to complete the patriation process at a federal-provincial conference held in January and September that year.

Although no agreement was reached, the conference gave the premiers the opportunity to articulate their criticism of section 91(1) that it "went too far." Prime Minister Louis St-Laurent agreed, and promised that the section could be repealed if the provinces agreed upon an overall domestic amending formula – which finally occurred in 1982. Also, during the conference, the issue of delegating exclusive powers from one order of government to another to deal with a potentially rigid amending formula was discussed – an issue that would reappear in subsequent proposals.

Between 1950 and 1960 not much discussion on patriation took place. This changed when Prime Minister John Diefenbaker announced his wish to secure a domestic amending formula, and a constitutional conference to do just that was convened in July 1960. At first, the federal government suggested that the UK Parliament be asked to relinquish its authority over the BNA Act and to pass a provision requiring unanimity to amend the Constitution, with Diefenbaker initially feeling that the federal and provincial governments could then arrive at a more flexible amending formula. He quickly came to believe, however, that it would be better to secure an amending formula first.[21]

The talks continued, and by the end of the conference the provinces agreed to what came to be known as the "Fulton Formula," after federal attorney general E. Davie Fulton, who chaired the meeting. The Fulton Formula echoed many of the provisions suggested in 1935, including the requirement of unanimity for fundamental amendments and bilateral amendments between the federal and provincial government(s).[22] New aspects were also introduced – most notably, a change in how general amendments would be put into effect. Recall that, in 1935, it was suggested that these should be put into effect with the consent of a majority of the provinces making up 55 per cent of the population. This was now changed to two-thirds of the provinces making up at least 50 per cent of the population, a formula that later would be referred to as the 7/50 rule, and that would be included in the final 1982 agreement. The Fulton Formula also included a special section dealing with education and a provision enabling delegation of provincial powers to the federal government.

Although the Fulton Formula did not receive unanimous consent, it became a building block for the next round of constitutional talks.

From the Fulton-Favreau Formula to the Victoria Charter

In September and October 1964, Prime Minister Lester Pearson and the provincial premiers met in Charlottetown, Prince Edward Island, to discuss and resolve the patriation issue. Chaired by then federal minister of justice Guy Favreau, the first ministers unanimously agreed to what came to be known as the "Fulton-Favreau Formula," a modified version of the Fulton Formula that included clarifications of sections 91(1) and 92(1),[23] and "a French version of the new act respecting the amending formula and the delegation of legislative authority in a schedule that would make the French version official."[24]

This unanimous agreement, however, was not enough to move ahead with the patriation process. By this time, the Quebec government had developed the practice of seeking the Quebec legislature's approval before giving formal consent to any proposed patriation package, and in 1965 Premier Jean Lesage duly submitted to it the Fulton-Favreau Formula. But before the legislature could discuss the proposed package, a seminar was held at the Université de Montréal on 18 March at which the general public had an opportunity to participate in the constitutional discussions. Supporting the Fulton-Favreau Formula, Pierre Laporte and René Lévesque, two ministers in the Lesage government, argued that it essentially would put into effect that which already existed in practice, and that would not change Quebec's ability to achieve *le statut particulier* (special status). In contrast, Jacques-Yvan Morin, a law professor at the Université de Montréal, argued that the proposed formula was not enough – that a revised division of powers providing Quebec "with all the exclusive and shared legislative powers it would need to ensure its own self-fulfillment within Canada" should accompany any proposal.[25] Without it, he said, the Fulton-Favreau Formula could become a straitjacket hindering Quebec's ability to achieve *le statut particulier*.

Premier Lesage, quickly recognizing the growing public support for Morin's position, withdrew his support for the formula. In January 1966 he wrote to Prime Minister Pearson informing him that the Quebec government would not support the Fulton-Favreau Formula, which accordingly was not adopted; "at that time, the federal government accepted the principle that fundamental changes in the Constitution of Canada must not be made without the consent of the Quebec government."[26]

To a certain extent, it is surprising that the Constitution was not patriated in 1964. The Fulton-Favreau Formula seemed to appease the various interests at play. Under the formula, provincial unanimity would have been required to amend fundamental aspects of the Constitution – notably, on matters dealing with language, Quebec, and the other provincial governments, essentially would have had a constitutional veto. Further, the 7/50 amending formula would have assured supporters of provincial rights that amending the Constitution would not be easy. It also would have protected the principle of equality of the provinces, as all would have had a relatively equal opportunity to support or reject any proposed amendment. But, alas, the formula was not enough. The proposed package did not include any immediate changes to the division of powers, which was of particular interest to the Quebec government. The ongoing Quiet Revolution, whereby the focus of Quebec nationalism evolved from one centred on *la survivance* to one fuelled by goals of development and expansion, affected the constitutional demands of the Quebec government.[27] Securing the powers acquired at Confederation was no longer enough: as evident in Morin's opposition to the Fulton-Favreau Formula, the Quebec government looked to secure powers it felt it needed to ensure that it would become *maître chez nous*.

After this failed attempt, a new era of constitutional politics in Canada emerged, one that Peter Russell has labelled "mega constitutional politics."[28] The search for a general domestic amending formula took place alongside concerns about the division of powers, regional disparity, and the need for a charter of rights and freedoms. As well, the Quiet Revolution under way in Quebec was increasing sentiments of nationalism and separatism, coupled with terrorist acts by the *Front de liberation du Québec*, which made the patriation issue all the more pressing. Moreover, not only did the provinces begin to take the initiative on constitutional issue, but the hitherto closed-door negotiations began to open up slightly, at least outside Quebec, with the public invited, not necessarily to engage in a meaningful discussion with the first ministers, but at least to observe constitutional conferences by way of television. In short, patriation was no longer just about a domestic amending formula, but also about Canadian identity and the type of Canada that Canadians envisioned and desired. Canadians began to get involved, first as spectators, and then, by 1981, as contributors to the conversation on an entrenched bill of rights.

The next round of constitutional talks began when Ontario premier John Robarts convened the aptly named Confederation of Tomorrow Conference in Toronto, 27–30 November 1967. However, with the federal government's decision not to attend and the premiers' realization that not much could be accomplished without its participation, the conference soon became a "public education exercise."[29] By way of television, the public was able to observe what was ostensibly an exercise in executive federalism. It also gave the premiers an opportunity to articulate their views on Canada and its future to a wider audience.

Capitalizing on the momentum the conference generated and attempting to win back Canadians, as "the federal government clearly lost points through its non participation,"[30] Prime Minister Pearson decided not only to add the Constitution to the agenda of an already scheduled 1967 first ministers' conference, but also to televise part of the proceedings. Prior to the conference, Pierre Trudeau, then federal minister of justice, delivered a speech in which he upped the ante by stating that his first priority with regard to constitutional renewal would be an entrenched bill of rights. In the ensuing years, Trudeau, who became prime minister in April 1968, would make an entrenched charter his primary goal. His address was followed by the release of a federal government White Paper, "Federalism for the Future," in which it outlined its position for the upcoming conference: strengthening the Canadian community would be achieved with "a constitutional statement on the rights of Canadian citizens" and the strengthening of central institutions, specifically the Senate and the Supreme Court of Canada; only when these two items were satisfied would the federal government discuss the division of powers.[31] Surprisingly, there was no mention of a general domestic amending formula. During the conference, Trudeau not only rejected Quebec's constitutional agenda; he was also adamant that a pan-Canadian identity and vision should shape future constitutional talks. In this vision, the rights of all Canadians would be secured by central institutions through a charter of rights.

By 1969, regional interests focusing on "bread and butter issues" emerged, curtailing the federal government's plans. For example, provinces with a strong economic base demanded a larger share of the tax field, while poorer provinces looked to secure strong fiscal powers for the federal government. Quebec, meanwhile, continued to question the federal government's presence in areas of provincial jurisdiction. By 1970, the first ministers, realizing a complete overhaul of the constitution was not feasible, began to discuss a more manageable plan. In a February 1971 working session, the agenda included a bill of rights, a commitment to overcome regional disparity, the constitutionalization of the Supreme Court, a domestic amending formula, and – to ensure Quebec's continued participation – social policy. Between February and June 1971, federal justice minister John Turner toured the country seeking to achieve consensus with the provinces; the process was federally driven, bilateral in nature and beyond public scrutiny.[32]

On 14 June 1971 the first ministers met in Victoria, British Columbia, to consider an agenda that included the amending formula, alongside other items. As Meekison has pointed out, "while the importance of establishing an amending formula was recognized, this topic received far less scrutiny than most of the other questions under consideration,"[33] demonstrating how vast the issue surrounding constitutional renewal had become. Nonetheless, on 17 June, the first ministers arrived at an intergovernmental agreement, known as the Victoria Charter, which differed starkly from previous such agreements. The Charter dealt with issues extending beyond a domestic amending formula to include a bill of rights, and provisions on language rights, the Supreme Court, and regional disparity. As well, and more important for the purposes of this chapter, it included an amending formula, known as the "Victoria Formula," which, while resembling previous proposals by including the bilateral and unilateral provisions, also contained what came to be understood as a regional formula, whereby all proposed amendments except for those that fall under the bilateral and unilateral provisions, would require the consent of Parliament and each province having more than 25 per cent of the population – effectively giving both Ontario and Quebec a constitutional veto – and two Atlantic provinces and two western provinces together having at least 50 per cent of the population.[34] This differed from the 1935, 1960, and 1964 proposals, where fundamental changes to the Constitution would require unanimity and general amendments would require the consent of two-thirds of the provinces making up at least 50 per cent of the population.

On 22 June, however, after some deliberation, the Quebec cabinet rejected the Victoria Charter, not, to be clear, because of the proposed amending formula, but because of the Charter's limited revisions to section 94(a) (on old age pensions and supplementary benefits),[34] and because it did not give Quebec enough to pursue its nation-building project.[35] Quebec's rejection of the Victoria Charter ended this round of constitutional talks.

A pattern thus became evident here: with Quebec's refusal to consent to them, the proposals of 1960, 1964, and now 1971 were shelved, and constitutional negotiations ended. In its 1981 *Quebec Veto Reference*, the Supreme Court rejected Quebec's argument that a convention had developed whereby its consent was required to legitimize any patriation package.[36] With the other political actors – the federal government and the other provinces – also failing to acknowledge this convention, the patriation of the Constitution in 1981 took place without Quebec's consent.

Patriation: The Final Haul

Between 1971 and 1978, while the issue of an overall domestic formula did not dominate Canadian constitutional politics, the political scene was changing, ultimately affecting the final, and successful, attempt at patriation. First, in 1972, a Special Joint Committee of the Senate and House of Commons, chaired by Senator Gildas Molgat and MP Mark MacGuigan, opened up constitutional talks to the public. This, as Russell states, was "Canada's first real attempt at popular participation in constitution-making."[37] Concluding that Canadians wanted a new Constitution, the committee offered some detailed recommendations that foreshadowed events to come. Two examples were its comments on the principle of self-determination, which was steadily gaining support in Quebec, and its sections on Indigenous peoples, who, until this point, had been excluded from constitutional talks. Second, in key cases dealing with Aboriginal and treaty rights, most notably the *Calder* case of 1973, the Supreme Court of Canada began recognizing the collective rights of Indigenous peoples. Third, the West's rising discontent with Canada's state of affairs became a noteworthy phenomenon. And fourth, in the 1976 Quebec provincial election, the Parti Québécois won enough seats to form the government; for the first time in Canadian history, a party committed to the independence of a province sat in power.

Such was the political environment when the first ministers met to discuss constitutional reform in October 1978 and again in February 1979. Regarding the amending formula, the first ministers faced three choices: "first, accept the Victoria Formula; second, modify the Victoria Formula; or third, find an acceptable alternative."[38] The Victoria Formula was quickly deemed unacceptable, as it would give Ontario and Quebec a perpetual veto. Canada, with this amending formula in place, would become a federation made up of equal regions and, in turn, first- and second-class provinces based on population. This fundamentally offended the provincial compact theory of Confederation, which promoted the idea that Canada was made up of equal provinces regardless of population, and thus that each province should be given an equal voice with respect to amending the Constitution. Moreover, as Meekison points out, in all the provinces except Ontario and New

Brunswick, a different party had come to power since 1971, when the Victoria Formula was agreed upon, so the formula's unacceptability was not surprising.[39] As an alternative, the "Toronto Consensus" was proposed, which suggested that general amendments should require the consent of Parliament plus two-thirds of the provinces representing 85 per cent of the population, while fundamental amendments, including natural resources (added to appease Alberta) should require unanimity. Like the Victoria Formula, the Toronto Consensus was criticized for favouring Quebec and Ontario, since, based on their share the population, the two provinces would continue to have a veto. At the February 1979 meeting, Alberta premier Peter Lougheed proposed yet another alternative: "provinces could opt out of any amendment which derogated from their existing legislative authority, propriety rights or provincial privileges contained within Constitution."[40] The conference ended, however, without an agreement.

As these constitutional meetings were under way, the federal and provincial governments established various task forces and special committees mandated to look at constitutional renewal.[41] In 1978, the federal government released its plan for constitutional renewal, entitled *A Time for Action*, which highlighted a strong role for Ottawa in the federation and the constitutional protection of individual rights. Also in 1978, the federal government tabled Bill C-60, which proposed to reform the Senate unilaterally. This was an interesting move by the Trudeau government that broke with past practices. When the composition and powers of the Senate had been discussed in previous constitutional conferences, provincial consent had always been considered: recall the Senate exceptions in the proposed formulas for unilateral constitutional change of 1935, 1960, and 1964, and the Victoria Formula's requirement of provincial consent to effect changes to the Senate. Controversy and provincial criticism of the bill led the federal government to refer the matter to the Supreme Court, which agreed with the provinces that, under s section 91(1), Ottawa did not have the authority to alter the Senate unilaterally.

By the time the first ministers met again on 2 June 1980, the political climate had shifted once again. In February, after a brief period in power by the Progressive Conservatives, the Liberals won the federal election, and Pierre Trudeau returned as prime minister determined to deal with Canada's constitutional issue. Then, in May, Quebecers voted no in the referendum on the Parti Québécois' sovereignty-association plan. These two events emboldened the federal government, and shifted the balance of power between the now-established protagonists of the constitutional impasse, Pierre Trudeau and René Lévesque. Further, the West's discontent reached new heights in 1980 with the implementation of the federal National Energy Program and the complete shutting out of Liberal candidates in that region in the February election. Both fuelled sentiments that the federal government was not equipped to represent the interests of the western provinces, and that the Constitution left the West vulnerable to the interests of central Canada. Finally, the National Indian Brotherhood, feeling excluded from the constitutional process and that Aboriginal peoples' interests were not being met, proceeded with plans to petition the Queen to block patriation.

Not much was accomplished at the June meeting, but it did lead to a televised constitutional conference held at the Château Laurier Hotel in Ottawa in September 1980, where the first ministers discussed a "best draft proposal" by the Continuing Committee of the Constitution. At the meeting, the provinces presented the federal government with a proposal entitled the "Château Consensus." Trudeau, however, dismissed the counteroffer as "another provincial shopping list,"[42] and the meeting ended with no resolution. In Russell's account, "it was one of the most acrimonious meetings on record."[43] The first ministers were nowhere near resolving the constitutional issue. And then the ball dropped.

On 2 October 1980 Trudeau announced on national television his intention to put his constitutional plan into effect and to proceed unilaterally to ask the UK Parliament to patriate the Constitution. Officially tabled as the "Joint Resolution to amend the Constitution," the plan included a bill of rights and two methods to amend the constitution: the Victoria Formula and referenda on constitutional amendments, but only in the event of a deadlock between the two orders of government and to be initiated only by the federal government. Labelling the Joint Resolution the "People's Package," the federal government initiated a well-orchestrated advertising campaign and held televised special parliamentary committee hearings where members of the public were invited to discuss and suggest changes to the proposed package (some were adopted).[44] Both approaches succeeded in generating public support for Trudeau's proposal, with the latter creating a sense of a charter belonging to Canadians and the sentiment that, with the "People's Package," ordinary Canadians finally had a role in constitutional politics.[45]

Again, Trudeau's action, like the 1979 Senate proposal, broke with tradition, since past discussions had operated on the assumption that, before asking the United Kingdom to relinquish authority over the BNA Act, Parliament would obtain provincial consent. The issue was not necessarily the proposed amending formula – although some provinces viewed it as problematic – but the method by which Trudeau planned to patriate the Constitution. And except for Ontario and New Brunswick, the provinces objected to Trudeau's initiative, as did various Indigenous groups, including the Union of BC Indian Chiefs, who launched a "Constitution Express," a protest train that travelled from Vancouver to Ottawa.[46] Quebec, Manitoba, and Newfoundland went further and challenged the initiative in their respective supreme courts. All three references reached the Supreme Court of Canada, where they were consolidated in the *Patriation Reference*.[47]

In the meantime, Trudeau indicated he would not proceed until the Supreme Court had ruled on the matter, and in the United Kingdom, the Kershaw Committee was established with a mandate to query the federal government's ability to act alone to request that the Constitution be patriated. Although the Kershaw Committee did not have open meetings, Indigenous groups submitted statements arguing for the Crown's continued treaty obligations towards Indigenous peoples. And, finally, the eight dissident provinces developed an alternative formula to Trudeau's that was similar to past proposals in requiring unanimity for fundamental amendments and the consent of two-thirds of the provinces making up at least 50 per cent of the population for general amendments, but with one important addition: any province that wished to opt out of an amendment that transferred powers from the province to the federal government could do so with full compensation.[48] The eight provinces also proposed not to agree to any other changes to the BNA Act until the UK Parliament relinquished authority over the Act. Here, however, they misread public reaction: by this time, Canadians had become both involved in constitutional issues and attached to Trudeau's proposed charter of rights and freedoms, and were not prepared to support a proposal that did not include a constitutionalized bill of rights.

In January 1981 the Kershaw Committee released its report, finding, first, that the federal government was not constitutionally authorized to ask the UK Parliament to patriate the Constitution over the objections of eight provinces and, second, that the Crown's treaty obligations to Indigenous peoples had been transferred to the federal government.

Then, in September, in the *Patriation Reference*, the Supreme Court delivered its opinion that, although nothing in law prevented the federal government from asking the UK Parliament to amend the Constitution without the prior consent of the provinces, a constitutional convention had developed that required Ottawa to obtain a substantial degree of provincial consent. This opinion led to the first ministers' renewed commitment to patriation, and on 3 November 1981, the federal government and the provinces, with the exception of Quebec, agreed to a constitutional package known as the "November Accord."

As Russell notes, "[t]he accord between the federal government and the provinces was truly an achievement of elite accommodation."[49] Both sides compromised. Trudeau agreed to the amending formula proposed by the provinces, provided the provinces agreed to exclude opting out with full compensation – they did, and the elimination of this clause served as one reason for Lévesque's rejection of the November Accord. The provinces agreed to Trudeau's proposed charter of rights, provided, first, that mobility rights included an affirmative action rider for provinces with an above-average unemployment rate – a change that was added to satisfy Newfoundland, which wanted to protect jobs in that province – and, second, that a "notwithstanding clause" enabling governments to override certain rights protected in the charter be implemented to appease provinces that feared the charter might compromise the principle of provincial legislative supremacy. Both compromises were adopted behind closed doors, beyond public scrutiny. In fact, the November Accord was often referred to as the "Kitchen Accord," as it was forged by Roy McMurtry and Roy Romanow, the attorneys general of Ontario and Saskatchewan, respectively, and Jean Chrétien, the federal justice minister, in a small, secluded room at the conference centre. The second compromise was more significant, as the notwithstanding clause (section 33) became an important element of the proposed charter. Suffice it to say this caused a public outcry, mainly by women's groups, which were active during the public parliamentary hearings; in response, section 28 was added to ensure that the clause would not apply to sex or gender equality. Also in response to public pressure, mainly by Indigenous peoples, the first ministers agreed to restore the recognition of Aboriginal rights, which had been dropped entirely in the original Accord, but only on the condition that the word "existing" precede Aboriginal rights. All Indigenous groups with the exception of the Métis Association of Alberta, however, opposed the package, with the Alberta Indian Association launching a legal challenge in the UK courts arguing that the Crown had treaty obligations towards Indigenous peoples. The UK courts, however, echoing the report of the Kershaw Committee, found that the Crown's treaty obligations had been transferred to the Canadian federal government.[50]

Two additional changes were made to the original November Accord in an attempt to secure Quebec's support: first, an accommodation of Quebec's education policy requiring immigrants to be educated in French, and, second, the inclusion of opting out with compensation, but only on matters dealing with education and cultural matters. Lévesque, however, to the chagrin of the other first ministers, continued to insist on full compensation on all matters, and refused to agree to the Accord.

While the first ministers, except for Lévesque, compromised on the details of the patriation package, there was little or no compromise on Canada's federal character. Indeed, equality of the provinces and the understanding of Canada as one nation trumped dualism and overshadowed a significant role for Indigenous peoples in the Canadian constitutional order. This is evident in the principle of provincial equality that underpins Part V of the Constitution Act, 1982: regardless of its population or of any claim to unique status or nationhood, every province, through the unanimity provision and the 7/50 rule, plays an equal role in future amendments to the Constitution. And although Quebec secured opting out in the areas of education and culture, it regarded this as insufficient to ensure its *statut particulier*. Further, although section 35 of the Constitution and section 25 of the Charter of Rights and Freedoms recognized Aboriginal and treaty rights, Indigenous peoples continue to have no role in the amending procedure where amendments potentially affect Aboriginal and treaty rights (for a broader discussion, see Christa Scholtz, Chapter 4 in this volume).

Regardless of ongoing objections to the patriation package and of the Quebec government's and Indigenous groups' vain attempts to challenge the November Accord constitutionally and legally, the other ten governments pushed ahead with the final agreed-upon package, which included five amending formulas. In December 1981 the Accord was passed by both the House of Commons and the Senate, and in March 1982 the Canada Act was passed in the UK Parliament. On 17 April 1982, at a ceremony held in Ottawa in the presence of the Queen, the Constitution Act, 1982 received Royal Assent.

Canada finally had patriated its constitution; it was now a fully sovereign nation. As Richard Gwyn of the *Toronto Star* exclaimed, Canadians were now "[m]asters in our own house!"[51] Such sentiments of jubilation, however, were not shared nationwide, particularly not among the political elite of Quebec or among Indigenous groups. Indeed, with the proclamation of the Constitution Act, 1982, Canada as one nation, made up of equal individuals and equal provinces, became and remains Canadian constitutional orthodoxy, despite the challenge of competing visions. Not surprisingly, then, not everyone or every province was satisfied that the constitutional renewal process was complete.

The Aftermath

The numerous attempts to establish a mutually agreed-upon constitutional amending formula and the long journey to patriation show that Canada's nation-building project remained incomplete. The debate about Canada's federal character and the articulation of different interests continued, and governments at both the federal and provincial levels repeatedly reopened constitutional talks.

In 1983, the Trudeau government and provincial premiers met to discuss constitutional matters with leaders of Indigenous groups, and another set of meetings was held with Indigenous groups in 1987, this time with Brian Mulroney as prime minister. Both sets of meetings came to an impasse, as political leaders were unable to agree upon a definition of Aboriginal self-government and how it would fit into Canada's federal character, still understood as a federation of two equal orders of government. Also in 1987, the first ministers met to discuss Quebec's place in the federation and to persuade Quebec premier Robert Bourassa to sign onto to the Constitution. An agreement known as the Meech Lake Accord was reached that would have recognized Quebec as a "distinct society," giving some credence to the dualist vision, but, in the end, the Accord failed to be ratified.[52] In 1992, to address some of the criticisms generated by the Meech Lake Accord – mainly the exclusion of citizens and Indigenous groups from the process and the privileges offered Quebec through the distinct society clause, the Mulroney government once again convened a constitutional conference involving the public and Indigenous groups. Once again, an agreement, the Charlottetown Accord, was reached, but in a nationwide plebiscite, Canadians turned down the proposed package.[53] In neither 1987 nor 1992, however, was reopening the amending formula on the agenda.

In another attempt to appease Quebec, the federal government passed An Act respecting Constitutional Amendments, 1996 (also referred to as the regional veto act).[54] Similar to the regional formula first introduced in the Victoria Charter, this law requires the federal government to secure the support of a "majority" of provinces – consisting of Ontario, Quebec, British Columbia, and at least two Atlantic provinces, together accounting for 50 per cent of the population – before proposing amendments to the Constitution regarding changes to parliamentary institutions, the creation of new provinces, and the division of powers between the federal and provincial governments. The law does not, however, cover amendments whereby a province may exercise a veto under sections 41 or 43 or dissent under section 38(3). Although the 1996 law is not part of the Constitution Act, 1982, it has added another step to the constitutional amendment procedure.

The exclusion of Indigenous peoples from the 1982 process and Quebec's refusal to sign on to the Constitution Act, 1982 continue to resonate, as manifested in, for example, the 1995 referendum on Quebec sovereignty, which 49 per cent of voters supported, and the Indigenous protest movement called Idle No More,[55] which exploded onto the scene in fall 2012. Although Canadian political leaders successfully patriated the constitution in 1982, ongoing events demonstrate that Canada remains far from having a constitutional order that is inclusive of all its peoples.

Notes

The author wishes to thank research assistant Shaun Maronese, BA, Laurentian University.

1 Peter H. Russell, *Constitutional Odyssey: Can Canadians Become a Sovereign People?* (Toronto: University of Toronto Press, 2004), 27.
2 Ibid., 7.
3 Ibid., 58.
4 J. Peter Meekison, "The Amending Formula," *Queen's Law Journal* 8 (1982): 100.
5 Russell, *Constitutional Odyssey*, 4.
6 Paul Gérin-Lajoie, *Constitutional Amendment in Canada*, vol. 3 (Toronto: University of Toronto Press, 1950), 222.
7 Ibid.
8 Russell, *Constitutional Odyssey*, 55.
9 Ibid., 56.
10 Ibid., 55.
11 James Ross Hurley, *Amending Canada's Constitution: History, Processes, Problems and Prospects* (Ottawa: Canada Communication Group, 1996), 26.

12 Gérin-Lajoie, *Constitutional Amendment in Canada*, 230.
13 Hurley, *Amending Canada's Constitution*, 27.
14 Ibid.
15 Gérin-Lajoie, *Constitutional Amendment in Canada*, 244.
16 No reason for New Brunswick's dissent was given.
17 Hurley, *Amending Canada's Constitution*, 29.
18 Gérin-Lajoie, *Constitutional Amendment in Canada*, 246–9; Hurley, *Amending Canada's Constitution*, 27–9.
19 Ibid., 249.
20 Ibid., 248–9.
21 Hurley, *Amending Canada's Constitution*, 32.
22 Daniel Dupras, "The Constitution of Canada: A Brief History of Amending Procedure Discussions" (Ottawa: Library of Parliament, Research Branch, 1992).
23 "S. 92: In each Province the Legislature may exclusively make Laws in relation to Matters coming within the Classes of Subjects next hereinafter enumerated; that is to say, (1): 1. The Amendment from Time to Time, notwithstanding anything in this Act, of the Constitution of the Province, except as regards the Office of Lieutenant Governor." This section was repealed by the Constitution Act, 1982.
24 Hurley, *Amending Canada's Constitution*, 34.
25 Ibid., 35.
26 Russell, *Constitutional Odyssey*, 72.
27 Ibid., 73.
28 "Constitutional politics at the mega level is distinguished in two ways from normal constitutional politics. First, mega constitutional politics ... addresses the very nature of the political community on which the constitution is based ... Second, mega constitutional politics is exceptionally emotional and intense"; ibid., 75.
29 Hurley, *Amending Canada's Constitution*, 36.
30 Ibid.
31 Russell, *Constitutional Odyssey*, 79.
32 Ibid., 87.
33 Meekison, "Amending Formula," 102.
34 Meekison, "Amending Formula," 102.
35 Russell, *Constitutional Odyssey*, 88.
36 *Reference Re: Attorney General of Quebec and Attorney General of Canada*, [1982] 140 D.L.R. (3d), 385.
37 Russell, *Constitutional Odyssey*, 92.
38 Meekison, "Amending Formula," 103.

39 Ibid.
40 Ibid., 105.
41 Russell, *Constitutional Odyssey,* 115.
42 Ibid., 111.
43 Ibid., 110.
44 Ibid., 114.
45 Ibid., 113–15.
46 For full details on the political and legal challenges launched by Indigenous groups, see Douglas E. Sanders, "The Indian Lobby," in *And No One Cheered: Federalism, Democracy, and the Constitution Act,* ed. Keith G. Banting and Richard Simeon, 311–32 (Toronto: Methuen, 1983).
47 *Reference: Re Amendment to the Constitution of Canada, (Nos. 1, 2, and 3),* [1981] 125 D.L.R. (3d) 1.
48 Meekison, "Amending Formula," 106.
49 Russell, *Constitutional Odyssey,* 120.
50 *R v Secretary of State for Foreign and Commonwealth Affairs: Ex parte Indian Association of Alberta* [1982] 2 All E.R. 118 (C.A.).
51 Richard Gwyn, "Masters in our own house!" *Toronto Star,* 17 April 1982, A1.
52 For a thorough account of the process that led to the Meech Lake Accord, as well as its content, reasons it was not ratified, and lessons learned, see Patrick J. Monahan, *Meech Lake: The Inside Story* (Toronto: University of Toronto Press, 1991).
53 For a thorough account of the process that led to the Charlottetown Accord, as well as its content, reasons it was not ratified, and lessons learned, see Nadia Verrelli, "Negotiating the Charlottetown Accord in Canada," in *Changing Federal Constitutions: Lessons from International Comparison,* ed. Arthur Benz and Felix Knupling, 161–90 (Leverkusen, Germany: Barbara Budrich Publications, 2012).
54 The regional veto act was introduced soon after the 1995 sovereignty referendum, in which 49.42 per cent of those who participated voted for an independent Quebec. During the referendum campaign, Prime Minister Chrétien promised that his government would not proceed with any constitutional changes without the consent of Quebec's National Assembly. The passing of this Act realized this promise.
55 Briefly, the Idle No More Movement is a grassroots protest movement that began in November 2012 to "help build sovereignty and the resurgence of nationhood" (see http://www.idlenomore.ca/vision). The movement was galvanized by the need to protest the 2013 federal omnibus budget bill (Bill C-45). Among other changes, Bill C-45 proposed amendments to the Indian Act, the Navigation Protection Act, and the Environmental Assessment Act.

To raise awareness of how these changes would affect Indigenous communities, rallies, teach-ins, round dances, flash mobs, and a National Day of Action were held across the country. The movement gained a large following and significant media attention. For a deeper understanding of the objectives of Idle No More, its impact on participants, and its meaning for Indigenous communities, see the website http://www.idlenomore.ca/ or Kino-nda-niimi Collective, *The Winter We Danced* (Winnipeg: Arbeiter Ring Publishing, 2014).

56 Dupras, "Constitution of Canada."

2 Uncovering the Wall Surrounding the Castle of the Constitution: Judicial Interpretation of Part V of the Constitution Act, 1982

ADAM DODEK

Constitutional amendment is almost always difficult. Such is the nature of a constitution as higher law that endures over generations, perhaps centuries. Although the requirements for amending a constitution are usually demanding, they are often straightforward and clear. Such is not the case in Canada, where constitutional amendment is not only difficult; it is also exceedingly complicated. We need only compare the provisions of Part V of the Constitution Act, 1982, consisting of twelve sections and numerous subsections to that of Article V of the US Constitution or section 128 of the Constitution of Australia, both of which consist of a single section.[1]

The complexity of the constitutional amendment procedure in Canada is compounded by several factors. Rather than being a well-constructed, albeit detailed, provision, Part V is complex and confusing, unclear in many respects, and raises many questions. This is perhaps surprising, given that the search for a domestic amending formula was a seven-decades-long journey and given the level and intensity of debate over the amending formula in the years preceding the adoption of the Constitution Act, 1982.[2] Part V was definitely not a constitutional afterthought; rather, it was the core of the deal struck between the premiers and the federal government in November 1981 that paved the way for patriation and the enactment of the Constitution Act, 1982 and the accompanying Charter of Rights and Freedoms.[3]

It is surprising that proposals that had been circulating for many months, years, and sometimes decades were not articulated in clearer terms. According to Stephen Scott, "many of the difficulties in Part V ... result from an attempt, in midnight drafting sessions, to adjust, in legal terms acceptable to all parties, language in another document incorporated by reference into the federal-provincial intergovernmental agreement of November 5, 1981."[4] The drafters and the participants clearly underestimated the complexity of Part V,[5] thus leaving the courts with much work to do to unravel its intricacies.

In terms of complexity and interpretive challenges within Part V, Scott likens section 43 to a Rubik's Cube without the instruction manual.[6] Perhaps the analogy could be extended to all of Part V: it is complicated, and its interlocking parts affect one another. However, Part V is actually more intricate than a Rubik's Cube. With a Rubik's Cube, we know its exact parameters; with Part V, we do not. With a Rubik's Cube, we know when we have "got it right"; with Part V, we do not, until the Supreme Court of Canada confirms it.

I prefer a different metaphor for Part V, one based on the Supreme Court's own metaphors. In recent cases dealing with Part V, the Court has taken to referring to the Constitution's "structure"[7] and "architecture."[8] In the *Provincial Judges Reference* (1997), one of the high-water marks for judicial rhetorical flourish, Chief Justice Antonio Lamer famously referred to the preamble as "the grand entrance hall to the castle of the Constitution."[9] If the Constitution is a "castle," then Part V is the wall that surrounds and protects it. The problem is that, like a good strategic defence system, much of the contours of the wall of Part V cannot be seen. And also like a good wall, Part V hides part of the "castle of the Constitution" it is designed to protect. Thus, Part V is more like the sort of invisible picture loved by children that is slowly revealed as you scratch a pencil over it: the contours of the picture appear piece by piece to expose the whole, but one has to work the pencil diligently over each part of the picture to reveal that part. So it is with Part V: bit by bit, the courts have scratched away its cover, revealing the pieces underneath.

As Peter Oliver describes, the open-ended definition the Supreme Court has given to "the Constitution of Canada" places a considerable burden on the Court to resolve the many questions likely to arise.[10] It is thus surprising that the body of judicial interpretation of Part V is rather thin, but more understandable when we realize how seldom issues regarding constitutional amendment come before the courts. The Supreme Court did not address Part V in any comprehensive manner until 2014, when two judgments – the *Supreme Court Act Reference* and the *Senate Reform Reference* – cast significant light on Part V, which had dwelled in the shadows for over three decades since its enactment in 1982.

In this chapter, I analyse what the courts have revealed of Part V to date, while also raising questions about other areas of Part V that remain hidden. I am cognizant and thankful that other contributors are addressing specific provisions of Part V, and so I say less about these issues. In the *Senate Reform Reference*, the Supreme Court explained that an analysis under Part V proceeds in two stages. First, it must be determined whether a contemplated change amends "the Constitution of Canada." Second, if so, then it must be determined which amendment procedures apply.[11] I follow and expand on this framework in the four sections of this chapter. Thus, in the second section, I analyse judicial interpretation of "the Constitution of Canada." This phrase is the entry point for Part V, and thus plays a critical role in constitutional amendment. The Supreme Court has applied different tests to determining whether something is part of "the Constitution of Canada," and open questions remain about whether various acts, doctrines, and principles are also part of it. This analysis therefore takes up the largest portion of the chapter. In the third section, I then examine the internal dynamics of the relationship between the different provisions of Part V of the Constitution Act, 1982. In the final section of the chapter, I examine judicial treatment of the relationship between Part V and other parts of the Constitution. Finally, I end with a brief discussion of various themes that emerge from judicial interpretation and additional questions still to be addressed in the unrevealed parts of Part V.

Triggering Part V: What Is "the Constitution of Canada"?

Starting (but Not Ending) with the Text

In most countries with a written constitution, its contents are readily identifiable: the castle is there for all to see. For example, the US Constitution consists of the text of the "Constitution of the United States" and amendments made thereto. It is a simple matter to determine whether a proposed law would amend the US Constitution, thus invoking the amending procedure. One must simply ask if the proposed law seeks either (1) to add a new provision to the Constitution or (2) to amend a provision in the text of the Constitution or any amendment thereto. This is not the case in Canada, which has no single, unified written text.

The phrase "the Constitution of Canada" is thus a critical and uncertain legal term of art. It is the castle that Part V is constructed to protect, but its scope is not certain. Part V is entitled "Procedure for Amending *the Constitution of Canada"* (my emphasis), and the phrase "the Constitution of Canada" is found in sections 38, 41, 42, 43, 44, and 47 of that Part. The phrase "the Constitution of Canada" has rightly been called "[t]he elusive thread that is interwoven throughout the five basic procedures of Part V."[12] Identifying "the Constitution of Canada" is the domain that necessitates entry by the passkeys set out in Part V. Simply put, if proposed legislation does not involve "the Constitution of Canada," the stringent requirements of Part V may be dispensed with and legislation may proceed by the ordinary legislative process, federal or provincial.[13] So what does "the Constitution of Canada" mean?

The constitutional text is the starting point; it reveals most, but not all, of "the Constitution of Canada." Moreover, judicial interpretation has not made clear how much more there is to "the Constitution of Canada" beyond the text. Section 52(2) of the Constitution Act, 1982 provides:

Constitution of Canada

(2) The Constitution of Canada includes

    (*a*) the *Canada Act 1982*, including this Act;

    (*b*) the Acts and orders referred to in the schedule; and

    (*c*) any amendment to any Act or order referred to in paragraph (*a*) or (*b*).

There are twenty-four acts or orders listed in the schedule. Thus, we know much of the contents of "the Constitution of Canada," but other hidden parts exist, and some of them have been recognized or revealed through judicial interpretation. For example, the Supreme Court held, in *New Brunswick Broadcasting v Nova Scotia* (1993),[14] that the definition of "the Constitution of Canada" in section 52(2) of the Constitution Act, 1982 was not exhaustive; it may also include unwritten concepts. The Supreme Court has subsequently thrice confirmed this.[15] In *New Brunswick Broadcasting*, the Court found that parliamentary privilege should be considered part of "the Constitution of Canada" on the basis that the preamble to the Constitution Act, 1867 proclaims the intention to establish "a Constitution similar in Principle to that of the United Kingdom."[16]

The Court's decision in *New Brunswick Broadcasting* holding that the definition of "the Constitution of Canada" in section 52(2) is not exhaustive was controversial, and the Court openly acknowledged this. In his earlier writings, Peter Hogg warned of "grave consequences (namely, supremacy and entrenchment …) of the inclusion of other instruments."[17] Justice Beverley McLachlin (as she then was), writing for the majority, quoted this and other passages from Hogg, and accepted "the spirit of the remarks of Hogg that additions to the 30 instruments set out in the Schedule to s. 52(2) of the Constitution Act, 1982 might have grave consequences" for the reasons Hogg mentioned above. However, she stated that, as Hogg himself had conceded, section 52(2) was clearly not intended to be exhaustive.[18]

Using the preamble to import parliamentary privilege into "the Constitution of Canada" was criticized in the dissenting opinion[19] and later by Hogg, who warned that "the Court's decision means that the definition is capable of judicial expansion by virtue of implications from other parts of the Constitution. This raises the possibility of further additions, which destroys the certainty, apparently afforded by the list of 30 instruments that is scheduled to s.52(2)."[20] Other commentators, however, have supported the decision. Thus, Patrick Monahan stated that "[b]y treating the definition of the Constitution of Canada in section 52 as non-exhaustive, the Court will retain the flexibility needed to ensure that such anomalous results are avoided. It goes without saying that the courts should be very cautious before deciding, if at all, to add an enactment or a legal rule to the list of matters included in section 52, given the significant legal consequences that would flow from such a decision."[21]

The open-ended definition of "the Constitution of Canada" is now settled law, although the nature of that open-endedness is still not clear. Monahan's warning that the courts should be cautious before adding to the list of matters included in section 52 has proved prescient. At first, however, the Supreme Court seemed to embrace an extremely open and broad approach to "the Constitution in Canada" – one that perhaps threatened overwhelm the definition of that phrase and Part V. In the *Quebec Secession Reference* (1998), for example, it stated that this term "embraces unwritten, as well as written rules."[22] The Court then referred to its decision in the *Provincial Judges Reference*[23] that would seem to indicate clearly that the unwritten principle of "judicial independence" it recognized in that case through the preamble – the grand entrance hall to the castle of the Constitution – is surely part of "the Constitution of Canada" and therefore subject to Part V. In the *Quebec Secession Reference*, however, the Court went even further. Quoting from the *Patriation Reference* (1981),[24] it stated that "the Constitution of Canada includes 'the global system of rules and principles which govern the exercise of constitutional authority in the whole and in every part of the Canadian state.'"[25] The Court had also stated in the *Patriation Reference* that constitutional conventions were also part of the Constitution.

These statements about "the Constitution of Canada" should not be taken to mean "the Constitution of Canada" for purposes of Part V, however, because the *Patriation Reference* both predated the use of that term in Part V and because the *Quebec Secession Reference* did not address Part V. Such statements should not be taken to expand "the Constitution of Canada" under section 52(2) and under Part V, but to reflect "the political constitution" rather than the "legal constitution" (that is, "the Constitution of Canada" in section 52(2) and Part V). Justice John Sopinka made this distinction in *Osborne v Canada (Treasury Board)* (1991)[26] in expressly rejecting the inclusion of constitutional conventions as part of "the Constitution of Canada." The same reasoning should apply to the sweeping statements made by the Supreme Court in the *Quebec Secession Reference*.

In contrast, the Supreme Court and lower courts have demonstrated a much more cautious and case-by-case approach to the incorporation of new documents or principles into "the Constitution of Canada." No full legislative enactment has been recognized as part of "the Constitution of Canada" under section 52. As discussed below, the Supreme Court recognized portions of the Supreme Court Act as part of "the Constitution of Canada" in the *Supreme Court Act Reference*. In a decision affirmed by the Ontario Court of Appeal, the Ontario Superior Court of Justice, in *O'Donohue v Canada* (2003),[27] held that the rules of succession in the Act of Settlement, 1701, were part of "the Constitution of Canada." Applying the holding in *New Brunswick Broadcasting* (1999) that parliamentary privilege was essential to the proper functional of the legislature, the Ontario Superior Court held that "Canada's structure as a constitutional monarchy and the principle of sharing the British monarch are fundamental to our constitutional framework." In *Teskey v Canada* (2014),[28] the Ontario Court of Appeal held that the rules of succession "are a part of the fabric of the constitution and incorporated into it."[29] These decisions implicate the "Office of the Queen" under section 41(a) in Part V (for more detail, see Philippe Lagassé and Patrick Baud, Chapter 12 in this volume). These cases revealed only small portions of Part V, but in 2014, however, the Supreme Court revealed large swathes of Part V in two cases.

Lessons from the Supreme Court Act Reference *and the* Senate Reform Reference

The disputed appointment of Justice Marc Nadon to the Supreme Court of Canada forced judicial resolution of an issue that otherwise would have lain dormant for decades: whether the high court is constitutionally entrenched as part of the "Constitution of Canada." The Supreme Court is the subject of separate comprehensive treatment by Erin Crandall in this volume (Chapter 10), as is the Senate by Emmett Macfarlane (Chapter 11). My point here is to attempt to analyse what the *Supreme Court Act* and *Senate Reform References* tell us about broader issues under Part V.

The Supreme Court's uncertain constitutional status derives from a paradox or a conflict in the Constitutional Act, 1982. On the one hand, the Supreme Court Act was not included in the list of statutes contained in the schedule of the Constitutional Act, 1982, or recognized as forming part of the "Constitution of Canada" in section 52(2). The Court is, however, expressly mentioned twice in Part V. Section 41(d) provides that amendments to "the composition of the Supreme Court of Canada" may be made only by way of Parliament and the unanimous consent of the provinces. Section 42(1)(d) provides that "subject to paragraph 41(d)," amendments to the Constitution in relation to "the Supreme Court of Canada" must be made in accordance with the general procedure.

In the *Supreme Court Act Reference*,[30] however, the Court held that it was constitutionally entrenched *prior* to the adoption of Part V of the Constitution Act, 1982. As the Court explained, "[t]he Supreme Court's constitutional status initially arose from the Court's historical evolution into an institution whose continued existence and functioning engaged the interests of both Parliament and the provinces. The Court's status was then confirmed by the *Constitution Act, 1982*, which reflected the understanding that the Court's essential features formed part of the Constitution of Canada."[31] The Court was not clear on when exactly it became constitutionally entrenched, which is not of particular importance for the Court under Part V, but it might be for the continued challenge of recognizing new institutions under "the Constitution of Canada."

I leave aside the Court's interpretation of "the composition of the Supreme Court" under section 41(d) because that phrase appears unique to the Court and provides little indication of any application beyond that institution (see Erin Crandall, in this volume). Rather, I focus on the Court's holding that "[e]ssential features of the Court are constitutionally protected under Part V of the *Constitution Act, 1982*."[32] The Court uses similar language in the *Senate Reform Reference*, holding that Part V protects "the fundamental nature and role of the institutions provided for in the Constitution" from being altered unilaterally either by a provincial government under section 45 or by the federal government under section 44.[33]

The language and the logic of these two decisions likely could be applied to other subjects in Part V. Thus, it is probable that, in interpreting "the Office of the Queen, the Governor General and the Lieutenant Governor of a province" under section 41(a), a court would find that this provision protects only the "essential features" of each institution. Thus, the power of a province to amend its own constitution under section 45 should allow it to make changes to the office of the lieutenant-governor so long as it does not impair the "essential features" of the office. The same should apply to Parliament's power under section 44 respecting changes to the office of the Queen and the governor general. For example, changes to the manner in which Royal Assent is granted are properly within the power of Parliament, acting alone under section 44.[34]

Thus, it is likely that parts of the "Letters Patent Constituting the Office of the Governor General and Commander in Chief of Canada" (1947) would be recognized as part of "the Constitution of Canada" in the same manner as the Supreme Court indicated that the Court's "essential features," rather than all the provisions of the Supreme Court Act, are constitutionally entrenched.[35]

The explicit mention of the Supreme Court twice in Part V makes it much easier to recognize the Court as constitutionally entrenched. However, we might consider other institutions that have evolved into important constitutional structures and whose "continued existence" engage the interests of both Parliament and the provinces. Could the chief electoral officer and the auditor general simply be abolished unilaterally by Parliament under section 44? We might also add political parties, which have come to play a vital constitutional role, but which have generally escaped public law or constitutional scrutiny.

Outside the Constitution of Canada: Provincial Constitutions (Generally)

Provincial constitutions are generally not part of "the Constitution of Canada." Some parts of provincial constitutions are contained within the Constitution Acts, 1867 to 1982, yet courts have held, rightly, that they are not part of "the Constitution of Canada," and thus can be amended unilaterally by the province under section 45.[36] Moreover, some provisions may be part of both the "constitution of the province" and "the Constitution of Canada" at the same time (for more on this, see Emmanuelle Richez, Chapter 8 in this volume). These provisions are constitutionally entrenched and subject to other amending procedures in Part V.

Several courts have held expressly that provincial constitutions are generally not part of "the Constitution of Canada."[37] Justice Jean Beetz's decision in *OPSEU v Ontario (Attorney General)* (1987)[38] should be taken as a leading expositor on the meaning of "the constitution of the province" in Part V, even though his decision was not interpreting Part V directly. In *OPSEU*'s strange procedural posture, it was argued in March 1986, after Part V had come into effect, but it related to legislation enacted before Part V had come into effect. Thus, the Court was interpreting the predecessor of section 45 – namely, section 92(1) of the Constitution Act, 1867. However, it clearly was interpreting the phrase "the constitution of the province" against the background of Part V, despite not formally expressing an opinion on the interpretation of that phrase in section 45.[39] The Court held that section 92(1) allowed provincial legislatures to enact amendments only in relation to "the operation of an organ of the government of the province provided it is not otherwise entrenched as being indivisibly related to the implementation of the federal principle or to a fundamental term or condition of the union."[40]

The Supreme Court subsequently indicated that *OPSEU*'s interpretation of section 92(1) remains relevant to interpreting section 45. In the *Senate Reform Reference*, the Court referred to sections 44 and 45 as "the successors" to sections 91(1) and 92(1),[41] ensuring the relevance of judicial decisions under sections 91(1) and 92(1) to the interpretation of sections 44 and 45. The Court held that sections 91(1) and 92(1) empowered the federal and provincial governments to amend their respective constitutions "provided that the amendments did not engage the interests of the other level of government."[42] And the Court relied on its decision in *OPSEU* quoted above.

There is conceptual and logical clarity to treating "the constitution of the province" as not being part of "the Constitution of Canada." The contrary view would treat the former as part of the latter, with the caveat that, generally, a province may make amendments to "the Constitution of Canada" that involve "the constitution of the province" unilaterally, unless an exception applies. The problem with this view arises not within Part V but outside it. If "the constitution of the province" is considered part of "the Constitution of Canada," the supremacy clause in section 52(1) would apply to it. This would have two effects. First, as I discuss below, amendments to "the Constitution of Canada" are not subject to attack on other constitutional grounds, especially on Charter grounds. Considering "the constitution of the province" as part of "the Constitution of Canada" thus would immunize such legislation – extremely broadly defined in *OPSEU* – from Charter scrutiny. This is directly contrary to the Supreme Court's holding in *OPSEU* and subsequent cases that such legislation was subject to the Charter.[43] Second, if "the constitution of the province" is considered part of "the Constitution of Canada," then laws inconsistent with it would be "of no force and effect" by virtue of section 52(1). This would be a radical constitutional change. It is thus clearer both legally and conceptually to exclude generally "the constitution of the province" from "the Constitution of Canada." This approach also provides consistency with the many subsequent Supreme Court decisions involving Charter challenges to legislation that must be considered part of "the constitution of the province."[44]

Several exceptions, however, bring aspects of "the constitution of the province" within "the Constitution of Canada." The first is found in the text of section 45, which is made expressly subject to section 41 (the unanimity procedure). The only provisions of section 41 that could be part of "the constitution of the province" are "the office of ... the Lieutenant Governor" (section 41(a)) and, "subject to section 43, the use of the English or the French language" (section 41(c)). In accordance with the *Supreme Court Act Reference*, the "essential features" of both these matters should be taken as constitutionally entrenched as part of "the Constitution of Canada," in addition to being part of the constitution of the province.

The second exception is where an aspect of "the constitution of the province" is entrenched elsewhere in the Constitution Acts, 1867 to 1982 – for example, section 133 of the Constitution Act, 1867. Warren Newman rightly suggests that the Supreme Court's twin 1979 decisions in *Blaikie* and *Forest* suggest that the "constitution of a province" may also in certain circumstances be part of "the Constitution of Canada."[45] The Supreme Court's decision in *R. v Mercure* (1988)[46] also supports this conclusion.

Where Things Stand: Multiple Tests for Determining "the Constitution of Canada"

There now appear to be two or possibly three tests for recognizing a document, institution, or principle as part of "the Constitution of Canada." The first is what I call the "incorporation test"[47] created in *New Brunswick Broadcasting*, where the Supreme Court used the preamble to recognize an addition to "the Constitution of Canada," and asked if the doctrine of parliamentary privilege was "a foundational premise of the Constitution." The incorporation test is backward looking, and focuses on the contents of "a Constitution similar in principle to that of the United Kingdom" in 1867, when that provision was enacted. I call this the "incorporation test" because it asks what doctrines were incorporated into "the Constitution of Canada" through the preamble to the Constitution Act, 1867. So far only parliamentary privilege and judicial independence have been so recognized.

The second is the "evolutionary test," which takes its name from language used in the *Supreme Court Act Reference*.[48] There, the Court stated that its constitutional status "initially arose from the Court's historical evolution into an institution whose continued existence and functioning engaged the interests of both Parliament and the provinces."[49] Elsewhere, it stated that the Supreme Court "is a foundational premise of the Constitution."[50] While using the same language as in *New Brunswick Broadcasting*, the Court cannot be referring to the same thing in the *Supreme Court Act Reference*. In the former, the Court was referring to the foundational premise in 1867, which could not include the Court, since it was not created until 1875 and did not obtain constitutional status as a final court of appeal until after the abolition of appeals to the Judicial Committee of the Privy Council in 1949. The *Supreme Court Act Reference* adds the requirement that the "continued existence and functioning" of the institution must engage "the interests of both Parliament and the provinces."[51] There is thus an obvious link between the evolutionary test and the "living tree" doctrine of constitutional interpretation.

The third test is the "constitutional structure/constitutional architecture test" inspired by the frequent use of these terms in both the *Supreme Court Act Reference* and the *Senate Reform Reference* (as well as in the *Quebec Secession Reference*).[52] Under this test, a legislative enactment, even if it does not alter the constitutional text, is taken to amend "the Constitution of Canada" if it alters the constitutional "structure" or "architecture." In the *Senate Reform Reference*, the Supreme Court stated that "[t]he concept of an 'amendment to the Constitution of Canada,' within the meaning of Part V ... is informed by the nature of the Constitution and its rules of interpretation ... [T]he Constitution should not be viewed as a mere collection of discrete textual provisions. It has an architecture, a basic structure. By extension, amendments to the Constitution are not confined to textual changes. They include changes to the Constitution's architecture."[53]

There is significant overlap between the evolutionary test and the constitutional structure test. This can be seen in the statement in the *Supreme Court Act Reference* that the Court "emerged as a constitutionally essential institution engaging both federal and provincial interests," which "was already essential under the Constitution's architecture as the final arbiter of division of powers disputes and as the final general court of appeal for Canada" prior to 1982.[54] According to the Court, Part V "confirmed" its status "as a constitutionally protected institution."[55] By 1982, the Court was already "an essential part of Canada's constitutional architecture."[56]

There is also a link between the incorporation test and the constitutional structure test. The Supreme Court does not make the link, but its approach and conclusion in the *Supreme Court Act Reference* flow logically from its decision in *New Brunswick Broadcasting*. Once "the Constitution of Canada" includes unwritten elements or doctrines – such as parliamentary privilege – then substance is elevated over form: the applicable test can no longer be whether a proposed government action alters the text of something in the Constitution Acts, 1867 to 1982 because there is no text to amend.

However, the choice of test might determine whether something is found to part of "the Constitution of Canada." The incorporation test favours recognizing doctrines or concepts, such as parliamentary privilege and judicial independence, as part of "the Constitution of Canada." The evolutionary test and the constitutional structure test favour recognizing institutions, such as the Supreme Court and the Senate. It is thus not altogether clear that parliamentary privilege would meet the requirements of the second or third test; however, it is likely that a doctrine such as responsible government would meet the requirements of each test.

The Relationship between the Different Provisions of Part V

Part V does not state how its different provisions relate to one another, but in the *Senate Reform Reference*, the Supreme Court stated that the process in section 38 is the default rule for amendments to the Constitution and that "the other procedures in Part V should be construed as exceptions to the general rule."[57] This is a different approach than the Newfoundland Court of Appeal took in *Hogan v Newfoundland (Attorney General)* (2000), where that court did not find any presumption in favour of a particular rule, but essentially adopted a "choose-the-best-procedure" approach. The rule created by the Supreme Court in the *Senate Reform Reference* thus creates the presumption that section 38 will apply unless a party is able to demonstrate that one of the other "exceptions" applies.

The procedures in Part V should be considered alternative, not cumulative. In *Hogan*, the Newfoundland Court of Appeal explicitly held that Part V creates alternative methods of amendment, not cumulative ones: "[t]he procedures for amending the Constitution are complex. The suggestion of the appellants would, because of minimal even tangential effect, invoke a more complex procedure."[58] The Supreme Court denied leave to appeal in *Hogan*,[59] so it did not explicitly rule on this subject, but its subsequent elaboration of Part V in the *Senate Reform Reference* would indicate the correctness of the approach in *Hogan*. Generally, the Court has never considered the possibility that more than one amending procedure could apply to a particular issue. In the *Senate Reform Reference* specifically, it stated that section 38 is "the procedure of general application for amendments to the Constitution of Canada. As a result, the other procedures in Part V should be construed as exceptions to the general rule."[60] Thus, in setting up the dichotomy of a general rule and exceptions, the Court implicitly has accepted the proposition in *Hogan* that the procedures in Part V are alternative, not cumulative.

Hogan was the most comprehensive treatment of Part V issues before the Supreme Court's twin decisions in the *Senate Reform Reference* and the *Supreme Court Act Reference*. For whatever reason, the Court did not comment on any aspects of *Hogan*, leaving the continued validity of certain statements in that decision unclear. In many ways, however, the Court's pronouncements and actions in the two 2014 references are consistent with the important rulings in *Hogan*. Thus, in *Hogan*, the Newfoundland Court of Appeal explicitly rejected the application of the general procedure to the amendment to the Newfoundland Act because it would have permitted an amendment to the Constitution that affected Newfoundland and Labrador to be passed without the province's consent. Without referencing *Hogan*, the Supreme Court called attention to this general problem in the *Senate Reform Reference*, explaining that, in such cases, the general procedure would "overshoot the mark." The Court further stated that "[s]ection 43 also serves to ensure that those provisions [which apply only to one or several, but not all, of the provinces] cannot be amended without the consent of the province for which the arrangement was devised."[61]

Section 45 empowers a province to amend provisions of "the constitution of the province" that are contained in the Constitution Acts, 1867 to 1982, but are not otherwise entrenched as part of "the Constitution of Canada" as I described above. Provinces may enact legislation that expressly or implicitly overrides provisions of the Constitution Act, 1867 or other statutes relating to the "constitution of the province." Provinces lack the power to repeal such provisions formally, but the legislation enacted must essentially repeal the provision; they cannot act inconsistently with such provisions.

These are the lessons from the Supreme Court's decision in *Re Eurig* (1998).[62] Section 53 of the Constitution Act, 1867 requires that bills imposing any tax shall originate in the House of Commons; section 90 makes this provision applicable to the provinces. The Court thus found that Ontario's probate levy, which had been created by regulation, was a direct tax *intra vires* the province pursuant to section 92(2) of the Constitution Act, 1867 that the combination of sections 53 and 90 of the Constitution Act, 1867 required that "all provincial bills for the imposition of any tax must originate in the legislature,"[63] and that the rationale underlying section 53 was "no taxation without representation" – that is, "by requiring any bill that imposes a tax to originate with the legislature ... [t]he Lieutenant Governor in Council cannot impose a new tax *ab initio* without the authorization of the legislature."[64] The Court also found that section 52(1) of the Constitution Act, 1982 (the supremacy clause) requires that any provincial legislation that seeks to amend the constitution of a province must do so expressly. Because it had not expressly amended "the constitution of the province" by making section 53 inapplicable to it, Ontario was required to comply with its requirements. Because the province had failed to do so, the tax at issue was rendered unconstitutional.[65] As Warren Newman states: "This decision must be read ... as addressed only to amendments to the provincial constitution that are intended to alter, amend or suspend the application of provisions that are found within the *Constitution Acts, 1867 to 1982* per se, and not to amendments to the constitution of the province that are in the nature of organic laws of public administration of the type contemplated in *OPSEU*, which do not seek or purport to amend the text of provisions within the *Constitution Acts*."[66]

Indeed, the courts have upheld laws as amendments to provincial constitutions that have the effect of altering provisions of the Constitution Act, 1867, as Newman discusses.[67] For example, section 85 of the Constitution Act, 1867 provides that sessions of the legislatures of Ontario and Quebec shall not extend longer than four years, but both provinces enacted legislation changing the maximum duration of their legislatures to five years. A challenge was brought to Ontario's extension, the Legislative Assembly Extension Act, 1942, but in 1943 the Ontario Court of Appeal upheld the Act's validity despite its clash with the express language of section 85 of the Constitution Act, 1867.[68] In 1997 the Quebec Superior Court upheld the constitutionality of the abolition in 1968 of Quebec's Legislative Council, which was explicitly provided for in the Constitution Act, 1867.[69] The same year, on similar grounds, the Manitoba Court of Queen's Bench rejected a similar challenge to the 1876 statute that abolished that province's Legislative Council.[70]

The Relationship of Part V to Other Provisions of the Constitution: Exclusivity

The requirements of Part V should be considered exclusive. To return to our metaphor of Part V as a wall surrounding the castle of the Constitution, portions of Part V might be hidden to us, but it is the only wall: there are no other "walls" to climb over in amending the Constitution except for those that make up Part V. Attempts frequently have been made to set up other barriers in addition to those contained in Part V, but the Supreme Court and lower courts properly have rejected such attempts.

The Supreme Court did not address exclusivity expressly in either the *Supreme Court Act Reference* or the *Senate Reform Reference*, but the issue is implied from the Court's decision in the latter case, where it described Part V as providing "the blueprint for how to amend the Constitution of Canada."[71] Several parties also pressed the Court to use unwritten constitutional principles to amplify or add to the requirements of Part V, but, without any comment, the Court refused to do so.

An earlier Supreme Court decision also points to the exclusivity of Part V. In *Native Women's Assn. of Canada v Canada* (1994),[72] the Court did not address Part V expressly, but, rather, constitutional discussions that potentially could lead to a process under Part V. The Court unanimously held that neither the Charter nor section 35 provides any group the right to participate in constitutional discussions. Thus, if there is no right to participate in discussions that serve as a prelude to Part V, it is difficult to see how there could be a right outside Part V that supplements the requirements of this part. As I discuss below, the Supreme Court's creation of a duty to negotiate in the *Quebec Secession Reference* should be considered a special case, restricted to secession.

The Newfoundland Court of Appeal did expressly address the exclusivity of Part V. In *Hogan*,[73] it held that Part V is a "complete code," meaning that additional requirements outside of this part may not be imposed on the amendment process. It adopted this term from Peter Hogg, who had stated and continues to state that Part V constitutes "a complete code of legal (as opposed to conventional rules which enable all parts of the 'Constitution of Canada' to be amended."[74] The Newfoundland court rejected the contention that there could be additional requirements to those contained in Part V before an amendment could be effective under the law of contract. The court held that, since the Terms of Union between Canada and Newfoundland were given the force of law by the Newfoundland Act, which is explicitly enumerated in the schedule to the Constitution Act, 1982 and therefore part of the Constitution, the provision in question – Term 17 – was subject to the amending procedures in Part V and nothing more.[75]

Similarly, the obligation to negotiate imposed by the Supreme Court in the *Quebec Secession Reference* should be seen either as lying outside Part V or as an exception to the general rule that Part V is a complete code. The better interpretation is to view the duty to negotiate as a special rule for secession that lies outside Part V, rather than as an additional requirement imposed on top of those contained in Part V. This is supported by the fact that the Court did not address Part V in the *Quebec Secession Reference*. Thus, we can imagine the unlikely scenario in which Quebec (or another province) might seek to secede from Canada, but without any negotiation between the province and the federal government and the other provinces, with all the parties complying instead with whatever the relevant amending procedure is determined to be. It seems highly unlikely that an opposing party would succeed in challenging the constitutionality of secession if the Court found that the correct procedure in Part V had been complied with. In *Hogan*, the Newfoundland Court of Appeal expressly rejected the application of the duty to negotiate to constitutional amendment outside the secession context.[76] At least in the context of secession, Warren Newman has argued that the duty to negotiate can be seen to flow from the right of the constitutional actors to engage the multilateral amending procedures under section 46 of the Constitution Act, 1982.[77] (Kate Puddister addresses further issues specific to secession in her contribution to this volume.)

The Charter, for its part, does not apply to most of the amending procedures set out in Part V. In *Penikett v Canada*,[78] the Yukon government challenged the Meech Lake Accord as violating the rights of Yukoners under the Charter in various respects. The British Columbia Court of Appeal, sitting as the Court of Appeal for the Yukon, held that section 32 of the Charter – the application clause – does not apply to procedures under Part V, and that a constitutional amendment is not a "matter" within the authority of either Parliament or the provinces within the meaning of section 32. Rather, the amending power under Part V "is vested in a joint decision of both federal and provincial authority."[79] The Northwest Territories Court of Appeal reached the same conclusion in a parallel appeal.[80] Finally, in 2000, the Newfoundland Court of Appeal affirmed the same principle in a different context.[81] Thus, a decade and a half later, it now appears clear – despite the lack of a definitive Supreme Court pronouncement – that the Charter does not apply to consideration of a proposed amendment under Part V.[82]

The Charter does apply, however, to Parliament's acting alone under section 44 and to provincial legislatures under section 45. This conclusion is reached as a matter of precedent, pragmatism, and doctrine. As a matter of precedent, courts have subjected legislation enacted by the federal and provincial governments under sections 44 and 45 to Charter scrutiny.[83] As a pragmatic matter, immunizing such legislation from Charter scrutiny would exempt a huge class of legislation from constitutional review, given the Supreme Court's broad definition of "constitution" in OPSEU. As a matter of doctrine, Hogg states that such legislation is caught by the literal language of section 32 of the Charter.[84] Moreover, as noted previously, the Charter does apply to amendments to provincial constitutions because they generally do not form part of "the Constitution of Canada."[85]

Unwritten constitutional principles should also not apply to Part V[86] – the Supreme Court has not clarified the relationship between these principles and Part V, and it appears that they cannot add to the requirements of Part V. Indeed, when pressed, the Court has demonstrated an unwillingness to consider, let alone rule, on the issue. Thus, in the Senate Reform Reference, several parties raised unwritten constitutional principles as potential factors influencing the choice of amendment procedures or as adding to the textual requirements. Several attorneys general of the provinces and territories relied particularly on the unwritten constitutional principle of federalism in the attempt to amplify the requirements of Part V,[87] while francophone minority interveners from outside Quebec relied heavily on the principle of the protection of minorities. Senator Serge Joyal argued that there was an obligation on the part of the federal government to consult with Aboriginal peoples,[88] and the Northwest Territories government argued that the federal government had a duty to "consult, consider and represent" the interests of citizens of the Northwest Territories who are excluded from Part V.[89]

The argument of the territories was very persuasive. How can it be that the Constitution essentially disenfranchises all Canadian citizens resident in the three territories? For the purposes of Part V, Canadians resident in the territories are a constitutional non-entity: they do not count in the population of Canada, and they have no voice in the actual amendment requirements. Section 38(1) provides for amendment by way of the general procedure through resolutions of the Senate and the House of Commons and "(b) resolutions of the legislative assemblies of at least two-thirds of the provinces that have, in the aggregate, according to the then latest general census, at least fifty per cent of the population of all the provinces." The only representation for the territories in this process is through their representatives in the Senate and the House of Commons. Furthermore, the territories have no distinct voice in the extension of a province into a territory (section 42(1)(e)) or in the establishment of new provinces (section 42(1)(f)) that could be created out of a territory. This is certainly a constitutional and democratic anomaly, which can be explained only by the constitutional view of the territories as essentially legal creatures of Parliament that would achieve constitutional recognition only if they were to become provinces. They are subject to the Constitution, but have no voice in its amendment.

Despite the compelling nature of such arguments, the Supreme Court did not address them in the *Senate Reform Reference*. Because they were put expressly before the Court, which issued a ruling inconsistent with such arguments, we should take them as not being accepted by the Court. Thus, the ruling of the Newfoundland Court of Appeal in *Hogan*[90] that unwritten constitutional principles cannot supplement the procedures of Part V should be accepted as an accurate statement of the law.

Conclusion

Constitutions are intended to be enduring statements of a nation's fundamental law. They stand above ordinary law in terms of both their normative status and the difficulty with which they can be changed.

The amendment clause of a constitution serves to both permit amendment and protect the constitution. In Part V of the Constitution Act, 1982, the drafters created a complex mechanism to facilitate amendment to "the Constitution of Canada." They left a difficult challenge for the Supreme Court, however, which was compounded by the drafters' failure to alter historical provisions in the Constitution Acts, 1867 to 1982 that had been superseded or "spent" by further legislative enactments. The Court has added to this complexity through the open-ended nature of the interpretation it has given to "the Constitution of Canada." As a result, we cannot even be sure of the scope of "the castle of the Constitution" that Part V exists to protect.

In 2014, the Supreme Court took a huge step in revealing wide swaths of Part V in the *Senate Reform Reference* and the *Supreme Court Act Reference*, but much of Part V has yet to be revealed. Multiple tests – the incorporation test, the evolutionary test, and the constitutional structure test – now exist for recognizing an enactment, institution, or a doctrine as part of "the Constitution of Canada," and the choice of test may determine whether or not something succeeds in being so recognized. Recognition thus remains the most critical and confounding question. If a proposed enactment does not impact upon "the Constitution of Canada," the analysis ends, and the province or the federal government may proceed by ordinary legislative process. If not, the Supreme Court must determine which amendment procedure in Part V applies.

On this issue, the Court provided much clarity in the *Senate Reform Reference* by designating the general amendment procedure in section 38 as the default formula and the others as exceptions. There is still much work to do in clarifying various provisions within Part V, and other contributors to this volume address some of these issues. Our collective efforts to reveal "the castle of the Constitution" and the wall that surrounds it – Part V – may assist future judicial interpretation, as the process of revealing the boundaries of Part V will continue in the courts for the foreseeable future.

Notes

Thanks to Emmett Macfarlane, Warren Newman, and Peter Oliver for their helpful comments. This chapter is dedicated to my friend, colleague, and University of Ottawa Public Law Group co-conspirator Peter Oliver. In appreciation for all.

1 US Constitution, art. V, and An Act to constitute the Commonwealth of Australia, 63 & 64 Victoria, c 12, s 128. Both of these have several exceptions and caveats, but are far simpler than Canada's Part V.

2 The search for an amending formula between 1926 and 1982 produced fourteen different attempts. See James Ross Hurley, *Amending Canada's Constitution: History, Processes, Problems and Prospects* (Ottawa: Canada Communication Group, 1996), 23–67. According to Hurley, the amending formula proposed by attorneys general in 1936 is "a distant mirror of the formula now in place" (xiv).

3 See Howard Leeson, *The Patriation Minutes* (Edmonton: University of Alberta, Faculty of Law, Centre for Constitutional Studies, 2011).

4 Stephen A. Scott, "Pussycat, Pussycat or Patriation and the New Constitutional Amendment Processes," *University of Western Ontario Law Review* 20 (1982): 250.

5 Thus, the explanatory notes for the April Accord agreed to between the premiers of all provinces except Ontario and Quebec, which subsequently formed the basis for Part V (see *Senate Reform Reference*, 2014 SCC 32, para. 30), identifies certain provisions as "self-explanatory" that clearly are not. See Constitutional Accord: Canadian Patriation Plan, 16 April 1981, Part A, paras 9(a), 10(a), and 10(b).

6 Stephen A. Scott, "The Canadian Constitutional Amendment Process," *Law and Contemporary Problems* 45, no. 4 (1982): 276.

7 See *Senate Reform Reference*, paras 3, 25, 26, 54, 55, 63, and 107; *Supreme Court Act Reference*, 2014 SCC 21, paras 82, 94, and 101; *Quebec Secession Reference*, [1998] 2 S.C.R. 217, paras 50, 51, 56, 62, 67, 70, 81, and 106.

8 See *Senate Reform Reference*, paras 27, 53, 54, 59, 60, 70, and 97; *Supreme Court Act Reference*, paras 82, 87, 88, and 100; and *Quebec Secession Reference*, paras 50 and 51.

9 *Provincial Judges Reference*, [1997] 3 S.C.R. 3, para. 109.

10 Peter Oliver, "Canada, Quebec, and Constitutional Amendment," *University of Toronto Law Journal* 49, no. 4 (1999): 579.

11 *Senate Reform Reference*, para. 21.

12 Warren J. Newman, "Defining the 'Constitution of Canada' since 1982: The Scope of the Legislative Powers of Constitutional Amendment under Sections 44 and 45 of the *Constitution Act, 1982*," *Supreme Court Law Review* (2d) 22 (2003): 429.

13 Of course, amendments to "the Constitution of Canada" under sections 44 and 45 proceed through the normal federal and provincial legislative processes, respectively. Thanks to Warren Newman for pointing out this obvious but important point.

14 [1993] 1 S.C.R. 319.
15 See *Quebec Secession Reference*, para. 32; *Supreme Court Act Reference*, paras 97–100; and *Senate Reform Reference*, para. 24.
16 [1993] 1 S.C.R. 319, 378.
17 Peter W. Hogg, *Constitutional Law of Canada*, 3rd ed. (Toronto: Carswell, 1992), 1: 1–7.
18 *New Brunswick Broadcasting Co. v Nova Scotia (Speaker of the House of Assembly)*, [1993] 1 S.C.R. 319, paras 112–14.
19 Ibid., para. 158 (Sopinka J., dissenting).
20 Hogg, *Constitutional Law of Canada*, 3rd ed., section 1.4.
21 Patrick J. Monahan, *Constitutional Law*, 2nd ed. (Toronto: Irwin Law, 2002), 181.
22 *Quebec Secession Reference*, para. 32.
23 [1997] 3 S.C.R. 3, para. 92.
24 *Reference re Resolution to Amend the Constitution*, [1981] 1 S.C.R. 753.
25 *Quebec Secession Reference*, para. 32, quoting ibid., 874.
26 *Osborne v Canada (Treasury Board)*, [1991] 2 S.C.R. 69, 88.
27 *O'Donohue v Canada*, [2003] O.J. No 2764, [2003] O.T.C. 623, 109 C.R.R. (2d) 1 (S.C.J.), aff'd [2005] O.J. No. 965 (Ont. C.A.).
28 2014 ONCA 612.
29 Ibid., para. 6
30 2014 SCC 21.
31 Ibid., para. 76.
32 Ibid., para. 74.
33 *Senate Reform Reference*, para. 48.
34 See Newman, "Defining the 'Constitution of Canada' since 1982," 434–5, citing Royal Assent Act, S.C. 2002, c. 15.
35 *Supreme Court Act Reference*, para. 94.
36 Scott, writing in 1982, took a contrary view; see "Canadian Constitutional Amendment Process," 262.
37 See *MacLean v Nova Scotia (Attorney General)* [1987] N.S.J. No. 2, 35 D.L.R. (4th) 306, 76 N.S.R. (2d) 296 (N.S.S.C.-T.D.); and *Dixon v British Columbia (Attorney General)*, [1986] B.C.J. No. 916, 7 B.C.L.R. (2d) 174, paras 43–7.
38 *OPSEU v Ontario (Attorney General)* [1987] 2 S.C.R. 2.
39 "It may well be thought that the coming into force of the amending procedure has not altered the power of the province to amend its own constitution but I refrain from expressing any view on the matter" (ibid., 33).
40 Ibid., 40, per Justice Beetz, quoted in *Senate Reform Reference*, 2014 SCC 32, para. 47.
41 Ibid., para. 48.
42 Ibid., para. 47.

43 See *OPSEU v Ontario (Attorney General)*.

44 See *Re Provincial Electoral Boundaries (Sask.)*, [1991] 2 S.C.R. 158, 179 [*Saskatchewan Boundary* reference]; and *MacLean v Nova Scotia (Attorney General)*.

45 Newman, "Defining the 'Constitution of Canada' since 1982," 488, citing Scott, "Canadian Constitutional Amendment Process," 262; *R. v Mercure*, [1988] 1 S.C.R. 234, 271, 280.

46 *R. v Mercure*, 271, 280.

47 This title is inspired by the incorporation doctrine under the US Bill of Rights; see, generally, Laurence H. Tribe, *American Constitutional Law*, 2nd ed. (New York: Foundation Press, 1988), 772–4.

48 Cf. *Supreme Court Act Reference*, para. 76 ("Evolution of the Constitutional Status of the Supreme Court").

49 Ibid., para. 76.

50 Ibid., para. 89.

51 Ibid., para. 76.

52 See *Senate Reform Reference*, paras 27, 53, 54, 59, 60, 70, and 97; *Supreme Court Act Reference*, paras 82, 87, 88, and 100; *Quebec Secession Reference*, paras 50 and 51.

53 *Senate Reform Reference*, para. 27.

54 *Supreme Court Act Reference*, paras 87 and 88.

55 Ibid., para. 88.

56 Ibid., para. 100.

57 *Senate Reform Reference*, para. 36.

58 *Hogan v Newfoundland (Attorney General)*, 2000 NFCA 12, para. 81.

59 [2000] S.C.C.A. No. 191.

60 *Senate Reform Reference*, para. 36.

61 *Supreme Court Act Reference*, para. 44.

62 [1998] 2 S.C.R. 565.

63 Ibid., 581.

64 Ibid.

65 Ibid., 583.

66 Newman, "Defining the 'Constitution of Canada' since 1982," 492.

67 Ibid., 440–4.

68 *Tolfree v Clark*, [1943] O.R.501 (C.A.). Section 85 of the Constitution Act, 1867 provides: "Every Legislative Assembly of Ontario and every Legislative Assembly of Quebec shall continue for Four Years from the Day of the Return of the Writs for choosing the same (subject nevertheless to either the Legislative Assembly of Ontario or the Legislative Assembly of Quebec being sooner dissolved by the Lieutenant Governor of the

Province), and no longer." This provision and the legislation effectively amending it are discussed in detail in Newman, "Defining the 'Constitution of Canada' since 1982," 440–1.

69 *R. v Montplaisir*, [1997] R.J.Q. 109 (S.C.), appeal denied C.A.M. 500–10–000687–960, discussed in Newman, "Defining the 'Constitution of Canada' since 1982," 442–3.

70 *R. v Somers*, [1997] M.J. No. 57, [1997] 3 W.W.R. 107 (Man. Q.B.), discussed in detail in Newman, "Defining the 'Constitution of Canada' since 1982," 443–4.

71 *Senate Reform Reference*, para. 28.

72 [1994] 3 S.C.R. 627, [1994] S.C.J. No. 93.

73 2000 NFCA 12.

74 Ibid., para 73; see Peter W. Hogg, *Constitutional Law of Canada*, 5th ed. supp. (Toronto: Carswell, 2008), section 4.1(a).

75 Constitution Act, 1982, schedule (renamed the Newfoundland Act, 1949); *Hogan*, para. 61.

76 *Hogan*, para. 104.

77 Warren Newman, *The Quebec Secession Reference – The Rule of Law and the Position of the Attorney General of Canada* (Toronto: York University, Centre for Public Law and Public Policy, 1999), 46.

78 (1988), 45 DLR (4th) 108, [1988] 2 WWR 481, 21 BCLR (2d) 1, [1987] BCJ No 2543 (BCCA).

79 Ibid.

80 See *Sibbeston v Canada* (1988) 48 DLR (4th) 691 (NWT CA).

81 See *Hogan*, para. 88 (holding that the Charter of Rights did not apply to an amendment under section 43 of the Constitution Act, 1982).

82 For general agreement, see Hogg, *Constitutional Law of Canada*, 5th ed. supp., section 4.2(d).

83 *Saskatchewan Boundary Reference*, 179; *MacLean v Nova Scotia (Attorney General)*.

84 Hogg, *Constitutional Law of Canada*, 5th ed. supp., section 4.2.

85 *Saskatchewan Boundary Reference*, 179; *MacLean v Nova Scotia (Attorney General)*.

86 Cf. *Hogan*, paras 105–25.

87 See SCC File No. 35203, Facta of British Columbia, paras 54–71; Manitoba, paras 4, 28, and 39; New Brunswick, paras 48 and 68; Newfoundland and Labrador, paras 106–23; Northwest Territories, paras 86–93; Nova Scotia, paras 4, 23, 32, and 50; Ontario, para. 36; Prince Edward Island, paras 12–19, 93–4, and 99.

88 Factum of the Hon. Serge Joyal, paras 145–8, 159–61.

89 Factum of the Northwest Territories, paras 85–93.

90 2000 NFCA 12.

3 The Federal Principle: Constitutional Amendment and Intergovernmental Relations

CARISSIMA MATHEN

Since its founding in 1867, Canada has pursued large-scale constitutional reform numerous times.[1] Success was finally achieved via the UK Parliament's Canada Act 1982.[2] For many Canadians, the constitution that emerged is best known for the rights entrenched in the accompanying Charter of Rights and Freedoms.[3] The state-citizen relationship illustrates the aspect of constitutionalism most likely to be of interest to citizens. But the Constitution implicates numerous other structural features of the Canadian state, including how the machinery of government is organized, the agreements by which resources are shared, and the rules ordering the exercise of authority, law making, and adjudication.

Canada is committed to many foundational ideals and principles, including: democracy and the rule of law, pluralism, social welfare, and minority rights. But, perhaps first and foremost, the country is a federation.[4] Many Canadians derive a deep sense of belonging from their provinces[5] – indeed, for some, provincial identity might be the more potent source of political affiliation.[6] With its distinctive features, history, and constitutional demands, Quebec springs to mind, but other regions have experienced alienation as well.[7]

Amending the Constitution of Canada is difficult. The formal procedure (found in Part V of the Constitution Act, 1982)[8] was arrived at after decades of failed negotiation. Part V leaves some kinds of change unspecified,[9] and renders the route to other kinds of change ambiguous.[10] The fact that Part V entails different amending procedures leads to additional conundrums.

In the morass of Part V, is there, nonetheless, a unifying principle?

In this chapter, I argue that there is: the country's essential federal character. Canada was formed through the coming together of several distinct communities,[11] whose distinctiveness has shifted, but not disappeared. Of course, the provinces exist within a larger political structure with a separate and powerful governing authority. Nonetheless, Canada remains a "federally constituted whole,"[12] a fact that has had a profound impact on the constitutional amending process. A variety of narratives bear this out: the negotiations themselves, the precise formulae laid out in Part V, and the analysis found in several opinions of the Supreme Court of Canada.[13]

The difficult hurdles to amendment – which some call a "constitutional straitjacket"[14] – are a by-product of the country's history and politics. I am sympathetic to the perceived need, reflected in Part V, to protect the country's essential federal character. There is no question, though, that Part V privileges the provinces' role in amendment to the exclusion of other means of determining support, and hampers the likelihood of achieving future constitutional change.

Pre-patriation: The Provincial Role in Amendment

The Dominion of Canada was formed by four colonies in British North America.[15] The new nation-state was to be governed by a document enacted by the Imperial British Parliament.[16] The document's preamble, which has been described as the "grand entrance hall to the castle of the Constitution,"[17] set forth its essential aims:

> Whereas the Provinces of Canada, Nova Scotia, and New Brunswick have expressed their Desire to be federally united into One Dominion under the Crown of the United Kingdom of Great Britain and Ireland, with a Constitution similar in Principle to that of the United Kingdom:
> And whereas such a Union would conduce to the Welfare of the Provinces and promote the Interests of the British Empire:
> And whereas on the Establishment of the Union by Authority of Parliament it is expedient, not only that the Constitution of the Legislative Authority in the Dominion be provided for, but also that the Nature of the Executive Government therein be declared:
> And whereas it is expedient that Provision be made for the eventual Admission in the Union of other Parts of British North America:[18]

Several points about the preamble are noteworthy.

First, it refers to certain provinces' desire to be "federally united in one Dominion," suggesting that the impetus for Canada's founding was to create a federal state.

Second, the preamble refers to the wishes of the constituent parties to adhere to a constitution "similar in principle to that of the United Kingdom." Since the UK Constitution is largely unwritten, the preceding phrase has been interpreted to mean that Canada's Constitution, too, is partially unwritten. That fact has had significant implications for amendment. In 1981, the Supreme Court confirmed the existence of an unwritten convention requiring substantial provincial consent for certain kinds of amendments.[19] Post-patriation, unwritten norms have featured in the Court's interpretation of Part V (in the *Supreme Court Act Reference* and the *Senate Reform Reference*).

Third, the preamble expresses an intention to define the nature and scope of legislative powers and the nature of the executive branch of government. An important effect of the new Constitution was to distribute authority between the national and subnational units.

The final point to be taken from the preamble is its reference to the admission of new territories. Section 146 of the Constitution Act, 1867 permitted such admissions through "the Queen, by and with the advice of [the Privy Council]" where requested by the relevant legislatures.[20] Thus, one method of constitutional change – enlarging the constituent political community – clearly anticipated that some consent by other parties in the federation would be required.

The Constitution Act, 1867 is marked by exhaustive detail to some matters and glancing treatment of others. Perhaps the most striking example of the latter is its lack of a general amending formula. For some scholars, that fact reflects a nonchalant attitude to the prospect of continued Imperial control.[21] For others, it suggests merely that the participants did not view amendment as an urgent matter because they assumed that a suitable formula would soon be achieved.[22]

In 1931 the United Kingdom decided it would no longer enact laws for its self-governing dominions without their explicit request and consent.[23] Through the Statute of Westminster, it also granted to colonies the authority to amend Imperial statutes that continued to apply to them. But the new law expressly exempted the Constitution Act, 1867 (and subsequent amendments to it). In 1949, a new clause was added to that document giving the Canadian Parliament the power to amend the Constitution "from time to time."[24] The new provision, section 91(1), appeared limited to relatively minor changes. Indeed, its powers subsequently were described as mere "housekeeping."[25] Section 91(1) was repealed in 1982.

Prior to the Canada Act 1982, Canada's Constitution was amended several times.[26] In each case, Westminster was presented with a joint resolution of both houses of the Canadian Parliament. Although the provinces were consulted, they played no formal role.[27] And at various times between 1927 and 1982, the country's political leaders sought to negotiate a new amending formula.[28] Each time, however, the provinces failed to achieve consensus (for more on this, see Nadia Verrelli, Chapter 1 in this volume). As Simone Chambers notes, the half-dozen or so attempts during this period were undertaken by "political elites behind closed doors."[29]

In 1964 the country came very close to securing a package. The provinces agreed to take the proposed package back to their respective jurisdictions for a sounding. But in Quebec the package was perceived as inadequate to meet the province's newfound sense of itself and of its role within Canada. Eventually, Quebec withdrew its support.

In 1971 the prime minister and all the premiers reached initial agreement on a comprehensive package known as the Victoria Charter. The Charter included an entrenched bill of rights, separate language rights, an amending formula,[30] and provincial input into appointments to the Supreme Court of Canada. Once again, however, Quebec dropped out, and the agreement withered.

In 1976, after the election of a separatist government in Quebec, Prime Minister Pierre Elliott Trudeau urged the provinces to pursue patriation once again. He also threatened to proceed unilaterally should consensus not be achieved.[31] In May 1980, after the Quebec government narrowly lost a referendum on whether to pursue "sovereignty-association,"[32] the prime minister reinitiated constitutional negotiations. By the fall, with discussions at a standstill, Trudeau had tabled in Parliament a resolution for a package with a Charter of Rights and an amending formula. The resolution was adopted by the House of Commons on 23 April 1981 and by the Senate the next day.

The prime minister's decision to proceed unilaterally precipitated a split between eight provinces opposed to the resolution and two (Ontario and New Brunswick) prepared to support it. The "Gang of Eight" resolved to challenge the constitutionality of the resolution by way of references initiated in various provincial courts of appeal. These were eventually appealed, and on 28 September, in the *Patriation Reference*, a majority of the Supreme Court advised that the federal government was legally entitled to seek patriation. Because the proposed package trenched on existing provincial powers, however, it triggered an unwritten constitutional convention requiring "substantial provincial consent." For the federal government to proceed unilaterally, the majority concluded, would be constitutional in the legal sense but not in the conventional sense.

As a result of a series of negotiations in November 1981, a resolution was put forward to the UK Parliament with the consent of the federal government and all the provinces save Quebec.[33] The new constitutional framework, including the amending formula, came into effect on 17 April 1982.

The Provincial Element of Part V

The amending formula consists of several processes, requiring varying degrees of provincial consent.

The general formula, section 38, requires resolutions of the Senate, House of Commons, and the legislative assemblies of at least seven provinces representing at least 50 per cent of the population of the provinces.[34] The so-called 7/50 rule anticipates a robust provincial role. A threshold of seven out of ten provinces, combined with a population quota that, in effect, requires the consent of either Ontario or Quebec,[35] anticipates a significant degree, across multiple levels, of national consensus. The importance of provincial input is further confirmed by the section's provision that changes derogating from provincial powers will have no effect in any province that signals its dissent.[36]

An even greater provincial role is found in section 41, which requires unanimous consent for changes to:

(a) the office of the Queen, the Governor General and the Lieutenant Governor of a province;
(b) the right of a province to a number of members in the House of Commons not less than the number of Senators by which the province is entitled to be represented at the time this Part comes into force;
(c) subject to section 43, the use of the English or the French language;
(d) the composition of the Supreme Court of Canada; and
(e) an amendment to this Part.[37]

Granting a veto to every actor in the Canadian federation, the unanimity formula represents the most stringent requirement for change.[38] One might, therefore, expect it to be strictly construed. Yet, as I discuss below, section 41 thus far has been given a generous, as opposed to constrained, interpretation.

Three other routes to amendment exist: section 43, which permits changes affecting only some provinces through resolutions by those provinces and by Parliament; section 44, which grants Parliament unilateral power over amendments in relation to the executive government of Canada, the Senate, and the House of Commons; and section 45, which allows each province to amend its own constitution unilaterally.[39]

A degree of internal logic unites the various amending procedures. The general formula, with its high threshold of agreement, signals the importance of the provinces to Canada's constitutional decisions.[40] Unanimity is required for a more limited set of changes to essential national institutions and practices. In the case of changes that do not implicate all the provinces, the "some but not all" formula of section 43 – which still requires federal input – is available. And changes limited to a single actor may proceed unilaterally.

Despite its internal logic, some aspects of Part V are curious.[41] The multiple routes to amendment, together with the elaboration of specific situations triggering one route as opposed to another, can lead to ambiguity. Below I address two such instances, one regarding the Senate and one regarding the Supreme Court. In addition, a canvassing of the relevant jurisprudence shows that the provinces have always been considered integral to the amendment process. Recent judicial opinions confirm the essential federal character of the Canadian state, and demonstrate how that character has supported deeper entrenchment of provincial consent as a precondition to fundamental constitutional change.

The Federal Principle Confirmed

The general formula has been very rarely used,[42] and the unanimity formula not at all. But the Supreme Court has considered the parameters for constitutional change in a number of advisory opinions, or references. In these opinions, a particular understanding of intergovernmental relations emerges as the central analytic principle.

In 1980 the Supreme Court considered whether Parliament enjoyed the unilateral authority to make various changes to the Senate. The *Reference Re Legislative Authority of the Parliament of Canada in Relation to the Upper House* (*Senate Reference*) concerned a federal proposal to amend the Senate through ordinary legislation.[43] The federal government argued that the proposed changes lay within its exclusive authority under the former section 91(1) of the Constitution Act, 1867, discussed above.[44]

The Court paid particular heed to the historical context behind Confederation. Quoting George Brown, the Court wrote that "the very essence of [the] compact [was] that the union shall be federal."[45] The Senate was created to respond to regional concerns about a body empowered to enact legislation for the country as a whole. Because the Senate's role was, in part, to maintain Canada's essential federal character,[46] the federal government could not abolish it unilaterally.

One year later, the Supreme Court issued the *Patriation Reference*. By a vote of 7–2, the Court advised that the federal government was legally entitled to call upon the United Kingdom to pass the Canada Act 1982.[47] But, by a vote of 6–3, it found that doing so in the absence of provincial consent would be at odds with constitutional convention.[48] The majority said that a constitutional convention exists if it is supported by relevant precedents, the affected parties believe that those precedents are binding, and the convention is supported by adequate reasons. In its discussion of the latter element, the majority cited a notion that it called "the federal principle": "Canada is a federal union … The federal principle cannot be reconciled with a state of affairs where the modification of provincial legislative powers could be obtained by the unilateral action of the federal authorities. It would indeed offend the federal principle that 'a radical change to ... [the] constitution [be] taken at the request of a bare majority of the members of the Canadian House of Commons and Senate.'"[49] Thus, the federal principle lent support to the idea that there was a constitutional convention requiring substantial provincial consent for a proposed amendment that would derogate from provincial powers.

The federal principle is not absolute. It does not, for example, justify a presumption of *unanimous* provincial consent. Nor does it support a veto for Quebec.[50] But, overall, the jurisprudence has tended to emphasize, rather than minimize, the principle's importance. The *Quebec Secession Reference* is a good example.[51] The reference dealt, not with amendment per se,[52] but with the legal framework that would apply in the event that a province sought to secede from the federation. In developing that framework, the Supreme Court articulated a set of unwritten principles that it described as part of the Constitution's "architecture."[53] The first unwritten principle the Court identified, federalism, was described as "a central organizational theme" of the Constitution and "a political and legal response to underlying social and political realities." The coming together of distinct political units into a federation was a precondition to the nation's founding, permitting the reconciliation of "diversity with unity."[54]

In the *Senate Reform Reference* (2014), the Supreme Court was asked whether Part V grants Parliament the unilateral power to implement a framework for consultative elections to guide Senate appointments, set fixed senatorial terms, and remove the property and net worth requirements for appointees. The Court also considered what degree of provincial consent would be required to abolish the Senate entirely.[55] It concluded that, save for the property requirement as it applies to non-Quebec senators,[56] Parliament could not achieve the proposed changes on its own, but would have to abide by the general amending formula (or, in the case of removing the property requirement for Quebec senators, the bilateral amending formula). The Court advised, as well, that abolition of the Senate could be achieved only via section 41 (unanimity).[57] According to the Court, a defining feature of Part V is its guarantee of provincial input into constitutional choices engaging provincial interests. Part V exists "to constrain unilateral federal powers to effect constitutional change ... In principle, no province stands above the others with respect to constitutional amendments, and all provinces are given the same rights in the process of amendment. The result is an amending formula designed to foster dialogue between the federal government and the provinces on matters of constitutional change, and to protect Canada's constitutional *status quo* until such time as reforms are agreed upon."[58]

In discussing possible changes to the Senate, the Court strongly emphasized the need to respect the Constitution's underlying architecture.[59] "Architecture," the Court explained, describes a basic structure of the Constitution that extends beyond "discrete textual provisions."[60] If a proposed change affects the Constitution's architecture, it must fit within the scheme of Part V. The Court described the Senate as "a core component of the Canadian federal structure of government"[61] – designed, in part, to respond to provincial concerns about a central law-making body through the incorporation of a regionalist perspective. Thus, changes to the institution could well implicate the Constitution's architecture.

The Court then interrogated the proposed changes, looking at their interaction with both textual and structural elements of the Constitution. With respect to consultative elections, for example, the attorney general of Canada argued that the determinative factor should be whether such elections could be implemented without changing either the text of the Constitution Act, 1867 or the actual appointment mechanism.[62] According to the Court, this argument privileged form over substance: "Th[e Attorney General's] narrow approach is inconsistent with the broad and purposive manner in which the Constitution is understood and interpreted ... While the provisions regarding the appointment of Senators would remain textually untouched, the Senate's fundamental nature and role as a complementary legislative body of sober second thought would be significantly altered."[63] The Court concluded that changes engaging "the interests of the provinces in the Senate as an institution forming *an integral part of the federal system*" required use of the general amending formula.[64] Using similar reasoning, the Court found that abolition of the Senate would structurally modify Part V itself: "Part V was drafted on the assumption that the federal Parliament would remain bicameral in nature ... As discussed, the notion of an amendment to the Constitution of Canada is not limited to textual modifications – it also embraces significant structural modifications of the Constitution. The abolition of the upper chamber would entail a significant structural modification of Part V."[65] As changes to the amending formula itself are permissible only under section 41(e), abolition of the Senate requires unanimity.

In the second advisory opinion of 2014, the *Supreme Court Act Reference*, the Supreme Court dealt with its own constitutional status (for more on this, see Erin Crandall, Chapter 10 in this volume). The reference dealt mainly with section 6 of the Supreme Court Act, which requires that three of the Court's nine judges be appointed "from among the judges of the Court of Appeal or of the Superior Court of the Province of Quebec or from among the advocates of that province."[66] Prime Minister Stephen Harper nominated a Federal Court of Appeal judge, Marc Nadon, to fill the seat vacated by a Quebec jurist. Because Justice Nadon was neither sitting on a Quebec court nor a current member of the Quebec bar, a question arose regarding his eligibility.

The federal government responded to the controversy by seeking an advisory opinion, as well as passing legislation declaring that section 6 of the Supreme Court Act includes *former* advocates.[67] This in turn led the Supreme Court to consider both the meaning of section 6 at the time of the appointment and the effect of the subsequent declaratory legislation (section 6.1). In a 6–1 opinion, the Court found that section 6 restricts eligible candidates to jurists on enumerated Quebec courts and current Quebec advocates.[68] Moving to the declaratory legislation, the Court found that section 6.1 was a federal attempt to alter the Court's "composition,"[69] which is specifically mentioned in section 41(d) of Part V. Therefore, such a change could occur only in accordance with the unanimity formula.

The *Supreme Court Act Reference* was a profound constitutional moment. Of particular significance is the Court's conclusion that parts of the Supreme Court Act are now protected against ordinary legislative change. That result was not obvious, for the Act was enacted, and has been amended numerous times, through ordinary parliamentary law-making.[70] Although the amending formula explicitly mentions the Supreme Court, the rest of the written Constitution does not. In other words, Part V protects an institution that does not appear to be otherwise entrenched.

This ambiguity had led some scholars to suggest that Part V's references to the Supreme Court were aspirational – that they would take effect only in the event of further amendments that specifically entrenched the Court within the Constitution.[71] The Court, however, rejected the aspirational argument. Intriguingly, it did so on the basis, not that Part V had *itself* entrenched the Court, but that Part V merely *recognized* the fact that the Court was *already* entrenched. That status, the Court emphasized, was predicated on and driven by the country's essential federal character. Since the abolition in 1949 of appeals to the Privy Council, the Court had fulfilled a role necessary in any federal system: that of impartial arbiter of jurisdictional disputes.[72] From then on, "the continued existence and functioning of the [Court] became a key matter of interest" to all actors in the federation.[73] Consequently, in negotiating the 1982 package, the relevant actors "accepted that future reforms would have to recognize the Supreme Court's position within the architecture of the Constitution."[74]

In the result, the federal government's declaratory legislation affected the Supreme Court in a way that now can be achieved only through constitutional amendment. In the case of changes to the Court's composition – which the Court took the eligibility criteria in section 6 to include – section 41 prescribes unanimity. Changes to the Court's other "essential features" require the general formula of section 38.

The Supreme Court's conclusion that Part V applies to portions of the Supreme Court Act has been controversial. What is important for this chapter is the role played by the federal principle. In the *Supreme Court Act Reference*, the federal principle, *inter alia*, propelled the conclusion that the Court has become constitutionally entrenched despite the lack of any formal change to the written Constitution.

Whither Constitutional Amendment?

Part V sets forth a rigorous template for constitutional amendment. On one hand, that is hardly surprising: the *raison d'être* of most constitutions is to complicate the prospect of enacting fundamental change. (Admittedly, in the Canadian context, the point might be muddied by the fact that, for so many years, amendment was achieved through parliamentary resolution endorsed by the United Kingdom.) On the other hand, Part V privileges provincial input over other methods of determining national preferences.[75] As a result, Part V might frustrate even very strong preferences. To be sure, if expressed vigorously enough, such preferences might exert some pressure on provincial actors. But both the general and unanimity formulas render the prospect of change vulnerable to idiosyncratic regional demands. In particular, the prospect that a single province could block an otherwise deeply popular change is open to criticism on the grounds of unfairness and, even, imperilling national unity.

When considering how formal change to the Constitution may be achieved, the Supreme Court has used the federal principle to support the most stringent possible route. This was evident in both the *Senate Reform Reference* and the *Supreme Court Act Reference*. The effect is particularly stark in the latter case. The Court has now rendered most modifications to itself subject to the general formula, and has protected its current "composition" under the even stronger standard of unanimity. The Court's conclusions probably make initiatives such as mandatory bilingualism for judges or a guaranteed Aboriginal seat – both of which have been mooted in the past several years – impractical. Leaving aside whether these changes would be desirable per se, there are costs to rendering most changes to such a significant institution unachievable.[76] Without a reasonable prospect of success, there is little incentive for actors to enter into debate – a value the Court itself has identified in Part V – and to explore possible common ground through which the Court's legitimacy and functioning might be enhanced. The *Supreme Court Act Reference* also leaves in a state of considerable ambiguity the prospect of future changes to the Court's appellate jurisdiction. Such changes, though not frequent, have occurred long since the elimination of Privy Council appeals. That the Court's current jurisdiction is now frozen under the auspices of Part V is a sobering, if not worrisome, prospect.

The dominant judicial approach to Part V runs the risk of reifying the federal principle at the expense of other values. Through its different routes to constitutional amendment, Part V might be seen to embody a sort of flexibility in which the "juristic whole" of the Canadian political unit is not always, or even generally, the most important precondition to change. Depending on the context, other values, such as debate or economy, might be equally important. Perhaps the unilateral and bilateral amending formulas are owed greater attention. It might be, too, that the federal power in section 44 has been given too short shrift. The link drawn between section 44 and former section 91(1), which operated in a very different constitutional context, has perhaps been overstated.

All that being said, when evaluating the federal principle, it is important to avoid a static conception of intergovernmental relations. For one, the principle does not necessarily precipitate an oppositional federal-provincial dynamic: the provinces themselves might have quite divergent perspectives. The legal arguments presented in the *Senate Reform Reference* are a case in point. The western provinces tended to side with the federal government's more lax approach to changing the Senate, while the central and eastern provinces argued that the Confederation bargain required the most stringent possible formula.[77] The split is partially explained by the fact that the original bargain could not perfectly predict the development of the Canadian state. For some, the current structure of the Senate entrenches an unfair advantage for certain provinces. Emphasizing the idea that political legitimacy is derived chiefly from representation based on population and direct election, newer provinces argue that it is wrong to use Part V to thwart modernizing, democratic reform. Older provinces stress that their Senate seats provide an independent basis of political legitimacy to law-making at the federal level that Part V clearly means to protect and that cannot be superseded by national popular will.

Nor does the federal principle necessarily work at cross-purposes with the national unit. Indeed, in 1995, the federal government itself embraced the principle. In the so-called regional veto statute, Parliament enacted legislation whereby "no Minister of the Crown" may propose an amendment (other than those under sections 41 or 43) in the absence of consent from five subregions.[78] Although not constitutional in nature, the legislation imposes a significant federal obstacle to proceeding with constitutional change unless a high degree of regional and/or provincial agreement obtains.

It is true that recent advisory opinions frustrated the Conservative government's specific policy goals. And the Supreme Court's rather expansive approach to Part V appears to be based, at least in part, on a determination not to subordinate provincial interests to federal ones. But the interests at risk of subordination are not uniform in every case. The extent to which the principle works for or against the federal government will depend upon the nature of the constitutional change, the party initiating that change, and the appeal of the status quo. Consider the occasional calls to amend the Constitution to include property rights. Some argue that such a change is achievable through bilateral amendment.[79] But it also could be argued that entrenching property rights constitutes an amendment to the Charter that would require, at least, the general formula.[80] A federal government that is wary of property rights, or that believes that securing greater provincial consent is appropriate, might well advocate that stricter approach.

The federal principle is one of the Constitution's most enduring, if complicating, features. It explains the choices made in 1867, it underscores the attempts at amendment over the ensuing one hundred and fifty years, it features heavily in the current formulas in Part V, and it has powerfully influenced interpretation of the mechanism of constitutional change. In the dynamics of amendment, the provinces have emerged as essential actors. No doubt, pressures at the regional level will pose obstacles to achieving substantial or unanimous consent. To the extent that this thwarts amendments that are popular or normatively desirable, the federal principle exacts a price – at times, a steep one. But it is the by-product of the country's continuing imperative to reconcile diversity with unity.

Notes

The author thanks Eric McGill for research assistance, and acknowledges the helpful comments provided by anonymous reviewers.

1 J. Peter Meekison, "The Amending Formula," *Queen's Law Journal* 8 (1982): 92.
2 Canada Act 1982 (UK), 1982, c.11. Note that certain aspects of Canada's governing structure continue to depend on the institution of the Crown, which, while thoroughly domesticated in the legal sense, remains tethered to the United Kingdom.
3 Canadian Charter of Rights and Freedoms, Part I of the Constitution Act, 1982, being Schedule B to the Canada Act 1982 (UK). Consider, for example, the fundamental freedoms in the Charter's section 2, its legal rights in sections 7–14, and the equality guarantees in section 15. Also worthy of mention is the Constitution's protection of Aboriginal rights in section 35, which falls outside the Charter.

4 The special status of the territories, and their role in constitutional amendment, is not discussed in this chapter. The facta submitted by Nunavut and the Northwest Territories in the *Senate Reform Reference* are available online at http://www.scc-csc.ca/case-dossier/info/af-ma-eng.aspx?cas=35203.

5 Statistics Canada, "Sense of Belonging to Canada, the Province of Residence and the Local Community" (Ottawa, 29 June 2015), available online at http://www.statcan.gc.ca/pub/89-652-x/89-652-x2015004-eng.htm.

6 Laura Howls, "N.L. residents feel strongest sense of belonging, survey finds," *CBC News*, 6 July 2015, available online at http://www.cbc.ca/news/canada/newfoundland-labrador/n-l-residents-feel-strongest-sense-of-belonging-survey-finds-1.3137979.

7 See Patrick James, *Constitutional Politics in Canada after the Charter: Liberalism, Communitarianism, and Systemism* (Vancouver: UBC Press, 2010), 5; William Johnson, "Quebec's long identity crisis," *Globe and Mail*, 17 April 2007, available online at http://www.theglobeandmail.com/globe-debate/quebecs-long-identity-crisis/article722736/?page=all; and Brian O'Neal, "Distinct Society: Origins, Interpretations, Implications," Background Paper BP-408E (Ottawa: Library of Parliament, Political and Social Affairs Division, December 1995), available online at http://www.parl.gc.ca/Content/LOP/researchpublications/bp408-e.htm.

8 Constitution Act, 1982, being Schedule B to the Canada Act 1982 (UK).

9 For example, foundational changes to Parliament, up to and including its abolition, are not specifically addressed. Neither are changes to the Charter of Rights and Freedoms. This latter point inspired some debate during the oral submissions for the *Senate Reform Reference*. See my discussion in "Living Originalism," *National Magazine*, 9 December 2013.

10 The reference, in sections 41(d) and 42(d) of Part V, to the Supreme Court of Canada is one example.

11 "In our own Federation we [will] have Catholic and Protestant, English, French, Irish and Scotch, and each by his efforts and his success [will] increase the prosperity and glory of the new Confederacy. . . . [W]e [are] of different races, not for the purpose of warring against each other, but in order to compete and emulate for the general welfare"; George-Étienne Cartier, cited in the *Parliamentary Debates on the subject of the Confederation* (1865), 60.

12 I borrow this phrase from Professor John Finnis, "Patriation and Patrimony: The Path to the Charter" (lecture delivered at Western University, London, ON, 8 April 2014), available online at https://www.youtube.com/watch?v=LiaSlgZ71oU.

13 *Reference re Supreme Court Act, ss. 5 and 6*, 2014 SCC 21, [2014] 1 S.C.R. 433; *Reference re Senate Reform*, 2014 SCC 32, [2014] 1 S.C.R. 704.

14 Andrew Coyne, "Take control of the Constitution away from the premiers, THEN fix the Senate," *National Post*, 13 November 2013.

15 At the time, Ontario and Quebec were united into the province of "Canada," but are considered to have joined the Dominion in their respective capacities.

16 Constitution Act, 1867, 30 and 31 Victoria, c. 3 (UK). Note the full title: An Act for the Union of Canada, Nova Scotia, and New Brunswick, and the Government thereof; and for Purposes connected therewith. The law was originally titled the British North America Act, and for accuracy's sake should be thus referred to for discussion about events pre-1982. For ease of reference, throughout this chapter I use Constitution Act, 1867.

17 *Reference re Remuneration of Judges of the Provincial Court (P.E.I.)*, [1997] 3 S.C.R. 3, para. 109.

18 Ibid.

19 *Re: Resolution to amend the Constitution*, [1981] 1 S.C.R. 753, and discussion of same in Carissima Mathen, "'The question calls for an answer, and I propose to answer it': The Patriation Reference as Constitutional Method," *Supreme Court Law Review* (2d) 54 (2011): 143–66.

20 In the case of the existing colonies of British Columbia, Prince Edward Island, and Newfoundland, their respective legislatures could make the request of the Imperial Parliament. In the case of the existing territories of Rupert's Land and the North-west Territory, the Parliament of Canada could make the request.

21 Simone Chambers, "Contract or Conversation? Theoretical Lessons from the Canadian Constitutional Crisis," *Politics & Society* 26, no. 1 (1998), 146.

22 Support for the latter view is found in the summary for the Dominion Conference of 1931 as cited in the *Patriation Reference*, 796.

23 Statute of Westminster, 1931, 22 Geo. V, c. 4 (UK).

24 As amended in 1949, section 91(1) reads as follows:

> The amendment from time to time of the Constitution of Canada, except as regards matters coming within the classes of subjects by this Act assigned exclusively to the Legislatures of the provinces, or as regards rights or privileges by this or any other Constitutional Act granted or secured to the Legislature or the Government of a province, or to any class of persons with respect to schools or as regards the use of the English or the French language or as regards the requirements that there shall be a session of the Parliament of Canada at least once each year, and that no House of Commons shall continue for more than five years from the day of the return of the Writs for choosing the House: provided, however, that a House of Commons may in time of real or apprehended war, invasion or insurrection be continued by the Parliament of Canada if such continuation is not opposed by the votes of more than one-third of the members of such House.

25 *Reference Re Legislative Authority of the Parliament of Canada in Relation to the Upper House* [1980] 1 S.C.R. 54, 65.
26 "The Amendment of the Constitution of Canada," published in 1965 under the authority of the Hon. Guy Favreau, who cited twenty-two such changes. Note that this does not cover amendments to provincial constitutions.
27 *Senate Reference*, 64. See also 69–70: "In our opinion, the word 'Canada' as used in s. 91(1) does not refer to Canada as a geographical unit but refers to the juristic federal unit. 'Constitution of Canada' does not mean the whole of the *British North America Act,* but means the constitution of the federal government, as distinct from the provincial governments. The power of amendment conferred by s. 91(1) is limited to matters of interest only to the federal government."
28 Meekison, "Amending Formula."
29 Chambers, "Contract or Conversation?" 146.`
30 The Victoria Charter provided that amendments to the Constitution of Canada could be made via a "general amending formula" requiring the agreement of every province having more than 25 per cent of the national population and at least two provinces, respectively, from the Atlantic and western regions; a bilateral formula involving issues affecting only one province; unilateral amendment by Parliament for matters concerning the House of Commons, the Senate, or the executive; and unilateral provincial amendment of provincial constitutions. Much of the Victoria Charter was replicated in Part V of the Constitution Act, 1982.
31 "But if unanimity does not appear possible, the federal government will have to decide whether it will recommend to Parliament that a Joint Address be passed seeking 'patriation' of the B.N.A. Act. A question for decision will then be what to add to that action"; Pierre Elliott Trudeau, cited in J. Peter Meekison, "Introduction," in *Constitutional Patriation: The Lougheed-Lévesque Correspondence* (Kingston, ON: Queen's University, Institute of Intergovernmental Relations, 1999), 3.
32 *Québec-Canada, a New Deal: The Québec Government Proposal for a New Partnership between Equals: Sovereignty-Association* (Quebec City: Éditeur official, 1 November 1979).
33 The override reads as follows: "**33.** (1) Parliament or the legislature of a province may expressly declare in an Act of Parliament or of the legislature, as the case may be, that the Act or a provision thereof shall operate notwithstanding a provision included in section 2 or sections 7 to 15 of this Charter." Exempted from the override are the Charter's democratic, mobility, and language rights. The override also cannot apply to Aboriginal rights, as those are not found in the Charter. For discussion of the override,

see my "Constitutional Dialogue in Canada and the United States," *National Journal of Constitutional Law* 14, no. 3 (2003): 403–67; and "Dialogue Theory, Judicial Review, and Judicial Supremacy: A Comment on 'Charter Dialogue Revisited,'" *Osgoode Hall Law Journal* 45, no. 1 (2007): 125–46.

34 Statistics Canada, "Sense of Belonging to Canada." Note that section 42 specifies that the following amendments require the formula found in section 38:

> 42. (1) An amendment to the Constitution of Canada in relation to the following matters may be made only in accordance with subsection 38(1):
>
> (a) the principle of proportionate representation of the provinces in the House of Commons prescribed by the Constitution of Canada;
> (b) the powers of the Senate and the method of selecting Senators;
> (c) the number of members by which a province is entitled to be represented in the Senate and the residence qualifications of Senators;
> (d) subject to paragraph 41(d), the Supreme Court of Canada;
> (e) the extension of existing provinces into the territories; and
> (f) notwithstanding any other law or practice, the establishment of new provinces.

35 The most recent census, conducted in 2011, places the population of Canada at 33,476,688, with 12,851,821 people residing in Ontario and 7,903,001 residing in Quebec. See Statistics Canada, *Census Profile, 2011 Census*, Cat. no. 98–316–XWE (Ottawa: Statistics Canada, 2012).
36 Constitution Act, 1982, Part V, section 38(2) and (3).
37 Ibid., section 41.
38 Warren J. Newman, "Living with the Amending Procedures: Prospects for Future Constitutional Reform in Canada," *Supreme Court Law Review* (2d) 37 (2007): 388–416.
39 Constitution Act, 1982, Part V, sections 43–5.
40 The 7/50 requirement is close to Article V of the US Constitution, which prescribes a two-stage process for amendment: confirmation of a proposal by two-thirds majorities in Congress, or application of the legislatures in two-thirds of the states; and ratification of that proposal by three-fourths of the states. Note that Article V prescribes one standard for all amendments regardless of their character.
41 One scholar has called Part V a "Rubik's Cube"; see Stephen A. Scott, "Pussycat, Pussycat or Patriation and the New Constitutional Amendment Processes," *University of Western Ontario Law Review* 20 (1982): 292–8.
42 *Constitutional Amendment Proclamation, 1983*. See SI/84–102. This amendment made changes, *inter alia*, to section 35.

43 *Senate Reference*, 57–8. The questions included whether Parliament could, in effect, abolish the Senate and whether it could change senators' tenure and method of appointment. These questions were again considered in the 2014 *Senate Reform Reference*.

44 *Senate Reference.*

45 Ibid., 67.

46 Support for the latter view is found in the summary for the Dominion-Provincial Conference of 1931, as found in the *Patriation Reference*, 796.

47 Manitoba, Newfoundland, and Quebec initiated the proceedings in their respective courts of appeal, which were then appealed to the Supreme Court; see Mathen, "'The question calls for an answer,'" 152–3.

48 Due to space constraints, I deal here only with the majority decision. For a fuller discussion of the reference, see ibid.

49 *Patriation Reference*, 905–6.

50 The majority in the *Patriation Reference* did not deal directly with the issue (see ibid., 875). But in the subsequent *Quebec Veto Reference*, the Court dismissed the argument that there was such a convention. See *Re: Objection by Quebec to a Resolution to amend the Constitution*, [1982] 2 S.C.R. 793.

51 *Reference re Secession of Quebec*, [1998] 2 S.C.R. 217.

52 Ibid., para. 2. The Court was asked the following questions:

> 1. Under the Constitution of Canada, can the National Assembly, legislature or government of Quebec effect the secession of Quebec from Canada unilaterally?
>
> 2. Does international law give the National Assembly, legislature or government of Quebec the right to effect the secession of Quebec from Canada unilaterally? In this regard, is there a right to self-determination under international law that would give the National Assembly, legislature or government of Quebec the right to effect the secession of Quebec from Canada unilaterally?
>
> 3. In the event of a conflict between domestic and international law on the right of the National Assembly, legislature or government of Quebec to effect the secession of Quebec from Canada unilaterally, which would take precedence in Canada?

53 The principles are federalism, democracy, constitutionalism and the rule of law, and respect for minorities; ibid., para. 32.

54 Ibid., para. 57. By calling federalism the "first" principle, I mean only that it was articulated first in the advisory opinion.

55 *Supreme Court Act Reference*, para 2.

56 Changes to the property qualifications of Quebec senators were held to require the consent of Quebec's legislative assembly; ibid., para. 86.

57 Ibid., para. 3.
58 *Constitutional Accord: Canadian Patriation Plan*, General Comment, in Part A, 1, cited in *Senate Reform Reference*.
59 To be sure, the concept of constitutional architecture had been mentioned before; see *Quebec Secession Reference*.
60 Ibid., para. 27.
61 Ibid., para. 77.
62 Ibid., para. 41. The attorney general argued in the alternative that, if consultative elections required a constitutional amendment, they would fall under the unilateral federal power in section 44.
63 Ibid., para. 52.
64 Ibid., para 75; emphasis added.
65 Ibid., paras 106–7.
66 *Supreme Court Act* reference; Supreme Court Act, R.S.C., 1985, c. S-26, s. 6.
67 Economic Action Plan 2013 Act, No. 2 (Bill C-4), S.C. 2013, c. 40, ss. 471, 472.
68 For discussion of this part of the reference, see Michael Plaxton and Carissima Mathen, "Purposive Interpretation, Quebec, and the *Supreme Court Act*," *Constitutional Forum* 22, no. 3 (2013): 15–26.
69 Justice Michael Moldaver, who dissented from the Court's interpretation of section 6, did not take express issue with the discussion of Part V, and he agreed that changes to the Court's composition are embraced under section 41(d), although he declined to opine on whether the specific professional standard articulated in section 6 would qualify. But he did not consider it necessary to answer the second question, since he found that Justice Nadon had always been eligible for appointment under section 6. See *Supreme Court Act Reference*, para. 114.
70 Supreme and Exchequer Court Act, S.C. 1875, c. 11, s. 4; and subsequent legislation.
71 This has been referred to as the "empty vessels" theory; its proponents include Peter W. Hogg, in *Constitutional Law of Canada*, 5th ed. supp. (Toronto: Carswell, 2008), 4–21.
72 *Supreme Court Act Reference*, para. 83, citing *Reference re Securities Act*, 2011 SCC 66, [2011] 3 S.C.R. 837.
73 Ibid., para. 85.
74 Ibid., para. 87.
75 It should be noted that Part V does privilege democratic preferences to the extent that it requires the approval of legislative assemblies, as opposed to the executive branch.
76 Perhaps one is overstating it to paint the unanimity formula as "unachievable." Unanimous consent of all of the actors in the federation

has been achieved – for example, in the Charlottetown Accord, although the package fell apart after an agreed-upon national referendum did not obtain the requisite level of popular approval.

77 On the question of abolishing the Senate, for example, Saskatchewan, Alberta, and British Columbia all argued (similar to the federal government) that an amendment under section 38 was sufficient. Ontario, Quebec, New Brunswick, Nova Scotia, Manitoba, and Newfoundland and Labrador argued that section 41 was required. Prince Edward Island argued that Part V was inapplicable and that negotiations would be required.

78 An Act respecting constitutional amendments, S.C. 1996, c.1. The law refers to the support of "a majority" in Quebec, Ontario, British Columbia, two of the four Atlantic provinces comprising 50 per cent of their population, and two of the three Prairie provinces comprising 50 per cent of theirs. Note that this essentially implies that referenda will be organized.

79 See, for example, Dwight Newman, "The Bilateral Amending Formula as a Mechanism for the Entrenchment of Property Rights," *Constitutional Forum* 21, no. 2 (2013): 17–22.

80 Because the Charter is not specifically mentioned in Part V, this suggests that the general amending formula would apply. The issue has yet to arise.

4 Part II and Part V: Aboriginal Peoples and Constitutional Amendment

CHRISTA SCHOLTZ

What is the role of Aboriginal peoples in constitutional amendment? The mobilization of Aboriginal peoples during and since the Patriation process clearly indicates that they now have a political role. And, according to section 35.1 of the Constitution Act, 1982, there appears to be a legally enforceable obligation on the part of governments to consult with Aboriginal peoples prior to amending any constitutional provision that specifically applies to them. Is it significant, however, that this commitment is found outside Part V? How one answers that question depends on the legal premises one marshals, yielding opposing conclusions. In this chapter I develop two arguments. In the first, I conclude that the role of Aboriginal peoples in formal constitutional amendment is solely political, despite section 35.1's enactment in 1983. In the second, I conclude there is a legally enforceable duty to consult, either because section 35.1 remains lawful or because it is unnecessary to ground the duty. In setting out these arguments, my goal is to be explicit about the premises on which they are built and the normative value of each premise. None of these premises is a "dead letter." Each merits serious consideration from those who care about what constitutionalism means. Each premise in either argument calls upon a set of important reasons, and the Canadian courts have endorsed each of them in their jurisprudence. As a result, neither argument is trivial. This renders complicated the choice of which argument is more persuasive, more appropriate, or more conducive to a kind of Constitution Canadians want to live with and under. To make a reasoned, versus arbitrary, choice between them, however, requires the introduction of other reasons. This I do not do – I stop short of campaigning for one argument over the other, but set that task aside to be tackled another day.

I do, however, position the question of the legal role of Aboriginal peoples in relation to Part V's procedures within the larger debate on the Constitution as written or unwritten. The particular case of the commitments of Part II and Part V shows how a satisfactory interpretation, defined for the moment as one that is faithful to both written text and unwritten principle, can be elusive.

Part II and Part V: Setting Out the Problem

Since I am addressing the role of Aboriginal peoples in the amendment of the Constitution, it bears setting out briefly how the two issues, formerly separate, came to be entwined. In September 1970, federal and provincial officials were busy preparing cabinet memoranda to support ongoing intergovernmental negotiations on constitutional reform, which eventually would culminate in the (short-lived) Victoria Charter of 1971. In their preparations, federal officials produced a five-page list of constitutional elements that already were, or would be, decided. The only mention of Canada's Indigenous peoples in this archival document was as constitutional marginalia, among "other matters (a number of unrelated and specific matters will require some further consideration after the main principles of a distribution of powers are dealt with ... : for example, citizenship and immigration, marriage and divorce, Indians and Eskimos, etc.)."[1] This archival snippet paints a singular picture of the role of Aboriginal peoples in constitutional amendment forty-five years ago: as objects of constitutional discussion, and irrelevant as agents at the constitutional bargaining table.

The process leading to patriation changed this dynamic. Through political and legal mobilization, Aboriginal peoples sought a central role at the constitutional bargaining table so that the rights for which they argued would be respected in the shared territory that is Canada. Their efforts did not yield all that they sought, but their mobilization did produce the following: the inclusion of the non-derogation clause (section 25) in Part I, the Charter of Rights and Freedoms; Part II (section 35); and Part IV (section 37). Upon its proclamation on 17 April 1982, Part II of the Constitution Act, 1982 consisted of section 35(1), "the existing aboriginal and treaty rights of the aboriginal peoples of Canada are hereby recognized and affirmed," and section 35(2), "[i]n this Act, 'aboriginal peoples of Canada' includes the Indian, Inuit and Métis peoples of Canada." Part IV set out a commitment undertaken by the prime minister to convene, within a year, a first ministers' conference on the issue of Aboriginal peoples and their rights, to which Aboriginal peoples would be invited.

Although the aforementioned sections were the tangible outcomes of Aboriginal constitutional mobilization, Aboriginal peoples were excluded from the Constitution Act, 1982's critical Part V, entitled the "procedure for amending the Constitution of Canada." It contains the set of tiered amendment formulas, where the size of the amending coalition varies according to the substantive nature of the amendment. Clearly stated in Part V are the terms for its own amendment: section 41(e) sets out that Part V's amendment requires the largest possible coalition – the unanimous consent of the Senate, House of Commons, and the legislative assemblies of each province. Henceforth, Canadian legal officials would no longer recognize the UK Parliament as having any power to amend the Constitution of Canada. Instead, section 52(3) of the Constitution Act, 1982 sets out that "amendments to the Constitution of Canada shall be made only in accordance with the authority contained in the Constitution of Canada."

The exclusion of Aboriginal peoples from the new procedures governing future amendments to the Constitution meant that the recognition and protection of Aboriginal rights through sections 35 and 25 were subject to future amendment, including repeal, through Part V's general amending procedure (the 7/50 rule), without Aboriginal consent. This weakness became one of the topics addressed at the March 1983 first ministers' conference that was struck pursuant to the Part IV commitment to consult. At that conference, the Assembly of First Nations (AFN) tabled a proposal to amend Part V. The AFN's proposal contained a number of elements, but two were the inclusion of a consultation requirement with Aboriginal representatives through the first ministers' conference mechanism, and Aboriginal consent to any formal amendment of those constitutional provisions directly implicating them.[2]

The AFN's proposal did yield some traction, but amending Part V proved unattainable. The issue was Quebec, whose political position under Premier René Lévesque during the March 1983 first ministers' conference was to participate only as a non-voting member, for to participate in the formal amendment of the Constitution Act, 1982 was to recognize the validity of the very Constitution that had been brought into being without Quebec's consent. Instead of amending Part V, the federal and provincial governments chose instead to amend Part II, subject to the general amending procedure, to include a new section 35.1, which reads:[3]

> The government of Canada and the provincial governments are committed to the principle that, before any amendment is made to Class 24 of section 91 of the "*Constitution Act, 1867*," to section 25 of this Act or to this Part,
>> (*a*) a constitutional conference that includes in its agenda an item relating to the proposed amendment, composed of the Prime Minister of Canada and the first ministers of the provinces, will be convened by the Prime Minister of Canada; and
>> (*b*) the Prime Minister of Canada will invite representatives of the aboriginal peoples of Canada to participate in the discussions on that item.

The failure to amend Part V in 1983 was subsequently addressed in the constitutional discussions of 1992, the so-called Charlottetown Accord, which would have inserted in Part V a section specifying that any amendments to the Constitution directly referring to Aboriginal peoples could be at their initiative and required their "substantial consent."[4]

Had the Charlottetown Accord proposals been subsequently enacted, the story arc of the preceding two decades would have been astounding. Aboriginal peoples would have clawed themselves out of the constitutional margins, been recognized as a third order of government, and anchored within Part V. Since the Charlottetown Accord's death in October 1992, Canadians and their politicians have recoiled from the mega-politics of formal constitutional amendment, and the courts have continued with the business of spelling out the scope and implications of Canada's Part II commitments within the Constitution. The focus to date has primarily been the development of section 35(1) jurisprudence. However, the status of section 35.1 has not been litigated, presumably because governments since 1982 have engaged in intergovernmental bargaining in consultation with Aboriginal peoples' representatives. It seems to work, if one limits this claim to procedural commitments. Why, then, should we continue to write about or poke at the issue of Aboriginal peoples' participation in formal constitutional amendment? It is clear that they are no longer irrelevant. But is that all we can now assert with any confidence?

Section 35.1 sits in an anomalous position. Herein lies a conundrum. On its face, it is a constitutionalized commitment on the part of the prime minister to initiate a consultative process between first ministers and Aboriginal peoples. It is clearly a commitment to do so *before* amending the Constitution, and as such, it is a procedure related to the amendment of the Constitution. Yet, it is not included in Part V, and it did not meet the unanimity criteria.[5] As such, is this provision of the Constitution actually legally enforceable? Rather, is it colonialism's hard truth that, in the courts, Part II's commitments must yield to Part V's procedural code, where Aboriginal peoples remain absent? To answer in the affirmative here is to conclude that the enforceability of this provision remains in the political realm, for governments to decide whether a political convention now exists that Aboriginal peoples must be consulted prior to effecting formal constitutional change that directly implicates them. The degree of solace that this conclusion brings to the reader is directly related to how the reader evaluates the place of political conventions in Canadian constitutionalism. It might bring no solace at all to the Aboriginal negotiators who endured the first ministers' conferences of the 1980s.

Or, on the other hand, can one build an argument where Part II plays the constitutional trickster, constraining Part V itself? To do so is to argue one of two ways. One could argue that the anomalous context of section 35.1's enactment does not void it of legal enforceability, despite the unambiguous unanimity requirement for Part V's amendment. Or one could try to argue that there are reasons outside section 35.1 itself that can independently ground a legally enforceable role for Aboriginal peoples in constitutional amendment, in the face of the textual silence of Part V on this point. To answer in the affirmative here is to accept an extensive judicial activism, where the judiciary is empowered to rewrite, not merely interpret, the democratic commitments of Canada's legislatures. This, too, is no small thing.

Part V Is Unconstrained: The Complete Procedural Code

Here I build an argument that Part II's commitments do not constrain Part V's procedures. For my purposes here, the conclusion of this argument is that Aboriginal peoples have no legally enforceable role to play in formal constitutional amendment. I stress that this should not be reduced to saying that Aboriginal peoples have no role whatsoever in constitutional amendment; rather, it is to define the norm of Aboriginal consultation as part of the amendment process as a political norm, enforceable, not in the courts, but through the political process.

It anchors the role of Aboriginal peoples as, first and foremost, a part of Canada's political Constitution.

The first premise of the argument is the simple idea that the constitutional text itself matters, and is at the very least the starting point in a process of legal reasoning. In a constitutional structure where legislatures are recognized as having the authority to make law and where a central role of the judiciary is to interpret legislated law and apply it to particular facts, then the words themselves should matter. The words that compose a constitutional text are often fraught with ambiguity, gaps, and outright contradictions, but there are also words over which there is shared or common understanding. To say that legal reasoning should be constrained by the text itself is not to deny that indeterminacy exists, or to say that the text is a perfect constraint on judicial reasoning. Whether the text is to be given a "living tree," or originalist, or other interpretation is part of how courts justify their subsequent conclusions. But it is to say that the text cannot be ignored, for this would upset the basic and sound idea that legislatures have a real job to do in a legal order. The Supreme Court of Canada has recognized the "primacy" of the constitutional text, and that judicial review should not "dispense with the written text of the Constitution."[6] Elsewhere, Justice Ian Binnie has written that "implicit principles can and should be used to expound the Constitution, but they cannot alter the thrust of its explicit text."[7] Although Part V has its fair share of ambiguous language, section 41(e) is very clear that the unanimity rule regulates the amendment of Part V itself.

The entrenchment clause – section 52(3) of the Constitution Act, 1982 – states that amendments to the Constitution "shall be made only in accordance with the authority contained in the Constitution of Canada." It is notable that such authority is not specifically limited to Part V, and it makes it arguable that text placed elsewhere in the Constitution may amend it. This is clearly possible for elements of the Constitution that included amendment clauses prior to 1982,[8] and the courts have yet to address possible contradictions between this authority and the terms of Part V. What should be clear from the constitutional text, however, is that, in the absence of any pre-existing constitutional authority, constitutional amendment post-1982 is regulated solely by Part V. To do otherwise would be effectively to gut (at least) the unanimity clause of any meaning, for it then would be possible to amend some other part of the Constitution using the 7/50 rule – to say that, notwithstanding Part V, the unanimity rule was repealed.

This outcome might be attractive for bringing some needed flexibility into our current constitutional rules, but that is beside the point. The wisdom of the unanimity criterion might be doubtful, but it was nevertheless enacted in accordance with the legal rules governing constitutional amendment prior to patriation.

The next premise is that Part V is, indeed, a complete procedural code.[9] It includes all of the procedures, or steps, that are related to the purpose of newly amending the Constitution. To say that it is a complete procedural code is to say that the only legally enforceable constraints or limitations placed on the governor general, the House of Commons, the Senate, and the provincial legislatures are included in the text of Part V. The Supreme Court has written that Part V "provides the blueprint for how to amend the Constitution of Canada."[10] Canadian courts have recognized the very strong implications that adding other procedures, grounded either in unwritten principles or judicial doctrines, would have, as to do so "would have the effect of adding an additional step to constitutional change – one not provided for in Part V of the Constitution Act, 1982. It is an argument which therefore must be approached with extreme caution because the effect of its acceptance would fly in the face of the constitutional text which has its own amendment mechanisms built in."[11] In addressing a direct question on the use of an equitable doctrine to ground a procedural rule not explicitly written into Part V, the Newfoundland Court of Appeal responded thus: "In effect, the appellants are requesting that the equitable doctrine of estoppel, a creation of the courts, be used to defeat a process of constitutional change mandated by the Constitution itself. If a provision of the Constitution is amended in accordance with Part V of the Constitution Act, 1982 the doctrine of estoppel cannot succeed in thwarting that process."[12]

In the paragraphs above, I have both set out and addressed the merit of the premises for the argument that clear constitutional text is primary to legal reasoning, that the unanimity provision in Part V is indeed clear, that Part V is the amending authority in the Constitution under section 52(3), and that Part V is a complete procedural code. If these premises are applied to Part II's amendment in 1983 with the addition of section 35.1, then the conclusion that follows is that section 35.1 was improperly enacted.

Given that there was no other possible textual authority in the Constitution that addressed the role of Aboriginal peoples in formal constitutional amendment, Part V's text solely governed any proposal for amendment that arose from the March 1983 first ministers' conference.

It is also clear that section 35.1 is understood to be a procedural commitment with regards to constitutional amendment. After all, it says that, "before any amendment" to the listed provisions are made, the federal and provincial governments commit themselves to the principle of engaging with Aboriginal peoples. This is, on its face, a procedure related to amendment. It is, therefore, an amendment to Part V, and the unanimity rule applies. And, as section 35.1 was not enacted with unanimous consent, it fails as a legally enforceable constraint on the amendment process.

One might respond that section 35.1 was lawfully enacted as an amendment to Part II because it is a principled commitment to a consultation procedure that engages only governments, not legislatures, and thereby is not a procedure for the purpose of amending Part V itself.[13] Legislatures and the governor general, after all, are actors with the legal power formally to amend the Constitution, not the political executive. This attempt to save section 35.1 as a legally enforceable procedural commitment runs into two difficulties that I can see. One is that the section still clearly pertains to constitutional amendment, and is not an open commitment to discuss constitutional issues with Aboriginal peoples outside the context of an amendment proposal. The other is that section 49 of Part V includes a constitutional commitment by the prime minister and the provincial premiers to review Part V itself. This section clearly broadens the scope of Part V to include consultative procedures related to constitutional amendment undertaken by actors beyond legislatures and the governor general.

It follows that section 35.1 fails as a properly enacted amendment, and therefore cannot be legally enforceable on those grounds. The question remains: does this particular constitutional commitment fall away all together? I argue that it does not, so long as one accepts that this procedural commitment is conventional. Lest one despair that political conventions can never compensate for legal powers, one might be reminded of their centrality in Canadian constitutionalism. After all, it is the political convention of responsible government that constrains the use of the governor general's legal powers; it is a political convention that the disallowance power is no longer invoked. The argument can be raised that a political convention of consultation with Aboriginal peoples prior to formal constitutional amendment now exists, ironically because the practice has become entrenched since 1983.[14] But it exists so long as Canadian governments agree to be bound by it.[15]

Arguably, as a political community, Canada has been pulled and pushed beyond the point where provincial and federal governments would seriously contemplate reversing this convention – the political costs are now too high. Since the federal government's 1969 White Paper on Aboriginal policy, Aboriginal political mobilization has changed the political dynamics of constitutional amendment, and those dynamics have left their trace on the constitutional text. It is grounded in the ability of Aboriginal actors to build and then prevail upon internal allies, so that constitutional recognition of Aboriginal and treaty rights was reinserted into the constitutional text in 1982, after it was promised in 1980 and mysteriously dropped in 1981. It is grounded in the reality that the 1980s first minister's conferences yielded actual amendment only when some level of common ground was achieved. It is grounded in the legacy of Elijah Harper in 1990, quietly and powerfully taking his place in the Manitoba legislature, raising the eagle feather, and refusing Premier Gary Filmon's motion to allow debate on the Meech Lake Accord. It is grounded in August 1992 in the political and personal convictions, forged through transformative dialogue with Aboriginal leadership, of politicians Joe Clark, Bob Rae, and Joe Ghiz, that Aboriginal amendments would not be negotiated behind closed doors while the Aboriginal constitutional negotiators Ovide Mercredi (AFN), Rosemarie Kuptana (Inuit Tapirisat of Canada), Yvon Dumont (Métis Council of Canada), and Ron George (Native Council of Canada) were not in the room.

I am well aware that, in the "Part V is legally unconstrained" argument presented above, I make no use of a premise anchored in a *sui generis* or special relationship between the Crown and Aboriginal peoples. The acceptance of Aboriginal peoples as special in some way has no consequence, either because the premises are applied the same regardless or because no additional or competing premises are generated. The soundness of the overall argument rests on its internal logical validity and the appropriateness of its premises, and the premises here address central and abiding concerns about the judicial versus legislative roles in constitutionalism. The appropriateness of each is supported with recourse to current jurisprudence. Note that had the Charlottetown Accord's "substantial consent" clause been integrated into Part V, these very same non-Aboriginal-specific premises would have protected the Aboriginal peoples' (limited) veto role in constitutional amendment against competing claims of groups who might assert a special or particular constitutional relationship on other grounds (such as anglophone or francophone minority language communities).

Part V Is Constrained: The Crown's Honour as Internal Limit

Here, I build a different argument about Aboriginal peoples and Part V. This argument starts from the normative position that Aboriginal difference requires us to engage with a different set of argumentative premises, each also justifiable according to key reasons. Where the first argument I set out rests most heavily on the primacy of the text in constitutional interpretation and Part V as a complete procedural code, this second argument relies on an old judicial doctrine that has been reinvigorated as an increasingly important proposition in section 35 jurisprudence: the honour of the Crown.[16] As a result, the prism of how one should legally interpret Parts V and II changes significantly. The conclusion of this argument is that the procedural commitment to consultation at the core of section 35.1 either rescues it from its constitutional anomalousness, so that it remains enforceable, or that, even if section 35.1 cannot be saved as a validly enacted constitutional amendment, the principle of consultation it enshrines survives independently of it, and therefore legally constrains Part V. In effect, the honour of the Crown as the starting premise in an argument can lead to the addition in Part V, in the absence of text, of a legally enforceable consultation procedure with Aboriginal peoples in the face of an amendment proposal.

The honour of the Crown is a concept rooted in a theory of the sovereign itself. Hobbes's sovereign came to be so when individuals in the state of nature covenanted with one another to renounce their individual rights to all things, so that one among them, the sovereign, could see to the preservation and security of all. The purpose of the sovereign is to effect our mutual preservation through the creation and enforcement of a legal order. The legitimacy of the sovereign to command her subjects' allegiance is eroded should she flout her unilaterally asserted power at will and without restraint. So long as she cares to be a lawful sovereign, rather than mere brute, she will hold herself (or be assumed by the judiciary to so hold herself) to the natural law standards of fairness and equity. She must "live up to the moral demands of Sovereignty," which is to say that "power cannot be exercised by a public body without a concomitant assumption of duties of fairness and reasonableness."[17] Evan Fox-Decent argues that the sovereign's obligation to *all* of her subjects is best thought of as grounded by a normative concept of trust – hence his characterization of the sovereign as fiduciary,[18] where the sovereign must act honourably in the use of her public power lest she diminish or squander her authority vis-à-vis her subjects. Ultimately, holding the mirror up to the sovereign, so that she may act honourably, is for the sovereign's continued protection, for without honour, her assertion as sovereign commands no allegiance. On this view of the sovereign as fiduciary, the subjects' duty to obey is derived, not from their continued consent, but from the conduct of the sovereign in providing for and respecting the core ideals of a legal order.

The use of the honour of the Crown in legal doctrine, not just in political theory, demonstrates both the limits and leverage of settler sovereignty for Aboriginal peoples involved in the amendment of a settler constitutional text. Judicial review starts from the central idea that the Crown's asserted sovereignty is itself not reviewable. The Crown is sovereign over Aboriginal peoples as over her other non-Aboriginal subjects. One cannot fashion from this place an obligation on the Crown to concede to Aboriginal peoples, for this would fly in the face of the Crown's assertion. One cannot get to a veto for Aboriginal peoples in constitutional amendment from here, for Aboriginal consent is precluded from the outset.[19] If the judicial acceptance of the Crown's assertion is the limit, then the leverage rests in the idea that the Crown's legality stems from the fulfilment of its obligations to those over whom it asserts its rule.

In Canadian Aboriginal law jurisprudence, the courts increasingly have made use of the honour of the Crown to ground and expand the Crown's legal duties to Aboriginal peoples. What legal duties the honour of the Crown can ground on its own – without making reference to the text of the Constitution – is unclear, and shifts as the courts develop this jurisprudence. I offer an understanding here. The Canadian courts are developing a *sui generis*, rather than a general, theory of the Crown as fiduciary, so that Aboriginal peoples can call on the Crown in a way that other groups cannot.[20] The Supreme Court has said that "the honour of the Crown is always at stake in its dealings with Aboriginal peoples."[21] The Crown's honour demands a fair consideration of Aboriginal interests, for to do otherwise would thwart the reconciliation of the Crown's sovereignty with Aboriginal pre-existence. From this the Supreme Court has fashioned a duty to consult and potentially to accommodate Aboriginal peoples, even in the absence of a proven legal right or interest.[22] In the event that the Crown assumes discretion over a cognizable Aboriginal interest, the honour of the Crown gives rise to a fiduciary obligation.[23] The Crown's honour demands that the Crown always intend to keep its promises; an honourable Crown does not make empty promises. From this the Supreme Court has fashioned a Crown duty "to act diligently in the pursuit of its obligations."[24] The Crown thus must act with diligence in the implementation of its commitments. Next, there shall be no appearance of sharp dealing, as even the appearance of such would besmirch the Crown. From this the Supreme Court has fashioned a general interpretive principle: that the Crown's promises be given a liberal and generous interpretation, with ambiguities resolved in the favour of Aboriginal peoples.[25]

The honour of the Crown and the legal duties that have come to stem from it present a very different way of understanding Part II and Part V of the Constitution. The honour of the Crown tells us that Part II as a whole should be interpreted liberally and generously, with ambiguities or anomalies in the text resolved in favour of Aboriginal peoples. Part II's provisions should also be interpreted to further a fair and just settlement between Aboriginal peoples and the Crown. Furthermore, the Crown's commitments should be diligently pursued. Section 35.1 was enacted in 1983 as an amendment to Part II, and represents a commitment on the part of the federal and most provincial legislatures to pursue high-level consultation with Aboriginal peoples in advance of formal amendment on Aboriginal provisions. It is not a Part V commitment, but a constitutional commitment it is nonetheless. The need to uphold the Crown's honour, the Supreme Court implicitly responds, is held in priority above other well-established constitutional considerations,[26] perhaps even those considerations that would deny section 35.1 as a proper or lawful enactment. Instead, the section needs to be read generously and to fulfil its reconciliatory purpose. The first ministers' conference with Aboriginal peoples at the table is an obligation the Crown entered into, and an honourable Crown does not make empty promises. A constitutional commitment "must be given meaningful content."[27] Therefore, section 35.1 must be interpreted as a solemn commitment to discuss constitutional provisions with Aboriginal peoples through the first ministers' conference mechanism. To make the content of section 35.1 meaningful is to make it legally actionable. The Crown must be held to implement diligently its promise of consultation.

However, to say that section 35.1 is a real constitutional procedural commitment that lies nonetheless in Part II is to say that, by necessary implication, Part V is not a complete procedural code. Here we arrive at a crossroads, the place where judges should proceed "with extreme caution."[28] It bears repeating how we got here. First, the courts have concluded that the Crown's assertion of sovereignty over Aboriginal peoples engages the Crown's honour in a way that its assertion over its other subjects does not. According to the Supreme Court, the Crown-Aboriginal relationship is *sui generis*, and it is therefore appropriate that it interpret and balance the Constitution's Aboriginal provisions differently than its other provisions. Hence, Part II's section 35.1 anomaly pierces Part V's completeness. Whether or not one sees this as an appropriate outcome, it is certainly significant. It is arguably one of the unintended consequences that Justices Marshall Rothstein and Michael Moldaver were concerned about in their dissent of the Supreme Court's jurisprudence with respect to the honour of the Crown.[29] It would be for the Court to effect a cut-and-paste, moving the section from Part II into Part V, explicitly amending the amendment procedures all by itself.

One could argue that I have been too quick to extend the ability of the honour of the Crown to resolve section 35.1's anomalous enactment in favour of Aboriginal peoples. However, even if the section were to fall away due to improper enactment and a procedural right was no longer explicitly recognized in the constitutional text, the honour of the Crown could still be used to ground a procedural right of consultation. Since 2004 the Supreme Court has recognized a Crown duty to consult with Aboriginal peoples in the absence of a proven and cognizable right. This argument could be extended to a possible procedural right during a process where the Crown considers the rights and protections it will afford Aboriginal peoples in the Constitution. Do Aboriginal peoples have the right to a consultative role in the amendment process? Perhaps, as the Court has said that "the honour of the Crown gives rise to different duties in different circumstances."[30] The Court has said that the Crown has a duty to consult if the answer is perhaps, not just when the answer is yes. The duty to consult, however, if so extended, need not demand a first ministers' conference in order to be honourably discharged, only that the consultation be "meaningful" and "appropriate to the circumstances."[31]

The use of the honour of the Crown in this manner would be tantamount to treating this concept as more than a common law or equitable doctrine, and more like an unwritten constitutional principle (contra *Hogan*). Indeed, the Supreme Court has already written that the honour of the Crown "has been confirmed in its status as constitutional principle."[32] In the 1998 *Quebec Secession Reference*, the Court took the position that, when the constitutional text is silent, unwritten principles can ground legal obligations on the Crown because of the principles' normative force.[33] In this respect, a duty to consult with Aboriginal peoples on amendments directly implicating them and the duty to negotiate in the advent of a clear majority on a clear secession question are of the same ilk. In the *Quebec Secession Reference*, the Court raised the possibility of constitutional amendment procedures generated on the basis of unwritten principles, outside the Part V text.[34]

Conclusion

If Part II's commitments pierce Part V's completeness, it is because judges have done so by using principles that are also central to constitutionalism, such as equity, fairness, and the moral limits of state power. Placing meaningful limits on the use of public power is at constitutionalism's core. This is the debate on the merits of unwritten constitutionalism, where those who defend judicial power through judicial recourse to unwritten constitutionalism (or common law constitutionalism) do so on the basis that written constitutions cannot capture all that is lawful, and that the judiciary should fill legal vacuums as it deems necessary. As Mark Walters notes, "[t]he political value of constitutionalism should be seen to be based upon confidence in the ability of people to construct normative order through making of law and writing constitutions, but also upon a sense of humility that arises from the knowledge that no amount of law-making or constitution writing will produce all of the law the people need."[35]

If Part V is unconstrained by Part II's consultative commitments, then it is because the written text serves as an important constraint – as the primary mechanism for past constitutional authors to fix the limits of constitutional meaning for future interpreters. Entrenchment is, after all, also at the core of constitutionalism. To the suggestion that the written Constitution's scribes should go about their task with humility is the countercharge that unwritten constitutionalism is the handmaiden of judicial hubris. The recourse to unwritten constitutionalism allows judges, it is charged, to elide their own obligation to humility by the use of inventive argumentation. Judges are engaging, in other words, in scope-creep, where their common-law project of constitutional renovation imposes their own particular vision for our constitutional enterprise, even while asserting that they are executing the designs of either the dead (via originalism) or the living (via "the living tree"). As a key voice on this side of the debate, contra Walters and others,

Jeffrey Goldsworthy writes with particular reference to parliamentary contexts such as Canada's:

> [C]laims that [unwritten or implied constitutional principles] are inherent in our concept of law; claims that they are inherent in a "common law constitution" that supposedly underpins our written constitutions; and claims that they are implied or presupposed by particular written constitutions ... are refuted once we take into account the doctrine of parliamentary sovereignty. This is the elephant in the room that is usually overlooked or ignored by those who seek to aggrandize our "ancient tradition" of "legality." The doctrine's predominance within Britain's actual constitutional tradition – inherited by countries such as Canada and Australia – is inconsistent both with the proffered analysis of our concept of law, and with the pretensions of common law constitutionalism.[36]

I situate the conundrum of how Parts II and Parts V fit together as another example of the fundamental tensions at play in the appropriate roles of judges and legislatures in constitutionalism generally.[37] What is valuable in this debate is to think about how a settler constitutionalism can be rendered less so, perhaps not by taking sides, but in seeing whether the development towards a truly reconciled and respectful constitutionalism requires at least the combination of both.

Notes

1 "Memorandum to Cabinet: Constitutional Review: Second Working Session of the Constitutional Conference: Federal Positions and Objectives," cabinet document 1065/70, 4 September 1970, appendix 4 (Part 1), 5.
2 Assembly of First Nations, "Proposals for Amendment and Additions to the Constitution Act, 1982" (Ottawa, 1983).
3 In the interest of inclusiveness, Part I was amended to change the wording of section 25(b), Part II was further amended to add sections 35(3) and 35(4), and Part IV(1) was added to hold another series of first ministers' conference (it was repealed on 17 April 1987). All these amendments were effected through the Constitutional Amendment Proclamation, 1983, SI/84–102.
4 A new section 45(1) of Part V was proposed to read:

> (1) An amendment to the Constitution of Canada that directly refers to, or that amends a provision that directly refers to, one or more of the Aboriginal peoples of Canada or their governments, including (a) section 2, as it related

to the Aboriginal peoples of Canada, class 24 of section 91, section 91A and section 95F of the Constitution Act, 1867, and (b) section 25 and Part II of this Act and this section, may be made by proclamation issued by the Governor General under the Great Seal of Canada only where the amendment has been authorized in accordance with this Part and has received the substantial consent of the Aboriginal peoples so referred to. (2) Notwithstanding section 46, the procedures for amending the Constitution of Canada in relation to any matter referred to in subsection (1) may be initiated by any of the Aboriginal peoples of Canada directly referred to as provided in subsection (1).

Library and Archives Canada, Joe Clark Fonds, RG6–7 MG26 Vol. 4, File 4–13 (author file: e-011089483.pdf).

5 This is the conclusion adopted in Bryan Schwartz, *First Principles, Second Thoughts* (Montreal: Institute for Research on Public Policy, 1986).

6 *Reference Re: Secession of Quebec*, [1998] 2 S.C.R. 217 [*Quebec Secession Reference*], para. 53.

7 *Eurig Estate (Re)*, [1998] 2 S.C.R. 565, para. 66.

8 Section 2 of the Constitution Act, 1871 reads: "The Parliament of Canada may from time to time establish new Provinces in any territories forming for the time being part of the Dominion of Canada, but not included in any Province thereof, and may, at the time of such establishment, make provision for the constitution and administration of any such Province, and for the passing of laws for the peace, order and good government of such province, and for its representation in the said Parliament."

9 Peter W. Hogg, in *Constitutional Law of Canada*, 4–4.

10 *Reference Re: Senate Reform*, 2014 SCC 32, para. 28.

11 *Hogan v Newfoundland*, 183 D.L.R. (4th) 225, para. 64.

12 Ibid., para. 71.

13 This position is offered by Hogg, *Constitutional Law*, 28–66, fn290.

14 See Neil Finkelstein and George Vegh, *The Separation of Quebec and the Constitution of Canada*, Background Studies of the York University Constitutional Reform Project 2 (North York, ON: York University, Centre for Public Law and Public Policy, 1992).

15 The Royal Commission on Aboriginal Peoples argued that a political convention now exists of substantial Aboriginal consent to all constitutional amendments, not only those directly related to them. The commission pointed to the inclusion of Aboriginal peoples in all constitutional working groups during the Charlottetown Accord negotiations, not solely in the Aboriginal peoples' working group. I certainly agree that the Charlottetown process established a precedent, but it is a considerable distance to go from precedent to convention. No such language was included in the

Charlottetown Accord itself, and Aboriginal peoples were denied a role in negotiations over intergovernmental agreements.

16 For a short summary of the doctrine's historical use in Canada, see Thomas Isaac, *Aboriginal Law: Commentary and Analysis* (Saskatoon: Purich, 2012), 312–14.

17 Evan Fox-Decent, *Sovereignty's Promise: The State as Fiduciary* (Oxford: Oxford University Press, 2011), 55, 37.

18 Ibid., 105–11.

19 For a contrary view that Aboriginal consent is required, see Patrick J. Monahan, "The Law and Politics of Quebec Secession," *Osgoode Hall Law Journal* 33, no.1 (1995): 33–67.

20 For example, see *Hogan*, para. 67, where the Newfoundland Court of Appeal writes that "the submission of the [Roman Catholic] appellants that a fiduciary duty *similar* to that owed by the Crown to aboriginal peoples is owed to the class represented by the appellants *cannot succeed*"; emphasis added.

21 *Haida Nation v British Columbia (Minister of Forests)*, [2004] 3 S.C.R. 512, para. 16.

22 Ibid. Elsewhere, the Court locates reconciliation as section 35's purpose – hence as an obligation consciously undertaken.

23 *Wewaykum Indian Band v Canada*, [2002] 4 S.C.R. 245.

24 *Manitoba Métis Federation, Inc. v Canada (Attorney General)*, 2013 SCC 14, para. 77.

25 The liberal and generous interpretation principle has been applied to treaty commitments (*Nowegijick v The Queen*, [1983]1 S.C.R. 29), statutory commitments (*Guerin v The Queen*, [1984] 2 S.C.R. 335), s.35 specifically (*R. v Sparrow*, [1990] 1 S.C.R. 1075), and now any constitutional obligation to Aboriginal groups (*Manitoba Métis Federation*, para. 91).

26 So contend Rothstein and Moldaver JJ (dissenting), in *Manitoba Métis Federation*, para. 254.

27 *Sparrow*, 1108.

28 *Hogan*, para. 64.

29 *Manitoba Métis Federation* (Rothstein and Moldaver JJ dissenting), paras 161, 214, 267.

30 *Haida Nation*, para. 18.

31 Ibid., para. 41.

32 *Beckman v Little Salmon/Carmacks First Nation* [2010] 3 S.C.R. 103, para. 42.

33 *Quebec Secession Reference*, para. 54.

34 This has been met with criticism and some trepidation; see, for example, Alan C. Cairns, "The Quebec Secession Reference: The Constitutional Obligation to Negotiate," *Constitutional Forum* 10, no. 1 (1998): 27.

35 Mark D. Walters, "Written Constitutions and Unwritten Constitutionalism," in *Expounding the Constitution: Essays in Constitutional Theory*, ed. Grant Huscroft (New York: Cambridge University Press, 2008), 275.
36 Jeffrey Goldsworthy, "Unwritten Constitutional Principles," in Huscroft, *Expounding the Constitution*, 312.
37 For a wander through the written versus unwritten constitutionalism debate in Canada in the post – *Quebec Secession Reference* context, see Warren J. Newman, "'Grand Entrance Hall,' Back Door or Foundation Stone? The Role of Constitutional Principles in Construing and Applying the Constitution of Canada," *Supreme Court Law Review* (2d) 14 (2001): 197–234.

PART TWO

The Procedures

5 Constitutional Amendment by Legislation

WARREN J. NEWMAN

The procedures for amending the Constitution of Canada found in Part V of the Constitution Act, 1982 contain the following striking feature. The multilateral procedures – that is, the general amending formula set out in section 38 and required as well for matters listed in section 42, the unanimous consent procedure encompassed in section 41, and the some-but-not-all provinces or special arrangements procedure of section 43 – all proceed by way of authorizing resolutions of the federal houses of Parliament and the provincial legislative assemblies, culminating in the proclamation of an amendment to the Constitution by the governor general under section 48. The multilateral process is triggered by the initiating power in section 46. However, Part V also contains two unilateral procedures set out in sections 44 and 45, and constitutional amendments made pursuant to those sections proceed by way of statutory enactments, not parliamentary resolutions. In other words, sections 44 and 45 embody grants of legislative authority, and the relevant actors are not the federal parliamentary chambers and provincial assemblies, but rather the Parliament of Canada on the one hand and the provincial legislatures on the other.

This is more than a pedantic terminological point or mere legal nicety. There is a distressing tendency on the part of some jurists and academics to employ the words "Parliament and the provincial legislatures" as a sort of short-hand for the Senate and House of Commons and the provincial legislative assemblies, as if the two sets of terms were identical. They are not, and failure to maintain the distinction can only lead to confusion as well as to numerous legal and practical difficulties. A parliamentary resolution, for example, is not an Act of Parliament, and only the latter has the force of law. The Parliament of Canada is, as section 17 of the Constitution Act, 1867 confirms, composed of the Queen, the Senate, and the House of Commons, and it is those three acting in concert in the passage and assent to bills that results in the enactment of legislation. So, too, the legislature of each province is composed of the lieutenant-governor and the legislative assembly. Resolutions of the federal houses of Parliament and the provincial assemblies, respectively, are formal expressions of the will of those houses, but they are not, in and of themselves, legislation.

So, Part V of the Constitution Act, 1982 is unique in that it contemplates two methods of achieving constitutional amendment. This chapter focuses on the method of legislative enactment by Parliament and the provincial legislatures, with particular emphasis on the scope of Parliament's legislative power to enact both amendments to the text of the Constitution of Canada and enactments that, while not amending the actual provisions of the Constitution, may be said to enhance the implementation of the text or advance the underlying structural principles of the Constitution.

Sections 44 and 45 of the Constitution Act, 1982

Sections 44 and 45 were enacted as part of the series of new amending procedures that replaced the largely convention-driven process of amendment that had grown up prior to 1982, whereby the Senate and House of Commons would make a joint address to the Queen to lay before the United Kingdom Parliament measures to alter provisions in the British North America Acts. Unlike the new multilateral procedures enacted in Part V of the Constitution Act, 1982, however, sections 44 and 45 are the direct successors of earlier provisions in the British North America (BNA) Act, 1867 – henceforth to be known as the Constitution Act, 1867 – that already granted to the Parliament of Canada and the provincial legislatures, respectively, some limited legislative powers of constitutional amendment. Since 1949, class 1 of section 91 of the BNA Act had provided that the legislative authority of Parliament extended to the "amendment from time to time of the Constitution of Canada," followed by a substantial list of exceptions, including the federal-provincial distribution of powers and minority rights. Since 1867, by class 1 of section 92 of the BNA Act, the legislature of each province was authorized to make laws amending "the Constitution of the Province, except as regards the Office of the Lieutenant Governor." Both of these heads of legislative power were repealed by the schedule to the Constitution Act, 1982, but, as antecedents to sections 44 and 45, their scope and interpretation have remained relevant, and I return to them later.

It is convenient at this point to set out the text of sections 44 and 45 of the Constitution Act, 1982:

44. Subject to sections 41 and 42, Parliament may exclusively make laws amending the Constitution of Canada in relation to the executive government of Canada or the Senate and House of Commons.
45. Subject to section 41, the legislature of each province may exclusively make laws amending the constitution of the province.

As the drafter's marginal headings indicate, section 44 deals with amendments by Parliament; section 45 with amendments by provincial legislatures. The parallelism is evident. Both provisions grant legislative authority, with important exceptions that are reserved to the multilateral procedures.

Statutory Alterations to the Constitution Act, 1867

As an Imperial statute extending to Canada, the BNA Act, 1867 was generally and directly amendable only by the exercise of the plenary legislative authority of the UK Parliament. From the beginning, however, the Act of 1867 contemplated at least certain indirect amendments or alterations by the Parliament of Canada and the provincial legislatures that were not entirely of a marginal character. For example, section 35 established the quorum of the Senate as a minimum of fifteen senators, but that provision commences with the words, "[u]ntil the Parliament of Canada otherwise provides." The exact same wording is found at the outset of section 40, providing for the electoral districts of the original four provinces; section 41, providing for the continuance of pre-Confederation election laws; section 47, dealing with the absence of the speaker of the House of Commons; sections 130 and 131, dealing with the transfer of provincial officers to and the appointment of new officers by Canada; and sections 103, in respect of auditing in relation to the Consolidated Revenue Fund, and 141, providing for penitentiaries, contain the same wording ("until the Parliament of Canada otherwise provides") at the end and in the body of those provisions, respectively. Section 105 fixed the salary of the governor general at £10,000, "[u]nless altered by the Parliament of Canada," and section 120 provided that all payments made under the BNA Act or in discharge of liabilities assumed by Canada would be made in such manner and form as determined by the governor in council "until the Parliament of Canada otherwise directs."

Most of these provisions were clearly of a transitional character, establishing or continuing baseline rules until Parliament (or in certain cases, the provincial legislatures) altered those rules by providing otherwise. Nonetheless, they demonstrate the truth of the proposition that at least some rules embodied in provisions of what is now called the Constitution Act, 1867 were amendable by ordinary statute law. Section 52 provides another salient example: "**52.** The Number of Members of the House of Commons may be from Time to Time increased by the Parliament of Canada, provided the Proportionate Representation of the Provinces prescribed by this Act is not thereby disturbed."

The principle of proportionate representation is protected from unilateral amendment today by paragraph 42(1)(a) of the Constitution Act, 1982 (where it is made subject to the general amending procedure of subsection 38(1)), and under section 44 (and its predecessor, the former class 1 of section 91 of the Constitution Act, 1867). Parliament has directly amended section 51 of the Constitution Act, 1867 with respect to the rules that apply to the readjustment of representation in the House of Commons, but the point for present purposes is that, once again, Parliament was granted legislative authority to alter constitutional rules and provisions indirectly and (since 1949 and again in 1982) directly by the Constitution Acts, 1867 to 1982.

The Supreme Court's Opinion in the First *Senate Reference*

In the original *Senate Reference* (*Reference re Authority of Parliament in relation to the Upper House*),[1] the amendments made expressly to the text of the BNA Act, 1867 by statutes of Parliament dealt with what the Supreme Court of Canada has described as "federal 'housekeeping' matters."[2] As of 1979, the year the Court issued its opinion, there had been five such legislative enactments. These included the aforementioned amendments to section 51 of the Constitution Act, 1867, in 1952[3] and again in 1974,[4] as well as two amendments in 1975 that increased the representation of the Northwest Territories in the House of Commons from one to two members and the total number of senators from 102 to 104, thereby providing for representation in the Senate for Yukon and the Northwest Territories, respectively.[5] Moreover, the BNA Act, 1965 amended section 29 of the 1867 Act by changing the tenure of senators from life to obligatory retirement at the age of seventy-five.[6]

In the original *Senate Reference*, the Supreme Court circumscribed the scope of Parliament's legislative authority to make constitutional amendments under class 1 of section 91 of the BNA Act, 1867. I noted above that this provision conferred upon Parliament the power to make laws in relation to "[t]he amendment from time to time of the Constitution of Canada," except as regarded a series of specific but important matters, including the federal-provincial distribution of powers and other entrenched guarantees. The Court held that "Canada" in this context meant "the juristic federal unit," and that the "Constitution of Canada" did not mean the whole of the BNA Act but, rather, "the constitution of the federal government, as distinct from the provincial governments." The amending power conferred by section 91(1) was thus "limited to matters of interest only to the federal government."[7]

Furthermore, the Court ruled that amendments to the Constitution that would "affect the fundamental features, or essential characteristics, given to the Senate as a means of ensuring regional and provincial representation in the federal legislative process" were beyond the scope of Parliament's legislative authority under section 91(1).[8]

Impact on the Scope of Section 44 of the Constitution Act, 1982

Section 44 of the Constitution Act, 1982 accordingly was framed in similar, relatively narrow and specific terms. As we have seen, Parliament was granted legislative authority to make amendments to the Constitution "in relation to the executive government or the Senate and House of Commons," and this section was made subject, *inter alia*, to section 42, which, in the case of the Senate, carved out and reserved to the general amending formula of section 38 the essential characteristics and fundamental features the Supreme Court identified as protected from ordinary legislative amendment – that is, amendments in relation to "the powers of the Senate and the method of selecting Senators" (para. 42(1)(b)) and "the number of members by which a province is entitled to be represented in the Senate and the residence qualifications of Senators" (para. 42(1)(c)).

Since 1982, three textual amendments to the Constitution have been made pursuant to section 44 of the Constitution Act, 1982: the two amendments to section 51 of the Constitution Act, 1867 effected by the Constitution Act, 1985 (Representation)[9] and the Fair Representation Act of 2011,[10] and the Constitution Act, 1999 (Nunavut),[11] providing for the newly established territory of Nunavut to be represented by one member each in the Senate and the House of Commons.

The Supreme Court's Opinion in the *Senate Reform Reference*

In 2006, the federal government introduced Bill S-4, An Act to amend the Constitution Act, 1867 (Senate tenure), the first of several successive bills over the years that proposed to amend section 29 of the Constitution Act, 1867 to alter the tenure of senators. As noted above, in 1965 Parliament amended this same constitutional provision to change the tenure of senators from life to retirement at age seventy-five. Theoretically, this meant that senators could still remain in the Senate for a maximum of forty-five years, assuming a hypothetical appointment as early as age thirty and retirement at seventy-five. In practice, senators' average and median lengths of service are considerably shorter. In any event, in Bill S-4 the government proposed an eight-year, renewable term of years,[12] and in Bill C-7 – the Senate Reform Act, introduced in 2011 – a nine-year, nonrenewable term.

In the *Senate Reform Reference*,[13] the governor in council submitted detailed questions to the Supreme Court on whether it was within the legislative authority of Parliament, acting pursuant to section 44 of the Constitution Act, 1982, to amend section 29 of the Constitution Act, 1867 to provide, *inter alia*, for a fixed term of nine years for senators, as set out in Bill C-7, or a fixed term of "eight years or less" or "ten years or more." The Court held that such alterations were beyond the scope of section 44's grant of authority to "make laws amending the Constitution of Canada in relation to ... the Senate." Rather, amendments to provide for a fixed term of years, however lengthy, for senators were held to come within the purview of the general amending procedure of section 38 of the Constitution Act, 1982, even though section 38 was not mentioned as a general exception to section 44 in the latter provision and an amendment in relation to senatorial tenure was not a matter covered by the specific exceptions to section 44 set out expressly in section 42. The Court held that the limited compass of section 44 did not embrace "all constitutional changes to the Senate which are not expressly included within another procedure in Part V," but that section 44, "as an exception to the general amending procedure, encompasses measures that maintain or change the Senate without altering its fundamental nature and role."[14] The type of textual amendment to the Constitution that *was* within the scope of section 44 would be the removal of the net worth requirement and a partial repeal of the real property requirement for senators under section 23 of the Constitution Act, 1867. The Court held that such amendments would not engage the interests of the provinces, but would "update" the constitutional framework without affecting the fundamental nature and role of the Senate.[15]

Legislation of a Constitutional, Quasi-constitutional, or Organic Character

Until now, I have discussed legislation that has made or proposed – successfully or unsuccessfully – essentially textual amendments to the Constitution. As we have seen, prior to 1982, and aside from the alterations implied in the words, "until the Parliament of Canada otherwise provides" and like expressions in the early and often transitional provisions of the BNA Act, legislative authority at the federal level for textual constitutional amendments flowed from subsection 91(1), enacted by the UK Parliament in 1949 as the British North America (No. 2) Act. We have seen as well that this provision was repealed by the schedule to the Constitution Act, 1982 and replaced with section 44 of that Act, which was henceforth the source of federal legislative authority for amendments to the text of the Constitution.

I turn now to another class of federal legislation with constitutional implications: legislation of a constitutional, quasi-constitutional, or organic character that does not alter the text of the Constitution, but that might be considered, in a broad, analytical sense, as a form of constitutional amendment or reform.[16]

In 1982 Professor Stephen Scott provided a striking illustration of what this means. "Much of the 'organic' law," he wrote, "dealing with the constitution and structure of the federal Parliament is to be found on the federal statute book. Are these enactments part of the 'Constitution of Canada'?"[17]

> Consider, by way of example, the existing rules of law (1) making a seat in the Senate incompatible with a seat in the House of Commons of Canada, and (2) making a seat in any house of a provincial legislature incompatible with a seat in the House of Commons ...
>
> Not many lawyers could venture, at any rate confidently, to say from memory exactly where, in terms of legal sources, these rules are to be found. At common law? In a federal statute? In an Imperial statute? Fewer lawyers still, I suspect, would venture to insist that the rules in these two

classes are inherently different in kind or quality so that one set is necessarily of a 'constitutional' nature and the other not.[18]

Professor Scott's point was that the first of these rules is to be found in section 39 of the Constitution Act, 1867, whereas the second is set out in the provisions of a federal statute: sections 22 and 23 of the Parliament of Canada Act.[19] He took the view that section 91(1) of the Act of 1867 "clearly – and even on the narrowest reading – has empowered the Parliament of Canada to enact and repeal such provisions" as the disqualification rules that are now to be found in the Parliament of Canada Act, but these provisions long predate the granting of that amending power in 1949: "It cannot seriously be doubted that they have been, from Confederation, within the legislative authority of Parliament to enact and repeal."[20]

"Peace, Order and Good Government": Section 91 of the Constitution Act, 1867

Whence, then, did Parliament's power to enact such organic or "constitutional" legislation come prior to 1949? Where had it arguably remained since, even with the advent of section 91(1)? The answer was, in the main, to be found in Parliament's general and residuary power to enact laws for the "Peace, Order and good Government of Canada."[21] Indeed, the first federal Official Languages Act had been upheld on that very basis. Chief Justice Bora Laskin, writing for a unanimous Supreme Court in the *Jones* case, stated:

> I am in no doubt that it was open to the Parliament of Canada to enact the *Official Languages Act* (limited as it is to the purposes of the Parliament and Government of Canada and to the institutions of that Parliament and Government) as being a "law for the peace, order and good government of Canada in relation to [a matter] not coming within the classes of subjects ... assigned exclusively to the Legislatures of the Provinces." ... The quoted words are in the opening paragraph of the *British North America Act*; and in relying on them as constitutional support for the Official Languages Act, I do so on the basis of the purely residuary character of the legislative power thereby conferred. *No authority need be cited for the exclusive power of the Parliament of Canada to legislate in relation to the operation and administration of the institutions and agencies of the Parliament and Government of Canada.* Those institutions and agencies are clearly beyond provincial reach.[22]

There is little doubt that the constitutional validity of many statutes of an organic or quasi-constitutional character enacted by Parliament prior to 1982 – including not only the Senate and House of Commons Act (as it then was) and the first Official Languages Act of 1969, but also the Demise of the Crown Act, the Governor General's Act, the Seals Act, the Succession to the Throne Act of 1937, the Royal Style and Titles Acts of 1947 and 1952, the Canadian Bill of Rights Act of 1959, and the Canadian Human Rights Act of 1977 – can generally be supported on the basis of the general and residuary power in the opening words of section 91 of the Constitution Act, 1867. These statutes did not amend the Constitution in any formal or textual sense, but they did modernize and advance, by way of ordinary legislative action, constitutional principles, values, and institutions of governance.

For example, in the *Jones* case, it had been claimed by those arguing against the validity of the 1969 Official Languages Act that it was in reality an amendment in relation to the use of the English and French languages and, as such, a matter protected by section 133 of the Constitution Act, 1867 and beyond the scope of section 91(1) – that is, the express amending power. Chief Justice Laskin responded, however, that, while certainly, what section 133 grants "may not be diminished" by Parliament, "if its provisions are respected," there was nothing in it that "precludes the conferring of additional rights or privileges or the imposing of additional obligations respecting the use of English and French, if done in relation to matters within the competence of the enacting Legislature."[23] Moreover, the fact that the first volume of the Final Report of the Royal Commission on Bilingualism and Biculturalism, published in 1967, and government documents such as *A Canadian Charter of Human Rights* and *Federalism for the Future*, both published in 1968, recommended the constitutional entrenchment of a range of language rights beyond the limited purview of section 133, was "hardly a support for the contention that there can be no advance upon section 133 without constitutional amendment."[24]

Sections 44 and 45 and Organic Legislation: The Significance of *OPSEU*

With the advent of the Constitution Act, 1982, the primary legislative authority for organic legislation that advances and implements constitutional values throughout the institutions of government remains, in principle, the general and residuary power in the opening words of section 91 of the Constitution Act, 1867. It is arguable, however, that section 44 of the Constitution Act, 1982 may provide an additional source of legislative power.

To understand why that is the case, one should begin with the reasoned analysis that the late Justice Jean Beetz employed in the *OPSEU* case.[25] Although the matter turned on the scope and application of section 92(1) of the Constitution Act, 1867, and Justice Beetz was prudent not to rule on whether, as might be imagined, section 45 of the Constitution Act, 1982 was identical in scope, it has been generally taken that it is, and the Supreme Court confirmed as much in the *Senate Reform Reference*. Section 45, like its predecessor, grants to provincial legislatures the power to amend the internal constitution of the province, subject to section 41 of the Constitution Act, 1982 – which expressly protects, as did section 92(1), the office of the lieutenant-governor from unilateral provincial amendment.

Just as the Supreme Court had done in the *Patriation Reference*[26] in 1981 in relation to the Constitution of Canada, Justice Beetz approached the constitution of the province – in this case, of Ontario – from a broad, principled, and purposive perspective. The constitution of Ontario included not only the relevant provisions of the Constitution Act, 1867 relating to the lieutenant-governor, the executive council, and the legislature, but also provisions "enacted by ordinary statutes of the Legislature of Ontario," including the Legislative Assembly Act, the Representation Act and the Executive Council Act. An enactment of the Ontario legislature, Justice Beetz indicated, is "constitutional in nature" if it satisfies at least some of the following indicia:

> [I]s the enactment in question, by its object, relative to a branch of the government of Ontario or, to use the language of this Court in *Attorney General of Quebec* v. *Blaikie*, [1979] 2 S.C.R. 1016, at p. 1024, does "it [bear] on the operation of an organ of the government of the Province"? Does it for instance determine the composition, powers, authority, privileges and duties of the legislative or executive branches or their members? Does it regulate the interrelationship between two or more branches? Or does it set out some principle of government?[27]

Of course, this definition was subject to further limitations, since Ontario is not a unitary state, but a province within the Canadian federation. It was not open to the provincial legislature, in the guise of amending the constitution of the province, to alter "provisions relating to the constitution of the federal state, considered as a whole, or essential to the implementation of the federal principle" – an "obvious example" being the federal-provincial distribution of legislative powers – nor would it have been within the purview of the legislature's amending power to alter "a fundamental term or condition of the union formed in 1867."[28] Nor did the power of provincial constitutional amendment "necessarily comprise the power to bring about a profound constitutional upheaval by the introduction of political institutions foreign to and incompatible with the Canadian system."[29]

In the event, Justice Beetz upheld the validity of provisions of the Ontario Public Service Act as an amendment to the constitution of the province, insofar as they bore on an organ of government (the public service) and gave legislative effect to a principle of government (the neutrality of the public service) that was itself a prerequisite of a larger constitutional principle: responsible government. Again, what is significant and relevant for present purposes is that the impugned provisions of the Public Service Act constituted "an ordinary legislative amendment of the constitution of Ontario, within the meaning of s. 92(1) of the *Constitution Act, 1867*."[30] And in the *Senate Reform Reference*, the Supreme Court confirmed that section 45 of the Constitution Act, 1982 has essentially the same scope as its predecessor.

The Supreme Court's Opinion in the *Senate Reform Reference* and Sections 44 and 45

Indeed, as I have emphasized, the Supreme Court held that sections 44 and 45 of the Constitution Act, 1982 "fulfill the same basic function" as their predecessors, sections 91(1) and 92(1) of what is now the Constitution Act, 1867, which "granted the federal and the provincial governments the power to amend their respective constitutions."[31] The successor provisions, sections 44 and 45, "give the federal and the provincial legislatures the ability" to amend unilaterally "certain aspects of the Constitution that relate to their own level of government, but which do not engage the interests of the other level of government." This "limited ability to make changes unilaterally" reflects a principle, the Court stated, that "Parliament and the provincial legislatures are equal stakeholders in the Canadian constitutional design." Neither body or level, acting on its own, could "alter the fundamental nature and role of the institutions provided for in the Constitution." That said, however, "those institutions can be maintained and even changed to some extent under ss. 44 and 45, provided that their fundamental nature and role remain intact."[32]

In the *Senate Reform Reference*, the Supreme Court held that federal legislative proposals[33] to provide for popular consultation at the national or provincial and territorial levels in the Senate appointments process would constitute an amendment to the architecture of the Constitution, even though the Constitution's provisions would not have been altered and the governor general would have continued to summon and appoint senators pursuant to sections 24 and 32 of the Constitution Act, 1867 on the advice of the prime minister.[34] The Court's reasoning was that, although no change was contemplated to the Constitution's text, the underlying structure would have been altered fundamentally by conferring upon senators what would have amounted to a popular mandate. This would be tantamount to changing the fundamental constitutional design of the Senate and, "by extension, would constitute an amendment to the Constitution."[35]

The Court held that the constitutional protection afforded by paragraph 42(1)(b) of the Constitution Act, 1982 in respect of amendments relating to the "method of selecting Senators" included "more than the formal appointment of Senators by the Governor General" and extended to the "entire process" by which senators are selected.[36] Having decided that the scope of paragraph 42(1)(b) was so broad, it was then a relatively easy matter for the Court to rule out the application of section 44, given that "the categories of amendment captured by s. 42 are removed from the scope of s. 44."[37] The Court made no direct allusion to the other source of legislative power invoked in the questions put by the governor in council to the Court on the issue of legislated popular consultations – the general and residuary power in section 91 of the Constitution Act, 1867 – but it is clear from the context that the fundamental structural changes to the Senate that would be brought about, in the Court's view, to the Senate's nature and role by "consultative elections" were beyond the scope of Parliament's legislative power under either section 91 of the Act of 1867 or section 44 of the Act of 1982.

Parliament's Legislative Authority Today

Where does that leave the Parliament of Canada today? It is evident that Parliament's legislative authority – whether to enact formal constitutional amendments pursuant to section 44 of the Constitution Act, 1982 or to enact organic legislation of an arguably "constitutional" or quasi-constitutional character pursuant to the general and residuary grant of legislative power in the opening words of section 91 of the Constitution Act, 1867[38] – cannot alter the basic structure of the Constitution or the fundamental nature and role of its protected institutions. On the other hand, federal legislation that enhances, rather than transforms, those central institutions or that otherwise implements and advances structural constitutional principles will find support for its validity and legitimacy in both the *Senate Reform Reference* and the *Supreme Court Act Reference*.

Parliament has enacted numerous statutes of this organic character since 1982. A few examples will illustrate the importance of these in fleshing out the Constitution's basic framework in relation to central institutions, in modernizing some aspects of those institutions, in giving additional legislative effect to some of the Constitution's fundamental postulates, and in carrying out its aims and requirements.

Examples of Recent Quasi-constitutional or Organic Legislation

In 1988 Parliament enacted a new Official Languages Act of a much broader and ambitious character than the original statute of 1969.[39] The preamble to the Act contains several references to the Constitution of Canada and the language rights enshrined therein, and the Act was clearly designed to implement constitutional requirements in respect of the equal status of English and French in the institutions of the Parliament and government of Canada, their use in proceedings before federal courts, and in communications with and services offered to the public. The Act built upon the enhanced guarantees of linguistic equality that were introduced into the Constitution through the provisions of the Canadian Charter of Rights and Freedoms in 1982, and also gave expression to the principle of advancement of the English and French languages that was set out in subsection 16(3) of the Charter, one of the stated purposes of the Act being to "support the development of English and French linguistic minority communities and generally to advance the equality of status and use of the English and French languages within Canadian society."[40]

In 1988 Parliament also enacted the Canadian Multiculturalism Act, which also invokes the Constitution of Canada numerous times in its preamble, notably in respect of its guarantees of human rights and freedoms, which builds upon the reference to "the preservation and enhancement of the multicultural heritage of Canadians" in section 27 of the Charter and which declares in solemn and eloquent terms the federal government's multiculturalism policy and provides measures for the implementation of that policy.[41]

In 1992 Parliament passed the Referendum Act, the long title of which is An Act to provide for Referendums on the Constitution of Canada. The Act enables the governor in council to "obtain by means of a referendum the opinion of electors on any question relating to the Constitution of Canada."[42] This optional mechanism was employed to consult Canadians on the Charlottetown Accord, an agreement in principle among first ministers to seek ratification, through the multilateral amending procedures of Part V of the Constitution Act, 1982, of a series of significant constitutional amendments.[43]

In 1996 Parliament enacted An Act respecting constitutional amendments,[44] which restrains federal ministers of the Crown from proposing a motion for a resolution to authorize an amendment under the general amending procedure – other than one in respect of which a legislative assembly may exercise its dissent under subsection 38(3) of the Constitution Act, 1982 – unless the amendment has first been consented to by a majority of the provinces that includes Ontario, Quebec, British Columbia, two or more of the Atlantic provinces, and two or more of the Prairie provinces.[45] The thrust of the legislation is to enhance the protection afforded to provincial interests under the general amending procedure by ensuring that a broad provincial consensus is reached before the federal government proceeds with such amendments.

In the aftermath of the Supreme Court's landmark opinion in the *Quebec Secession Reference*,[46] Parliament enacted the Clarity Act,[47] which deals with the role of the House of Commons and the federal government in respect of a referendum on the secession of a province from Canada. The Act, which recognizes in a detailed preamble that "any proposal relating to the break-up of a democratic state is a matter of the utmost gravity," provides a legal framework to guide the conduct of the House, "the only political institution elected to represent all Canadians," and imposes certain duties on the federal government. The Act invokes the constitutional principles that the Supreme Court found were essential to a resolution of the question – federalism, democracy, constitutionalism and the rule of law, and the protection of minorities – in responding to the Court's findings.

In 2002 Parliament enacted the Royal Assent Act,[48] which recognizes, in its preamble, that the granting of assent to bills passed by both Houses of Parliament is the "constitutional culmination of the legislative process," and facilitates the signifying of Royal Assent by written declaration, while preserving, at least twice in each calendar year, the signifying of Royal Assent in the more ceremonial and traditional setting "in Parliament assembled." The Act, of course, did not alter the fundamental constitutional requirement that, for a bill to become law, it must first receive assent by the governor general in the Queen's name, pursuant to section 55 of the Constitution Act, 1867, but it modernized and rendered more flexible the ways and means, or modalities, by which Royal Assent is granted.

In 2007 Parliament enacted amendments to the Canada Elections Act[49] to provide for a four-year cycle for general elections within the five-year maximum life of the House of Commons set by section 50 of the Constitution Act, 1867. Elections are, in principle, to be held on the third Monday of October in the fourth calendar year after the polling day for the previous general election, but subject always to the "powers of the Governor General, including the power to dissolve Parliament at the Governor General's discretion."[50]

In 2012 Parliament enacted amendments to the Governor General's Act[51] and the Income Tax Act[52] that repealed provisions exempting the governor general's salary from income tax and adjusted his salary commensurately. These changes, while made so as to treat the governor general's salary in a manner similar to that of other public office holders, could hardly be construed as amendments to the Constitution in relation to the office of the governor general, as neither the text of the Constitution was altered nor the constitutional status, dignity, or powers of the governor general affected or undermined in any way.

It is also noteworthy that, in 2013, Parliament enacted the Succession to the Throne Act, 2013,[53] which signified its assent to changes proposed in a bill pending before the UK Parliament to alter the common law rule of male primogeniture and the archaic statutory bar against heirs to the throne marrying Roman Catholics. In the Canadian statute, which came into force on 26 March 2015, Parliament assented in accordance with the action contemplated by the constitutional convention recorded in the second recital of the preamble of the Statute of Westminster, 1931, itself a part of the Constitution of Canada:

> And whereas it is meet and proper to set out by way of preamble to this Act that, inasmuch as the Crown is the symbol of the free association of the members of the British Commonwealth of Nations, and as they are united by a common allegiance to the Crown, it would be in accord with the established constitutional position of all the members of the

Commonwealth in relation to one another that any alteration in the law touching the Succession to the Throne or the Royal Style and Titles shall hereafter require the assent as well of the Parliaments of all the Dominions as of the Parliament of the United Kingdom[.]

This Canadian parliamentary assent to the modernization of the rules of royal succession is at least arguably in keeping with statutory precedents, Canadian constitutional principles, and Charter values.[54]

Conclusion

Sections 44 and 45 of the Constitution Act, 1982 grant legislative authority to Parliament and the provincial legislatures to enact a narrow but significant range of constitutional amendments: in the case of Parliament, to make laws amending the Constitution in relation to the executive government of Canada or the Senate and House of Commons; in the case of the provincial legislatures, to the constitution of the province; and subject, in both cases, to important exceptions. Section 101 of the Constitution Act, 1867 grants Parliament legislative authority to provide for the continuing maintenance and organization of another central federal institution, the Supreme Court of Canada. Laws that would amend the text and provisions of the Constitution of Canada or that might alter the Constitution's underlying architecture to a degree that would be tantamount to a formal constitutional amendment, must henceforth respect the Supreme Court's rulings in the *Supreme Court Act Reference* and the *Senate Reform Reference*.

At the same time, there remains great potential in the Parliament of Canada's legislative authority to enact generically "constitutional," quasi-constitutional, and organic legislation, whether pursuant to section 44 of the Constitution Act, 1982 – on the view that section 44 should have the same scope as the provincial power to enact organic legislation as well as formal constitutional amendments under section 45 – or, as is more likely to be common, pursuant to the opening words of section 91 of the Constitution Act, 1867 and other grants of undoubted legislative power, such as section 18, which deals with the privileges and immunities of the Senate and the House of Commons.

Legislation that is constitutional in *character* without being constitutional in *status* possesses two potential drawbacks that are also, viewed another way, two virtues: it is neither supreme nor entrenched law. As such, it provides the Parliament and government of the day a more flexible means of engaging in constitutional experimentation and innovation, which thereby might permit the advancement of constitutional principles while paving the way for future amendments that do engage the multilateral procedures and do entrench the innovations as part of Canada's supreme law.

As well, where the experimentation proves unsuccessful in some ways, errors might be corrected more easily by statutory amendments or in a better formulation of the provisions, borne of experience with the statutory regime, in the drafting of formal constitutional amendments. And thus, the statutory Canadian Bill of Rights experiment begat, in certain respects, enhanced guarantees in the Canadian Charter of Rights and Freedoms – notably with respect to equality rights – and the first Official Languages Act begat enhanced Charter guarantees and, in turn, a broader and more effective new Act.

As long as the handiwork of Parliament (and the provincial legislatures) continues to give life to the Constitution's provisions and its underlying principles, and modernizes the contours of its institutional architecture without transforming its essential features, then constitutional amendment or enhancement by legislation will continue to be a valuable means of constitutional implementation and reform.

Notes

The views expressed in this chapter are presented from an academic perspective, and do not necessarily represent the position of the federal Department of Justice.

1 [1980] S.C.R. 54. The Court's unanimous and *per curiam* opinion was rendered on 21 December 1979. The bench was composed of eight judges: Chief Justice Laskin and Justices Martland, Ritchie, Pigeon, Dickson, Estey, Pratte, and McIntyre.

2 Ibid., 65.

3 British North America Act, 1952, 1 Eliz. II, c. 15 (Can.); repealed by the schedule to the Constitution Act, 1982.

4 British North America Act, 1974, 23 Eliz. II, c. 13, Part I (Can.); styled the Constitution Act, 1974 by the schedule to the Constitution Act, 1982. This amendment was later repealed by further amendments to section 51 of the Constitution Act, 1867.

5 British North America Act, 1975, 23–24 Eliz. II, c. 28, Part I (Can.); British North America Act (No. 2), 1975, 23–24 Eliz. II, c. 53 (Can.); styled the

Constitution Act, 1975 and the Constitution Act (No.2), 1975 by the schedule to the Constitution Act, 1982.

6 British North America Act, 1965, 14 Eliz. II, c. 4, Part I (Can.); styled the Constitution Act, 1965 by the schedule to the Constitution Act, 1982.

7 [1980] 1 S.C.R. 54, 70.

8 Ibid., 78.

9 R.S.C. 1985, Appendix II, No. 47. This amendment repealed and replaced subsection 51(1) – the version enacted by the Constitution Act, 1974 – of the Constitution Act, 1867.

10 S.C. 2011, c. 26. This amendment also replaced subsection 51(1) – the version enacted by the Constitution Act, 1985 – of the Constitution Act, 1867.

11 S.C. 1998, c. 15, Part II.

12 The legislative history of Bill S-4, including study by two Senate committees, is set out in some detail in Warren J. Newman, "Living with the Amending Procedures: Prospects for Future Constitutional Reform in Canada," *Supreme Court Law Review* (2d) 37 (2007): 410–16.

13 *Reference re Senate Reform*, 2014 SCC 32, [2014] 1 S.C.R. 704. The Court's opinion, as in the first *Senate Reference* in 1979, was rendered unanimously and *per curiam* by an eight-judge bench, this time composed of Chief Justice McLachlin and Justices LeBel, Abella, Rothstein, Cromwell, Moldaver, Karakatsanis, and Wagner. I disclose that I was one of counsel representing the Attorney General of Canada in this reference.

14 Ibid., para. 75.

15 Ibid., paras 90, 94. A full repeal of the property requirement would engage the bilateral procedure under section 43 of the Constitution Act, 1982 because of the impact on the scope and application of subsection 23(6) of the Constitution Act, 1867, a special arrangement for Quebec senators that permits them to reside in the electoral division for which they are appointed or simply to fulfil their real property qualification by holding property in that division; see para. 93 of the Court's opinion.

16 "These statutes are what the French call organic laws, namely, laws which are looked upon as constitutional, not because of some special or formal method of enactment (which is the same as that used for ordinary statutes) but by their content – the fact that the subject material of these statutes is constitutional in its nature ... [Federal statutes that have] established the franchise, adjusted the provincial subsidies, created new government departments, provided for the trial of controverted elections, and a host of others are all organic laws ... Inasmuch as large sections of the provincial constitutions are in the form of provincial statutes, these parts fall entirely in this category"; R. MacGregor Dawson, *The Government of Canada*, 4th ed.,

revised by Norman Ward (Toronto: University of Toronto Press, 1963; reprinted 1967), 67–8.

17 Stephen A. Scott, "Pussycat, Pussycat or Patriation and the New Constitutional Amendment Processes," *University of Western Ontario Law Review* 20 (1982): 266.

18 Ibid.

19 R.S.C., c. P-1. At the time he was writing in 1982, Professor Scott cited the predecessor provisions in what was then the House of Commons Act, R.S.C. 1970, c. H-9.

20 Ibid., 267.

21 Other important grants of legislative authority to Parliament to enact organic legislation of a generically "constitutional" character include section 18 (with respect to the privileges, immunities, and powers of the Senate and the House of Commons and their members) and section 101 (to establish and maintain a general court of appeal for Canada and federal courts) of the Constitution Act, 1867. For further analysis of these provisions, see Warren J. Newman, "Parliamentary Privilege, the Canadian Constitution and the Courts," *Ottawa Law Review* 39, no. 3 (2008): 573–609; and idem, "The Constitutional Status of the Supreme Court of Canada," *Supreme Court Law Review* (2d) 47 (2009): 429–43.

22 *Jones v Attorney General of New Brunswick*, [1975] 2 S.C.R. 182, 189.

23 Ibid., 192–3.

24 Ibid., 192.

25 *OPSEU v Ontario (Attorney General)*, [1987] 2 S.C.R. 2, 37–47.

26 *Re: Resolution to amend the Constitution*, [1981] 1 S.C.R. 753, 876–8.

27 *OPSEU*, 39.

28 Ibid., 39, 40.

29 Ibid., 40.

30 Ibid., 46.

31 *Reference re Senate Reform*, paras 46–7. The Court adverted to its earlier opinion in the original *Senate Reference* and to Justice Beetz's judgment in the *OPSEU* case in support of its understanding of the scope of the provisions.

32 Ibid., para. 48.

33 Specifically mentioned in the reference questions put to the Court were Bill C-20, the Senate Appointment Consultations Act, which had been introduced in 2006, and Bill C-7, the Senate Reform Act, introduced in 2011.

34 "In practice, convention requires the Governor General to follow the recommendations of the Prime Minister of Canada when filling Senate vacancies" (*Senate Reform Reference*, para. 50).

35 Ibid., para. 60.

36 Ibid., para. 65. One can only advert at this stage to the significant interpretative issues to which this finding will give rise in the future; see Warren J. Newman, "Putting One's Faith in a Higher Power: Supreme Law, The *Senate Reform Reference*, Legislative Authority and the Amending Procedures," *National Journal of Constitutional Law* 34, no. 2 (2015): 99–120.

37 *Senate Reform Reference*, para. 69.

38 And possibly enacted pursuant as well to section 44 of the 1982 Act, if sections 44 and 45 are to retain symmetry (since section 45, on the reasoning in *OPSEU* that was approved in the *Senate Reform Reference*, supports both textual constitutional amendments and organic legislation). See Warren J. Newman, "Defining the 'Constitution of Canada' since 1982: The Scope of the Legislative Powers of Constitutional Amendment under Sections 44 and 45 of the *Constitution Act, 1982*," *Supreme Court Law Review* (2d) 22 (2003): 423–98.

39 This is in no way to gainsay the importance of the 1969 Act, which paved the way for the official language guarantees embodied in sections 16 and 20 of the Charter, itself part of the Constitution Act, 1982.

40 An Act respecting the status and use of the official languages of Canada, S.C. 1988, c. 38, s. 2. See Warren J. Newman, "The Official Languages Act and the Constitutional and Legislative Recognition of Language Rights in Canada," in *Language and Governance*, ed. Colin Williams, 196–234 (Cardiff: University of Wales Press, 2007).

41 An Act for the preservation and enhancement of multiculturalism in Canada, R.S.C. 1985, c. 24 (4th Supp.).

42 S.C. 1992, c. 30, s. 3.

43 Following the failure of the package to receive general popular support, the amendments were not proceeded with and the formal Part V procedures were not engaged, with the exception of a bilateral amendment to the Charter to recognize the equality of the English and French linguistic communities in New Brunswick.

44 S.C. 1996, c. 1.

45 More precisely, two or more of the Atlantic provinces that have, according to the then latest general census, a combined population of at least 50 per cent of the population of all the Atlantic provinces, and two or more of the Prairie provinces that have, according to the then latest general census, a combined population of at least 50 per cent of the population of all the Prairie provinces.

46 [1998] 2 S.C.R. 217. I disclose that I was one of counsel who appeared on behalf of the Attorney General of Canada in this reference.

47 An Act to give effect to the requirement for clarity as set out in the opinion of the Supreme Court of Canada in the Quebec Secession Reference, S.C. 2000, c. 26.

48 An Act respecting royal assent to bills passed by the Houses of Parliament, S.C. 2002, c. 15.
49 An Act to amend the Canada Elections Act, S.C. 2007, c. 10.
50 Ibid., section 56.1 of the Canada Elections Act (as amended). For interpretation and discussion, see *Conacher v Canada (Prime Minister)*, 2009 F.C 920, [2010] 3 F.C.R. 411; 2010 FCA 131, [2011] 4 F.C.R. 22; and Warren J. Newman, "Of Dissolution, Prorogation, and Constitutional Law, Principle and Convention: Maintaining Fundamental Distinctions during a Parliamentary Crisis," *National Journal of Constitutional Law* 27 (2009): 217–29.
51 An Act respecting the Governor General, R.S.C. 1985, c. G-9, as amended by the Jobs, Growth and Long-term Prosperity Act, S.C. 2012, c. 19, s. 16.
52 Paragraph 81(1)(n) of the Income Tax Act, R.S.C. 1985, c. 1 (5th Supp.), as also amended by the Jobs, Growth and Long-term Prosperity Act, S.C. 2012, c. 19, s. 3.
53 S.C. 2013, c. 6.
54 See Peter W. Hogg, "Succession to the Throne," *National Journal of Constitutional Law* 33, no. 1 (2015): 83–94. A challenge to the constitutional validity of the Succession to the Throne Act, 2013, was dismissed in a judgment rendered on 16 February 2016 by Justice Claude Bouchard of the Quebec Superior Court in *Motard and Taillon v Canada (Attorney General)*. A challenge to Canada's participation in the Commonwealth agreement leading to the enactment of the legislation was denied in *Teskey v Canada (Attorney General)* by the Ontario Superior Court of Justice on 9 August 2013 *per* Hackland J., on grounds of standing and justiciability; appeal rejected by the Ontario Court of Appeal (2014 ONCA 612); leave to appeal to the Supreme Court of Canada refused 19 February 2015.

6 *U*2: *Unanimity* versus *Unilateralism* in Canada's Politics of Constitutional Amendment

RAINER KNOPFF

No, not U2, the Irish rock band, but the two "*U*"s – unanimity and unilateralism – that so often compete in Canada's modern politics of constitutional reform. The archetypical example of these conflicts is the patriation process that gave us the Constitution Act, 1982. In the politics of that reform, the Trudeau government threatened to impose unilaterally what most provinces insisted required unanimous (or at least substantial) provincial consent. A variety of post-1982 initiatives – including the 1996 regional veto act,[1] fixed-election-date legislation,[2] and the Harper government's Senate reform proposals – replicate this clash between unilateralism and either "substantial" provincial consent (as found after 1982 in the 7/50 amending formula) or "unanimous" provincial consent (as set out in the section 41 amending formula). This chapter focuses on the *U*2 conflict, unilateralism versus unanimity, although it will sometimes be helpful to refer to its close cousin, unilateralism versus substantial consent.

After reviewing the competing claims of unilateralism, unanimity, and substantial consent in the politics of patriation, I briefly show how all three principles found their way into the Constitution Act, 1982. I then trace the ongoing clash between unanimity and unilateralism in Canada's post-1982 politics of constitutional amendment, using as primary examples the federal regional veto legislation and fixed-election-date legislation. I conclude by exploring the conflicting constitutional logics of proposed or actual legal challenges to such laws.

Unanimity versus Unilateralism in the Political of Patriation

As Nadia Verrelli details in Chapter 1, Pierre Trudeau's threat to unilaterally ask the UK to enact patriation and the Charter led to the colloquially labelled *Patriation Reference*.[3] Central to the provincial challenge to Trudeau's plan was the claim that constitutional convention required unanimous consent for such a substantial reform.[4] The Trudeau government replied that the convention of unanimity either did not exist or was not legally binding.

Ottawa's courtroom attempt to deny the existence of a convention of unanimous consent was arguably included for completeness – to cover all the bases, so to speak – rather than out of real conviction. Indeed, in introducing his constitutional proposals on national television, Trudeau identified the "tyrant" of unanimity as the cause of "fifty-three years of constitutional paralysis."[5] He clearly wished to depose this tyrant, but, as I have previously observed, "one need not (indeed one cannot) depose a tyrant who is not in power."[6] In his rhetoric outside the courtroom, Trudeau essentially conceded (and deplored) the convention of unanimity insisted upon by most of the provinces. Ottawa's more important case was thus to evade the tyrant's claims by insisting that they were not legally binding.

The Supreme Court famously split the difference between the Trudeau government and its provincial opponents. On the one hand, it agreed with Ottawa that constitutional convention was indeed not *legally* binding. According to the Court, "[t]he very nature of a convention, as political in inception and as depending on a consistent course of political recognition by those for whose benefit and to whose detriment (if any) the convention developed over a considerable period of time is inconsistent with its legal enforcement."[7] On the other hand, the Court found that unilateralism would infringe a constitutional convention of provincial consent. Having admitted that they could not "enforce" this convention, the judges nevertheless insisted on their legitimate capacity to "recognize" it.[8] Moreover, they went out of their way to emphasize that, "while they are not laws, some conventions may be more important than some laws."[9] In short, while giving a *legal* green light to Trudeau's unilateralism, the Court simultaneously placed a *conventional* red light in its path.

Although unilateralism did not receive the clear endorsement the Trudeau government desired, neither did the principle of unanimous consent that had preoccupied almost everyone on both sides of the dispute. Strikingly, the Supreme Court adopted the novel suggestion of a single province, Saskatchewan, that the convention required only "substantial" provincial consent.[10] The logical coherence of this middle-ground judgment, however, has been called into question. If it is true that the "political" nature of convention "is inconsistent with its legal enforcement," what business did a court of law have in recognizing a political convention? And why choose a conventional position advanced by only one of the governments before the Court?

For Adam Dodek, the "distinction between 'recognizing' and 'enforcing' conventions" is "artificial and untenable."[11] He observes that, although reference-case judgments and judicial declarations against the attorney general are also formally unenforceable, "we expect compliance by government" with such rulings. References, he notes, "are not accorded less precedential value on the grounds that they are merely advisory." Similarly, the judicial recognition of a convention, although technically nonbinding, often will be difficult to distinguish from practical enforcement.[12] As Andrew Heard has observed, "[a]ny pronouncement by a court of the terms of a convention can and often does amount to a political enforcement of the convention" because judicial conclusions, especially those of the Supreme Court, are "portrayed as authoritative."[13]

Peter Russell has similarly discerned "questionable jurisprudence" in the Court's distinction between enforcing and recognizing conventions. But Russell also refers to this "questionable jurisprudence" as "bold statescraft" because it enabled the Court to broker new negotiations and compromise between Ottawa and the provinces.[14] Thus, the Trudeau government could no longer proceed unilaterally without facing the serious political charge of violating important constitutional convention. At the same time, if the provinces blocked the publicly popular goals of patriation and the Charter for too long, unilateralism, which did after all have a *legal* green light, might become politically viable. The Court's statescraft gave both Ottawa and the dissenting provinces new incentives to return to the bargaining table. The resulting negotiations generated the Constitution Act, 1982, which secured the consent of Ottawa and nine of the ten provinces.

Nine out of ten provinces was deemed sufficiently "substantial" in the subsequent *Quebec Veto Reference*,[15] even though the dissenting jurisdiction was Quebec, which understood itself as one of two founding nations, not just one of ten provinces. Had the Supreme Court recognized the widely supported convention of unanimous consent in its 1981 judgment, Quebec's dissent might have stopped the 1982 reforms. Similarly, had the Court, perhaps with greater logical coherence, steered clear of convention altogether and simply given Ottawa its legal green light, we might have seen Trudeau's package imposed over the opposition of most provinces – hardly an auspicious beginning for a new constitutional order. In other words, the establishment of the Constitution Act, 1982, and the success and support it has enjoyed through most of Canada, was arguably facilitated by the Court's 1981 rejection of both unilateralism and unanimity in their simple or extreme versions.

The Persistence of Unanimity, Unilateralism, and Substantial Consent

Nevertheless, both unilateralism and unanimity survived the process. Indeed, they constitute the two poles of the continuum of amending formulas found in Part V of the Constitution Act, 1982. At the easier end of that continuum, Canadian governments can change parts of their own constitutions through unilateral statutes under sections 44 (federal) and 45 (provincial), as Warren Newman discusses in Chapter 5. Here, I am concerned primarily with section 44, the federal provision (Emmanuelle Richez addresses section 45 – especially with respect to Quebec – in Chapter 8). Section 44's unilateralism is obviously much narrower in reach than the unilateralism at issue in the *Patriation Reference*. The kind of mega-constitutional change Trudeau threatened to pursue unilaterally is certainly beyond the scope of section 44.

At the other end of Canada's formal amendment continuum, section 41 requires some amendments to secure the very difficult – some might say impossible – consent of Parliament and all ten provincial legislatures. Thus, the kind of unanimity the Court found too stringent for Trudeau's ambitious reforms is required for certain constitutional amendments. But section 41 uses unanimity to protect a set of matters much more restricted than the changes most provinces claimed were subject to unanimity in the *Patriation Reference*; it requires unanimity only for amendments "in relation to" a limited set of five matters (see the full provision in the Appendix to this volume). Like unilateralism, in other words, unanimity persists after 1982, but in significantly attenuated form.

Although unanimity and unilateralism survived 1982, the principle of substantial consent flourished in the 1982 Constitution. Indeed, in the *Senate Reform Reference*, the Supreme Court depicted the "general" (or 7/50) amending formula in the Constitution Act, 1982 as the formalization of the substantial-consent convention recognized in the *Patriation Reference*.[16]

Just as all three principles at stake in the *Patriation Reference* found their way into the Part V amending continuum, so did the political conflict among them. That is, Canada's post-1982 politics of amendment has continued to display the clash between federal unilateralism and either substantial or unanimous provincial consent.

Unanimity versus Unilateralism after 1982

In its post-1982 clashes with unanimity, legislative unilateralism takes several forms. One of these was triggered by the controversy about the Harper government's attempt to appoint Justice Marc Nadon to the Supreme Court. When Nadon's eligibility was called into question, Ottawa unilaterally enacted declaratory legislation designed to flesh out the eligibility requirements in sections 5 and 6 of the Supreme Court Act – in ways that supported Nadon's appointment, of course.[17] In Ottawa's view, this amendment to its own legislation effected no change at all; it merely clarified what had always been the eligibility requirements. Critics, by contrast, insisted that the legislative amendment unilaterally altered requirements for "the composition of the Supreme Court of Canada," one of the five matters that can be changed only via a constitutional amendment under the section 41 unanimity formula. This critical view won the day in *Reference re Supreme Court Act, sections 5 and 6*.[18]

I concern myself in this chapter, however, not with the kind of declaratory legislation at issue in the *Supreme Court Act Reference*, but with unilateral legislation that openly strives to achieve or promote constitutional change. Such legislation takes two forms. First, proponents of a constitutional reform that might plausibly require amendment under one of the more difficult formulas sometimes claim that it can actually be achieved unilaterally under section 44. This is what Robert Hawkins calls "formula shopping."[19] For Hawkins, formula shopping is one kind of "constitutional workaround," defined as a way "of achieving change of a constitutional nature that works around the complex requirements of the section 38 (general) and section 41 (unanimous) formal amending procedures."[20] The Harper government's attempt to establish term limits for senators is an example of formula shopping. The government maintained that term limits could be achieved unilaterally through a statute passed under section 44, while the government's opponents insisted they could be achieved only through a 7/50 amendment. In Hawkins's terms, the government shopped for the section 44 formula, while its opponents shopped for the 7/50 formula.

If section 44 does actually apply, of course, one could question using the term "workaround" to describe its legitimate use. The term applies more readily and universally to Ottawa's pursuit of constitutional change via a second form of unilateral legislation, which occurs when formula shopping for section 44 is not an option – that is, when the desired constitutional reform can be made legally binding only via the 7/50 or unanimity procedures. Because this kind of unilateral legislation bypasses Part V of the Constitution Act altogether, it is for Hawkins a workaround that "seeks change of a constitutional nature through a regular act of Parliament rather than through formal constitutional amendment."[21] Hawkins uses the term "ordinary legislation" to distinguish this kind of workaround from formula shopping. In Chapter 9, Dennis Baker and Mark Jarvis call this kind of unilateral legislation "informal amendment."

Although a unilateral statute justified by section 44 remains a formal constitutional amendment, an "ordinary legislation" workaround of Part V must avoid formal amendment. It typically does so by encouraging, rather than requiring, the desired reform. Hawkins considers such attempts "to do indirectly what cannot be done directly" to be constitutional "so long as they are non-binding on the political actors to whom they are addressed." That is, they are constitutional to the extent that they do not "fetter the discretionary powers that the constitution grants to public servants, and politicians, charged with operationalizing Canada's fundamental law."[22]

The Harper government's strategy regarding Senate elections illustrates unilateralism in the form of Hawkins's "ordinary legislation" (or Baker and Jarvis's "informal amendment"). Knowing full well that the Constitution expressly required an unlikely 7/50 amendment to change "the method of selecting senators," the government attempted unilateral legislation promoting the nonbinding consultation of provincial electorates. Such legislation was constitutional in the government's view because, far from formally changing "the method of selecting senators," it merely encouraged a new source of advice to the prime minister, who remained free to reject that advice. Hawkins agreed that such "advisory or consultative" elections were sufficiently nonbinding to be constitutional.[23] Critics, arguing that democratic norms would soon make the so-called electoral "advice" binding in practice, insisted that government was illegitimately attempting to do indirectly through unilateral legislation what it could do directly only through the 7/50 formula.[24] This chapter's two main examples of the post-1982 clash between unilateralism and unanimity – the 1996 regional veto legislation and fixed-election-date legislation – pose the same issues.

Regional Veto Legislation

Several attempts have been made to heal the wound of Quebec's rejection of the 1982 Constitution, including the spectacular failures of the Meech Lake and Charlottetown accords. The demise of those mega-constitutional initiatives has led to more incremental attempts to placate Quebec, such as the regional veto statute passed by the Chrétien government in 1996. The Act fulfilled Prime Minister Jean Chrétien's promise during the 1995 independence referendum to restore Quebec's veto over constitutional amendments. The familiar necessity of extending to other provinces or regions a benefit designed for Quebec came into play, however, and so Quebec became one of five regions that gained veto power under the Act. The other four were Ontario, British Columbia, two or more Atlantic provinces having at least 50 per cent of the Atlantic region's population, and two or more Prairie provinces having at least 50 per cent of the Prairie population. The Act specified that "no [federal] Minister of the Crown shall propose a motion for a resolution to authorize" a 7/50 amendment without the consent of all five regions.[25] In effect, Ottawa had loaned its veto to each of the specified regions. Because of Alberta's weight in the Prairie region, it gained, in practical terms, the same kind of single-province veto given to Quebec, Ontario, and British Columbia. So, whereas no province held a veto under the 7/50 formula, four now did because of the regional veto act.

The constitutionality of the regional veto law was in question from the outset. For example, Andrew Petter, then chairman of the British Columbia government's National Unity Committee, saw a clash between "the provincial consensus required by the 1982 Constitution" and the "unilateralism" of Ottawa's law. As a constitutional lawyer, Petter knew that the five items subject to the unanimity requirement included "an amendment to this Part" – that is, to Part V of the Constitution Act, 1982. This meant that "changes to the amending formula of the Constitution – unlike most other changes – require approval of all of the provinces and the federal government." Because the regional veto act sought to "alter" the 7/50 formula, making it possible for an amendment that otherwise met the 7/50 test to be stopped by a single region, it could be achieved only through a unanimous-consent amendment. Instead, Ottawa was unconstitutionally making the change "with no consultation."[26]

The federal government vigorously defended the constitutionality of its law against the kind of critique made by Petter. In testimony before the Senate committee considering the Bill, Justice Minister Allan Rock conceded that "Part V [of the Constitution Act, 1982] cannot be amended except with unanimous consent," but insisted that the Act "does not amend Part V." In his view, the 7/50 formula continued to apply as written. The "federal consent" required by that formula still had to "be expressed through resolutions of the House of Commons and Senate," just as the formula specifies. The Bill "merely sets out the conditions that the government will look to in determining whether to participate in the process." That is, the Bill only specified when federal government *ministers* would agree to introduce a "resolution to authorize" a 7/50 amendment in Parliament; it did not affect Parliament's formal authority to consider and approve such amendments.[27]

But Parliament's formal authority can remain unaffected only to the extent that "resolutions to authorize" 7/50 amendments could be introduced by nonministers. Liberal Senator Allan MacEachen made this point several times during the hearings. For MacEachen, the Bill placed "no limitation ... on the power of Parliament; it is on the behaviour of ministers, that is all." Although ministers cannot introduce a resolution for amendment that has not secured the level of consent specified by the regional veto law, other members of Parliament could do so. For example, "the Leader of the Opposition in the House of Commons or an individual senator could "launch a constitutional amendment and, with a level of consensus of 7-50, amend the Constitution."[28] A Commons backbencher could similarly introduce the requisite resolution.[29]

McGill University law professor Stephen Scott supported this view in his testimony before the Senate committee. Noting that the Bill addressed "only ministers of the Crown and only the single action of proposing – that is, introducing – a motion of the relevant kind," Scott concluded that, once an amendment resolution had been introduced by a nonminister, "every member of each house, including any minister of the Crown, is perfectly free ... to vote in its favour."[30]

Osgoode Hall Law School's Patrick Monahan similarly considered the Bill constitutional because "[i]t doesn't deal with the ability of the House to dispose of resolutions, but focuses on the ability of ministers to introduce them." David Schneiderman agreed: the Bill "sets the ground rules for the federal government's exercise and leaves the rest of the amending formula intact."[31]

Scott even mused that, "if, in violation of the legislation, a minister of the Crown were to introduce a motion, it is likely that ... its origin would become in law irrelevant, so that, if duly passed, it would be as valid as if it had been properly introduced by a non-minister." In other words, the law might not be binding even on the ministers to whom it was explicitly addressed. Moreover, Scott emphasized, it was always open to Parliament to repeal the law,[32] a point Hawkins also made.[33] Scott speculated that the unilateral regional veto legislation might be justified by "section 44 of the Constitution Act, 1982, as an amendment of the Constitution 'relating to the executive Government of Canada or the Senate and House of Commons.'"[34] This would put it in the same category as the Harper government's proposed legislation of term limits for senators. But Scott's claims about the law's nonbinding character suggest it could equally fall into Hawkins's category of nonsection 44 "ordinary legislation," which is where Hawkins himself placed it.[35] Ultimately, Hawkins and Scott agreed that the law is constitutional to the extent that it is nonbinding.

This view, as we have seen, did not impress Andrew Petter. Nor did it persuade Andrew Heard, for whom it was not the law's possible loop-holes, but its "pith and substance" – that is, its "essential intended purpose and effect" – that determined the issue of constitutionality. For Heard, the law's "purpose" was clearly to introduce provincial vetoes over con-stitutional amendments that did not exist under the 7/50 formula, and its "effect" would be to "impose almost insurmountable obstacles" to needed "constitutional renewal." He noted that, although the 7/50 for-mula allowed for amendments "with the consent of seven provinces that represent as little as 50.3 per cent of the population," the regional veto law required "combinations of provinces that, at a minimum, would rep-resent 92.2 per cent of the Canadian population." Taking both purpose and effect into account, the law could be understood only as a "deliberate attempt to alter fundamentally the nature of the constitutional amend-ment process ... in a manner that is substantively inconsistent with section 38 of the Constitution Act, 1982." It might not have changed the wording of the Constitution directly, but it unconstitutionally sought "to achieve indirectly that which Parliament cannot achieve directly: the uni-lateral, fundamental transformation of the amending process outlined in the Constitution."[36]

Senator Gérald Beaudoin, a noted constitutional scholar, came to a similar conclusion. Although it might be true that the law "doesn't change the Constitution," he argued, "if the effect of the statute is to change the Constitution indirectly, then there are grounds to say it is unconstitutional."[37] Law professor Douglas Schmeiser agreed, observing that "there is constitutional authority that suggests that this legislation is contrary to general constitutional rules and conventions and is quite inappropriate."[38] Political scientists Roger Gibbins[39] and Ted Morton,[40] among many other observers, also considered the Act unconstitutional.

Critics of the law clearly took no comfort from the technically non-binding character emphasized by its defenders. Disagreeing with Scott, they argued that the law would be practically impossible to repeal.[41] They similarly doubted the prospects of having nonministers introduce an amendment resolution that violated the spirit of the law. For the critics, one might say, this technically nonbinding law launched a new and binding constitutional convention.

Heard would later make the same argument against consultative Senate elections. It would be "all but impossible," he wrote, "for a government to ignore the clear wishes of the people in a nominee election process conducted with all the seriousness and substance of a regular election for members of the House of Commons." If such allegedly "consultative" elections "were enacted, *it would not take long for a constitutional convention to be established* that Prime Ministers should only recommend elected nominees for selection to the Senate."[42] Peter Russell agreed, arguing that consultative elections would become just as binding in practice as the convention transferring the governor general's discretion to appoint senators to the prime minister.[43] In Heard's words, "the theoretical discretion left to the Prime Minister and Governor General" by legislated "consultative" elections would "quickly prove to be a mirage."[44]

Heard clearly thought that a similar and equally problematic convention would overwhelm the "theoretical discretion" left by the regional veto law. Indeed, it is only by stimulating a convention that such loophole-ridden and repealable "ordinary legislation" could actually achieve indirectly what requires unanimity to achieve directly – namely, the effectively binding transformation of the 7/50 amending formula.

Hawkins, who considers "ordinary legislation" workarounds to be legitimate as long as they are nonbinding in the formal legal sense, concedes that they sometimes might lead to practically binding constitutional conventions. This does not change his mind, however, about the constitutionality of such workarounds. "The evolution of conventions," he notes, "is a legitimate path to constitutional amendment." Accordingly, "[t]he fact that a non-binding change might one day evolve into a convention is no reason to say that the non-binding change is void at the outset because of its potential to amend the constitution."[45]

Note the elements of time and conditionality in Hawkins's analysis. He emphasizes, first, the "evolution" over time of a nonbinding statute into a binding constitutional convention and, second, that this evolution "might" (hence, might not) occur. If the initial statute is actually nonbinding, it does not itself (and "at the outset") amend the Constitution. The convention to which the statute eventually "might" contribute, by contrast, effectively *would* amend the Constitution, but such conventional amendment – outside of any formal or legal amending procedures – must be legitimate. Otherwise, says Hawkins, "we might still be waiting for a formal constitutional amendment to authorize the principles of responsible government."[46]

The critics of the regional veto law might well have agreed with Hawkins about the legitimacy of constitutional amendment through the gradual evolution of convention, but they saw no gradualism in this case. In their view, the statute simply could not be described as "a non-binding change [that] *might* one day *evolve* into a convention."[47] They saw no "might" about how things would evolve, and not much evolution either. For the critics, the regional veto law created the practical conditions of a binding convention in one fell swoop, or at least very quickly. In their view, such nonevolutionary amendment of the Constitution must occur through a prescribed Part V amending formula – in this case, the unanimity formula – and not by unilaterally using "ordinary legislation" to create an instantaneous convention.

Given the controversy about the regional veto law's constitutionality, one might have expected to see it challenged in court. Senator Beaudoin certainly foresaw a legal challenge,[48] and Alberta's premier, Ralph Klein, publicly mused about launching one.[49] Roger Gibbins, who was then advising Klein, supported this course of action.[50] So did Stephen Harper, then the Reform Party's national unity critic: "I think Alberta should pursue [a legal challenge]," he said; "I feel there is a case to be made."[51] Such a challenge, invoking the precedent of the *Patriation Reference*, likely would have asked the courts to address the issues of convention raised by this formally nonbinding law.

As it turned out, Klein never launched his legal challenge at the time of the law's enactment. Neither did the British Columbia government, despite the strong claims of unconstitutionality raised by Andrew Petter, one of its cabinet ministers. Andrew Heard actually predicted that neither of these provinces would proceed with legal action against the regional veto law. Both provinces had enacted legislation requiring proposed constitutional amendments to be put to a provincial referendum before being brought to the legislative assembly, as constitutionally required. Heard considered these unilateral provincial statutes to be just as unconstitutional as the federal regional veto law and "for the same reasons" – namely, that they "fundamentally" changed the amendment process prescribed in Part V of the Constitution Act, 1982. Just as the federal regional veto law limited the constitutionally secured discretion of Parliament in considering constitutional amendments, so the Alberta and British Columbia referendum laws constrained the constitutional discretion of provincial legislative assemblies in considering such amendments. In both cases, the changes attempted through unilateral legislation required a unanimous-consent amendment under section 41 of the Constitution Act, 1982. Would Alberta and British Columbia bring a challenge to the federal law that would logically "backfire" against their own, equally suspect legislation? Heard did not think so.[52]

Heard speculated (perhaps hoped) that other Canadian jurisdictions – one of the territorial governments, for example – might launch a court case,[53] but in fact no challenge has ever materialized. Actual federal use of the veto legislation might have prompted legal action, but to date there has been no occasion to invoke the law. The federal fixed-election-date legislation, by contrast, did end up in court.

Fixed-Election-Date Legislation

Like the regional veto statute, unilateral fixed-election-date legislation is constitutional only to the extent that it is formally nonbinding. Just as section 41 requires unanimity to enact a formal amendment to the 7/50 formula (or any other aspect of Part V), so it requires unanimity for amendments "in relation to … the office of the Queen, the Governor General and the Lieutenant Governor of a province." The viceregal offices include the traditional discretion to call new elections at any time, although this discretion is exercised, by convention, on the advice of first ministers. Thus, the traditional power of first ministers to trigger "snap" elections can be removed, in a legally binding way, only through a unanimous-consent constitutional amendment. Because formula shopping for a unilateral section 44 or 45 amendment is not an option, the "ordinary legislation" enacted by Ottawa and several provinces to fix election dates must be nonbinding.

Although the nonbinding character of the regional veto legislation was not evident on its face – it had to be brought to light and emphasized by the law's defenders – Canada's unilaterally enacted fixed-election-date laws explicitly announce their nonbinding status. British Columbia, which took the lead in enacting such legislation in 2001, subjects its fixed dates to the continuing discretion of the lieutenant-governor to "dissolve the Legislative Assembly when [he or she] thinks fit,"[54] and all provincial fixed-date laws since then contain similar provisions. So does the federal fixed-date law enacted by the Harper government in 2007, which emphasizes in its first clause that "nothing in this section affects the powers of the Governor General, including the power to dissolve Parliament at the Governor General's discretion"[55] – a discretion, of course, that is exercised by convention on the prime minister's advice.

When Prime Minister Harper famously used this loophole to have Parliament dissolved in 2008, prior to the 2009 statutory date, he was vilified for contravening his own law,[56] and Duff Conacher, head of Democracy Watch, challenged the early election in court.[57] Note that Conacher's case was quite different from the challenge against the regional veto law's constitutionality threatened by Premier Klein or the reference-case questions actually raised about the constitutionality of the Harper government's Senate reform agenda. Conacher challenged, not the constitutionality of the fixed-date legislation, but the Harper government's failure to comply with it. Instead of launching a "constitutional challenge" to the validity of the fixed-date law, in other words, Conacher brought what might be called a "compliance challenge." Needless to say, a challenge of the latter kind makes sense only if the law at issue is assumed to be constitutionally valid. One cannot reasonably complain of the failure to comply with an unconstitutional law.

An analogous compliance challenge with respect to the regional veto law would have taken the federal government to task for supporting Parliament's passing of a 7/50 amendment over the objection of any of the five regions specified by the Act. With respect to consultative Senate elections, a compliance challenge such as Conacher's would have challenged a prime minister's decision to appoint someone who had not received electoral approval. In these hypothetical compliance challenges, as in Conacher's actual one, it is the discretionary use of formal legal loopholes that is treated as illegitimate.

But if obvious legal loopholes are not legitimately available, it must be because they have been closed by constitutional convention.

Thus Conacher argued that the technically nonbinding fixed-date law was actually designed to inaugurate a new and binding convention preventing federal prime ministers from calling snap elections. From this perspective, the legal loophole protecting discretionary early elections exists mainly to accommodate circumstances in which a minority government loses the confidence of the House of Commons. That is, the convention closes the law's formal and explicit loophole only with respect to the government, not with respect to the opposition. In other words, the new convention inaugurated by the fixed-date statute, according to Conacher and his supporters, permits early election calls when a government is defeated on a matter of confidence, but prevents an undefeated prime minister from calling a snap election, as Harper did in 2008.[58]

Interesting questions can be raised about the political coherence of a convention that essentially transfers the power of triggering snap elections from the prime minister to the opposition in minority government circumstances.[59] If stabilizing minority government for a four-year cycle had been a central purpose of the fixed-date law, one might have expected more thought about how to achieve "constructive non-confidence" votes by the opposition – that is, votes that defeat a government but simultaneously install an alternative government without new elections. New Zealand has established a confidence protocol that encourages such constructive nonconfidence votes, and a number of European countries require them in most circumstances. But, although the federal fixed-date law was passed during a lengthy period of minority government, it came early in that period and against a background in which infrequent spells of minority government were the exception that proved the general majority-government rule.[60] This context did not generate much thought about fixed dates and constructive nonconfidence.

Systems of constructive nonconfidence have arisen in regimes where, mainly because of proportional representation, majority government is not a reasonable expectation. And, indeed, the New Zealand confidence protocol received some Canadian attention a few years ago when provinces were considering more proportional electoral systems.[61] In the debates about the federal fixed-date law, however, it was widely assumed that nonconfidence votes would not be constructive – that is, that they would lead mostly to new elections, as they generally have in the past. In this context, one can expect the game of chicken[62] that actually occurred during the first Harper minority, as the government, sensing the electoral winds blowing in its favour, tried to goad the opposition into nonconfidence votes.[63] The opposition, sensing the same winds, refused to take the bait, but, so as not to appear too weak, insisted that it would trigger an election at a time of its choosing. "The power [of calling an election] has been given to me," said Stéphane Dion. "I will use it. Be ready at any time."[64] Using the opposition's early-election rhetoric as rhetorical cover, Prime Minister Harper eventually exploited the fixed-date law's loophole himself. An asymmetrical convention that constrained only the prime minister and not the opposition, in other words, was arguably destined to fail in minority-government circumstances.

However that may be, it was this asymmetrical convention that Conacher and his supporters hoped the Federal Court would recognize, much in the manner that the Supreme Court had recognized a convention of substantial consent in the *Patriation Reference*. They knew, of course, that courts cannot enforce conventions, but, to recall Heard's formulation, the "pronouncement" of a convention by an "authoritative" court "can and often does amount to a political enforcement of the convention." To repeat, the convention Conacher had in mind would fundamentally alter viceregal discretion to call elections at any time upon the advice of an undefeated prime minister.

As it turned out, Conacher lost both at trial[65] and at the Federal Court of Appeal.[66] Moreover, the Supreme Court denied Conacher's application for leave to appeal. Opponents of the Harper government's early election call were naturally dismayed. They thought the trial and appeal decisions were profoundly wrong, and hoped that the Supreme Court would hear the case and come to a different conclusion. Dodek reports that the editors of TheCourt.ca "singled out Conacher [as] the most disappointing refusal of leave to appeal in 2010."[67]

In fact, however, for those opponents of Harper's 2008 election call who also opposed his government's proposal for consultative Senate elections, the *Conacher* loss might have been a blessing in disguise. As I show in the conclusion of this chapter, winning a compliance challenge to an "ordinary legislation" workaround might mean losing a constitutional challenge to another such law.

Conclusion: The Politics of Conflicting Constitutional Logics

A major point of debate in *Conacher v Canada* was whether or not a domestic convention could be established more or less instantaneously – that is, without the evolution of precedents – through the explicit agreement of relevant political actors (expressed in this case via legislative enactment). Justice Michel Shore of the Federal Court denied this possibility, and was upheld by the Federal Court of Appeal.

Many commentators – including Peter Russell[68] and Andrew Heard – disagreed. Heard contends that "scholars who have made any significant study of the matter" accept that "conventions can be created through undertakings by the relevant actors," and he believes that the federal fixed-date law was such an undertaking. Justice Shore, in short, had "missed the mark"; he should have found that the law had indeed established a new constitutional convention, and that Prime Minister Harper's 2008 election call was in "breach of a clear conventional obligation."[69]

But surely this conclusion poses a conundrum for anyone who believes that other workarounds in the form of "ordinary legislation" are unconstitutional to the extent that the conventions they inaugurate rapidly overwhelm their formal loopholes. Critics of the regional veto law, for example, consider it constitutionally suspect precisely to the extent that it quickly becomes conventionally (if not legally) binding. To that extent, unilateral legislation has secured – via instantaneous convention – the kind of constitutional amendment that requires unanimous consent under section 41. Similarly, critics consider the legislation of consultative Senate elections to be unconstitutional if the alleged "consultation" would "quickly prove to be a mirage" – if, that is, the legislation would, in fact, unilaterally achieve what formally requires a 7/50 amendment.

It follows that a *Conacher*-analogous "compliance challenge" to a government's failure to fulfil the conventional spirit of the regional veto statute or the proposed consultative elections legislation could succeed only because of the kind of binding convention that would underlie a "constitutional challenge" to the validity of the same laws. The two kinds of legal challenge – constitutional and compliance – seem mutually incompatible with respect to "ordinary legislation" workarounds.

Of course, we have not seen such incompatible challenges with respect to any one of the laws under consideration. With respect to the regional veto law or the consultative elections initiative, only constitutional challenges were proposed or launched. And with respect to the fixed-date law, only a compliance challenge was brought.

Here we confront interesting questions of litigation timing. Suppose someone had succeeded in constitutionally challenging the regional veto law because, legal loopholes aside, it had unconstitutionally established a binding convention. Surely this would have caused difficulty for Conacher's later attempt to secure compliance with the convention allegedly established by the fixed-date law. In other words, Conacher and his supporters, including those who previously had favoured a constitutional challenge to the regional veto law, arguably should have been grateful that no such challenge ever materialized.

Suppose now that Conacher's compliance challenge had succeeded, thus implying that the loopholes of an "ordinary legislation" workaround could be conventionally closed without impugning the statute's constitutionality. Would this not have made it subsequently more difficult to mount the successful constitutional challenge to the Harper government's proposal for consultative Senate elections? In other words, those who supported the constitutional challenge to consultative Senate elections, including some who had favoured Conacher's compliance challenge, arguably should be grateful for Conacher's loss.

Indeed, one cannot help wondering whether the prospect of a constitutional challenge to the Harper government's Senate reform proposals helps explain the Supreme Court's denial of leave to appeal in *Conacher*. Adam Dodek speculates that the Court sidestepped the issues of convention raised by the fixed-election-date legislation for one of two reasons: either the Court did not discern "a serious allegation regarding established constitutional convention" or the Court "simply saw the case as inherently political and not requiring judicial intervention."[70] It is also possible, of course, that at least some of the Court's judges thought Conacher had a serious case for the judicial recognition of a new, legislatively induced convention regarding fixed dates. This possibility generates a third speculation to explain the denial of leave: that the Court strategically ducked Conacher's compliance challenge to avoid complicating a later constitutional challenge to consultative Senate elections, which had generated considerable public controversy by the time the Court addressed Conacher's leave application. Had the Court heard Conacher's case and decided in his favour, the jurisprudential route to its 2014 judgment in the *Senate Reform Reference* would have become more difficult. At the same time, this Senate reform judgment now surely weighs against the constitutionality of the regional veto statute, as Emmett Macfarlane observes in Chapter 11 – although Dennis Baker and Mark Jarvis wonder in Chapter 9 whether the outcome of the *Supreme Court Act Reference* implies the constitutional entrenchment of the veto law.

Just as constitutional law is the most political of laws, so constitutional politics is a particularly legal politics, often fought out in the courtroom – or in its shadow. In these battles, constitutional doctrines are chosen not just for their own sake but also because they support favoured outcomes. But doctrines that help secure the desired outcome on one issue might set counterproductive precedents with respect to constitutionally related issues. The problem is compounded by the fact that related issues come to court (or fail to get there) in erratic and unpredictable ways. In this context, short-term goals often dominate particular battles, and the luck of the draw – including the accidents of litigation sequence – affects broader political and constitutional outcomes. Strategic behaviour based on long-term considerations remains possible, however. Clearly, the interaction of political agendas and constitutional logics can be a tricky business.

Notes

I wish to acknowledge the School of Politics and International Relations at the Australian National University, which provided a supportive and congenial setting for researching and writing much of this chapter. I am also grateful for the helpful comments provided by Dennis Baker and Peter McCormick.

1 An Act respecting constitutional amendments, S.C. 1996, c. 1.
2 An Act to amend the Canada Elections Act, S.C. 2007, c. 10.
3 *Reference re Resolution to Amend the Constitution*, [1981] 1 S.C.R. 753 (*Patriation Reference*).
4 Seven of the "gang of eight" supported unanimous consent; the one exception was Saskatchewan.
5 Rainer Knopff, "Legal Theory and the 'Patriation' Debate," *Queen's Law Journal* 7, no. 1 (1981): 43.
6 Ibid.
7 *Patriation Reference*, 774–5.
8 Ibid., 853, 885.
9 Ibid., 883.
10 Ibid., 904–5.
11 Adam Dodek, "Courting Constitutional Danger: Constitutional Conventions and the Legacy of the Patriation Reference," *Supreme Court Law Review* (2d) 59 (2011): 127.
12 Ibid., 129–30.

13　Andrew Heard, "*Conacher* Missed the Mark on Constitutional Conventions and Fixed Election Dates," *Constitutional Forum* 19, no. 1 (2010): 129.
14　Peter H. Russell, "Bold Statecraft, Questionable Jurisprudence," in *And No One Cheered: Federalism, Democracy and the Constitution Act*, ed. Keith G. Banting and Richard Simeon, 210–38 (Toronto: Methuen, 1983).
15　*Re: Objection by Quebec to a Resolution to amend the Constitution*, [1982] 2 S.C.R. 793.
16　*Reference re Senate Reform*, [2014] 1 S.C.R. 704. See especially paras 29 and 32; see also paras 34, 53, and 67.
17　*Reference re Supreme Court Act ss.5 and 6*, [2014] 1 S.C.R. 433, para. 12.
18　Ibid.
19　Robert E. Hawkins, "Constitutional Workarounds: Senate Reform and Other Examples," *Canadian Bar Review* 89, no. 3 (2010): 516.
20　Ibid.
21　Ibid.
22　Ibid., 517.
23　Ibid., 517, 523–5.
24　For example, Andrew Heard, "Constitutional Doubts about Bill C-20 and Senatorial Elections," Working Papers on Senate Reform (Kingston, ON: Queen's University, Institute of Intergovernmental Relations, 2008).
25　An Act respecting constitutional amendments, S.C. 1996, c. 1.
26　Andrew Petter, "Why B.C. would veto the veto bill, if it could: The Ottawa legislation turns Canada away from provincial equality, flexibility and consensus-building," *Vancouver Sun*, 8 February 1996, A15.
27　Proceedings of the Special Senate Committee on Bill C-110, 22 January 1996, testimony of Allan Rock.
28　Ibid., comments of Senator Allan MacEachen.
29　Hawkins, "Constitutional Workarounds," 536.
30　Proceedings of the Special Senate Committee on Bill C-110, 25 January 1996, testimony of Stephen Scott.
31　Murray Campbell, "Legality of regional veto questioned: Constitutional mini-industry gears up again as scholars and lawyers debate whether bill exceeds Ottawa's powers to affect amending formula," *Globe and Mail*, 3 February 1996, A4.
32　Proceedings of the Special Senate Committee on Bill C-110, 25 January 1996, testimony of Stephen Scott.
33　Hawkins, "Constitutional Workarounds," 535.
34　Proceedings of the Special Senate Committee on Bill C-110, 25 January 1996, testimony of Stephen Scott.
35　Hawkins, "Constitutional Workarounds," 522–6.

36 Proceedings of the Special Senate Committee on Bill C-110, 30 January 1996, testimony of Andrew Heard.

37 Campbell, "Legality of regional veto questioned."

38 Ibid.

39 Tom Arnold and Marta Gold, "Klein promises not to use veto," *Calgary Herald*, 8 December 1995, A1.

40 F.L. Morton, "Why Chrétien's proposal won't wash in the West," *Globe and Mail*, 30 November 1995, A21.

41 Ibid.

42 Heard, "Constitutional Doubts about Bill C-20," 11; emphasis added.

43 Sean Fine, "A guide to the battle for Senate reform," *Globe and Mail*, 12 November 2013, A3.

44 Heard, "Constitutional Doubts about Bill C-20," 11.

45 Hawkins, "Constitutional Workarounds," 525–6.

46 Ibid.

47 Ibid.; emphasis added.

48 Campbell, "Legality of regional veto questioned."

49 Brian Laghi, "Chrétien offers a deal; Klein enraged over veto proposal in three-pronged unity plan," *Edmonton Journal*, 28 November 1995, A1.

50 Arnold and Gold, "Klein promises not to use veto."

51 Sheldon Alberts, "Reform urges Klein to act," *Calgary Herald*, 1 December 1995, A3.

52 Proceedings of the Special Senate Committee on Bill C-110, 30 January 1996, testimony of Andrew Heard.

53 Ibid.

54 Constitution Act, RSBC 1996, c. 66, s. 23.

55 An Act to amend the Canada Elections Act, S.C. 2007, c. 10, s. 56.1 (1).

56 Peter Aucoin, Mark D. Jarvis, and Lori Turnbull, *Democratizing the Constitution: Reforming Responsible Government* (Toronto: Emond Montgomery, 2011), 61–5; Peter H. Russell, "Learning to Live with Minority Parliaments," in *Parliamentary Democracy in Crisis*, ed. Peter H. Russell and Lorne Sossin (Toronto: University of Toronto Press, 2009), 138–41.

57 Aucoin, Jarvis, and Turnbull, *Democratizing the Constitution*, 81–6.

58 Heard, "*Conacher* Missed the Mark," 135–8; Peter H. Russell, *Two Cheers for Minority Government: The Evolution of Canadian Parliamentary Democracy* (Toronto: Emond Montgomery, 2008), 60.

59 Gary Levy, "A Crisis Not Made in a Day," in Russell and Sossin, *Parliamentary Democracy in Crisis*, 23; Heard, "*Conacher* Missed the Mark," 137–8.

60 Elsa Piersig, "No Confidence in Non-Confidence Votes: Would the New Zealand Confidence Protocol or Constructive Non-Confidence Restore the

Canadian Confidence Convention?" (MA thesis, University of Calgary, 2014), chap. 1.

61 Peter Aucoin and Lori Turnbull, "Removing the Virtual Right of First Ministers to Demand Dissolution," *Canadian Parliamentary Review* 27, no. 2 (2004): 16–19.

62 Russell, *Two Cheers for Minority Government*, 55.

63 Levy, "A Crisis not Made in a Day," 23.

64 Kevin Werner, "Dion promises to call election soon," *Hamilton News, Mountain Edition*, 14 March 2008, 5; see also Russell, *Two Cheers for Minority Government*, 60.

65 *Conacher v Canada (Prime Minister)*, 2009 FC 920.

66 *Conacher v Canada (Primer Minister)*, 2010 FCA 131.

67 Dodek, "Courting Constitutional Danger," 139.

68 Russell, "Learning to Live with Minority Parliaments."

69 Heard, "*Conacher* Missed the Mark," 139.

70 Dodek, "Courting Constitutional Danger," 140.

7 Understanding the Section 43 Bilateral Amending Formula

DWIGHT NEWMAN

Further constitutional amendment in Canada is sometimes seen as requiring the use of an amending formula under which constitutional change is unwieldy or even impossible.[1] The prospect of amendment seems particularly daunting when the constitutional amending formulas are combined with various practices or principles associated with their use, as well as further statutory requirements.[2] Recent case law might seem to reinforce this stultifying impression, with the Supreme Court of Canada's *Senate Reference*,[3] in particular, potentially rendering constitutional change into a species as endangered as the unicorn.[4]

Yet there is hope. Some of that hope comes from the often-underexamined section 43 of Part V, which provides for the possibility of a constitutional amendment by just the federal Parliament and one or more affected provinces.[5] This so-called bilateral amending formula provides an accessible route to some constitutional changes and, without a lot of attention to the point, it has been the mechanism used for a meaningful number of post-1982 constitutional amendments.[6]

At the same time, some seem to remain wary about section 43 or to encounter some kind of intellectual struggle with it. The *Senate Reference* somewhat peculiarly adopted a 1982 description of section 43 as "the 'Rubik's Cube' of Part V," while referring to "[t]he determination of its scope and of the effects of its interaction with other provisions of Part V" as "present[ing] significant conceptual difficulties" that led the Court to "limit our remarks on s. 43 to what [wa]s necessary" in the case before it.[7]

In this chapter, building upon the appropriate interpretive approach to Part V, I seek first to justify a primary reference to the text and then to examine the textually expressed purposes of section 43, as contextualized in Part V more generally. My claim, in part, is that section 43 is precisely formulated to create certain kinds of constitutional flexibility. Second, I show that the accepted uses of section 43 make clear that a reading that embraces the full possibility of its text is in fact in place. I argue that the Supreme Court's pronouncements in the *Senate Reference* ultimately do not alter the vibrant possibilities of section 43. Third, I argue that the implication is that there is much unexplored potential for routes to easier constitutional change in a variety of contexts, and I present a number of examples of contexts in which section 43 could be used to achieve meaningful changes, and show how these tangible examples also flesh out some implicit limits on section 43. I conclude the chapter by showing that realities of section 43 incidentally call into question in a broader way some of the ways the Supreme Court has engaged recently with constitutional change in the *Senate Reference* and the *Nadon* case.[8]

The Textually Expressed Purposes of the Bilateral Amending Formula

Part V presents a carefully developed code concerning the legal requirements for constitutional amendment. More detailed constitutional provisions, like those in Part V, are properly interpreted with special attention to their carefully developed and negotiated text. That principle arguably is especially significant in the context of the amending formulas, which were subjected to some fourteen rounds of painstaking constitutional discussions from 1926 to 1982.[9]

In order to understand Part V generally or section 43 specifically, the text must properly be the starting point for any discussion of the amending formulas. This legal approach is proper even though the Supreme Court of Canada largely failed to attend to this textual priority in the politicized context of its decision in the *Senate Reference*. That reference purports to adopt a universalized "rule" of constitutional interpretation that all constitutional documents "be interpreted in a broad and purposive manner and placed in their proper linguistic, philosophic, and historical contexts."[10] Closer attention reveals that the sentence reproduces essentially verbatim a sentence in the majority judgment in *Nadon*, along with the same purportedly supporting citations.[11]

There are reasons, however, to give limited weight to this "rule" in understanding the law in this area. The citations involved do not actually support this rule directly; rather, they are a set of materials that the rule, as stated, purports to draw together. Two of the cases cited, however, pertain to the interpretation of more open-textured provisions of the Charter of Rights and Freedoms and to the "living tree" principle from the *Persons* case.[12] The latter case actually employed close textual reading of specific constitutional wording, and its metaphorical portions do not necessarily have the implications they are sometimes taken to have.[13] More generally, none of these precedents properly bears on a highly detailed text concerning the amending formulas, but other precedents do specifically support the idea that this detailed text is to be interpreted based on its contents.[14] As confirmed in other cases dealing with detailed constitutional texts,[15] the specificity of these textual provisions means that the text must be particularly significant to interpretation if the Constitution itself is to be respected.

In terms of the bilateral amending formula itself, the text of section 43 relates in broad terms to "[a]n amendment to the Constitution of Canada in relation to any provision that applies to one or more, but not all, provinces, including (a) any alteration to boundaries between provinces, and (b) any amendment to any provision that relates to the use of the English or the French language within a province."[16] The text is specific that this provision concerns provisions of the Constitution of Canada, as opposed to provisions of provincial constitutions, which are subject by unilateral amendment by the province pursuant to section 45.[17] The language of the text clearly is not exhaustive concerning the types of provisions at issue, with nonexhaustiveness fitting not only the normal language of the provision, but also the wide array of province-specific provisions in the Constitution. Incidentally, it has also been confirmed by the *Senate Reference*, where the Supreme Court confirmed that it considered section 43 to apply to Quebec-specific dimensions of the property-holding requirement for senators.[18]

In the context of the broad range of existing or potential province-specific provisions of the Constitution, section 43 permits flexible constitutional amendment with the agreement just of "each province to which the amendment applies," along with that of the federal Parliament.[19] Such a well-accepted approach to province-specific amendments was present without issue in the draft amending formulas discussed over a period of decades. Writing shortly after the final adoption of section 43 as part of Part V, Justice Jean Beetz, in a Supreme Court judgment, summarized in passing the nature of section 43 as "a flexible form of constitutional amendment" designed to allow particular provinces to develop in diverse ways.[20] Justice Beetz's language presages the reality that section 43 permits not only the amendment of existing province-specific provisions, but also constitutional change that establishes province-specific provisions. This point used to be debated,[21] but it is now clear and accepted that section 43 can be used for the adoption of new provisions.[22] Thus, the text of section 43, considered in the context of Part V, provides for a variety of constitutional amendments if their effect is limited to one or several provinces.

Accepted Uses of Section 43

Section 43 was carefully drafted to allow for certain types of constitutional flexibility, and, in fact, has been used in a flexible manner to achieve various types of constitutional change on a number of occasions since 1982. Various provinces, in conjunction with the federal government, have made use of it to carry out amendments to the Constitution on matters particularly affecting them. Newfoundland has used it on four occasions, three in relation to modifying denominational school rights[23] and the fourth to change the name of the province officially to Newfoundland and Labrador.[24] Quebec used it to end denominational school rights.[25] Prince Edward Island used it to allow a bridge instead of a ferry for its constitutionally guaranteed mainland link.[26] New Brunswick used it to add section 16.1 to the Charter, which guarantees equality of status to the English and French linguistic communities in that province.[27] Thus, section 43 has been the clear source for a number of significant constitutional amendments. The uses by Newfoundland and Quebec were subjected to judicial challenges, with their respective Courts of Appeal upholding the amendments to denominational school rights as valid and the Supreme Court of Canada denying leave to appeal in each case.[28] These judicial interpretations help to shed further light on the well-accepted use of section 43.

The Newfoundland Court of Appeal specifically faced the question of the scope of application of the provision, and considered an argument that one must go to another amending formula where there was "any effect on a matter which would require a more complex amending formula."[29] In response to this argument, however, Justice Margaret Cameron held that "[i]t is not the type, nature or subject matter of provision being amended which is critical – it is the scope of the application of the provision."[30] The judgment did offer other reasoning that reached the same result, but at this point the Court of Appeal held that the scope of the provision's application was determinative.

To the extent that minority denominational school rights affected certain communities at a more national level, the amendment might have been thought to have broader effects. Ultimately, however, it pertained legally only to the effects of the Canadian Constitution in Newfoundland, which meant that the Court of Appeal held that the amendment was a valid use of section 43.[31]

In the context of the Quebec Court of Appeal's consideration of the amendment of denominational school rights in a case called *Potter*,[32] the Court considered the effects of section 93(4) of the Constitution Act, 1867, which gave the federal Parliament the power to make remedial laws to implement denominational school rights in a province to which section 93 applied if the province had failed to implement such rights effectively. The removal of Quebec's section 93 rights would also effectively remove this federal power. The Quebec Court of Appeal described the section 93(4) federal power as a merely "ancillary power," and also suggested that the federal government would not lose this power because it would continue to apply in provinces other than Quebec.[33] The Federal Court affirmed and adopted this reasoning when it considered issues related to the interpretation of section 16.1 of the Charter in *Société des acadiens du Nouveau-Brunswick v Canada*.[34] There, Justice Johanne Gauthier wrote that, "[l]ike the Quebec Court of Appeal, I believe that Parliament may alter its own obligations in respect of a province, in particular by way of section 43."[35] Interestingly, then, it becomes possible even to say that the scope of a change that affects only a single province does not relate to whether there is some effect on the scope of federal power in that province.

The fact that section 43 has been used to amend such sensitive matters as minority rights provisions on denominational school rights and linguistic rights, even with effects on the power of the federal government in a particular province, suggests that section 43 is accepted as having a wide scope. The fact that it has supported the introduction of an entirely new subsection on linguistic rights into the Charter similarly shows that it is not subject to unexpressed formalistic limits. Section 43's use to pursue aims of appropriate provincial diversity within the Canadian Constitution has been accepted through government practice and judicial review of that practice.

In addition to these already substantial clearly accepted uses of section 43, there is also the possibility that section 43 offers a means of interpreting in constitutional terms another significant phenomenon – namely, that of modern treaties. In the context of various Aboriginal communities, especially where federal and provincial governments are still dealing with unresolved land claims, there has been a significant use of tripartite agreements, acceded to by the federal and provincial governments along with Aboriginal communities themselves, to establish new terms of the relationship with the Aboriginal community involved. The adoption of these treaties has not followed the form of section 43, but the fact that their tripartite negotiation follows the same consent requirement as for section 43 arguably legitimates their constitutional effects.

Despite their widespread use, the precise constitutional character of these agreements has not always been clear, and there have even been challenges to the constitutional ability of the federal and provincial governments to enter into them. In the context of a constitutional challenge to the Nisga'a Agreement in British Columbia at a time when the British Columbia treaty process was especially controversial, the trial court that upheld the Agreement found a way to do so without deciding that it modified any constitutional powers by suggesting that the Agreement merely recognized the ongoing presence of inherent governmental powers outside the division of powers enumerated in the Constitution Act, 1867.[36]

Later judicial reasoning, however, has been more forthright in simply acknowledging the possibility that a modern treaty actually might effect a constitutional amendment of sorts by becoming an agreement recognized under section 35(3) of the Constitution Act, 1982.[37] In particular, in considering the James Bay and Northern Quebec Agreement in the *Moses* case,[38] Supreme Court justices Marie Deschamps and Louis LeBel held – in dissent, but not specifically on this point – that the Agreement qualified as a modern treaty, and thus took on a "constitutional status."[39] The Agreement resulted in the ouster of aspects of certain federal environmental jurisdiction in favour of a joint management approach within the Agreement. One might read the Agreement, then, as also having implicitly adjusted the scope of federal power within Cree territory in northern Quebec.

One might try to read these sorts of changes as flowing simply from a residual sort of power to enter into treaties. However, to the extent that modern treaties have a constitutional character and might even effect a constitutional amendment, such as to the scope of federal powers within certain areas, a possible way of reading constitutional processes more harmoniously would be to regard the establishment of modern treaties through tripartite agreements as deriving constitutional legitimacy from the section 43 bilateral amending formula. To the extent that this thesis is the case, the section 43 power has actually been employed on dozens of further occasions beyond the clearly accepted cases to recognize, enhance, and entrench diversity within the Canadian federation.

The Potential of Section 43

Given both the clear cases of section 43's use and its possible implicit role in a wider array of cases as well, section 43 thus has application to effect constitutional changes that affect just one (or several) provinces with the support of Parliament and the provincial legislature(s) in question. There are no extra restrictions to read into this. Some of the changes have modified rights, while others have modified legislative powers, but both types of changes have been accepted as legitimate uses of section 43. The result is that section 43 actually has significant potential for various scenarios, including some that have been the subject of more open discussion and others that have not.

One area in which the potential use of section 43 has been openly mooted by legislators – and even put on the agenda via private members' bills[40] – is the possible introduction of a constitutional property rights provision in a particular province.[41] Out of a variety of historical circumstances, the Charter does not include a property rights provision, even though such a provision had long been on the agenda of many of those promoting or agreeing to the Charter.[42] There remains today much interest in securing such a protection, and section 43 would appear to provide a plausible basis for the entrenchment of provincially differentiated property rights. Some instinctively find it peculiar that Charter rights might differ from province to province, but this is already the case with such provisions as section 16.1, adopted under the section 43 provision.[43]

This example, though, illustrates immediately one possible set of limits on the potential of section 43. In the Canadian context, the entrenchment of property rights (other than Aboriginal property rights) traditionally has occasioned both governments' worry about constraints on their policy-making and thus political division.[44] The use of section 43 to entrench property rights in a particular province can proceed only when there is democratic willingness to do so simultaneously at both the provincial and federal levels. Moreover, any entrenched property right also would seem to be subject to later removal by different governments through the same section 43 procedure, unless such removal was seen as politically impossible as a sort of removal of established rights, a scenario that certainly would be possible if a province became sufficiently convinced of the value of entrenched property rights as to pursue a section 43 amendment.

Recognizing that section 43 can be used to establish different arrangements in each province, whether on property rights or on the sorts of established section 43 practices already discussed, potentially highlights the possibility of using the section more broadly to craft forms of asymmetrical federalism. Some scholars have argued that the relatively unrestricted use of section 43 provides a possible means to develop asymmetrical arrangements for Quebec within the Constitution.[45] In highlighting the flexibility of section 43, I perhaps have suggested that this possibility might be legally viable, even in the face of past government caution about using section 43 in such a way.[46] There is reason, however, to consider carefully whether this example also illustrates some issues related to the fine line on when other provinces' interests are actually at stake in a particular constitutional amendment, thus taking particular possibilities out of section 43.

Here, it is worth highlighting the innovative argument of David Cameron and Jacqueline Krikorian, who suggest that section 43 could be used to entrench an interpretive provision that would modify the application of the Charter to Quebec.[47] They shy away, however, from proposing the term "distinct society," both because of the uncertain impact of that text and because it "would evoke memories of earlier divisive and unsuccessful efforts at recognizing Quebec."[48] Only somewhat later do they note that "[w]e also think it is worth noting that one of the main reasons that the Meech Lake and Charlottetown Accords were so strongly contested was not simply the fact that the amendments required the consent of other provinces but also that each purported to declare something about the country as a whole."[49] They seem to think that a "distinct society" clause still could be adopted through section 43 – although it is not the main idea they advocate – but they do not explain why a clause that would say something about Canada as a whole does not take it out of the scope of section 43.

Section 43's text concerning "any provision that applies to one or more, but not all, provinces" has not blocked provinces from making changes to denominational school rights, even though those changes implicitly impacted on the affected minorities in Canada as a whole. Judicial consideration has emphasized the formal legal matter of where the constitutional effect is located,[50] rather than the more symbolic effect of an amendment that one might have thought potentially sub-ject to consideration.[51] But a larger constitutional statement, such as a "distinct society" clause, that has been previously discussed in the context of a nationally debated constitutional amendment arguably would call for a rereading of this line. Where the formal legal effects of an amendment are confined to one province, that presumptively puts it within the scope of section 43, but there is arguably an exception for an amendment that nonetheless fundamentally alters the country as a whole through further-reaching effects – even at some level of holistic constitutional interpretation – that affect the country more generally.

The exact shape of this limit on the use of section 43 is admittedly open to some argument. Some might propose that section 43 could be used to add province-specific rights to the Charter, but not to take away rights on a province-specific basis. That claim would be consistent with the addition of linguistic rights in New Brunswick through the addition of section 16.1. Its consistency with the removal of denominational school rights, though, depends on either a formalistic distinction between the Charter and other parts of the Constitution or some denigration of denominational school rights. It is not clear that there is any formal line between using section 43 to add or remove rights on province-specific bases, although it is subject to the limit that a purportedly province-specific amendment cannot alter the country as a whole.

Overall, section 43 might offer the real possibility of developing some asymmetric relationships that have relatively specific legal shape, but these cannot be asymmetries that have any sort of legal knock-on effect on other provinces. So, there are real limits that must be acknowledged. That said, there are real possibilities here as well for certain forms of flexible constitutional adaptation in more specific legal forms.

As I suggested earlier, section 43 arguably has been used implicitly in the context of tripartite agreements with Aboriginal communities. However, considering simply the general rules concerning section 43, there might be other possible uses of it in the Aboriginal rights context. At hearings before the Joint Committee of the Senate and House of Commons leading up to the Charlottetown Accord, the president of the Métis National Council referred to the possible future use of section 43 for the protection of Métis rights in specific provinces without the need for other amending formulas, and his suggestion appeared not to have attracted further commentary from the committee.[52] The possibility of using section 43 to craft special arrangements around Aboriginal rights, such as Métis rights, in specific provinces would appear to be a live possibility. Whether it is more or less pertinent after ongoing litigation concerning the division of powers and Métis communities remains to be seen.[53]

Section 43 could be used in Aboriginal rights contexts in other ways as well, albeit not necessarily ones governments rush to moot openly. In committee testimony concerning the Constitution Act, 1982, there was, notably, a brief mention of the possible use of section 43 by the federal government and a province to alter Aboriginal rights in a province. Then-justice minister Jean Chrétien's key testimony on the point was as follows: "I said the general amending formula will apply in the case of aboriginal rights. If it were to be a very clear case where it would be just a local situation, it might be that a decision would be that it is possible to amend by a provincial or the national government."[54] That testimony engaged even with the possibility of a post-1982 extinguishment of an Aboriginal right, something not permitted in the context of section 35 generally in the post-1982 constitutional context. Governments could use section 43 to effect a constitutional amendment to rights in a local context were they to consider, for instance, resource development overly hamstrung by particular judicial interpretations.[55] One counterargument would see such amendments as inherently changing something about Canada as a whole, but it seems that localized amendments would fit the general rules for section 43 and specific evidence concerning the Joint Committee's intentions for the section.

Interesting questions also arise over to what extent constitutional proposals to amend section 35 rights were themselves subject to the duty to consult doctrine, something that has been unclear in respect of legislation generally.[56] In this particular section 35 context, there are some rich questions – some of them discussed further by Christa Scholtz in Chapter 4 – concerning how Part V must interact with other parts of the Constitution Act, 1982, with Part V obviously having to take priority on the modalities of amendment, but that priority also being something that should not vitiate the rest of the Constitution.[57]

However, the possibility of section 43 constitutional amendments that modified specific features of particular Aboriginal rights contexts – including even amendments that effect post-1982 extinguishment in specific contexts – is in keeping with testimony before the Joint Committee relating to the intention of the section, with its implicit use in the context of modern treaties – which entrench both modern treaty rights and the surrender of previously unceded Aboriginal rights – and with the established law on section 43. This seldom-contemplated possibility bears significantly on certain current issues, such as those related to particular resource development projects, and, again, illustrates the potential of section 43 to establish different forms of constitutional flexibility.

Whether in the context of a right where views might differ in different parts of the country on its appropriateness for the Charter, or over the big issues of some carefully crafted constitutional asymmetries for Quebec, or over complex Aboriginal rights questions, there are many larger possibilities for constitutional flexibility than is sometimes presumed. Section 43 has the potential to contribute to the resolution of some of the toughest constitutional logjams that have given rise to some of the most intractable situations. It is an important tool of constitutional amendment.

Conclusions: Learning about Constitutional Amendment from the Section 43 Context

The lessons of section 43 are, of course, arguably broader in several different ways. First, as I concluded above, understanding section 43 means understanding that there may be a tool for greater constitutional flexibility than is often realized. As I showed earlier in the chapter, there have been many already accepted uses of section 43 to adapt the Constitution flexibly in response to the needs of particular provinces.

Second, that conclusion means that it is highly unfortunate there has not been greater development of a section 43 jurisprudence or a better understanding of what jurisprudence there is. The cases decided at the appellate level on which the Supreme Court has denied leave are instructive as to the flexibility that section 43 creates. It is peculiar, then, that the Court's latest reference to section 43, the *Senate Reference*, sounds more ominous notes on the Court's apparent confusion about it. The reference does show a pertinent application of the section, consistent with the broader picture that has emerged here. Indeed, the strong historical, textual, and purposive foundations of section 43 actually call into question some overreaching aspects of some of the Court's rhetorical pronouncements in the *Senate Reference*, so it might be worth highlighting that the Court itself arguably already has had implicitly to retreat from some of those. In the *Senate Reference*, the Court ended up referring to section 38 as the "general procedure for constitutional amendment," with section 44 "as an exception to the general procedure."[58] Section 44, of course, contains some language that explicitly subjects it, through section 42, to section 38's prevailing on certain matters.[59] So the Court's statement should not be read too generally, particularly when any overly general reading of it would be inconsistent with the long-standing historical and textual roots of provisions such as section 43. Moreover, to the extent that the *Senate Reference* saw the Court drawing on general values of federalism to reread the constitutional text, the majority of the Court more recently has held against using general values of federalism to rewrite specific constitutional arrangements, marking some move away from that dimension of the *Senate Reference*.[60] That case should not be read as posing a legal barrier to section 43.

Third, quite frankly, the presence of negotiated provisions in the text that make the amending formulas responsive to Canada's complex needs reinforces, once again, the appropriateness of the courts' applying the constitutional text on amendments. Surely this is better than trying to invent broader structural reasoning that might make things even more challenging, or that, at least, marks a seizure of judicial power over amendment, rather than a respect for the textual provisions in the Constitution that are responsive to Canada's needs and diversity. Section 43 has a lot to tell us when we understand its text, its practices, and its potential.

Notes

I am grateful for discussions on section 43 with, among others, Warren Newman, Scott Reid, and John Whyte, and for comments on the draft chapter from Emmett Macfarlane, Michael Plaxton, and two anonymous reviewers.

1 See, for example, Michael Lusztig, "Constitutional Paralysis: Why Canadian Constitutional Initiatives are Doomed to Fail," *Canadian Journal of Political Science* 27, no. 4 (1994): 747–71.
2 See, for example, Guy Régimbald and Dwight Newman, *The Law of the Canadian Constitution*, 1st ed. (Markham, ON: LexisNexis, 2013), 27–8 (discussing provincial legislation), 40 (possible expectations of referendums to establish support through popular sovereignty), 38–9 (effects of unwritten principles), 40–1 (federal regional veto legislation).
3 *Reference re Senate Reform*, 2014 SCC 32, [2014] 1 S.C.R. 704 (*Senate Reference*).
4 However, for the view that it is possible to work within the amending formulas, see also Warren J. Newman, "Living with the Amending Procedures: Prospects for Future Constitutional Reform in Canada," in *A Living Tree: The Legacy of 1982 in Canada's Political Evolution*, ed. Graeme Mitchell et al., 747–80 (Markham, ON: LexisNexis, 2007).

5 Constitution Act, 1982, s. 43.

6 Aside from the discussion below, see also Dwight Newman, "The Bilateral Amending Formula as a Mechanism for the Entrenchment of Property Rights," *Constitutional Forum* 21, no. 2 (2013): 17–22.

7 *Senate Reference*, para. 43, citing Stephen A. Scott, "Pussycat, Pussycat or Patriation and the New Constitutional Amendment Processes," *University of Western Ontario Law Review* 20 (1982): 292–8.

8 *Reference re Supreme Court Act, ss. 5 and 6*, 2014 SCC 21, [2014] 1 S.C.R. 433 [*Nadon*].

9 For a discussion of this history, see Régimbald and Newman, *Law of the Canadian Constitution*, 21–7. For a more detailed explanation of the fourteen rounds, see James Ross Hurley, *Amending Canada's Constitution: History, Processes, Problems and Prospects* (Ottawa: Canada Communication Group, 1996), 23–67.

10 *Senate Reference*, para. 25.

11 *Nadon*, para. 19, with the sentence stating that sections 5 and 6 of the Supreme Court Act, which the Court suddenly held to be "constitutionally protected," must "be interpreted in a broad and purposive manner and understood in their proper linguistic, philosophic and historical context."

12 The citations are to *Hunter v Southam*, [1984] 2 S.C.R. 145, 155–6; *R. v Big M Drug Mart Ltd.*, [1985] 1 S.C.R. 295, 344; and *Edwards v Canada (Attorney General)*, [1930] A.C. 124, 136 (P.C.).

13 See Bradley W. Miller, "Origin Myth: The Persons Case, the Living Tree, and the New Originalism," in *The Challenge of Originalism*, ed. Grant Huscroft and Bradley Miller, 120–44 (Cambridge: Cambridge University Press, 2011); Scott Reid, "The Persons Case Eight Decades Later: Reappraising Canada's Most Misunderstood Court Ruling" (2013), available online at http:// papers.ssrn.com/sol3/papers.cfm?abstract_id=2209846.

14 *Native Women's Association of Canada v Canada*, [1994] 3 S.C.R. 627; *Hogan v Newfoundland (Attorney General)*, 183 D.L.R. (4th) 225, para. 125 (Nfld. C.A.), leave to appeal refused [2000] S.C.CA. No. 191. See also *Reference on Amendment of Canadian Constitution (Quebec Veto Reference)*, [1982] 2 S.C.R. 793, 806, stating that the Constitution Act, 1982 "contains a new procedure for amending the Constitution of Canada which entirely replaces the old one in its legal as well as in its conventional aspects."

15 *Canadian Egg Marketing Agency v Richardson*, [1998] 3 S.C.R. 157, paras 50–4 (discussing detailed text of section 6 mobility rights); *Mahe v Alberta*, [1990] 1 S.C.R. 342, 369 (discussing the section 23 minority language educational rights provision as a comprehensive code). See also Régimbald and Newman, *Law of the Canadian Constitution*, 699, 706, 714.

16 Constitution Act, 1982, s. 43. The French-language version of the text, it bears noting, has some more restrictive features. To the extent that it does, however, there has been an authoritative ruling that these elements were not meant to restrict its scope as compared to the English-language text: *Potter v Québec (Procureur général)*, [2001] R.J.Q. 2823, J.E. 2001–2166, paras 44–6; leave denied: [2002] C.S.C.R. no. 13.

17 Section 43 refers to an amendment of the Constitution of Canada, as distinct from the constitution of a province. The amendment of the constitution of a province is governed by section 45 of the Constitution Act, 1982: "Subject to section 41, the legislature of each province may exclusively make laws amending the constitution of the province." This section arguably simply replaced section 92(1) of the Constitution Act, 1867, brought forward into Part V of the Constitution Act, 1982 for purposes of codifying together all constitutional amendment formulas. Under section 45, there is no need for federal involvement at all: a province has the power to amend its own provincial constitution. On the special concept of provincial constitutions generally, see Régimbald and Newman, *Law of the Canadian Constitution*, 34–5, where we also refer to other scholarly writing on the concept.

18 *Senate Reference*, para. 86.

19 Constitution Act, 1982, s. 43. The French-language text refers to the agreement of the *"provinces concernées,"* potentially distinguishable according to some arguments from those to which a provision applies. For example, some have tried to argue that provinces with a similar provision are concerned by a change to a parallel provision. The English text is clearer, and better achieves the flexibility at which the provision's text is fundamentally aimed. Its expression of a possible reading of the French text should be the reading adopted.

20 *Association of Parents for Fairness in Education, Grand Falls District 50 Branch v Société des acadiens du Nouveau-Brunswick*, [1986] 1 S.C.R. 549, 579. See also Kathy Brock, "Diversity within Unity: Constitutional Amendments under Section 43," *Canadian Parliamentary Review* 20, no. 1 (1997): 24, where she states that "[s]ection 43 reflects and further enshrines the principle of provincial diversity."

21 For authors who adopted the narrow reading, see, for example, Jacques-Yvan Morin and José Woehrling, *Les constitutions du Canada et du Québec*, 3rd ed. (Montreal: Thémis, 1994), 516; and Henri Brun and Gérard Tremblay, *Droit constitutionnel*, 2nd ed. (Cowansville, QC: Yvon Blais, 1990), 228.

22 Benoît Pelletier, *La modification constitutionnelle au Canada* (Toronto: Carswell, 1996), 236; David R. Cameron and Jacqueline D. Krikorian, "Recognizing Quebec in the Constitution of Canada: Using the Bilateral Constitutional

Amendment Process," *University of Toronto Law Journal* 58, no. 4 (2008): 407–11; Newman, "Living with the Amending Procedures," 18.

23 Constitution Amendment Proclamation, 1987 (Newfoundland Act), S.I./88–11, C.Gaz. 1988.II.887; Constitution Amendment Proclamation, 1997 (Newfoundland Act), S.I./97–55, C.Gaz. 1997.II.1; Constitution Amendment, 1998 (Newfoundland Act), S.I./98–25, C.Gaz. 1998.II.339.

24 Constitution Amendment, 2001 (Newfoundland and Labrador), S.I./2001–117, C.Gaz. 2001.II.2899.

25 Constitution Amendment, 1997 (Quebec), S.I. 97/141, C.Gaz. 1997.II.1.

26 Constitution Amendment, 1993 (Prince Edward Island), S.I/ 94–50, C.Gaz. 1994.II.2021.

27 Constitution Amendment Proclamation, 1993 (New Brunsswick), S.I./93–54, C.Gaz. 1993.II.1588.

28 *Hogan; Potter c. Québec (Procureur général)*, [2001] R.J.Q. 2823, J.E. 2001–2166, leave denied: [2002] C.S.C.R. no. 13.

29 *Hogan*, para. 80.

30 Ibid., para. 82.

31 See also *Potter*, paras 47–51, rejecting the argument that Quebec's removal of denominational school rights interfered with a historic bargain among a number of provinces.

32 Ibid.

33 Ibid., paras 22–3.

34 2005 FC 1172, [2006] 1 F.C.R. 490. This judgment was reversed on other grounds; see *Société des acadiens et acadiennes du Nouveau-Brunswick v Canada*, 2006 FCA 196, [2007] 2 F.C.R. 177.

35 2005 FC 1172, para. 60.

36 *Campbell v British Columbia (Attorney General)*, 2000 BCSC 1123, 189 D.L.R. (4th) 333.

37 Constitution Act, 1982, s. 35(3), concerning treaties rights established after 1982 also receiving protection.

38 *Quebec (Attorney General) v Moses*, [2010] 1 S.C.R. 557.

39 Ibid., para. 106.

40 In early 2011 federal MP Scott Reid and Ontario MPP Randy Hillier announced their intention to introduce bills to effect such protection in Ontario, and they continued to discuss this for some time. In 2014 federal MP Jim Hillyer served notice of a private member's bill in respect of Alberta. Thus far, no such bill has been adopted.

41 The Reid-Hillier resolution would have added section 7.1(1) to the Charter, stating that "[i]n Ontario, everyone has the right not to be deprived, by any Act of the Legislative Assembly or by any action taken under authority of

an Act of the Legislative Assembly, of the title, use, or enjoyment of real property or of any right attached to real property, or of any improvement made to or upon real property, unless made whole by means of full, just and timely financial compensation."

42 On this history, see Dwight Newman and Lorelle Binnion, "The Exclusion of Property Rights from the *Charter*: Correcting the Historical Record," *Alberta Law Review* 52, no. 3 (2015): 543–66.

43 See, generally, Newman, "Bilateral Amending Formula."

44 See Newman and Binnion, "Exclusion of Property Rights from the *Charter*."

45 Cameron and Krikorian, "Recognizing Quebec in the Constitution of Canada." Note also that Pelletier has written of this:

> Dans un autre ordre d'idées, soulignons que l'article 43 semble receler un potentiel énorme à l'heure actuelle, malheureusement trop peu exploité par nos acteurs politiques. Ainsi, nous croyons que cette disposition pourrait autoriser un certain nombre d'asymétries constitutionnelles. Il pourrait s'agir, par exemple, de certaines ententes bilatérales ou multilatérales que l'on voudrait "enchâsser" dans la Constitution du Canada, ou encore d'autres dispositions constitutionnelles que l'on désirerait ajouter à nos textes actuels. Toutes ces ententes ou ces nouvelles mesures constitutionnelles devraient toutefois, pour pouvoir être effectivement visées par l'article 43 de la Loi de 1982, répondre à une condition essentielle, à savoir: n'être applicables, tant dans leur esprit que dans leur libellé, qu'à une ou à quelques-unes des provinces canadiennes.

Benoît Pelletier, "Les modalités de la modification de la Constitution du Canada," *Revue juridique Thémis* 33, no. 1 (1999): 1.

46 It does bear noting that the Joint Committee of the Senate and House of Commons chaired by Gérald Beaudoin leading up to the Charlottetown Accord did not comment at length on section 43, but was more sceptical of its use "to grant an asymmetric legislative status to any one province." See Report of the Special Joint Committee of the Senate and the House of Commons on the Process for Amending the Constitution of Canada, 2nd Sess., 34th Parl., 20 June 1991, 28 [hereafter Special Joint Committee].

47 Cameron and Krikorian, "Recognizing Quebec in the Constitution of Canada," 416–17.

48 Ibid., 417.

49 Ibid., 417–18.

50 *Hogan*, para. 82.

51 Cf. the quote in Pelletier, "Modalités," 1n46.

52 Special Joint Committee, 18 April 1991, 23:75.

53 *R. v Daniels*, 2014 FCA 101, with an appeal still to go to the Supreme Court of Canada, addresses this issue, with one of the complicating features to the case being possible effects on the Métis settlements system in Alberta.

54 Minutes of Proceedings and Evidence of the Special Joint Committee of the Senate and House of Commons on the Constitution of Canada, 1st Sess., 32nd Parl., 3 February 1981, 52:66.

55 Confidential sources have informed me that several years ago some senior-level bureaucrats were starting to discuss the possibility of constitutional amendments in relation to some of the implications of the duty to consult doctrine if they found it to be overly constraining and to create serious constitutional imbalance.

56 On the duty to consult, see, generally, Dwight G. Newman, *Revisiting the Duty to Consult Aboriginal Peoples* (Saskatoon: Purich, 2014).

57 In other states, that tension has given rise to the notion of "constitutional structure" and features of the constitution that cannot be amended through constitutional means. I do not seek to explore those possibilities in the scope of this chapter.

58 *Senate Reference*, para. 75.

59 Constitution Act, 1982, s. 44, opening with "[s]ubject to sections 41 and 42," and 42(1), making aspects of the Senate specifically subject to section 38.

60 See *Quebec (Attorney General) v Canada (Attorney General)*, 2015 SCC 14 (*Quebec Firearms*), in which the majority declined to use unwritten principles of federalism to modify constitutional text on federalism, emphasizing the importance of constitutional text, for instance, at para. 18.

8 The Possibilities and Limits of Provincial Constitution-Making Power: The Case of Quebec

EMMANUELLE RICHEZ

Section 45 of the Constitution Act, 1982 provides that "[s]ubject to section 41 [which references the Crown, the use of the English and French languages, and other exceptions], the legislature of each province may exclusively make laws amending the constitution of the province."[1] This might come as a surprise to some who thought Canadian provinces did not have constitutions of their own. This is because important components of provincial constitutions are unwritten, and those that are written are not labelled "constitution." In fact, only British Columbia has a document called "constitution" that specifies the workings of its major institutions.[2] In this chapter, I examine the scope, use, and amendment of provincial constitutions. More specifically, I ask whether the amending procedure found in section 45 provides rigidity or flexibility for provinces that seek to distinguish themselves from others on the constitutional playing field. By using the latest Parti Québécois proposal for a new Quebec constitution, I argue that the provincial amending formula gives provinces latitude in terms of carving a distinct model of democratic representation, but not in terms of identity building.

Defining Provincial Constitutions

As determined in *Ontario (A.G.) v OPSEU*, provincial constitutions encompass unwritten and written elements – the latter include statutory rules, common law rules, and constitutionally entrenched rules.[3] Each province has a "Constitution similar in Principle to that of the United Kingdom,"[4] meaning that significant elements of provincial constitutions are unwritten and, as such, are defined by conventions.[5] The principle of responsible government, which is as the heart of the

Westminster parliamentary system, is the most fundamental convention of provincial constitutions.[6] Other important conventions include the position and powers of the premier and the provincial cabinet.[7]

Fundamental laws, which are statutory in nature and articulate the functioning of government, are essential parts of provincial constitutions as well.[8] Statutes that detail the rules of the provinces' electoral systems, legislative processes, and executive governances fall into this category.[9] As they regulate the operations of government, judicature acts[10] and human rights codes[11] can also be considered integral parts of provincial constitutions. Rights protection statutes have been described as quasi-constitutional as they have precedence over other ordinary statutes.[12]

Another significant source of provincial constitutional characteristics is the written Canadian Constitution.[13] Part 5 of the Constitution Act, 1867, labelled "Provincial Constitutions," characterizes the office of the lieutenant-governor and the role of the Crown in provincial governance, as well as some aspects of the composition and functioning of provincial legislatures.[14] It was determined in *Fielding v Thomas*, however, that provincial constitutions encompass more than the provisions laid out in Part 5.[15] Of interest is the division of powers found in sections 91 to 95, which define provincial spheres of jurisdiction.[16] Canada's old Constitution also provides for the intervention of Parliament in provincial affairs through different powers, although they have fallen into disuse.[17] Sections 96 to 100 establish the provincial courts structure,[18] and section 133 guarantees the use of the English and French languages in the Quebec legislature.[19]

Constitutional scholars disagree on whether the Canadian Charter of Rights and Freedoms, which is entrenched in the Constitution Act, 1982, simply limits provinces' constitutions or is an integral part of them.[20] The constitutional supremacy clause found in section 52 of the Constitution Act, 1982 provides that all Canadian laws shall be consistent with the provisions of the Charter. As for section 24, it gives courts the power to enforce constitutional provisions in the provinces.[21] At the same time, the Charter, with its democratic rights (sections 3–6), combined with the preamble of and the general structure of the Constitution Act, 1867 oblige provinces to have freely elected representative legislatures.[22] In this sense, the Charter does more than limit the legislative power of provinces; it structures it.

Lastly, pre-Confederation constitutional documents such as the Quebec Act, 1774, the Constitutional Act, 1791, and the Act of Union, 1840 are also essential parts of provincial constitutions.[23] The same can be said of other federal statutes[24] that determine the terms of the union of provinces admitted to Canada after Confederation.[25] Provinces joined Canada on somewhat different terms:[26] some had to guarantee certain language[27] and denominational rights,[28] while others did not. Still, they all had to adhere to a similar parliamentary system of constitutional monarchy. The question is whether the provincial constitution amending formula found in section 45 provides the necessary flexibility for provinces to innovate, constitutionally speaking, and to differentiate themselves from one another.

The Section 45 Amending Formula: Rigidity or Flexibility?

Some authors argue that the provinces have considerable discretion in shaping their constitutional architecture under section 45,[29] while others are unsure.[30] With the adoption of the new constitution, section 92(1) of the Constitution Act, 1867 was repealed and replaced by section 45. As enacted, section 92(1) provided that:

> 92. In each Province the Legislature may exclusively make Laws in relation to Matters coming within the Classes of Subjects next hereinafter enumerated; that is to say,
>
>   1) The Amendment from Time to Time, notwithstanding anything in this Act, of the Constitution of the Province, except as regards the Office of Lieutenant Governor.

Although section 92(1) identified only one explicit limit to the provincial constitution amending formula – the office of the lieutenant-governor – section 45 identifies the use of English and French as an additional explicit limit. Section 45 is subject to section 41 of the Constitution Act, 1982, which states that the unanimity rule[31] is required for amendments relating to the Crown, which includes the office of the lieutenant-governor, and for the use of English and French in certain circumstances described below.

According to several legal scholars, the case law that applied to section 92(1), also applies to section 45.[32] With regard to the Crown and the office of the lieutenant-governor, it was determined in *Bureau Métropolitain des écoles protestantes de Montréal v Québec, 1976* that section 92(1) targets only the position of lieutenant-governor, not the lieutenant-governor in council, which would mean government as a whole.[33]

According to *In re Initiative & Referendum Act (Manitoba), 1919*, provinces cannot unilaterally amend the position of lieutenant-governor as an integral part of the legislative process or as the constitutional chief of their legislature.[34] The power of Royal Assent and reserve was confirmed as being outside the scope of section 45 in *Re Manitoba Language Rights*.[35] Similarly, all the powers of the lieutenant-governors provided for by the Constitution Act of 1867, like that of creation and dissolution of provincial legislatures, can be amended only by section 41(a) of the Constitution Act, 1982.[36] This was confirmed *obiter dictum* by Justice Jean Beetz in *OPSEU*.[37] Finally, the oath of allegiance to the Crown that members of provincial legislatures must make before taking office, as per section 128 of the Constitution Act, 1867, is likely not in the scope of section 45.[38]

Constitutional provisions relating to the use of the English and French languages cannot be modified according to the rule laid out in section 45. Rather, they have to be either amended by the rules laid out in sections 41(c) or 43(b), depending on the issue. The latter provides that an amendment to the use of English or French that concerns one or more, but not all, provinces can be passed only with the approval of Parliament and the legislatures of the provinces to which the amendment applies (for more on bilateral amendments, see Dwight Newman, this volume). All other amendments pertaining to language require the unanimity rule, as per section 41(c). Section 133 of the Constitution Act, 1867 and section 23 of the Manitoba Act, 1870 pertaining to the use of French and English in the legislature and courts of Quebec and Manitoba, respectively, are limits to section 45, and fall under the purview of section 41(c).[39] Sections 16 to 22 of the Charter, which provide for institutional bilingualism in New Brunswick, are also a limit to section 45, and fall under the purview of section 43(b).[40] As for the minority language educational rights found in section 23 of the Charter, they are subject to debate. Although some constitutionalists consider that they must be amended via section 41(c) since they concern all the provinces,[41] others believe they could be amended via section 43(b).[42] Still others stipulate that an amendment to section 23 requires the general amending formula found in section 38,[43] as it pertains to a set of rights that differs from those relating to institutional bilingualism.[44] Nevertheless, what is clear is that section 23 is not subject to section 45.[45] Yet provinces are not prohibited from granting new rights and privileges to official-language communities under section 45, as long as these are compatible with existing language rights provisions.[46]

Several implicit constitutional issues also limit the scope of section 45. For one thing, provinces cannot unilaterally amend their constitution in a way that would jeopardize the conditions of the 1867 union or the federal principle.[47] For example, it was decided in *A.G. of Quebec v Blaikie* that the Quebec component of section 133 of the Constitution Act, 1867 did not fall within the scope of section 92(1).[48] Rather, it was characterized as indivisible from the federal part, as it represents a political arrangement that made Confederation possible.[49] The same can be said of section 93 of the Constitution Act, 1867,[50] which recognizes denominational education rights, and therefore is a limit to section 45.[51] Furthermore, provisions considered indispensable for the implementation of the federal principle were declared *ultra vires* to section 92(1) in *OPSEU*,[52] and thus escape the scope of section 45. Accordingly, the unilateral secession of a province was deemed unconstitutional in *Reference re Secession of Quebec*.[53]

Another important implicit limit to the unilateral modification of provincial constitutions is constitutional rights and freedoms. Every right protected in the Charter constitutes a limit to section 45.[54] The only way to circumvent this limit is for a province to invoke the notwithstanding clause found in section 33. Then again, this clause applies only to sections 2 and 7–15 of the Charter, and has a five-year sunset clause. Even before the entrenchment of the Charter, there was the belief that the Canadian Constitution encompassed an implied bill of rights.[55] This theory was based on the fact that the Constitution was similar in principle to that of the United Kingdom. Although not all constitutionalists agree on the merits of this theory, it could still be a limit on section 45.[56]

Furthermore, provincial legislatures cannot delegate their powers – for example, via deliberative referendums – under section 45.[57] This conclusion is based on *In re The Initiative & Referendum Act (Manitoba)*, which posited that allowing provincial laws to be adopted or modified directly by citizens instead of the legislature was *ultra vires* section 92(1).[58] It was also confirmed *obiter dictum* in *OPSEU*.[59] Finally, provinces cannot unilaterally remove subject-matter jurisdictions from section 96 courts, which are administered by the provinces but appointed by the federal government, as determined by case law.[60]

Despite these explicit and implicit limits, the provinces do retain some flexibility in defining their internal constitutional arrangements. Section 45 mainly provides for latitude in the definition of provincial modes of representative government.[61] The provincial executive and legislative bodies are defined broadly in the Canadian Constitution, and provinces benefit from much interpretational space to articulate the details of their functioning.[62] Since the enactment of section 45, the provinces' power to amend their own constitutions has been used quite often, though not often explicitly.[63] In British Columbia, for example, the provincial constitution was modified to permit executive dominance over the scope and organization of the machinery of government.[64] In the same vein, provinces could easily amend their constitutions to put additional constraints on their executive power.[65]

One area where provinces have important constitutional discretion is in determining their electoral system, as long as they respect the democratic rights (sections 3–5) protected in the Charter.[66] Section 45 allows provinces to adopt laws on fixed election dates[67] and electoral spending limits[68] and to modify electoral boundaries. Provinces can also unilaterally amend their voting system. For example, many provinces have attempted to exchange, but without success, their single-member plurality system for a mixed-member proportional or single transferable vote system. Some authors have even suggested that provinces could adopt a modified presidential system, in which the premier would be elected separately from the legislature, as long as arrangements for consultation were made between the premier, the legislative assembly majority leader, and the lieutenant-governor.[69] This, however, arguably would affect the office of the lieutenant-governor and therefore not be permissible.

The provincial constitution amending procedure also offers flexibility in terms of shaping legislative power. Under section 92(1), the provinces have unilaterally abolished their upper houses, for example,[70] but under section 45, they could also bring them back.[71] Although jurisprudence would prohibit deliberative referendums, a province could use section 45 to put in place a system that requires the approval of the population, as well as that of the legislature, for some laws to be passed.[72] Consultative referendums, whether facultative or obligatory, could also be put in place.[73] In addition, it is possible for provinces to enact popular initiative laws,[74] such as British Columbia's.[75]

More interesting for the focus of this chapter, section 45 does not prevent provinces from adopting a new written constitution.[76] This would not necessarily involve making substantive changes to an existing provincial constitution, but, rather, consolidating existing rules in one coherent document.[77] As Campbell Sharman suggests, "more ambitiously it might involve an attempt to express broader constitutional principles either by appending explicatory preambles or by reducing matters at present left to convention to statements of positive law."[78] Furthermore, a province could decide to render its new constitution supreme, meaning that it would have primacy over other ordinary legislation. Several Canadian statutes that are considered quasi-constitutional already do this with the inclusion of a primacy clause.[79]

Section 45 does not dictate the type of majority required for a provincial constitutional amendment to pass, but it does require, at a minimum, the passing of a normal law by the legislature.[80] Nonetheless, making a provincial constitution supreme likely would require a supermajority to be passed with legitimacy. Similarly, once enacted, a supermajority might also be required to amend its provisions.[81] However, some have argued that asking for a supermajority to amend a provincial constitution could go against the rule that "that a legislature cannot bind itself or a future legislature."[82] Yet this rule is arguably no longer valid in Canada since the adoption of constitutional supremacy in 1982. Furthermore, most constitutionalists agree that requiring a supermajority for constitutional amendments is necessary for the protection of rights.[83]

The Parti Québécois Proposal for a New Quebec Constitution

To date, no province has adopted a comprehensive written constitution with primacy status. However, the desire to do so in Quebec has been present for a long time, as part of a wider nation-building strategy.[84] A new constitution would allow Quebec to express its distinctive values within the Canadian constitutional edifice, and even challenge the Canadian Constitution in certain areas of the law.[85] It could also act as an antecedent to an independent Quebec.[86] The idea of a new Quebec constitution picked up steam at the beginning of this century, but it was the crisis surrounding the debate on reasonable accommodations in 2007 that pushed the Parti Québécois to make a formal proposal for a new constitution.[87] During this period, many Quebecers felt that their values, identity, and way of life were being threatened.

The latest formal proposal for a new written Quebec constitution was made by Pauline Marois and Daniel Turp, who respectively introduced the Quebec Identity Act (Bill 195)[88] and the Quebec Constitution (Bill 196)[89] in the National Assembly. The first Bill aimed at identifying the process by which a new constitution could be enacted and the criteria for Quebec citizenship,[90] while the second was the draft of a constitution. Without the support of Jean Charest's Liberal government, both

Bills died on the order paper. Despite their fate, it is worth analysing whether Quebec could have adopted these Bills under section 45.

Bill 195 laid out the process by which an eventual Quebec constitution would be enacted. To begin, it provided that the National Assembly would be responsible for drafting the constitution: "The National Assembly must provide for the drafting of a Québec Constitution that will set forth the fundamental values of the Québec nation, establish Québec citizenship, present its national symbols, enshrine human rights and freedoms and fundamental linguistic rights, and describe Québec's parliamentary, government and judicial institutions. Such a Constitution must also provide for its own revision and ensure its own supremacy."[91]

More specifically, Bill 195 required the National Assembly to create a thirty-two-member[92] Select Committee on the Québec Constitution,[93] tasked with drafting a Quebec constitution, based on Bill 196, and to make recommendations on its entrenchment process.[94] The committee was to hold public meetings and deliberative meetings, as well as a general consultation,[95] and to report within two years of its creation to the president – equivalent to the speaker in other provincial legislatures – of the National Assembly.[96] The committee could easily have recommended that the entrenchment of a new Quebec constitution be submitted to popular approval by way of a referendum. As long as it also required the approval of the members of the National Assembly and Royal Assent, it would have been considered constitutional under section 45.

Altthough the Parti Québécois constitution proposal did not require a supermajority for its adoption, it did so for its modification. Bill 196 stated that "[a] bill to amend this Constitution may be introduced by the Prime Minister or jointly by at least 25% of the Members of the National Assembly. Such an amending bill must be supported by a two-thirds majority of Members of the National Assembly."[97] As previously mentioned, this provision could have contravened the rule that "a legislature cannot bind itself or a future legislature,"[98] but this rule likely was revoked with the adoption of constitutional supremacy in 1982. Bill 196 additionally provided for the supremacy of the new Quebec constitution,[99] which would have been permissible under section 45.

An important part of the proposed constitutional package was the entrenchment of existing fundamental laws relating to the powers of the National Assembly, the Quebec government, and the courts of justice.[100] In that sense, it did not contemplate reform of the province's mode of representative government; rather, the proposal was more interested in provincial identity-building. Bill 196 provided for the constitutional recognition of Quebec's fundamental values, citizenship, national territory, national cultural and natural heritage, national capital, official language, national symbols, and national holiday.[101] Only the enumerated fundamental values were novel here. The draft constitution notably provided that "Québec contributes to the maintenance of peace and international security. Québec supports social progress, economic development and cultural diversity throughout the world. Québec acts in accordance with the principles of human development and sustainable development."[102] It must be noted, however, that these fundamental values were declaratory in nature, and did not include substantive rights provisions.

Where the Parti Québécois constitutional proposal really tried to carve out a unique constitutional status for Quebec was in its proposal to entrench rights provisions, some of which could have conflicted with Canada's existing constitutional edifice. To begin, the preamble of Bill 196 stated that "Québec has an inalienable right to freely choose its political system and determine its legal status."[103] This right declaration was taken almost word for word from the declaration made to the same effect in An Act Respecting the Exercise of the Fundamental Rights and Prerogatives of the Québec People and the Québec State, 2000 (Bill 99).[104] This law was enacted by the National Assembly as a direct response to the *Reference re Secession of Quebec, 1998* and the federal Clarity Act, 2000, which prevent Quebec's unilateral secession from Canada and mandate the federal government to negotiate secession only in the event of a "yes" vote in referendum that has a "clear" question and a "clear" majority.[105] Instead, Bill 99 provides that Quebec can separate from Canada if a plurality of Quebecers (50 per cent + 1) vote in favour of such a move.[106] The constitutionality of Bill 99, however, is currently being challenged before the Quebec Superior Court.[107] As separation would directly affect the conditions of the union of 1867, it certainly would require more than the amending formula contained in section 45 to be effective (for more on this, see Kate Puddister, Chapter 13 in this volume).

Bill 196 also constitutionally established Quebec citizenship and specified that it would be regulated by law.[108] Concurrently, Bill 195 proposed to amend the Civil Code of Québec[109] to detail the statutory criteria for Quebec citizenship: "A person is a Québec citizen if the person (1) is a Canadian citizen and is domiciled in Québec on (insert the date of coming into force of this Act); or (2) was born in Québec after (insert the date of coming into force of this Act), or was born abroad after (insert the date of coming into force of this Act) to a parent who, at that time, was a Québec citizen."[110] Under this provision, Canadian citizens who had established domicile in Quebec after the passing of Bill 195 would not have obtained Quebec citizenship automatically, but would have had to be naturalized as Quebec citizens. The proposed law also provided, however, that naturalization was conditional not only on Canadian citizenship and six months' Quebec residency, but also on having "an appropriate knowledge of the French language," as well as knowledge of "Québec and of the responsibilities and advantages of citizenship."[111] Unilingual anglophone or allophone Canadians thus would not have been able to obtain Quebec citizenship.

Bill 195 also specified that Quebec citizens would have the right to "run in municipal, school and legislative elections," to "participate in the public funding of political parties," and to "petition the National Assembly for the redress of grievances." The proposed law was silent on whether Canadian citizens residing in Quebec without Quebec citizenship status would have been forbidden to exercise those rights.[112] If so, Bill 195 likely contravened section 3 of the Charter, which protects the right of every Canadian to run in legislative elections. It also likely contravened section 15 of the Charter, which protects equality rights. Although language is not an enumerated ground for discrimination under section 15, it has been considered an analogous ground.[113] Furthermore, although the proposed Quebec citizenship was conditional on Canadian citizenship, its establishment likely would have been *ultra vires* the powers of the National Assembly, as "naturalization" is an exclusive federal jurisdiction.[114] Therefore, Quebec would not have been able to amend its current constitution unilaterally, by way of section 45, to institute a Quebec citizenship as defined in Bill 195, but would have had to use the general amending formula found in section 38.

The Parti Québécois' constitution project proposed other important measures to promote Quebec's French language and public culture. First, it recognized Quebec as a "French-speaking nation,"[115] with the promotion of the French language to be one of its fundamental values.[116] These provisions were declaratory in nature and did not create new substantive rights that could conflict with existing language rights, such as that of the English-speaking community in Quebec. Second, Bill 196 sought to entrench sections 2 to 6 of the Charter of the French language,[117] which establish French as the official language of Quebec and lay out the fundamental right of Quebecers to a French public culture.[118] These provisions have thus far peacefully coexisted with the Canadian Constitution, and their constitutionalization is believed to be possible via section 45.

Bill 196 also provided for the constitutional entrenchment of sections 1–48 of the Quebec Charter of Human Rights and Freedoms (CHRF), which already enjoys a quasi-constitutional status. There exists no obstacle to the constitutionalization of the CHRF as it currently stands via section 45.[119] The CHRF has coexisted with the Charter for more than three decades, and the former has not been challenged on the basis of the latter.[120] Although the CHRF protects a more comprehensive set of rights than does the Charter,[121] this is permitted by section 26 of the Charter.[122]

The originality of the Parti Québécois' constitution project, however, was in its proposed adoption of a clause to guide the interpretation of the CHRF: "Those sections must be interpreted and applied with due regard for the historical heritage and fundamental values of the Québec nation and, in particular, the importance of ensuring the predominance of the French language, protecting and promoting Québec culture, guaranteeing equality between women and men, and preserving the secularity of public institutions."[123] *Prima facie*, the elements of this interpretative clause were not inconsistent with other rights provisions protected in the Canadian Constitution, and the provision could have been adopted via section 45. For example, "the importance of ensuring the predominance of the French language" was recognized in *Ford v Quebec (A.G.)*.[124] Nonetheless, certain policies that would use this interpretative clause as justification for their existence could be found unconstitutional.

One can draw a parallel between the protection of Quebec's historical heritage and fundamental values and the protection of Canada's multicultural heritage that is provided for in section 27 of the Charter.[125] Yet the protection of Quebec's historical heritage must be discussed in the context of the final report of the Bouchard-Taylor Commission on reasonable accommodations, which argued that separating state from church should have precedence over protecting the historical religious heritage of the majority.[126] It must be noted that elected officials unanimously refused the commissioners' recommendation to remove the crucifix hanging above the president's chair in the National Assembly. Several cities also rebuked the commissioners' recommendation to stop the recitation of prayers at municipal council meetings. Interestingly, the Supreme Court of Canada determined, in *Mouvement laïque québécois v Saguenay (City)*,[127] that municipal council prayers violate the freedom of conscience and religion protected in section 3 of the CHRF.[128]

Finally, the proposed interpretive clause aimed to "preserv[e] the secularity of public institutions" and to "guarante[e] equality between women and men." The term secularity, or secularism, can have different meanings. Open secularism must be distinguished from restrictive secularism. The expected outcomes of the former are "the moral equality of people," as well as "freedom of conscience and religion."[129] The "separation of church and state" and "state neutrality in respect of religious and deep-seated secular convictions" must be defined according to these ends.[130] In contrast, restrictive secularism seeks secular institutional structures at all costs, even if it means sacrificing the moral equality of people and freedom of conscience and religion.[131] The establishment of a restrictive secularism such as the Parti Québécois proposed in Bill 60 – the Charter affirming the values of State secularism and religious neutrality and of equality between women and men, and providing a framework for accommodation requests, 2013[132] – is problematic in terms of rights.

Bill 60 proposed forbidding public employees from wearing religious symbols, such as the kippa, the turban or the hijab, that overtly indicate a religious affiliation.[133] The Bill also provided that persons giving and receiving public services would have to do so with their face uncovered.[134] It additionally specified that requests for accommodations on religious grounds would have to be "consistent with the right for equality between women and men." Although Bill 60 died on the order paper following the electoral defeat of the Parti Québécois in spring 2014, it was unlikely to have withstood a constitutional challenge. First, the Supreme Court of Canada has declared that bans on religious signs in the public sphere, such as the one on kirpans in schools[135] and the one on niqabs before tribunals in certain circumstances, are unconstitutional.[136] Second, the precedence of the equality of men and women over freedom of religion goes against the "no hierarchy of constitutional rights" doctrine adopted by the Supreme Court.[137] The adoption of restrictive secular measures thus would require the section 38 amending formula as opposed to the section 45 one.

Conclusion

If Quebec were to adopt a new written constitution, it would become the only province with such a document, in that sense making Quebec stand out in the Canadian constitutional edifice.[138] Nonetheless, the amending formula found in section 45 imposes important barriers to constitutional innovation and asymmetry. It notably restricts the provinces' capacity to adopt provisions that would enhance their cultural identity – but the desire to do this is the driving force behind the idea of a Quebec constitution. As seen in the case of the Parti Québécois' constitutional proposition, Quebec would not be able unilaterally to entrench a distinct citizenship that requires the knowledge of French or a restrictive secular model. To do that, Quebec would need to pass its package with the bilateral amending formula (section 43(b)) and the general amending formula (section 38), respectively. History has shown that Quebec is unlikely to secure the support of other federal partners for its constitutional endeavours.

In sum, provinces have the capacity to enact written constitutions with primacy status. However, although consolidating existing constitutional rules in one coherent document is within reach, constitutional innovation is severely hindered by the explicit and implicit limits of the amending formula. As seen in the case of Quebec, promoting a unique provincial cultural identity through constitutional means that are at odds with Canada's cultural identity is impossible. Provinces can entrench fundamental values and identity-based rights provisions only as long as they do not violate existing Canadian ones. Section 45 only gives provinces flexibility in shaping their mode of representative democracy. Then again, provinces cannot unilaterally get rid of the Westminster parliamentary system, nor can they implement direct democracy. The provincial constitution-making power under section 45 thus participates in promoting constitutional symmetry between the provinces.

Notes

1 Constitution Act, 1982, being Schedule B to the Canada Act 1982 UK, 1982, c 11, section 41 reads:

> An amendment to the Constitution of Canada in relation to the following matters may be made by proclamation issued by the Governor General under the Great Seal of Canada only where authorized by resolutions of the Senate and House of Commons and of the legislative assembly of each province:
>
> (a) the office of the Queen, the Governor General and the Lieutenant Governor of a province;

(b) the right of a province to a number of members in the House of Commons not less than the number of Senators by which the province is entitled to be represented at the time this Part comes into force;
(c) subject to section 43, the use of the English or the French language;
(d) the composition of the Supreme Court of Canada; and
(e) an amendment to this Part.

2 The Constitution Act, RSBC 1979, c 62; see Campbell Sharman, "The Strange Case of a Provincial Constitution: The British Columbia *Constitutional Act*," *Canadian Journal of Political Science* 17, no. 1 (1984): 87–108.
3 *Ontario (A.G.) v OPSEU*, [1987] 2 SCR 2, 41 DLR (4th) 1, paras 83–5.
4 Constitution Act, 1867, 30 & 31 Victoria, c 3 (UK), preamble.
5 Daniel Turp, "La constitution québécoise: une perspective historique," *Revue québécoise de droit constitutionnel* 2 (2008): 22; Gerald Baier, "Canada: Federal and Subnational Constitutional Practices," in *Constitutional Dynamics in Federal Systems: Sub-national Perspectives*, ed. Michael Burgess and G. Alan Tarr, 174–92 (Montreal; Kingston, ON: McGill-Queen's University Press, 2012), 176.
6 *OPSEU*, para. 85; Michael Burgess and G. Alan Tarr, "Introduction: Subnational Constitutionalism and Constitutional Development," in *Constitutional Dynamics in Federal Systems: Sub-national Perspectives*, ed. Michael Burgess and G. Alan Tarr, 3–40 (Montreal; Kingston, ON: McGill-Queen's University Press, 2012), 5; Nelson Wiseman, "In Search of a Quebec Constitution," *Revue québécoise de droit constitutionnel* 2 (2008): 130; idem, "Clarifying Provincial Constitutions," *National Journal of Constitutional Law* 6 (1996): 272.
7 Sharman, "Strange Case," 88.
8 See ibid., 90; Turp, "Constitution québécoise," 22; Baier, "Canada," 181; Burgess and Tarr, Introduction," 5.
9 *OPSEU*, para. 83.
10 Christian L. Wiktor and Guy Tanguay, eds., *Constitutions of Canada: Federal and Provincial* (Dobbs Ferry, NY: Oceana, 1987).
11 Maxime St-Hilaire, "The Codification of Human Rights in Canada," *Revue de Droit, Université de Sherbrooke* 42 (2012): 543; Wiktor and Tanguay, *Constitutions of Canada*.
12 St-Hilaire, "Codification of Human Rights," 543.
13 Sharman, "Strange Case," 88–90; Turp, "Constitution québécoise," 22; Jacques-Yvan Morin, "Une constitution nouvelle pour le Québec: le pourquoi, le contenu et le comment," *Revue québécoise de droit constitutionnel* 2 (2008): 6.
14 Constitution Act, 1867, sections 58–90.
15 [1986] AC 600 (PC).

16 Sharman, "Strange Case," 88–9.
17 Ibid., 89; Sharman mentions the power of reservation (section 90), the power of disallowance (sections 56 and 62), and the declaratory power (section 92(10)(c)). Also worth mentioning is the Peace, Order and Good Government clause (section 91), as well as the Parliament of Canada's power to intervene in provincial affairs to protect denominational rights (section 93(4)).
18 See Baier, "Canada," 179.
19 Burgess and Tarr, "Introduction," 4–5; Wiseman, "In Search of a Quebec Constitution," 138; Baier, "Canada," 177–8.
20 See Baier, "Canada," 178–9; Wiseman, "In Search of a Quebec Constitution," 138; Burgess and Tarr, "Introduction," 5.
21 See Sharman, "Strange Case," 89–90.
22 Constitution Act, 1867, preamble. See Sharman, "Strange Case," 90; Burgess and Tarr, "Introduction," 5.
23 Wiseman, "In Search of a Quebec Constitution," 136–7; idem, "Clarifying Provincial Constitutions," 275; Morin, "Constitution nouvelle pour le Québec," 5.
24 Manitoba Act, 1870, RSC 1970, App II; Order in Council admitting British Columbia into the Union, dated the 16th Day of May, 1871; Order of Her Majesty in Council admitting Prince Edward Island in the Union, dated the 26th day of June, 1873; Saskatchewan Act, 1905, 4–5 Edw VII, c 42 (Can); Alberta Act, 1905, 4–5 Edw Vii, c 3 (Can); British North America Act, 1949, 12–13 Geo VI, c 22 (UK).
25 Baier, "Canada," 178; Wiseman, "In Search of a Quebec Constitution," 136–7; idem, "Clarifying Provincial Constitutions," 278–9.
26 See Wiseman, "Clarifying Provincial Constitutions," 279.
27 Constitution Act, 1867, section 133; Manitoba Act, 1970, section 23.
28 Constitution Act, 1867, section 93(2).
29 Sharman, "Strange Case," 105; Baier, "Canada," 175.
30 Wiseman, "Clarifying Provincial Constitutions," 293; idem, "In Search of a Quebec Constitution," 138.
31 Amendments made under the Constitution Act, 1982, section 41 require the approval of the House of Commons, the Senate, and every provincial legislature.
32 Benoît Pelletier, *La modification constitutionnelle au Canada* (Scarborough, ON: Carswell, 1996), 133; Peter W. Hogg, *Constitutional Law of Canada*, Student ed. (Scarborough, ON: Carswell, 2012), 4–33; Warren J. Newman, "Living with the Amending Procedures: Prospects for Future Constitutional Reform in Canada," in *A Living Tree: The Legacy of 1982 in*

Canada's Political Evolution, ed. Graeme Mitchell et al. (Markham, ON: LexisNexis, 2007), 753–4.

33 *Bureau métropolitain des écoles protestantes de Montréal v Ministre de l'Éducation du Québec,* [1976] CS 430, 83 DLR (3d).

34 In re Initiative and Referendum Act, [1919] AC 935.

35 [1985] 1 SCR 721, 19 DLR (4th) 1, para. 135 [*Manitoba Language Rights*].

36 Pelletier, *Modification constitutionnelle,* 148.

37 *OPSEU,* para. 108.

38 Pelletier, *Modification constitutionnelle,* 148–9; *A.G. of Quebec v Blaikie et al.,* [1979] 2 SCR 1016, [1979] 101 D.L.R. (3rd) 394, 1024.

39 *Blaikie; Manitoba Language Rights.*

40 Pelletier, *Modification constitutionnelle,* 143–5.

41 See, for example, André Braën, "Les recours en matière de droits linguistiques," in *Les droits linguistiques au Canada,* ed. Michel Bastarache et al. (Montreal: Yvon Blais, 1986), 503–4; Jacques-Yvan Morin and José Woehrling, *Les constitutions du Canada et du Québec (du régime français à nos jours),* 2nd ed., vol. 1 (Montreal: Thémis, 1992), 520.

42 See Charles-Emmanuel Côté and Guy Tremblay, "Un remède durable." *La Presse* [Montreal], 24 November 2009; Guy Tremblay, "La portée élargie de la procédure bilatérale de modification de la constitution," *Revue générale de droit* 41, no. 2 (2011): 417–49.

43 The Constitution Act, 1982, section 38(1) reads: "An amendment to the Constitution of Canada may be made by proclamation issued by the Governor General under the Great Seal of Canada where so authorized by (*a*) resolutions of the Senate and House of Commons; and (*b*) resolutions of the legislative assemblies of at least two-thirds of the provinces that have, in the aggregate, according to the then latest general census, at least fifty per cent of the population of all the provinces."

44 See, for example, Pelletier, *Modification constitutionnelle,* 138–9; Henri Brun and Guy Tremblay, *Droit constitutionnel,* 2nd ed. (Cowansville, QC: Yvon Blais, 1990), 754.

45 Pelletier, *Modification constitutionnelle,* 139.

46 Ibid., 140–1. In *Jones v A.G. of New Brunswick,* [1975] 2 SCR 182, 45 DLR (3d) 583, paras 192–3, this power was recognized as that of the federal government under the Constitution Act, 1867, s. 91(1).

47 Newman, "Living with the Amending Procedures," 754; Wiseman, "Clarifying Provincial Constitutions," 283; Pelletier, *Modification constitutionnelle,* 130–3.

48 *Blaikie,* 1026–7.

49 Ibid., 1025.

50 *Reference re Bill 30, An Act to Amend the Education Act (Ont.)*, [1987] 1 SCR 1148, 40 DLR (4th) 18, para. 29.
51 Pelletier, *Modification constitutionnelle*, 167–79.
52 *OPSEU*, para. 88.
53 [1998] 2 SCR 217, 161 DLR (4th) 385 [*Secession Reference*].
54 Pelletier, *Modification constitutionnelle*, 154.
55 See, for example, *Reference re Remuneration of Judges of the Provincial Court (P.E.I.)*, [1998] 1 SCR 3, 155 DLR (4th) 1.
56 Pelletier, *Modification constitutionnelle*, 150–3.
57 Ibid., 161–2.
58 *In re The Initiative & Referendum Act (Manitoba)*, [1916] 27 Man R 1 (CA Man).
59 *OPSEU*, para. 111.
60 See *Re Residential Tenancies Act, 1979*, [1981] 1 SCR 714, 123 DLR (3d) 554; *McEvoy v Attorney General for New Brunswick et al.*, [1983] 1 SCR 704, [1983] SCJ No 51 (QL); *MacMillan Bloedel Ltd. c. Simpson*, [1995] 4 SCR 725, 130 DLR (4th) 385.
61 Sharman, "Strange Case," 90.
62 Ibid.
63 Guy Régimbald and Dwight Newman, *The Law of the Canadian Constitution*, 1st ed. (Markham, ON: LexisNexis, 2013), 35; Wiseman, "Clarifying Provincial Constitutions," 280–1.
64 Sharman, "Strange Case," 105.
65 Gerald Baier, "Canada," 183.
66 Sharman, "Strange Case," 106; Baier, "Canada," 183–4; Wiseman, "In Search of a Quebec Constitution," 147.
67 Régimbald and Newman, *Law of the Canadian Constitution*, 35; Some Canadian provinces have amended their constitutions to adopt fixed election dates laws. See Constitution (Fixed Election Dates) Amendment Act, 2001, SBC 2001, c 36; An Act to amend the Election Act for the purpose of establishing fixed-date elections, RSQ 2013, c 13.
68 Pelletier, *Modification constitutionnelle*, 158–9.
69 Sharman, "Strange Case," 106; Wiseman, "In Search of a Quebec Constitution," 147.
70 Newman, "Living with the Amending Procedures," 754; Sharman, "Strange Case," 105; Wiseman, "Clarifying Provincial Constitutions," 280–1; Pelletier, *Modification constitutionnelle*, 160.
71 *Reference re Authority of Parliament in relation to the Upper House*, [1980] 1 SCR 54, 74; see Pelletier, *Modification constitutionnelle*.
72 Pelletier, *Modification constitutionnelle*, 164; Sharman, "Strange Case," 105; Baier, "Canada," 180.

73 Ibid.
74 Pelletier, *modification constitutionnelle*, 165; Sharman, "Strange Case," 105.
75 Recall and Initiative Act, RSBC 1996, c 398.
76 Turp, "Constitution québécoise," 16–17; Sharman, "Strange Case," 106.
77 Sharman, "Strange Case," 106–7.
78 Ibid., 107.
79 See St-Hilaire, "Codification of Human Rights," 543–52.
80 Wiseman, "Clarifying Provincial Constitutions," 280.
81 Baier, "Canada," 186.
82 Wiseman, "In Search of a Quebec Constitution," 145.
83 Ibid.
84 For a history of proposed constitutions in Quebec, see Morin, "Nouvelle constitution"; Turp, "Constitution québécoise."
85 Morin, "Nouvelle constitution."
86 Wiseman, "In Search of a Quebec Constitution," 136.
87 Turp, "Constitution québécoise."
88 Bill 195, Québec Identity Act, 1st Sess, 38th Leg, 2007 (first reading 18 Octobre 2007).
89 Bill 196, Québec Constitution, 1st Sess, 38th Leg, 2007 (first reading 18 Octobre 2007).
90 Bill 195 also suggested measures to strengthen the Charter of the French Language, LRQ, c C-11, to better integrate newcomers into Quebec's culture, and to consolidate the French and Quebec history school curriculum.
91 Bill 195, section 2.
92 Ibid., section 5, reads:

> The Committee is to consist of 32 members, namely,
>
> (1) 16 Members of the National Assembly appointed by the recognized parliamentary groups proportionately to their representation in the National Assembly; and
> (2) 16 civil society representatives, with each parliamentary group appointing the same number of civil society representatives as it did Members of the National Assembly under subparagraph 1.
>
> Each of the groups mentioned in the first paragraph must consist of an equal number of women and men.
>
> A list of the Committee members is to be submitted by the parliamentary groups to the President of the National Assembly not later than seven days after the coming into force of this Act.
>
> The Committee is to be co-chaired by a woman and a man. The Committee members are to designate one co-chair from among the Members of the National Assembly and one from among the civil society representatives.

93   Ibid., section 3.
94   Ibid., section 4.
95   Ibid., section 6.
96   Ibid., section 8.
97   Bill 196, section 13.
98   Wiseman, "In Search of a Quebec Constitution," 145.
99   Bill 196, section 14.
100 Ibid., sections 9–12.
101 Ibid., sections 1–7.
102 Ibid., section 1.
103 Wiseman also sees this provision as problematic for the same reasons; see "In Search of a Quebec Constitution," 143.
104 An Act Respecting the Exercise of the Fundamental Rights and Prerogatives of the Québec People and the Québec State, LRQ, c E-20.2, section 2.
105 *Secession Reference*; Clarity Act, SC 2000, c 26.
106 Fundamental Rights and Prerogatives of the Québec People, sections 3–4.
107 "Harper government joins court challenge of Quebec's right to secede," *CBC News*, 19 October 2013, available online at http://www.cbc.ca/news/canada/montreal/harper-government-joins-court-challenge-of-quebec-s-right-to-secede-1.2126690.
108 Bill 196, section 2.
109 Civil Code of Québec, LRQ, c C-1991.
110 Bill 195, section 10.
111 Ibid.
112 During the 2012 Quebec election campaign, the leader of the Parti Québécois, Pauline Marois, revived her idea to establish a Quebec citizenship conditional on an appropriate knowledge of French. She wanted to prevent newcomers, Aboriginals, and anglophones from running for office if they did not have an appropriate knowledge of French.
113 *Entreprises W.F.H. Ltée v Québec (Procureure Générale du)*, [2001] RJQ 2557, paras 90–1.
114 Constitution Act, 1867, section 91(25).
115 Bill 196, preamble.
116 Ibid., section 1.
117 Ibid., section 8.
118 Charter of the French Language, sections 2–6, reads:

   1. French is the official language of Québec.
   2. Every person has a right to have the civil administration, the health services and social services, the public utility enterprises, the professional

orders, the associations of employees and all enterprises doing business in Québec communicate with him in French.

3. In deliberative assembly, every person has a right to speak in French.
4. Workers have a right to carry on their activities in French.
5. Consumers of goods and services have a right to be informed and served in French.
6. Every person eligible for instruction in Québec has a right to receive that instruction in French.

119 David Sneiderman, "Dual(ling) Charters: The Harmonics of Rights in Canada and Quebec," *Ottawa Law Review* 24, no. 1 (1992): 235–63.
120 For a discussion on the compatibility of the two charters, see Schneiderman, "Dual(ling) Charters"; St-Hilaire, "Codification of Human Rights."
121 For a discussion on the additional rights protected by the CHRF, see St-Hilaire, "Codification of Human Rights," 551.
122 Part I of the Constitution Act, 1982, being Schedule B to the Canada Act 1982 (UK), 1982, c 11 [Charter], section 26 reads: "The guarantee in this Charter of certain rights and freedoms shall not be construed as denying the existence of any other rights or freedoms that exist in Canada."
123 Bill 196, section 8.
124 [1988] 2 SCR 712, 54 DLR (4th) 577.
125 Section 27 of the Charter reads: "This Charter shall be interpreted in a manner consistent with the preservation and enhancement of the multicultural heritage of Canadians."
126 Gérard Bouchard and Charles Taylor, *Building the Future: A Time for a Reconciliation* (Quebec City: Commission de consultation sur les pratiques d'accommodement reliées aux différences culturelles, 2008).
127 *Mouvement laïque québécois v Saguenay (City)*, 2015 SCC 16.
128 In May 2013, the Quebec Court of Appeal upheld the City of Saguenay's municipal prayer in *Saguenay (Ville de) v Mouvement laïque québécois*, 2013 QCCA 936.
129 Bouchard and Taylor, *Building the Future*, 20.
130 Ibid.
131 Ibid.
132 Bill 60, Charter affirming the values of State secularism and religious neutrality and of equality between women and men, and providing a framework for accommodation requests, 1st Sess, 40th Leg, 2007 (first reading 7 November 2013).
133 Ibid., section 5.
134 Ibid., sections 6–7.

135 *Multani v Commission scolaire Marguerite-Bourgeoys*, [2006] 1 SCR 256, 2006 SCC 6.
136 *R. v N.S.*, [2012] 3 SCR 726, 2012 SCC 72.
137 Mark Carter, "An Analysis of the 'No Hierarchy of Constitutional Rights' Doctrine," *Review of Constitutional Studies* 12, no. 1 (2007): 19–51.
138 Wiseman, "In Search of a Quebec Constitution," 148; Baier, "Canada," 188.

9   The End of Informal Constitutional Change in Canada?

DENNIS BAKER AND MARK D. JARVIS

In its spring 2014 session, the Supreme Court of Canada delivered two blockbuster reference opinions regarding the amendment of the Constitution of Canada. With the *Reference re Supreme Court Act, ss. 5 and 6* and *Reference re Senate Reform*, the Court effectively constrained the practice of informal constitutional change – addressing constitutional controversies through ordinary statutes – that had taken root in the years since the last formal multiparty attempt to amend the Constitution of Canada (1992's Charlottetown Accord). The Court curbed this practice of informal change both by insisting that the formal process be used and by making informal change much more uncertain. Whereas one might have hoped that these decisions – the first to fully interpret Part V of the Constitution Act, 1982 since its enactment – would provide clarity, one might argue that they have instead left Canadians with a confused approach to constitutional amendment that is likely to inhibit change of any sort.

In this chapter, we discuss the emergence of informal constitutional change in Canada, the advantages and disadvantages of such approaches, the prospects for informal "amendments" in light of the Supreme Court's bolstering of the formal amending process, and, finally, some lessons learned from the informal process that may help proponents of constitutional reform meet the high threshold of the newly resurgent formal process. Our position is that the Supreme Court's recent decisions will have a "chilling effect," at least for the near-to-medium term, on informal constitutional change, leaving formal amendment as the sole avenue for constitutional reform in the immediate future. In the longer term, it is not likely to signal a complete end to informal adaptation because such statutes can be politically advantageous. If informal constitutional change is to continue, we conclude with some "basic principles" that might better govern such acts. If formal change remains "off the table" to avoid the political instability and national discord that characterized the Meech Lake and Charlottetown processes, and if there is a retreat from informal constitutional change, then we are left with a Constitution that is adaptable only through the decisions of the Supreme Court of Canada. We discuss the consequences of exclusive judicial control of constitutional development throughout the chapter.

Informal Constitutional Change

If a constitution is codified as a written document or documents, it should contain some explicit means of altering or adding to it. Unless one expects a constitution to arrive fully formed, perfect, and timeless at the time of its inception, it will be necessary to have some formal process of amendment. The importance of having such a clause is particularly well understood in Canada. For almost a half-century, the patriation of the Canadian Constitution from the United Kingdom was delayed largely because the provinces and federal governments failed to agree upon an amending formula. Assisted by a Supreme Court decision that recommended a convention-based amending formula (the "substantial consent" of the provinces) that would never be used again, the federal Parliament and the provinces (with the exception of Quebec) agreed to what is now Part V of the Constitution Act, 1982. This part provides five different amending formulas prescribing different procedures depending on the subject of the amendment (see the Appendix).

Canadian political elites have shown very little appetite for "opening the Constitution" – that is, using sections 38 and 41, the "general" and "unanimity" procedures, respectively – and routinely shy away from even the suggestion of formal constitutional change. Indeed, this was clearly part of the federal government's strategy for Senate reform, and the Supreme Court's decision has done little to make formal amendment more palatable. Responding to the *Senate Reform* decision, Prime Minister Harper called it "a decision for the status quo" since there "is no desire of anyone to reopen the constitution and have a bunch of constitutional negotiations."[1]

Such antipathy to the prospect of formal amendment is not restricted to the Senate issue, but more generally reflects a Canadian disposition against constitutional negotiations of any sort. Some scholars even go so far as to conclude that the Canadian Constitution is now "constructively unamendable."[2] John Whyte suggests that "few political realities are better understood than the virtual impossibility of constitutional reform, including reform that might be considered nothing more than constitutional modernization."[3] At the root of this aversion to formal change is the fear of opening the "Pandora's Box" of constitutional complaints that inevitably lead to the horse-trading and compromises that characterized the Meech Lake and Charlottetown accords. The instability and national discord that marked that era mean that suggestions for constitutional reform are often rejected even before considering their merits, precluding even minor democratic reforms.

Given how few changes are actually attempted, one might suggest that this amounts to an unwarranted degree of defeatism on the part of Canada's leaders. Nevertheless, the record of recent formal constitutional amendment is clear. Although there have been eleven amendments since 1982, two were unilateral amendments adjusting the apportionment of seats in the House of Commons and eight were bilateral amendments that affected only a single province (five of them altered provincial school systems, for example). Other than these discrete unilateral or bilateral amendments, formal amendment essentially has been abandoned in Canada in the wake of the failed megaconstitutional negotiations of the late 1980s and early 1990s. Since Part V was enacted in 1982, the general amending formula (section 38) has been used successfully only once: in 1983, primarily to satisfy a requirement of the 1982 Act that a constitutional conference on Aboriginal rights be held. There have been no successful uses of the unanimity formula (section 41) to amend the Constitution on matters of national significance, although matters requiring constitutional attention arose in this period. Indeed, the post-Charlottetown environment, which included a divisive referendum on Quebec secession, left plenty of issues in need of resolution. Although constitutions are meant to provide continuity and to persist in the face of temporary passions, even the most-well-devised constitutions require "housekeeping" to keep abreast of technological and social change.

What the record of formal inactivity suggests is that the management, if not the resolution, of these controversies or necessary modernizations has taken a different 'informal' form. In the US context, scholars have argued that the substance of that country's Constitution has changed dramatically without any correlative amendment to the text.[4] As Heather Gerken suggests, constitutional change is "hydraulic": where the unavailability of formal constitutional change "effectively redirects those constitutional energies into different, potentially more productive" informal measures.[5] Richard Albert identifies a number of phenomena that might be considered "functionally equivalent to a formal amendment" – namely, "informal amendment by executive action, major legislation, judicial interpretation, political practice, treaty, and by extracanonical norms."[6]

In the Canadian context three obvious alternatives to formal constitutional change present themselves: (1) judicial amendment through interpretation; (2) the employment of constitutional conventions; and (3), perhaps most controversially, constitutional change through ordinary statutory enactment. All three alternatives share an explicit *informality*. To be considered *informal* means that such changes must not contradict what is actually in the formal Constitution.[7] If the Constitution declares "x," the informal measure can never say "not x." For example, in order for a judicial interpretation to be legitimately *interpretive*, the judicial application must be grounded in the wording of the Constitution, and, even if it is an expansion or elaboration of that wording, it can never expressly contradict that text. Although there is some controversy over whether conventions can alter the formal legal rules of the Constitution,[8] the orthodox position is that conventions must yield to the legal authority of the formal written parts of the Constitution. With respect to statutes, by virtue of section 52(1) of the Constitution Act, 1982, any statute that is "inconsistent" with the Constitution is "of no force or effect."

But prohibiting such explicit conflicts still leaves ample scope for informal measures to add, modify, or clarify the formal Constitution. Judicial interpretations sometimes take this form by expanding upon the constitutional language to apply it to a particular case or controversy. Similarly, conventions contextualize the formal Constitution by adding an extra layer of agreed-upon rules by political actors that, while remaining legally unenforceable – thus always remaining subject to the written Constitution – can govern political behaviour and produce outcomes in a fashion virtually indistinguishable from the legal authority of the formal Constitution. It is within this matrix of informality that we ask whether ordinary statutes might also play a role in constitutional change.

This is not an abstract question. Canadian political actors frequently have resorted to statutory instruments to address constitutional controversies. Robert Hawkins has provocatively called such statutes "constitutional workarounds."[9] For Hawkins, workarounds "seek a *de facto* constitutional change without following the formal constitutional process for achieving such a change."[10] Hawkins identifies three different forms of workarounds: formula shopping (that is, seeking an amending formula that demands no or less provincial consent), ordinary legislation (where attempting constitutional change is attempted via a simple statutory change), and declaratory statements (where constitutional-style change is sought by declaring how the executive branch should exercise its constitutionally granted powers). He outlines a series of examples of each type of workaround. These workarounds have included attempts to "loan" the federal veto over constitutional change to the regions, recognition of Quebec as a nation, fixed-election-date legislation, and, repeated – and now failed – attempts to reform the Senate, as well as recent legislation aimed at altering the line of Royal succession in Canada. Table 9.1 summarizes each of these informal changes.

In this chapter, we focus primarily on the discussion of "ordinary" statutes that purport to remedy apparent constitutional deficiencies, but we also recognize that some of these statutes incorporate elements of "formula shopping" or "declaratory statements." Although we appreciate Warren Newman's insistence on distinguishing between resolutions and legislation (see his chapter, in this volume), we question whether it is possible to make such "bright line" distinctions when resolutions might be as politically enforceable as a convention – but we share Newman's desire for clarity and its importance in identifying legal effect. Newman suggests some additional "organic" legislation that takes on a quasi-constitutional form, and we are mindful that the table – largely based on the measures discussed in Hawkins's article – might not capture the full extent of statutory measures that have some constitutional grounding. Finally, we hesitate in adopting Hawkins's terminology because "workaround" might imply all such actions are illegitimate; they are better described as informal constitutional changes, and judged on their merits.

In addition to the measures listed in Table 9.1, the potential for further informal changes seems strong, at least prior to the most recent Supreme Court decisions, and particularly in the area of parliamentary practices. For example, in March 2013, Ontario MPP Catherine Fife (NDP) introduced a private member's bill explicit aimed at restricting the ability of Ontario premiers to advise the lieutenant-governor to prorogue unilaterally without the legislature's consent. The bill further required the premier to advise the lieutenant-governor "to call it back within the time frame set out in the Assembly's resolution." A motion similar to Fife's bill was tabled at the federal level in 2010 by Jack Layton. Fife's bill, like Harper's Fixed Election Date Act, declared that nothing in it "alters or abridges the powers of the Crown, including the power

Table 9.1 Examples of Informal Constitutional Changes

Informal Change	Mechanism	Description
Quebec's status as a distinct society	Declaratory statements	The House of Commons passed declarations recognizing Quebec's unique status in Canada on three occasions between 1995 and 2006. On 11 December 1995, the House adopted a motion recognizing the "French-speaking majority, unique culture and civil law tradition" made Quebec "a distinct society within Canada." On 25 November 1997, the House passed a motion endorsing the Calgary Declaration. And, on 27 November 2006, the House passed a motion put forward by the Harper government that recognized "that the Québécois form a nation within a united Canada."
Federal spending power	Declaratory statements	Several declaratory statements have been made since 1995 circumscribing the federal government's spending power in areas of provincial jurisdiction, ascribing conditions for exceptions, and establishing allowances for opting out of cost-sharing programs.
Regional veto statute	Statutory	An Act respecting constitutional amendments, SC 1996, c 1, commonly referred to as the "regional veto" statute. The Act effectively shares the veto power granted to the House of Commons via section 38 of the general amending formula with the regions of Canada, including Quebec.
Clarity Act	Statutory	An Act to give effect to the requirement for clarity as set out in the opinion of the Supreme Court of Canada in the *Quebec Secession Reference*, SC 2000, c 26, commonly referred to as the "Clarity Act." The Act empowered the House of Commons to determine whether both the question and results of any referendum were sufficiently clear to initiate secession negotiations.
Fixed-Date Election Act	Statutory	An Act to amend the Canada Elections Act, SC 2006, c 16, commonly referred to as the "Fixed Date Election Act." The Act sets future election dates in the fourth year following the previous general election without binding the governor general's discretion to dissolve Parliament.
House of Commons prorogation	Declaratory statements	In 2010 the House of Commons passed a motion declaring "the prime minister shall not advise the Governor General to prorogue any session of any Parliament for longer than seven calendar days without a specific resolution of this House of Commons to support such a prorogation." This motion has already been ignored: in the fall of 2013 the House of Commons was prorogued for thirty days, delaying its return from summer recess.

Senatorial term limits constitutional amendment	Formula shopping	Bill C-10, An Act to amend the Constitution Act, 1867 (Senate Term Limits), introduced in the House of Commons, 29 March 2010, died with the dissolution of the 40th Parliament on 26 March 2011. The relevant provisions of the Bill would have limited senators to a single term of eight years. The government held that section 44 was an appropriate amending formula because term length was not one of the four noted exceptions to its use regarding the Senate.
Senatorial Selection Bill	Statutory	Bill S-8, An Act respecting the selection of senators (Senatorial Selection Act), introduced in the Senate on 27 April 2010, died with the dissolution of the 40th Parliament on 26 March 2011. The Bill would have provided a framework for provinces to hold consultative elections to fill vacant Senate seats, which the prime minister would have been obliged to consider but not follow.
Succession to Throne Act	Statutory	An Act, introduced in 2013, intended to amend the line of succession to the Canadian throne to end sexual discrimination by assenting to the Succession to the Crown Bill passed by the UK Parliament.
Supreme Court Act, ss. 5.1 and 6.1	Declaratory provisions	Enacted as part of the omnibus Economic Action Plan 2013 Act (Bill C-4), these provisions sought to provide "greater certainty" that candidates for judicial office were qualified if they had been a member of a bar of a province for ten years "at any time."
Governor General Appointment and Removal Procedure Act	Statutory	A private member's bill introduced in 2014 that seeks to formalize the use of an advisory committee to make nonbinding recommendations to the prime minister on the selection of governors general and to introduce a procedure for removing governors general from office.

to prorogue, dissolve or summon the Legislature." And like the Fixed Election Date Act, it is not clear if Fife's bill would actually have bound any of the relevant actors – including the premier.[11] Instead of a statutory change, a clearer and more effective mechanism for reform would be an explicit constitutional amendment, via the provincial amending formula (section 45). Even then, section 41 – which requires unanimity to change the office of the lieutenant-governor – might stand in the way of a formal unilateral amendment by the province.

Beyond the most obvious advantage informal constitutional change presents – that it is achievable! – statutory measures can be useful in other ways. First, they could address "symbolic" concerns that might not require the force of a legally binding amendment. For example, the November 2006 motion in the House of Commons recognizing "that the Québécois form a nation within a united Canada" arguably deflated some sovereigntist rhetoric, or at least that of the Bloc Québécois, which was agitating for a similar motion.[12] The motion met what many of the proponents recognizing Quebec as a "distinct society" had sought: formal recognition without any actual legal effect. Although the motion might have fallen short of constitutional recognition, the agreed-upon formulation in the Charlottetown Accord was as an "interpretive clause" that was expressly designed not to derogate from the "powers, rights and privileges" of any government actor. It might not have had the same impact on judicial interpretations of rights, but the 2006 motion came very close to meeting the "constitutional recognition" aspects demanded by proponents of Charlottetown.

Second, these informal measures are not "permanent," and thus allow for experimentation and modification with relative ease. Unlike formal constitutional amendments, which are in most areas nearly impossible to attain, legislative and declaratory amendments can be modified or retracted more simply. This could mean introducing constitutional-like changes for periods of time and/or facilitating the adoption of different approaches in different subnational jurisdictions to observe what impact the changes have before formally adopting constitutional changes or revising the statutes.

For example, Fife's bill aimed at preventing governments from unilaterally suspending the legislature to escape scrutiny. However, because the bill required only a simple majority to pass a motion sanctioning prorogation, the norms of party discipline virtually guarantee that a majority government would be able to meet this threshold, supplanting the intent of the bill. Although the first-past-the-post electoral system can lead to some particularly large majority governments,[13] a two-thirds majority threshold would help ensure that at least one other party would have to support a premier's request to prorogue in most instances. Where prorogation was routine, gaining the necessary support from the opposition might not be difficult. But if prorogation were to be used as a partisan tool, as it was by the McGuinty government, the opposition might be able to block an abusive government.[14] If the bill passed as written and a majority government in Ontario followed McGuinty's example of suspending the legislature to avoid scrutiny, it would be easy for a new legislature to bolster the law to enact a more suitable threshold.

Third, informal constitutional-like changes can lead to more traditional constitutional change if they alter the political expectations of actors such that the political consequences of deviating from them essentially amount to the same certainty that a legally binding amendment would provide. In this way, informal constitutional change can set the stage for the establishment of constitutional conventions. Because conventions are not legally enforceable, they rely on shared understanding and are only politically "binding." The Supreme Court has adopted Sir Ivor Jennings's (1959) three-part test for identifying a convention: there must be at least one previous case where the rule appeared to be enacted (a precedent), the actors involved in the situation must have believed themselves to be bound by the rule, and there is a reason for the rule's existence. In light of the Court's uneven experience with Jennings's test (particularly its dubious *Quebec Veto* decision of 1982),[15] alternative formulations have been sought. Andrew Heard, for example, argues that conventions do not actually demand a precedent, but can be born simply of "express agreement of the main political actors."[16] Despite the uncertain path to becoming a formal convention, informal changes through statutes[17] or declaratory devices (such as cabinet manuals) can serve as a good first step towards establishing or clarifying the "rules" through a broad, shared understanding – especially where an effort is made to seek the explicit agreement of the relevant political actors. Statutes such as the ones we are discussing, if followed over time, could attain conventional status. Once again, though, the line between informal and formal change becomes difficult to identify.

All that said, the statutory approach has some obvious weaknesses – primarily that, without being legally binding, they may be abandoned when they are politically inconvenient. Moreover, attempts to avoid the formal constitutional mechanism might distort both policies and principles in pursuit of an easier enactment. The fixed-election-date law reveals the potential to use statutes in place of formal constitutional change to engender confusion, and even cynicism, with respect to fundamental aspects of our democratic system. Further, recent events have demonstrated how a breakdown in shared understanding over conventions can weaken, if not jettison entirely, their utility. Debates over the existence of conventions, what they actually require, and how and when they evolve might undermine the ability of conventions to bind the behaviour of actors or potentially reduce the political consequences of breaching them.[18]

The Supreme Court and the End of Informal Constitutional Change

With its most recent decisions, the Supreme Court of Canada has significantly altered the viability of informal constitutional change. By exhibiting an ambivalence regarding the relationship between substance and form, and by tilting the table towards formal amendment over informal adjustment, the Court has not only narrowed the potential for future informal changes; it has also cast doubt upon existing measures. The net effect has been to reassert the pre-eminence of formal change under Part V.

Such an approach is not necessarily problematic: strict adherence to the formalities of Part V at least would clarify the "rules of the game." Writing prior to the delivery of the *Senate Reference*, Warren Newman argued that Part V "is fundamentally a rules-based part of the Constitution; its provisions are not openly and broadly textured, or inviting infinite variations on some impressionist theme."[19] Actors must "be able to understand just what the scope and ambit of the rules are: the procedural rules must, in principle, be cognizable in advance, so that rational actors can plan their proposed reforms and devote their energy and public resources accordingly."[20] Strict formality, in theory, could achieve these ends by having actors adjust their expectations accordingly.

But the Court did not restrict itself to constitutional formalities. While not "inviting infinite variations," the *Senate Reference* and the *Supreme Court Act Reference* – particularly when considered in combination – are "openly and broadly textured." According to the Court, constitutional documents, including Part V, must "be interpreted in a broad and purposive manner and placed in their proper linguistic, philosophic, and historical contexts."[21] Using this approach, the Court generally favoured expanding Part V's domain; so, "Composition of the Supreme Court" in section 41(d) now includes all "eligibility requirements" and the "method of selecting Senators" in section 42(b) "includes more than the formal appointment."[22] And once we accept that Court's view that "the Constitution should not be viewed as a mere collection of discrete textual provisions,"[22] we have all but conceded a judicial liberty to intervene even when the constitutional text does not support it. Indeed, the meta-rule seems to be whether the Court deems a change to be mere "housekeeping" or a "fundamental" change.[23] Here "context" is likely to collapse into whether a change is desirable or not:[24] a change that is consistent with one's understanding of the underlying principles is more likely to be "housekeeping" and a change – no matter how minor – that runs contrary to that understanding is likely to be seen as part of a "fundamental" shift.

Compare the fates of the property qualifications for senatorial appointments in section 23(4) of the BNA Act, 1867 with sections 6 and 6.1 of the Supreme Court Act. The "net worth" requirement in section 23(4) requires senators to hold $4,000 in property. In 1867 the provision was obviously meant to ensure that senators were to be drawn from the "moneyed class"; for Canadians today, the requirement is obviously too low to achieve that purpose, but also contrary to the modern sense that wealth should not be a precondition for public service. A Court insistent on enforcing the constitutional text could easily interpret the clause "purposively" – and here there is an absolutely clear purpose of ensuring that senators came from the moneyed class – by simply updating the amount to an equivalent sum, taking inflation into account. The Court explains, however, that the repeal of section 23(4) is "precisely the type of amendment that the framers … intended to capture under s. 44" because "[i]t updates the constitutional framework relating to the Senate without affecting the institution's fundamental nature and role."[25] Why is the abandonment of the moneyed class purpose not a fundamental alteration of the institution? Is it "housekeeping" simply because the Court approves of the change?

From this perspective, one might argue that section 6(1) of the Supreme Court Act is also a form of "housekeeping." Section 6 of the Act requires "[a]t least three of the judges shall be appointed from among the judges of the Court of Appeal or of the Superior Court of the Province of Quebec or from among the advocates of that province." Did "from among" mean only current members of the Barreau du Québec were eligible or would former members satisfy the requirement?

This ambiguity in section 6 manifested itself when the federal government appointed Marc Nadon – a Quebecer who had studied and taught law at the Université de Sherbrooke and was a member of the Barreau du Québec for almost two decades before being appointed a Federal Court judge in 1993 – to the Supreme Court in 2013. Because he had let his bar membership lapse while on the bench (as most judges do), Nadon's appointment became the subject of a private citizen's challenge, ultimately provoking the government to refer the question to the Supreme Court. In addition to the reference, the government enacted a declaratory provision, section 6(1), as part of its omnibus budget Bill, reading that "[f]or greater certainty, for the purpose of section 6, a judge is from among the advocates of the Province of Quebec if, at any time, they were an advocate of at least 10 years standing at the bar of that Province." As Michael Plaxton and Carissima Mathen argue, the textual hurdles to the Nadon appointment were significant – and their argument was emphatically *textual*: "The text matters. It has an independent force of its own."[26] And yet the substantial effect is minimal: a *current* bar membership would hardly ensure knowledge of Quebec's Civil Code, the very reason for the three-judge requirement, since a practising criminal lawyer from Quebec, dealing exclusively in public law, would be eligible. Moreover, as Justice Michael Moldaver noted in dissent, returning to the bar – even for a day – before appointment apparently would satisfy the formal requirement. The "current membership" requirement is perhaps the definition of a "mere formality." If so, might the Court have seen section 6(1) as the type of "housekeeping" that "updates the constitutional framework ... without affecting the institution's fundamental nature and role"?

The federal government's declaratory provision – stating the law "as it is and always was" – was not an amendment to the Constitution using the unilateral section 44 power. By virtue of section 42(1)(d), any *constitutional* change with respect to the Supreme Court would require the formal amending process (either section 38 or section 41). The government clearly considered section 6(1) a statutory clarification of, not a constitutional change to, the Supreme Court Act. The Supreme Court saw it differently. In its decision, the Court essentially entrenched the Supreme Court Act – or at least portions of it – as part of the Constitution of Canada.[27] While section 52 of the Constitution Act, 1982 does define the Constitution of Canada inclusively, the entrenchment of the Supreme Court Act as a constitutional text is surprising. During the Meech Lake and Charlottetown negotiations, one of Quebec's central demands was entrenchment of its three seats on the Supreme Court; this has now been achieved through constitutional litigation. Moreover, it is not just the *principle* of Quebec's representation on the Court that is constitutionally protected; it is the specific "eligibility requirements" in section 6 that are constitutionally mandated.[28] Given this judicial entrenchment, section 6(1) was *ultra vires* because a declaratory provision cannot run counter to constitutional text. It remains unclear if the entire Supreme Court Act is now untouchable by statutory means or just sections 5 and 6, but the decision likely will be understood as making bilingualism a requirement for Supreme Court judges – previously thought to be subject to ordinary legislation – possible only through formal constitutional amendment.[29]

The Court's decision to entrench the Act naturally raises the question of what other statutes are similarly unalterable by ordinary legislation. From the standpoint of informal constitutional change, the elevation to constitutional status offers both perils and possibilities. As with the Supreme Court Act, entrenching any particular statute in its current form means that any imperfections will be preserved (unless remedied by judicial or formal amendment). This could limit the flexibility and potential for experimentation that informal constitutional change might provide. However, judicial entrenchment can also address the weakness of informal change, since an entrenched statutory provision cannot be abandoned when it is politically expedient to do so. Like conventions, informal constitutional change via statute may become more binding as time passes and precedents are created; unlike conventions, however, they could become judicially enforceable. In this view, only the Supreme Court gets to decide when a statute becomes officially part of the entrenched Constitution of Canada. Should the federal government ever proceed with a formal amendment over the "veto" of Quebec or Ontario, in contravention of the Regional Veto Act, there is little doubt the Court would be called upon to block its passage. Whereas it was once assumed that the Act would simply be repealed in such an eventuality – indeed, this was commonly cited as a weakness of the Act – the *Supreme Court Act Reference* opens the possibility that the Veto Act is similarly entrenched.

Although the Court emphasizes the textual details in the *Supreme Court Act Reference*, it is much more ambivalent on the issue of substance and form in the *Senate Reference*. Consider the Court's treatment of the substantial effect of "consultative" elections. The Court suggested it would not be fooled by the mere form of the elections: while it is true "in theory" that a prime minister could ignore a nonbinding election, the Court would not "assume that future prime ministers will defeat this purpose by ignoring the results of costly and hard-fought consultative elections."[30] The "theoretical" fact that the prime minister would not be bound by the election was to have no constitutional significance. Any other approach "privileges form over substance."[31] Without any sheepishness about having privileged the form of section 6 of the Supreme Court Act over its substance a month earlier, the Court made it clear that the actions of other actors will be evaluated on substantial grounds even if they otherwise comply with constitutional forms. Sébastien Grammond summarized the decision as essentially saying "[d]on't try to do indirectly what you cannot do alone according to the Constitution."[32]

This emphasis on substance offers the gravest threat to informal constitutional change. By suggesting that constitutional change could not be defended on the grounds it preserved the constitutional formality – like the prime minister's choice not to appoint the winner of the consultative election – the Court cast doubt on a number of informal constitutional acts that rely heavily on such a distinction. Virtually all of the constitutional workarounds Hawkins identified manage to achieve their effect by explicitly claiming that they are not in fact altering constitutional forms. The Regional Veto Act, for example, purports to "lend" the federal veto to the regions; if the federal government would never "defeat the purpose" of the Act by refusing to veto on behalf of a region, then, in substance, the amending formula has been changed from what is detailed in Part V. Similarly the Fixed Date Election Act explicitly declared that it did not alter the governor general's power to dissolve Parliament and call an election; ironically, the federal government's nonadherence to the Fixed Date Election Act actually might be its best constitutional defence! The invalidation of federal "consultative" elections also might imperil Alberta's senatorial elections, which have led to the appointment of four elected senators,[33] since they are similarly constructed to achieve in substance (elected senators) what is denied in form (a binding requirement to appoint the winner). In this respect, the Supreme Court might have put an end to claims that sweeping institutional reform can be achieved piecemeal. But if Alberta persists with its elections and the prime minister continues to appoint the winner, the Supreme Court's *Senate Reference* eventually might be put to the sword: was it lack of provincial input that led to the rejection of the government's proposal or was it the substantial change without formal amendment? All it would take is a challenge to one elected senator's appointment.

The controversy over Justin Trudeau's Senate reform proposals is illustrative of the confusion created by this passage of the *Senate Reform Reference*. In a surprise announcement in January 2014, Trudeau expunged all thirty-two sitting Liberal senators from the party's caucus, and promised that, should he become prime minister, he would introduce a new, "open, transparent and non-partisan appointment process for Senators" that would be "informed by other non-partisan appointment processes, such as that of the Supreme Court Justices and Order of Canada recipients" in an attempt to transform the partisan nature of the Senate. The broad strokes of Trudeau's proposal are consistent with Harper's Advisory Committee on Vice-Regal Appointments, established in November 2012 to provide nonbinding recommendations to the prime minister on the selection of the governor general, lieutenant-governors, and territorial commissioners.[34] In the wake of the *Senate Reference*, there are now serious questions about the constitutionality of all of these appointment processes.

Hugo Cyr, writing in the *Toronto Star*, noted that the decision put Trudeau's proposal in jeopardy.[35] Citing the reference decision, Cyr interpreted the Supreme Court as concluding that

> any change to "the method of selecting senators" requires a constitutional amendment. The court went further, saying this would "include more than the formal appointment of senators," but also "the entire process by which senators are 'selected.'" The eight justices spoke even more specifically to what Trudeau had proposed when they said the prime minister could not be constrained by a list of candidates from which he would "be expected to choose" when making appointments.... [Thus,] in just two paragraphs, the Supreme Court made absolutely clear that any binding, non-partisan process for selecting senators, as Justin Trudeau had suggested, would require constitutional change.[36]

Others, such as Peter Russell, citing the precedents of other appointment advisory bodies noted above, have suggested this amounts to "reading too much into [the decision] to be certain."[37] Emmett Macfarlane, who advised the Liberals on Trudeau's reform, maintains that "as long as reforms don't bind [prime ministerial] discretion" no constitutional amendment should be required.[38] But, of course, the "consultative elections" did not formally bind that discretion, either. That even relatively benign proposals to mitigate partisanship and encourage outstanding candidates are now questionable on constitutional grounds highlights the problem.

The uncertainty introduced by the Court is likely to "chill" future debates on institutional reform in Canada. Given the reverence paid to the Court's decisions and the tendency to give them their widest application, it is now easier to label any attempt at reform as "unconstitutional" and inhibit discussion of its actual merits. It is not hard to advance a *plausible* – if not correct – argument based on these decisions to insist that a particular reform is unconstitutional. If one assumes that the House of Commons, for example, is also in part a reflection of some federal character, it is perhaps possible that any change to its core function and practices requires formal amendment. Bills limiting prorogation or perhaps even changes to representation (normally thought to be "housekeeping") might be vulnerable to such an argument. Although Russell may be right that this is "reading too much" into the decisions, it is also probably inevitable that the question of constitutional validity will be raised and treated as a serious impediment to otherwise sound proposals. In this respect, the burden on reform has grown significantly as a result of the Court's ambiguous extralegal commentary.

One can defend the Court's decisions as protecting an inclusive form of federalism. As it did in the *Patriation Reference*, the Court in both cases checked unilateralism by the federal Government and insisted that provincial interests be considered.[39] To do so, however, it invoked a series of hitherto unknown levels of constitutional depth. After finding a convention of "substantial provincial consent" in the *Patriation Reference* by a method that proved jurisprudentially problematic in the *Quebec Veto* decision, the Court moved on to "unwritten principles"[40] and now to "constitutional architecture."[41] At one time, the Court told Canadians that "constitutional conventions plus constitutional law equal the total constitution of the country";[42] now Canadians have learned to expect novel constitutional components to appear whenever they are necessary to determine the outcome of a particular constitutional controversy. If it is not in the text, perhaps it is in the architecture? By failing to restrict itself to constitutional *law*, the Court has expanded the potential effect of constitutional entrenchment. Whatever the "constitutional architecture" is, it appears to be beyond the reach of ordinary statutes.

And given that "constitutional architecture" might bolster an argument that one must consider not only the form but also the substance of a reform, it becomes important for other political actors to know precisely what it entails. While we can read the constitutional text, we can only guess what the Court sees behind it. There is a certain irony in that, as the Court delves further into more informal and expansive interpretations in judgments across a variety of fields,[43] it forces other political actors to undertake more formal and narrow amendments.

This approach privileges the Court over other institutions in controlling the content of the Constitution. Such strategic behaviour on the part of the Court with respect to the structure of the Constitution has been noted before. Christopher Manfredi, for example, has argued that the growing appreciation of the political unavailability of the notwithstanding clause (section 33) has led to a less deferential and more interventionist Court.[44] If the practical unavailability of section 33, as Manfredi argues, has prompted the Court to enhance its own power and influence, might the presumed unavailability of the amending formula also provide an opportunity for the Court to fill the vacuum left by other political actors? As Macfarlane notes, the Court has adopted similar power-enhancing strategies when deciding whether issues are justiciable, which parties to hear from, and what types of evidence it is willing to consider.[43] From this perspective, the more the Court privileges formal amendment, the more it privileges itself. As Kate Glover writes, "it is likely that future attempts at formal constitutional amendment will be steered by the courts, whether directly through litigation or indirectly through the chilling effect of unfavourable interpretations."[45] The court-centric approach to judicial amendment is unsatisfying on democratic grounds, and hinges on the courts' self-recognition of their institutional capacity, whereas greater scope for informal change can allow for a broader range of institutions to play an active role in constitutional development.

The Future of Formal and Informal Constitutional Change

Even if the Supreme Court finds itself benefiting from such an approach, it does not mean that its insistence on the formal amendment process is wrongheaded. The judiciary checks other institutions, one might say, and here is a good example of the Court's protecting constitutional forms from their derogation. And, from this perspective, why should formal amendment not be difficult? Why should it be otherwise, if we expect constitutions to constrain our immediate and perhaps passing passions? But if even relatively noncontroversial discrete issues cannot be addressed adequately, or even attempted, using the formal process, then Canadians have a real problem with constitutional stasis.

Consider the politics of the Succession to the Throne Act: the discrete issue (addressing gender inequality in the selection of the sovereign) was uncontroversial and unlikely to be addressed through litigation (any section 15 equality challenge would likely be nonjusticiable), but the federal government clearly feared using the formal amendment process because it assumed the discrete issue would have been subsumed by larger debates on the existence of the monarchy and the place of Quebec in the federation. Here, the availability of an informal option gave the government the means to address an important but minor issue, while avoiding the possibility of inviting larger issues of state. Used in a limited fashion, informal amendment can help alleviate the unavoidable pressure for at least some constitutional correction, and make the Constitution "work" when it might otherwise be "paralyzed."[46]

If Canadian political actors are to continue to employ methods of informal constitutional change, we suggest the following "basic principles." First, the use of formal amending processes should be explored fully, and perhaps even attempted in good faith, before assuming a statutory instrument is necessary. Although some might suggest a failed formal amendment would, *prima facie,* impugn the legitimacy of any subsequent informal amendment, we argue that, if the failure could be attributed entirely to the process (that is, the horse-trading), and not related to the merits, an informal measure might be acceptable. We concede, however, that it would be difficult to make this distinction and to ensure that the prospect of a unilateral informal resolution did not itself undermine negotiations for multilateral formal amendment. Second, unlike a formal amendment that has freedom to alter anything in the constitutional text, any statutory amendment must demonstrate due regard for existing constitutional forms and may not directly contradict the text. Third, such statutes should not be passed as part of an omnibus package, particularly if they are not directly and explicitly related to the rest of the content of the Bill. Fourth, political actors enacting such informal changes should avoid hyperbole about the potential positive effects of their reforms, and be clear about the practical limitations of the approaches. In this respect, it would be useful for legislators to articulate their understanding of the constitutional forms at issue in a statutory preamble. Finally, we encourage legislators to be selective and restrained when choosing to engage in constitutional ambiguities. Although we are not optimistic that politicians will always restrict themselves to such practices, clearly articulated norms might help guide and encourage responsible legislators.

Whatever the prospects for informal constitutional change, a number of lessons for the formal process can be gleaned from the informal experience of the past twenty years. As Manfredi and Lusztig have discussed, Canadian megaconstitutional politics has been plagued by "amending process overload."[47] With their flexible process (in fact, the routine legislative process), specificity of statutory language, and finite subject matter, informal amendments such as those we have discussed are clearly more practical and less subject to the "overload" Manfredi and Lusztig describe. A formal amendment strategy based on lessons learned from informal amendments would look quite different from the Meech and Charlottetown approaches. It would focus on discrete issues to be enacted quickly, not "packages." The celerity of the process should be paramount. Although the Constitution prescribes upper limits on the time for constitutional ratification (three years), nothing prevents actors from imposing shorter limits (backed by the threat of revocation). The informal acts we have discussed have resulted from swift and decisive action – sometimes with very little consultation. And although we do not encourage hastily drafted constitutional amendments, a shortened period of consideration might help keep the focus on independent and discrete issues.

Indeed, the key lesson from the informal experience is the eschewing of packages in favour of the resolution of discrete issues. This avoids the "log-rolling," agenda-increasing bargaining that fits awkwardly with the enactment of constitutional principles. As per Prime Minister Pierre Trudeau: we need "not trade fish for rights."[48] Negotiation is perhaps unavoidable with the formal amendment process, since it ultimately hinges on having actors with different interests agree, but any single actor could put out a resolution with a single position and invite other actors to agree to it (or make a counterproposal on the discrete issue). This might degenerate into the same bargaining as the megaconstitutional process, but it might not. We note that most of the informal "ordinary statutes" have resolved issues in a manner that has generated considerable consensus. The Clarity Act is an important and contentious exception, but others, such as the Regional Veto Act, suggest that a divisive issue in megaconstitutional negotiations actually might be relatively uncontroversial when it is not a "bargaining chip." By avoiding the integrative bargaining of the "around-the-table" approach, it might be possible to keep issues relatively independent of each other. This offers the best chance Canadians have to a sound and principled reform of their Constitution.

Notes

An earlier version of this chapter was presented at the International Political Science Association's World Conference on Political Science in Montreal in July 2014. The authors would like to thank Rainer Knopff, Emmanuelle Richez, Lawrence Buhagiar, Emmett Macfarlane, and the anonymous reviewers for their helpful comments. The views expressed in the chapter are the authors' alone.

1 Jordan Press and Steward Kennedy, "Harper 'disappointed' with Supreme Court ruling that he can't reform Senate without provincial agreement," *Canada.com*, 24 April 2014, available online at http://www.canada.com/news/Harper+disappointed+with+Supreme+Court+ruling+that+reform+Senate/9775020/story.html.
2 Richard Albert, "Constructive Unamendability in Canada and the United States," *Supreme Court Law Review* (2d) 67 (2014): 181.
3 John Whyte, "Senate Reform: What Does the Constitution Say?" in *The Democratic Dilemma: Reforming the Canadian Senate*, ed. Jennifer Smith (Montreal; Kingston, ON: McGill-Queen's University Press), 97–8.
4 The most famous iteration is Bruce Ackerman's "constitutional moments"; see Bruce Ackerman, *We the People: Foundations* (Cambridge, MA: Harvard University Press, 1991). Others, however, have made similar observations. See, for example, Sanford Levinson, "How Many Times Has the United States Constitution Been Amended? (A) <26; (B) 26; (C) 27; (D) >27: Accounting for Constitutional Change," in *Responding to Imperfection: The Theory and Practice of Constitutional Amendment*, ed. Sanford Levinson, 13–36 (Princeton, NJ: Princeton University Press, 1995); Mark Tushnet, *Taking the Constitution Away from the Courts* (Princeton, NJ: Princeton University Press, 1999); and Barry Friedman and Scott Smith, "The Sedimentary Constitution," *University of Pennsylvania Law Review* 147, no. 1 (1998): 1–90.
5 Heather K. Gerken, "The Hydraulics of Constitutional Reform: A Skeptical Response to Our Undemocratic Constitution," *Drake Law Review* 55 (2007): 927.
6 Richard Albert, "Constitutional Amendment by Constitutional Desuetude," *American Journal of Comparative Law* 62 (2014): 3.
7 See Dennis Baker, *Not Quite Supreme: The Courts and Coordinate Constitutional Interpretation* (Montreal; Kingston, ON: McGill-Queen's University Press, 2010), 70–1.
8 Andrew Heard, *Canadian Constitutional Conventions: The Marriage of Law and Politics* (Toronto: Oxford University Press, 2014), 24.

9 Robert E. Hawkins, "Constitutional Workarounds," *Canadian Bar Review* 89, no. 3 (2010): 513–43.

10 Ibid., 517.

11 Prorogation is a Royal prerogative power. In Ontario, that power is legally held by the lieutenant-governor; in practice, the premier advises the lieutenant-governor to prorogue. To date, no lieutenant-governor or governor general has ever refused the advice of a premier or a prime minister to prorogue. See Peter Aucoin, Mark D. Jarvis, and Lori Turnbull, *Democratizing the Constitution: Reforming Responsible Government* (Toronto: Emond Montgomery, 2011).

12 Hawkins, "Constitutional Workarounds."

13 At the federal level, in 1958 John Diefenbaker's Progressive Conservatives elected 208 MPs in a House of 265 seats (78.5 per cent), and in 1984 Brian Mulroney's Progressive Conservatives elected 211 members to the House's 282 seats (74.8 per cent). Some provinces have seen even stronger majorities. For example, Danny Williams's Progressive Conservatives won 44 of the 48 seats (91.6 per cent) in the Newfoundland and Labrador legislature in 2007.

14 See Aucoin, Jarvis, and Turnbull, *Democratizing the Constitution*; and Mark D. Jarvis, "Mark Jarvis on the Real Story in Ontario: Prorogation," *Maclean's*, 16 October 2012, available online at http://www.macleans.ca/politics/ottawa/mark-jarvis-on-the-real-story-in-ontario-prorogation/.

15 *Re: Objection by Quebec to a Resolution to amend the Constitution* [1982] 2 SCR 793.

16 Heard, *Canadian Constitutional Conventions*, 7. Heard notes that this view of conventions was rejected by Justice Michel Shore in *Conacher v Canada* (2009).

17 This relationship between statutes and conventions is not uncontroversial. In *Osborne v Canada (Treasury Board)* [1991] 2 SCR 69, 87 (1991), Justice John Sopinka resisted the notion that statutes embodying constitutional conventions could be entrenched: such statutes "retain their status as ordinary statutes. If that were not the case, any [such] legislation ... would have the affect of an amendment to the constitution which would have escaped the rigorous requirements of the constitutional amendment process" (87; see also Heard, *Canadian Constitutional Conventions*, 103). An alternate view would hold the convention to be in abeyance while the statute was in force.

18 Aucoin, Jarvis, and Turnbull, *Democratizing the Constitution*.

19 Warren Newman, "Putting One's Faith in a Higher Law: Supreme Law, Senate Reform, Legislative Authority and the Amending Procedures" (draft paper presented to Osgoode's 2013 Constitutional Case Conference, Osgoode Hall Law School, North York, ON, 11 April 2014).

20 Ibid.

21 *Reference re Senate Reform*, 2014 SCC 32, para. 25 [*Senate Reform Reference*].

22 Ibid., para. 27.

23 In this respect, the decisions resemble the earlier Senate *Reference*, *Re: Authority of Parliament in relation to the Upper House* (1980), 65–6, interpreting section 91(1) of the British North America Act, 1867.

24 The Court explicitly denies doing this, noting that the desirability of any particular reform is "not a question for the Court"; see *Reference re Senate Reform*, 2014 SCC 32, para. 4.

25 Ibid., para. 90.

26 Michael Plaxton and Carissima Mathen, "Purposive Interpretation, Quebec and the Supreme Court Act," *Constitutional Forum* 23, no. 3 (2013): 13.

27 *Senate Reform Reference*, para. 105.

28 The Court hedges a bit by saying "any *substantive* change in relation to those eligibility requirements is an amendment to the Constitution" (para. 105; emphasis added), but then says "[a]ny change to the eligibility requirements for appointment to the three Quebec positions on the Court *codified in s.6* therefore requires the unanimous consent of Parliament and the 10 provinces" (para. 105; emphasis added). It is hard to escape the conclusion that section 6 has been entrenched in the Constitution. Even if emphasis was to be placed on the modifier *substantive*, the Court provides no basis for understanding what constitutes a substantive change and again simply relies on its subjective interpretation.

29 See Crandall, Chapter 10 in this volume.

30 *Senate Reform Reference*, para. 62.

31 Ibid., para. 52.

32 Quoted in Cristin Schmitz, "SCC says no 'form over substance' in making changes to Constitution," *Lawyers Weekly*, 9 May 2014, available online at http://www.lawyersweekly.ca/index.php?section=article&articleid=2132.

33 Alberta's four elected senators are Stan Waters, Bert Brown, Douglas Black, and Betty Unger. Black and Unger are still sitting.

34 The Advisory Committee on Vice-Regal Appointments followed the prime minister's use of an ad hoc advisory committee to assist his recommendation of David Johnston as governor general in 2010; see more online at http://news.gc.ca/web/article-en.do?nid=704949.

35 Hugo Cyr, "Justin Trudeau's Senate reform plan has no teeth," *Toronto Star*, 11 May 2014, available online at http://www.thestar.com/opinion/commentary/2014/05/11/justin_trudeaus_senate_reform_plan_has_no_teeth.html.

36 Ibid.

37 Joan Bryden, "Baloney meter: NDP says Trudeau Senate plan requires constitutional amendment," *CTVNews*, 1 May 2014, available online at http://www.ctvnews.ca/politics/baloney-meter-ndp-says-trudeau-senate-plan-requires-constitutional-amendment-1.1800914.

38 Ibid.

39 For more on this, see Warren Newman, Chapter 5 in this volume.

40 See *Reference re Secession of Quebec* [1998] 2 SCR 217, para. 54.

41 *Senate Reform Reference*, para. 27.

42 *Re: Resolution to amend the Constitution* [1981] 1 SCR 753, 883–4.

43 Emmett Macfarlane, *Governing from the Bench: The Supreme Court of Canada and the Judicial Role* (Vancouver: UBC Press, 2013), 55.

44 Christopher Manfredi, "Strategic Behaviour and the Canadian Charter of Rights and Freedoms," in *The Myth of the Sacred: The Charter, the Courts, and the Politics of the Constitution in Canada*, ed. Patrick James, Donald E. Abelson, and Michael Lusztig, 147–70 (Montreal; Kingston, ON: McGill-Queen's University Press, 2002).

45 Kate Glover, "Structure, Substance and Spirit: Lessons from the *Senate Reform Reference*" (draft paper presented to Osgoode's 2013 Constitutional Case Conference, Osgoode Hall Law School, North York, ON, 11 April 2014), 22.

46 For more on this, see Philippe Lagassé and Patrick Baud, Chapter 12 in this volume.

47 Christopher P. Manfredi and Michael Lusztig, "Why Do Formal Amendments Fail? An Institutional Design Analysis," *World Politics* 50, no. 3 (1999): 380.

48 Barry L. Strayer, *Canada's Constitutional Revolution* (Edmonton: University of Alberta Press, 2013), 123.

PART THREE

The Issues

10 DIY 101: The Constitutional Entrenchment of the Supreme Court of Canada

ERIN CRANDALL

One purpose of a constitution is to reduce uncertainty. Politics is a messy business, but a well-constructed constitution can introduce a measure of structure and clarity to public life. Yet it is precisely because politics is messy that constitutions, themselves the product of political processes, are so frequently riddled with ambiguity, silences, and contradictions. A frequent remedy for such confusion is a high court tasked with interpreting these inevitably broad constitutional provisions. In the case of Canada, however, there is a further complication: until 2014, it was unclear whether the country's highest court, the Supreme Court of Canada, was entrenched in the Constitution at all. Although this ambiguity was generally viewed as more of a nuisance than a threat to the Court's institutional integrity, it has meant that discussions on reform necessarily have been framed from a more abstract starting point, focused not on what constitutional amending procedure was needed, but whether the amending procedures should apply at all. And in what is arguably a fitting end to such a political peculiarity, it was the Court itself that finally provided the definitive answer to the question of its constitutional status. In *Reference re Supreme Court Act, ss. 5 and 6*, 2014 SCC 21 (*Supreme Court Act Reference*, usually referred to as the *Nadon Reference*), the Court confirmed that its essential features are constitutionally protected under Part V of the Constitution Act, 1982.

This unusual constitutional journey is the focus of this chapter. By considering the Supreme Court's historical origins, attempts at constitutional reform, the earlier academic debates concerning its constitutional status, and finally the *Nadon Reference*, the Court's circuitous constitutional route is made apparent. I conclude by considering what the *Nadon Reference* might mean for future reforms, particularly recent proposals that would require Supreme Court judges to be bilingual.

The Supreme Court's Founding and Constitutional Reform (1867–1982)

Unlike Parliament, the Supreme Court was not established by the Constitution Act, 1867. Instead, its creation was merely contemplated, granting Parliament the power to provide for the "Constitution, Maintenance, and Organization of a General Court of Appeal for Canada and for the Establishment of any additional Courts for the better Administration of the Laws in Canada," under section 101. It was not until 1875, in fact, that Parliament actually exercised this power, establishing the Supreme Court via a simple federal statute (*Supreme and Exchequer Courts of Canada Act*, RS 1900, c 154). Considering the political importance of today's Supreme Court, its creation by federal statute alone might seem odd, but with the United Kingdom's Judicial Committee of the Privy Council acting as Canada's final court of appeal until 1949, few viewed the Court as critical in these early years.[1] Rather, it was the absence of any procedures for constitutional amendment in the Constitution Act, 1867 that ultimately drove interest in constitutional reform.[2]

Despite political aspirations to patriate the Constitution in the decades that followed the passage of the Statute of Westminster (1931),[3] it was not until 1964 that a proposal for a domestic amending formula, known as the Fulton-Favreau Formula, was publicly presented. The Quebec government eventually rejected this proposal in 1966 as too constraining and insufficient for the province's governing needs. The failure of Fulton-Favreau marked an important shift for future negotiations: moving forward, the mandate for constitutional reform was expanded, putting all political institutions and jurisdictions, including the Supreme Court, on the table.

The first serious attempt at comprehensive constitutional reform arose following a series of first ministers' conferences in 1969. The Victoria Charter, presented in 1971, was the eventual product of these talks. Although never at the top of the agenda for the federal government or the provinces, the view from the beginning was that the Supreme Court, including its composition, jurisdiction, and procedures, should be entrenched in the Constitution.[4] Both the Victoria Charter and later the federal government's Bill C-60 (1978) contained measures that would have entrenched the Court in the Constitution, but for reasons other than

Supreme Court reform, the proposals failed (for more detail on the history of the amending formula, see Emmett Macfarlane, Introduction, in this volume; and Nadia Verrelli, Chapter 1 in this volume).

Decades of constitutional negotiations finally culminated in 1981 in a reform package that would become the Constitution Act, 1982. That Act contains a number of important provisions – the Charter of Rights and Freedoms, an amending formula, and the recognition of Aboriginal rights are likely the best known – but it is also notable for what it lacks: the clear entrenchment of the Supreme Court. Given that the Court had been part of every major reform package until then and, more important, seemed to be one of the least contentious issues on the political agenda, its absence is odd.

There seems to be no single, straightforward explanation for this outcome. Entering the final four-day conference in November 1981, the federal government and the eight opposing provinces were still far apart, and negotiations focused on what divided them – particularly the Charter, minority-language education rights, the amending formula, and control over natural resources. It is interesting to note that, on the third and final day of full meetings, Saskatchewan proposed a constitutional package aimed at achieving a compromise that did not include reforms to the Supreme Court. In his description of the events that led to the final package later that evening, Howard Leeson, then Saskatchewan's deputy minister of intergovernmental affairs, makes no note of the Supreme Court.[5] In the bustle of this final round of negotiations, with proposals on contentious items trading back and forth, some issues, including the Supreme Court and the Senate, apparently were pushed aside in the effort to strike a final deal.

This is not to say that there is no reference to the Supreme Court in the Constitution Act, 1982. If that were the case, this story would be an easy one: Parliament would continue to have the authority to modify, by simple statute, all aspects of the Supreme Court under section 101 of the Constitution Act, 1867. Instead, the amending formula enacted as Part V of the Constitution Act, 1982 makes explicit reference to the Supreme Court. Section 41(d) provides that constitutional amendments relating to the "composition of the Supreme Court of Canada" require the unanimous consent of the Senate, the House of Commons, and all ten provincial legislatures. Section 42(1)(d) provides that other constitutional amendments relating to the Court require the consent of the Senate, the House of Commons, and the legislatures of seven provinces that together have at least 50 per cent of the country's population (the 7/50 formula).

True, the Supreme Court was not expressly entrenched in the Constitution Act, 1982, and the Supreme Court Act is not in the schedule of acts and orders included in the Constitution as set out in section 52(2),[6] but the amending procedure for its future reform was included. And therein lies the peculiarity that divided constitutional scholars and muddied the water for future reform efforts over the next thirty years: did reference to the Supreme Court in Part V of the Constitution Act, 1982 mean that the Court was entrenched in the Constitution?

Academic Debate on the Constitutional Status of the Supreme Court

Academic views on the interpretation of Part V were divided leading up to the Supreme Court's ruling in the *Nadon Reference*. By Paul Daly's account, at least three interpretative approaches to Part V were at play; he terms them (1) the formal approach, (2) the teleological approach, and (3) the intermediate approach.[7]

For those who take a formal approach to interpreting Part V, two steps must be followed. First, it must be determined if there has been an amendment to the Constitution; second, if an amendment has indeed occurred, it must be determined which section of Part V applies. For those who argued that the Supreme Court was not constitutionally entrenched (Peter Hogg is certainly the best known), analysis begins and ends with this first step of the formal approach. According to Hogg and others, sections 41 and 42 of the Constitution Act, 1982 apply only to amendments to the Constitution, and because the Supreme Court Act was not, by their view, part of the Constitution, it followed that the Supreme Court could be amended by a simple parliamentary statute under section 101 of the Constitution Act, 1867.[8] With this understanding, references to the "Supreme Court" in sections 41 and 42 acted as "empty vessels," which could be filled only when the Supreme Court was expressly entrenched in the text of the Constitution.[9]

Over the years, this position received considerable pushback. Writing in 1982, Stephen Scott emphasized the seeming contradiction that would exist if the Supreme Court were not entrenched in the Constitution: "[t]o argue that *none* of the federal statute law dealing with the Supreme Court of Canada forms part of the 'Constitution of Canada' is to say, in effect, that Parliament may continue to legislate on the subject exactly as it pleases ... This can scarcely have been what the eight 'opposing' premiers had in mind when they signed their 'April Accord'[10] from which sections 41(d) and 42(1)(d) were taken."[11] As Patrick Monahan and Byron Shaw argue, the underlying purpose of the April Accord was not to constitutionally entrench unilateral federal power, but to constrain federal powers to effect constitutional change.[12] By this view, sections 41 and 42 should be interpreted in a manner consistent with the underlying intention of the drafters. Such consideration of the philosophical and historical context of the provisions of Part V, including the understanding of the drafters, is consistent with what Daly terms the teleological approach.

Finally, there is the intermediate approach, which functions as a hybrid of the first two, adopting the two-step analysis of the formal approach, while also accepting the spirit of the teleological approach. With the intermediate approach, the analysis of whether an amendment to the Constitution has been proposed considers (1) "the matters listed in Part V, which are a guide to the matters thought sufficiently important as to require constitutional amendment"; and (2) "the 'fundamental' or 'essential' features of the institutions of government."[13] Although what constitutes the "essential" features of the Supreme Court is a source of debate, Monahan and Shaw, for example, suggest the following: the status of the Supreme Court as a general court of appeal for Canada and a superior court of record; the number of judges; the requirement that three members of the Court be appointed from the bar of Quebec; and the mode of appointment, tenure, and removal of judges.[14]

Altogether, much divided legal scholars on the question of the Supreme Court's constitutional status in the years that followed the passage of the Constitution Act, 1982, and, more important, these differences had major implications for Supreme Court reform. If Hogg's view was indeed correct, for example, Parliament continued to exercise, unfettered, the powers conferred by section 101 of the Constitution Act, 1867, including the power to abolish the Supreme Court. Consensus, however, could be found on at least one point: that the references to the Supreme Court in sections 41(d) and 42(1)(d) of the Constitution Act, 1982 had created, in Hogg's words, "an intolerably confusing situation."[15]

Formal and Informal Reform of the Supreme Court (1982–2015)

Given the nature of this confusion, two avenues for resolution were available: (1) use the amending procedures under Part V so that features of the Supreme Court were expressly made part of the Constitution, or (2) task the Supreme Court with interpreting Part V and ruling on its own constitutional status. Ultimately, the second approach was taken, but only after two failed attempts at entrenching the Court (the Meech Lake and Charlottetown accords) and a number of efforts to circumvent constitutional reform altogether. It is to these latter events that I now turn.

Because the Quebec government did not sign on to the Constitution Act, 1982, there was a general view that constitutional politics in Canada remained unfinished. Following the election wins of the Progressive Conservative Party federally (1984) and the Liberal Party in Quebec (1985), a new round of constitutional talks began whose primary objective was to bring Quebec into the constitutional fold. The deal finally struck in 1987, the Meech Lake Accord, proposed comprehensive reforms to the Supreme Court, including: express provision for the Court in the Constitution, a new appointments process that would give significant powers to the provinces, and changes to the amending formula so that any future constitutional amendment in relation to the Supreme Court would require the unanimity amending procedure.[16] The Accord came close to passing, but it eventually expired in 1990 when Manitoba and Newfoundland and Labrador failed to ratify it. Following this failure, a new round of constitutional negotiations began almost immediately. When agreement on a deal, the Charlottetown Accord, was reached once more in 1992, the proposals for the Supreme Court were very similar to those in Meech Lake: explicit provision of the Court in the Constitution, a new appointments process, and modifications to the amending formula.[17] The Charlottetown Accord, too, failed, turned down in a national referendum.

The Supreme Court's constitutional ambiguity would have been resolved had either of these proposals succeeded. However, their failure meant that by 1992 the Court's constitutional status was no closer to a resolution than a decade earlier, when the Constitution Act, 1982 had been passed. Despite their failure, the Meech Lake and Charlottetown accords are nonetheless important parts of Canada's constitutional history for many reasons. For the purposes of this chapter, of particular interest is whether the political actors who negotiated these accords viewed the Supreme Court as already constitutionally entrenched via Part V of the Constitution Act, 1982. A review of the federal government's approach to the Charlottetown Accord indicates that the answer is no. In its 1991 position paper on constitutional reform, "Shaping Canada's Future Together: Proposals," for example, the federal government describes the Court as a "creature of a federal statute."[18] It appears, then, that the federal government approached the constitutional negotiations following the entrenchment of Part V of the Constitution Act, 1982 still under the assumption that the Supreme Court was not part of the Constitution.

Following the defeat of these reform efforts, the federal government deliberately turned away from constitutional reform, making it increasingly unlikely that the Supreme Court's status would be addressed in the near future. However, although comprehensive constitutional reform was not on the table following these failed efforts, the issues that Meech Lake and Charlottetown tried to address, of course, did not simply go away. For the Supreme Court, in particular, its growing political importance since the entrenchment of the Charter in 1982 meant that its centralized appointments process, with the prime minister's nearly unfettered discretion to choose appointees to the bench, received increased scrutiny and calls for reform.[19]

Such calls were largely ignored during the tenure of Liberal prime minister Jean Chrétien (1993–2003), but gained a receptive ear when Paul Martin became leader of the Liberal Party in December 2003. As prime minister (2003–6), Martin's reform interests included a "democratic deficit" agenda, which, among a number of measures, sought to reform how senior government appointments were made.[20] As part of this agenda, Martin requested that the House of Commons Standing Committee on Justice and Human Rights (JUST) consult on how best to implement prior review of appointments of Supreme Court justices.

The JUST Committee presented its recommendations in a May 2004 report, "Improving the Supreme Court of Canada Appointments Process." Although every opposition party included a dissenting report, all parties agreed that "whatever the quality of judgments produced by the Supreme Court, the process by which Justices are appointed to that body is secretive or, at the very least, unknown to Canadians. This could lead to the perception that appointments may be based upon improper criteria."[21]

Not surprisingly, the federal government accepted nearly in their entirety the recommendations set out in the majority report authored by the Liberal committee members.[22] The proposed process charged the minister of justice with putting forward a shortlist of five to eight candidates to an advisory committee composed of a Member of Parliament from each of the elected political parties, representatives from the provinces, members of the judiciary, members of the legal profession, and lay members. The committee would provide the minister with a shortlist of three to five names from which the final nominee would be chosen. Following the final selection, the minister of justice would appear publicly before the JUST Committee to explain the selection process and qualifications of the selected appointee.

With a few minor caveats, the New Democratic Party (NDP) accepted the Liberals' recommendations. The two parties differed, however, in their reasons for taking this approach to Supreme Court reform. Left unaddressed in the Liberals' majority report was the issue of the constitutionality of reforms to the Court appointments process. The NDP, however, noted:

> This constitutional question probably cannot be resolved without, ironically enough, a reference to the Supreme Court of Canada. In the absence of this, the safest route to follow is to assume that no change to the Supreme Court Act is possible without constitutional amendment. This means that the final decision on appointments must continue to rest with the Governor-in-Council. Thus, suggestions such as binding Parliamentary confirmation hearings or a Parliamentary veto can be presumed to be unconstitutional. This report is written on that assumption, with the caveat that the constitutional question has never been firmly resolved.[23]

It was actually the Conservative Party, in its own minority report, that proposed the "confirmation hearings" the NDP described as constitutionally questionable. Although the Conservatives acknowledged the potential for conflict, explaining that "[t]he form of ratification must not infringe on the constitutional right of the Governor-in-Council to make the actual appointment,"[24] the party provided no details about the nature of this constitutional right, nor how it should be respected.

The NDP's minority report, I believe, provides some useful insight into how both the Liberal and later Conservative governments approached attempts to reform the Supreme Court. Although not publicly acknowledged by the Liberals, all parties would have been aware of the Court's uncertain constitutional status, and have designed their reforms accordingly. This is to say that the Liberal and Conservative governments chose to pursue informal reforms, at least in part, to avoid the threat of a constitutional challenge. This was most apparent with the Conservatives' approach to the appointments process. In 2004 the party was calling for parliamentary ratification of Supreme Court nominees, but when Stephen Harper's Conservatives formed the government just two years later, parliamentary ratification was no longer part of its reform agenda. Instead, after taking over mid-process the task of selecting a new Supreme Court judge to replace the retiring Justice John Major in 2006, only one feature of the Liberals' process (described above) was modified: rather than having the minister of justice appear before a committee to explain his or her judicial nominee, it was the nominee who would appear. Importantly, however, members of this ad hoc committee would have no power of confirmation.[25]

It is worth noting that none of these measures was set out formally in legislation, and the power of the governor in council to make appointments remains unchanged. The informality of these reforms is well demonstrated by the fact that, of the eight judges selected to the Supreme Court while this process was in place, in only four cases was this process actually followed.[26] With the appointment of Suzanne Côté in November 2014, the Conservative government indicated it was abandoning these reforms altogether in favour of the previous status quo.[27] Altogether, although these changes to the appointments process were far from permanent, and generally left most unsatisfied,[28] their informality meant that questions concerning the Supreme Court's constitutional status were unlikely to arise. This risk-averse approach was unexpectedly upturned in October 2013, however, when the Conservative government announced that its next appointment to the Supreme Court would be Judge Marc Nadon.

The *Nadon Reference* and a Step towards Constitutional Clarity

To understand how an appointment to the Supreme Court could lead to a constitutional challenge and long-sought clarity on the Court's constitutional status, it is first useful to note one of its unique compositional features: three of its nine members must come from Quebec. This requirement is a consequence of the nature of Canada's legal system: unlike the rest of Canada, which practices common law, Quebec has a civil law system. By mandating that a third of the bench be staffed with Quebec judges, the Court is assured of being prepared to hear any case that comes before it, regardless of the legal system in which it originated.

Judge Nadon was selected to replace the retiring Justice Morris Fish, who occupied one of the three Quebec seats on the Court. As a member of the Federal Court of Appeal, however, Nadon quickly faced questions as to whether he met the technical qualifications of a "Quebec judge." Section 6 of the Supreme Court Act specifies that three justices must be drawn "from among the judges of the Court of Appeal or of the Superior Court of the Province of Quebec or from among the advocates of that Province." As a Federal Court of Appeal judge, Nadon sat on none of the specified courts, and although he had once been a member of the Quebec Bar for more than ten years, his membership had lapsed some twenty years earlier. The Conservative government, anticipating that questions concerning Nadon's status might arise, circulated a legal opinion from a former Supreme Court justice affirming that Nadon's background qualified him to occupy one of the Court's Quebec seats.[29] On 7 October 2013, however – the same day Nadon was sworn in as a Supreme Court justice – an Ontario lawyer, Rocco Galati, filed a legal challenge to the appointment.

Facing an inevitable legal showdown and mounting condemnation from Quebec, the Conservative government took two actions. First, in an effort to clarify the qualifications for being appointed to the Court, it included in a budget implementation bill "declaratory provisions" that added two subsections to the Supreme Court Act, stating (1) that a person with at least ten years standing at the bar of Quebec is qualified to sit as a Quebec judge, and (2) that a person with at least ten years' standing at the bar of a province is qualified to be appointed as one of the other six Supreme Court judges.[30] Second, the government referred two questions to the Supreme Court in order to receive final clarification on who qualifies as a Quebec judge, and whether Parliament had the power to modify the Supreme Court Act unilaterally.[31]

The Supreme Court released its ruling on 21 March 2014. With one justice in dissent, the six-member majority concluded that Quebec judges must be from the Quebec Court of Appeal or the Superior Court or be a *current* member of the Quebec bar. By the majority's understanding, the pool of eligible Quebec candidates was thusly limited to "ensure expertise in civil law and that Quebec's legal traditions and social values are reflected in the judges on the Supreme Court, and to enhance the confidence of the people of Quebec in the Court" (para. 59). As a judge of the Federal Court of Appeal, Nadon did not meet these qualifications, and was therefore ineligible to serve.

It is the second question, concerning Parliament's ability to modify sections 5 and 6 of the Supreme Court Act unilaterally, that is of particular interest here. In his factum, the attorney general of Canada argued that, because the Court was never constitutionally entrenched, Parliament retained the plenary power to amend the eligibility criteria for appointments under section 101 of the Constitution Act, 1867. The Court, however, disagreed, ruling that the "essential features" of the Court are constitutionally protected under Part V of the Constitution Act, 1982.

According to the majority, the express mention of the Supreme Court in section 42(1)(d) was intended to ensure the Court's proper functioning by providing constitutional protection to its "essential features." These "essential features," the majority continued, are to be understood in light of the role that the Court had come to play in the Canadian constitutional structure by the time of patriation, and include, at the very least, the Court's jurisdiction as the final general court of appeal for Canada, including in matters of constitutional interpretation, and its independence (para. 94). As such, changes to these features require constitutional amendment via section 42(1)(d) (the 7/50 formula). Further, changes to the composition of the Supreme Court, such as the eligibility of its Quebec judges, can be made only under the procedure provided for in section 41(d) (unanimous consent). Consequently, the declaratory provisions passed by Parliament were ruled to be *ultra vires*.

Interestingly, although much of the debate on the Supreme Court's constitutional status until the *Nadon Reference* had focused on whether Part V of the Constitution Act, 1982 had constitutionalized the Court, the majority in Nadon chose to understand the Court's constitutional status in terms of its "historical evolution into an institution whose continued existence and functioning engaged the interests of both Parliament and the provinces" (para. 76). In particular, the abolition of appeals to the Judicial Committee of the Privy Council in 1949 meant that the Court had inherited the power and jurisdiction of that body (para. 83) and, as a result, had emerged as a "constitutionally essential institution" (para. 87). Rather than the Court being constitutionalized as a result of the Constitution Act, 1982, the majority reasoned that the Act instead "enhanced the Court's role under the Constitution and *confirmed* [my emphasis] its status as a constitutionally protected institution" (para. 88). Returning to Daly's three interpretative approaches to Part V, the majority clearly adopted an intermediate approach in the *Nadon Reference* – using the Court's historical role and the matters listed in Part V as a guide to understanding what should be understood as sufficiently important to require constitutional amendment.

Concluding Thoughts

What does the *Nadon Reference* mean for the Supreme Court going forward? The ruling has confirmed once and for all that the Court is constitutionally entrenched and, in effect, has drastically reduced the scope for change to the Supreme Court by ordinary federal statute. However, it remains to be seen just how reduced that scope will be. A decades-old question has been answered, but new questions have emerged, particularly in regards to what features of the Court are and are not constitutionally protected. Writing in 1982, Stephen Scott reflected on the strikingly different results that various courses of interpretation could bring. For example, if all statute law dealing with the Supreme Court were considered part of the Constitution, Scott speculated that the rule requiring appellants' factum covers to be coloured buff and respondents' factum covers to be coloured green would require a constitutional amendment to be changed.[32] If true, factum covers stood the prospect of being frozen in time no matter how unfashionable their colours became. A review of the Rules of the Supreme Court of Canada shows that by 2002 appellants' factum covers had, in fact, changed from buff to a more fashion-forward beige, indicating that not everything related to the Supreme Court is now constitutionally protected (nor, incidentally, more colourful). Indeed, the majority in the *Nadon Reference* noted that section 42(1)(d) does not apply the 7/50 amending procedure to all provisions of the Supreme Court Act, but only to the essential features of the Court (para. 94).

Then what is entrenched? The *Nadon* majority expressly laid out a number of provisions: the Supreme Court's jurisdiction as the final court of appeal (including over matters of constitutional interpretation), its independence, and its composition. Yet, coming out of the *Nadon Reference*, we still do not have an exhaustive list of the Court's "essential" features, leaving considerable uncertainty as to what future reforms will or will not require constitutional amendment. What falls under section 41(d) "the composition of the Supreme Court of Canada," and therefore requires unanimity to be reformed, also appears prime for dispute. I have focused on the majority's ruling, but Justice Michael Moldaver's dissenting opinion provides insight into how conflicting interpretations of the Court's composition appear likely. Although concurring with the majority that the Court is constitutionally entrenched and that changes to Quebec's guarantee of three seats would require unanimity (para. 114), Justice Moldaver expressed scepticism about the majority's conclusion that the government's disputed declaratory changes to the Supreme Court Act fell under the "composition" of the Court (para. 115). That this disagreement arose at the first opportunity to interpret the Supreme Court's constitutional status makes it seem inevitable that any proposed statutory reform will be greeted with considerable uncertainty moving forward.

Considering Canada's difficulty in achieving reform via constitutional amendment, in practice the Supreme Court might end up unpacking its own composition and "essential features" on a case-by-case basis. On this point, a contender for future constitutional challenge is the issue of bilingualism on the Court. Since 2008 the NDP has introduced a series of private members' bills calling for Supreme Court candidates to be able to understand both French and English without the assistance of an interpreter. The Harper Conservative government voted against these bills, but the now-governing Liberals also support the principle of a bilingual Supreme Court, so that the NDP's bill, or something similar to it, might well be passed. Given that language requirements seem to touch on the "composition" of the Court in a manner comparable to the criteria required to qualify as a Quebec judge, it now appears an open question whether Parliament alone can pass such a bill or whether it requires the unanimous consent of Parliament and the provinces under section 41(d). Indeed, a number of this volume's contributors anticipate that the *Nadon Reference* has closed the door on a legislative option to mandating bilingualism on the Court (see the chapters by Baker and Jarvis, Macfarlane, and Mathen, in this volume).

If a constitutional amendment is required to mandate bilingualism on the Court, the prospect for this and other reforms seems fairly bleak. The Court's focus on its role in the *Nadon Reference*, however, hints that its constitutionalized features might not track directly to specifiable legislative provisions, but instead might arise from practice.[33] For example, if, in practice, the Court had become bilingual, then there might be room for a bill, like the NDP's, to be passed by ordinary federal statute. That the Court has affirmed that language rights must be interpreted purposively and in a manner consistent with the preservation and development of official-language communities[34] might help establish the purpose of this practice. Such a rationale, of course, remains untested. The majority in the *Nadon Reference* made clear that the federal government's unilateral power to modify the Supreme Court under section 101 of the Constitution Act, 1867 has been overtaken by the Court's evolution in the structure of the Constitution, as recognized in the amendment formula of Part V. As a result section 101 is now limited to changes that serve to maintain and protect "the essence of what enables the Supreme Court to perform its current role" (para. 101). To what extent bilingualism strikes at the "essence" of the Supreme Court's role is certainly a difficult point to measure. The complexities of the issue, however, illustrate how murky the constitutional waters remain for the Supreme Court.

For all the new questions it raises, the *Nadon Reference* is a major marker on the Supreme Court's strange constitutional journey. The next steps – determining what elements of the Court are and are not constitutionally protected – appear destined for an equally circuitous route. Arguably, what does appear clear is who will lead. As noted in this volume's Introduction, the judiciary's role in interpreting the amending formula wields tremendous power, setting the conditions for political actors to follow, and determining not only which issues fall under the various amending procedures listed in Part V, but also their scope. In the *Nadon Reference*, the Supreme Court clearly stated its willingness to determine the contours of its own constitutional status.

Notes

1 James G. Snell and Vaughan Frederick, *The Supreme Court of Canada: History of the Institution* (Toronto: University of Toronto Press, 1985).

2 Peter H. Russell, *Constitutional Odyssey: Can Canadians Become a Sovereign People?* 3rd ed. (Toronto: University of Toronto Press, 2004).

3 The Statute of Westminster allowed Canada and other Commonwealth countries to patriate their constitutions.

4 Canada, "Federalism for the Future: A Statement of Policy by the Government of Canada" (Ottawa: Queen's Printer, 1968); idem, "The Constitution and the People of Canada: An Approach to the Objectives of Confederation, the Rights of People and the Institutions of Government" (Ottawa: Queen's Printer, 1968).

5 Howard A. Leeson, *The Patriation Minutes* (Edmonton: University of Alberta, Faculty of Law, Centre for Constitutional Studies, 2011), 48.

6 Section 52(2) of the Constitution Act, 1982 sets out that the Constitution of Canada includes: (a) the Constitution Act, 1982; (b) the acts and orders referred to in the schedule; and (c) any amendment to any Act or order referred to in paragraph (a) or (b).

7 Paul Daly, "Submission to the Senate Standing Committee on Legal and Constitutional Affairs Re Modifications to the Supreme Court Act" (Ottawa: Senate of Canada, 2013).

8 Peter W. Hogg, *Constitutional Law of Canada*, vol. 5 (Scarborough, ON: Carswell, 2007); Benoît Pelletier, *La modification constitutionnelle au Canada* (Scarborough, ON: Carswell, 1996); Katherine Swinton, "Amending the Canadian Constitution: Lessons from Meech Lake," *University of Toronto Law Journal* 42, no. 2 (1992): 139–69.

9 The "empty vessels" metaphor was employed by the majority in the *Nadon Reference* to describe this view (para. 97).

10 Prime Minister Pierre Elliott Trudeau's comments upon the tabling of the constitutional accord in the House of Commons arguably provide some insight: "As for the amending formula, it is, with one exception, exactly the same as the formula negotiated and accepted by the province of Quebec and the Group of Eight and made public on April 16 of this year [that is, the April Accord]. In other words, I want my fellow citizens in Quebec to understand that Quebec has retained the same veto right and the same opting-out right they were offered in the April 16 agreement, an agreement which received the approval of Premier Lévesque." See Pierre Elliott Trudeau, "Commons Debates" (Ottawa: Parliament of Canada, 5 November 1981), 12537.

11 Stephen A. Scott, "The Canadian Constitutional Amendment Process," *Law and Contemporary Problems* 45, no. 4 (1982): 261.

12 Patrick Monahan and Byron Shaw, *Constitutional Law*, 4th ed. (Toronto: Irwin Law, 2013), 204.

13 Daly, "Submission to the Senate Standing Committee," 23. Legal scholars who adopt some variant of the intermediate approach include Henri Brun, Guy Tremblay, and Eugénie Brouillet, *Droit constitutionnel*, 5th ed. (Cowansville, QC: Les Editions Yvon Blais, 2008); William R. Lederman, "Constitutional Procedure for the Reform of the Supreme Court of Canada," *Cahiers de droit* 26, no. 1 (1985): 195–204; Monahan and Shaw, *Constitutional Law*; Warren J. Newman, "The Constitutional Status of the Supreme Court of Canada," *Supreme Court Law Review* 47 (2d) (2009): 429–43; Peter Oliver, "Canada, Quebec, and Constitutional Amendment," *University of Toronto Law Journal* 49, no. 4 (1999): 519–610; and Scott, "Canadian Constitutional Amendment Process."

14 Monahan and Shaw, *Constitutional Law*, 205.

15 Peter W. Hogg, *Meech Lake Constitutional Accord Annotated* (Scarborough, ON: Carswell, 1988), 30.

16 Ibid., 27–36.

17 The Charlottetown Accord also called for the role of Aboriginal peoples in relation to the Supreme Court to be established in a future political accord, and for the provincial and territorial governments to develop a reasonable process for consulting representatives of Aboriginal peoples in the preparation of lists of candidates to fill vacancies on the Supreme Court.

18 In this report, the government committed itself to introducing a constitutional amendment on Supreme Court appointments using the 7/50 amending formula. However, on the issues of the entrenchment and composition of the Supreme Court, the report notes that these would be

included only "if it were found desirable to proceed with unanimity items in the final package." This dual approach to reform was undoubtedly a strategic response to the perceived missteps of the Meech Lake Accord, which bundled all amendments in a single package, making unanimity necessary for all items. Political prudence aside, the federal government's approach in this report means that it conceivably would have accepted a version of the Charlottetown Accord that entrenched the Supreme Court's appointments process, but not the Court itself – an unusual possibility in an already unusual story. Canada, "Shaping Canada's Future Together: Proposals" (Ottawa: Minister of Supply and Services Canada, 1991), 21–5.

19 Erin Crandall, "Intergovernmental Relations and the Supreme Court of Canada: The Changing Place of the Provinces in Judicial Selection Reform," in *The Democratic Dilemma: Reforming Canada's Supreme Court*, ed. Nadia Verrelli, 71–85 (Montreal; Kingston, ON: McGill-Queen's University Press, 2013).

20 Peter Aucoin and Lori Turnbull, "The Democratic Deficit: Paul Martin and Parliamentary Reform," *Canadian Public Administration* 46, no. 4 (2003): 427–49.

21 Canada, Parliament, House of Commons, Standing Committee on Justice, Human Rights, Public Safety and Emergency Preparedness, "Improving the Supreme Court of Canada Appointments Process" (Ottawa, 2004), 4.

22 Irwin Cotler, "The Supreme Court Appointment Process: Chronology, Context, and Reform," *University of New Brunswick Law Journal* 58 (2008): 131–46.

23 Canada, Standing Committee on Justice, "Improving the Supreme Court of Canada Appointments Process," 21.

24 Ibid., 16.

25 For later appointments, the Conservative government also changed the composition of the advisory committee tasked with creating the shortlist of nominees. Whereas the Liberals' committee included members of elected federal parties (one each), the legal community, the provinces, and the public, committees convened by the Conservatives consisted only of MPs, and membership was distributed according to parties' representation in the House of Commons. Consequently, after the Conservatives formed a majority government in 2011, Conservative MPs made up the majority of committee members.

26 Justice Thomas Cromwell (2008), Justice Clément Gascon (2014), and Justice Suzanne Côté (2014) did not appear before an ad hoc committee prior to their appointments.

27 Tonda MacCharles, "Quebec lawyer Suzanne Côté named to Supreme Court of Canada," *Toronto Star*, 27 November 2014.

28 For comprehensive analysis of this period of Supreme Court appointments and discussion of the inadequacies of the process, see Adam M. Dodek, "Reforming the Supreme Court Appointment Process 2004–2014: A Ten Year Democratic Audit," Working Paper Series WP 2014–07 (Ottawa: University of Ottawa, Faculty of Law, 2014); and Andrea Lawlor and Erin Crandall, "Questioning Judges with a Questionable Process: An Analysis of Committee Appearances by Canadian Supreme Court Candidates," *Canadian Journal of Political Science* 48, no. 4 (2015): 863–83.

29 Ian Binnie, "RE: Eligibility of Federal Court Judges for Appointment to the Supreme Court of Canada" (letter to Department of Justice, Ottawa, 9 September 2013).

30 Canada, Department of Justice, "Government of Canada takes steps to clarify certain eligibility criteria for Supreme Court justices," News Release, 22 October 2013, available online at http://news.gc.ca/web/article-en.do?nid=782979, accessed 4 January 2015.

31 The two questions referred to the Supreme Court are: (1) "Can a person who was, at any time, an advocate of at least 10 years standing at the Barreau du Québec be appointed to the Supreme Court of Canada as a member of the Supreme Court from Quebec pursuant to sections 5 and 6 of the Supreme Court Act?" and, (2) "Can Parliament enact legislation that requires that a person be or has previously been a barrister or advocate of at least 10 years standing at the bar of a province as a condition of appointment as a judge of the Supreme Court of Canada or enact the annexed declaratory provisions as set out in clauses 471 and 472 of the Bill entitled Economic Action Plan 2013 Act, No. 2?"

32 Stephen A. Scott, "Pussycat, Pussycat or Patriation and New Constitutional Amendment Processes," *University of Western Law Review* 20, no. 2 (1982): 272.

33 Robert Leckey, "Constitutionalizing Canada's Supreme Court," *International Journal of Constitutional Law Blog*, 25 March 2014, available online at http://www.iconnectblog.com/2014/03/constitutionalizing-canadas-supreme-court, accessed 4 January 2015.

34 *R. v Beaulac*, 1 SCR 768 (1999).

11　The Uncertain Future of Senate Reform

EMMETT MACFARLANE

In the spring of 2014, the Supreme Court of Canada rendered decisions in the *Supreme Court Act Reference*[1] and the *Senate Reform Reference*,[2] which together marked the first comprehensive examination by the Court of the constitutional amending formula in Part V of the Constitution Act, 1982. In this chapter I critically examine the *Senate Reform Reference* from the perspective of its coherence in interpreting the various amending procedures. I argue that the underlying logic of the Court's reasoning, specifically with respect to the method of selecting senators and senatorial term limits, creates ambiguity, and risks unintended consequences for future attempts at constitutional amendment generally and for Senate reform particularly.

The federal Conservative government had long sought to implement Senate reform through ordinary statute, a policy that was a key feature of the Conservative Party's electoral platforms since it formed the government in 2006. The objective was to implement terms limits for senators and "consultative elections" as part of the Senate appointments process. After repeated efforts to pass a bill, the government finally acquiesced to critics who argued that the changes required formal constitutional amendment, and submitted to the Supreme Court a set of reference questions asking it to determine whether Parliament could enact such reforms without the approval of the provinces.

The reference also asked what procedure under Part V was required to abolish the Senate.[3] The constitutional formula under Part V includes five to seven different procedures for amendment, depending on how they are counted. Of particular relevance for the *Senate Reform Reference* questions are:

- the general procedure,[4] requiring the consent of Parliament and at least seven provinces representing at least 50 per cent of the population;

- section 41,[5] which mandates unanimous consent of the provinces for particular changes, including changes to Part V itself;
- section 42(1)(b), which specifically states that amendments pertaining to "the powers of the Senate and the method of selection senators" must be done under the general formula;[6] and
- section 44, which states that "Subject to sections 41 and 42, Parliament may exclusively make laws amending the Constitution of Canada in relation to the executive government of Canada or the Senate and House of Commons."

The Court reached a unanimous opinion that provincial consent for term limits and consultative elections is required under the general amending procedure, and that unanimity is required for abolition.

The Court's approach to assessing the constitutional amending procedures begins with a point articulated in the *Secession Reference*: that constitutional interpretation involves examining "the constitutional text itself, the historical context, and previous judicial interpretations of constitutional meaning."[7] The justices noted as well that "constitutional interpretation must be informed by the foundational principles of the Constitution, which include principles such as federalism, democracy, the protection of minorities, as well as constitutionalism and the rule of law."[8] It is through these principles that the Court concluded, as it had invoked in earlier cases,[9] that the Constitution ought to be regarded as having an "internal architecture" or "basic constitutional structure," meaning that the Constitution "must be interpreted with a view to discerning the structure of government that it seeks to implement. The assumptions that underlie the text and the manner in which the constitutional provisions are intended to interact with one another must inform our interpretation, understanding, and application of the text."[10]

Describing the Constitution's "architecture" is in line with a purposive approach to interpretation that seeks to capture the meaning of specific constitutional provisions and to prevent interpretations that conflict with or contradict the application of other components of the Constitution. It also underscores, as the justices pointed out, that amendments to the Constitution are not limited to textual changes but also apply to changes in the way the Constitution operates. Therefore, on the one hand, an appreciation of the constitutional architecture ensures specific provisions are interpreted to operate as parts of a coherent whole. On the other hand, however, too much dependence on the fundamentally vague notion of the basic structure of the Constitution might divorce specific provisions from their textual underpinnings and basic meaning.

A reliance on the concept of the Constitution's architecture also gives the justices a lot of discretion in choosing how to locate and define specific issues, depending on how they view the broader governing structure. Interpreting specific constitutional provisions with too much focus on the indeterminate constitutional structure, rather than rooting analysis more directly in the text, thus risks a great level of dependence on the justices' ability to describe accurately the various institutions, conventions, and processes that animate the Constitution.

In what follows, I argue that the Court relies too heavily on the concept of constitutional architecture in its reasons, when a slightly narrower, textually rooted approach would be sufficient to arrive at a coherent dividing line between the various amending procedures and to establish a clear standard for future assessments of which procedures are required for changes relating to the Senate. Further, while the justices tread too far in exploring aspects of the constitutional architecture, they do not go far enough in examining the amending formula's specific provisions, such as section 44 of Part V of the Constitution Act, 1982. Here, for example, they fail to provide a logical justification for the minimal role they outline for Parliament in effecting changes to the Senate. I elaborate on this critique of the justices' logic relating to changes that would enact consultative elections and term limits for senators, while also briefly explaining why the Court arrived at the correct conclusion with respect to the abolition of the Senate. In the remainder of the chapter, I examine the implications of the Court's reasoning.

Consultative Elections

With respect to consultative elections, the federal government posed the following questions to the Supreme Court:

2. Is it within the legislative authority of the Parliament of Canada, acting pursuant to section 91 of the *Constitution Act, 1867*, or section 44 of the *Constitution Act, 1982*, to enact legislation that provides a means of consulting the population of each province and territory as to its preferences for potential nominees for appointment to the Senate pursuant to a national process as was set out in Bill C-20, the *Senate Appointment Consultations Act*?

3. Is it within the legislative authority of the Parliament of Canada, acting pursuant to section 91 of the *Constitution Act, 1867*, or section 44 of the *Constitution Act, 1982*, to establish a framework setting out a basis for provincial and territorial legislatures to enact legislation to consult their

population as to their preferences for potential nominees for appointment to the Senate as set out in the schedule to Bill C-7, the *Senate Reform Act*?

Under section 42(1)(b), changes to "the powers of the Senate and the method of selecting Senators" must be made according to the general amending procedure. The federal government argued that, under a system of strictly advisory elections, the prime minister would retain full discretion to make the final decision on senatorial appointments, and therefore its implementation would not constitute a change to the selection process. The judges did not give much credence to this argument, noting that, although in theory the prime minister might refuse to make appointments based on electoral outcomes, the very purpose of the reforms the government sought was "to bring about a Senate with a popular mandate. We cannot assume that future prime ministers will defeat this purpose by ignoring the results of costly and hard-fought consultative elections."[11] The justices thus stated that the federal government's argument incorrectly privileged "form over substance" in its interpretation of the meaning of section 42(1)(b).[12] If advisory elections were advisory in name only, their implementation effectively would provide a loophole to escape the requirements of the general amending procedure.

It is worth noting that this finding privileged a particular conception of "method of selection." The narrow reading the federal government espoused views the executive's final decision-making authority as the central element. From a certain perspective, there is a logical coherence to this view. Until now, the actual process that precedes the formal recommendation of the prime minister and appointment by the governor general has been at the virtually unfettered discretion of the prime minister, who has been free to canvass and consult anyone for names to consider. Candidates are routinely selected on the basis of patronage and often as a result of past work of a partisan nature, but in theory the prime minister has been free to make the final determination as the result of a committee of staffers in the Prime Minister's Office, the recommendation of cabinet colleagues, or even the flip of a coin. In a narrow respect, the Court's decision arguably created an absurdity: a prime minister is free to consult with whomever he or she wishes except for the voting public.

Yet the Court's reasoning also made clear that the prime minister is not free to bind his or her decision-making authority in all practical sense. It is difficult to dispute the justices on this point: elections, even if technically consultative, come with the baggage of democratic legitimacy that makes it difficult to foresee the appointment of winners of senatorial election campaigns becoming anything other than normal practice. As a result, advisory elections would mark a significant change in the way the final, formal decision to appoint is made, even if by conventional practice and not as a matter of formal law. In the result, the Court's reasoning here provided at least a legitimate legal grounding for interpreting section 42(1)(b) so that it applies to the institution of advisory elections.

However, the justices extended their rationale for this conclusion beyond the scope of a contextual analysis of how section 42(1)(b) applies with respect to establishing advisory elections. In line with its emphasis on the constitutional architecture concept, the Court described the impact consultative elections would have on the operation of the Senate as an institution. The justices pointed out that the "framers sought to endow the Senate with independence from the electoral process to which members of the House of Commons were subject, in order to remove Senators from a partisan political arena that required unremitting consideration of short-term political objectives."[13] The justices argued that "the choice of executive appointment for Senators was also intended to ensure that the Senate would be a *complementary* legislative body, rather than a perennial rival of the House of Commons ... This would ensure that they would confined themselves to their role as a body mainly conducting legislative review, rather than as a coequal of the House."[14] This conception of the Senate "shapes the architecture" of the Constitution Act, 1867.[15] Advisory elections would constitute a significant change to the function of the Senate, which, as it is a federal institution, would require provincial consent.

A number of problems flow from the Court's foray into describing the Senate's function. First, the justices' description of the Senate as a body of "sober second thought" and one that engages primarily in "legislative review" is somewhat simplistic. Studies of the upper house show that the classic sober second thought depiction is overstated, in part because the Senate has more legislative influence than is normally recognized.[16] As David E. Smith notes, the Senate has a major role to play in constraining majority governments.[17] It has even, for a time, been involved in scrutinizing draft bills before their introduction in the House (pre-study), which has had an important impact on legislative drafting. None of this is to suggest the Senate has been a competitive, rather than a complementary, body, but there are important nuances to the Senate's function that the Court's depiction did not fully address.

Second, the Court's emphasis on the proposed reform's impact – specifically, giving the upper house a "democratic mandate" – belied other potential changes that might affect the Senate's role vis-à-vis the House of Commons. It is not surprising that the Court left unaddressed what other reforms to the appointments process might be permissible without requiring the general amending procedure. The justices were addressing the questions before them, and wading too deeply into hypothetical scenarios would have been fraught with difficulty (and is generally avoided in the context of reference cases). Nonetheless, by not resting their reasons on the determination that the particular electoral reform proposal falls under the ambit of section 42(1)(b), the justices clouded the issue of whether other, more modest reforms to the process are possible when they invoked the Senate's general attitude as a deferential body of sober second thought. Nor did the Court's opinion settle solely on the fact that the proposed process would, in practice, be binding on the prime minister's discretion; the justices also emphasized that the specific nature of elections – and the democratic mandate they would give the Senate itself – were particularly likely to alter the Senate's function.

The Court's opinion not only failed to provide guidelines about what changes Parliament might make to rules governing senatorial selection or even a consultative process that might draw up a list of potential candidates for appointment; it also arguably clouded the issue more than if it had simply rested its reasons on its discussion of section 42(1)(b). This problem is more than hypothetical, because by the time the Court rendered its opinion, other proposals had already been put forward in political debate.[18] Liberal leader Justin Trudeau proposed abolishing partisanship and patronage as factors in the senatorial selection process.[19] A nonpartisan appointments process would mark a departure from past practice and, in the extreme, over time, could remove partisanship as a feature from the Senate entirely. Moreover, the Liberals promised an "open, transparent and non-partisan appointment process for Senators ... informed by other non-partisan appointment processes, such as that of the Supreme Court Justices and Order of Canada recipients."[20]

Although the specific details of the proposal remain to be seen, the prospect of an arm's-length committee of nonpartisan members developing a shortlist of candidates (or even propose nominees) for the prime minister raises a number of interesting questions in light of the Court's reasons. The Court suggested this might require an amendment under the general procedure, depending on how much emphasis is given to the electoral nature of the impugned proposals, when it wrote:

> The words "the method of selecting Senators" include more than the formal appointment of Senators by the Governor General ... The proposed consultative elections would produce lists of candidates, from which prime ministers would be expected to choose when making appointments to the Senate. The compilation of these lists through national or provincial and territorial elections and the Prime Minister's consideration of them prior to making recommendations to the Governor General would form part of the "method of selecting Senators." Consequently, the implementation of consultative elections falls within the scope of s. 42(1) (*b*) and is subject to the general amending procedure.[21]

It is not clear whether this applies to any list produced by any process from which the prime minister would be "expected" to choose names when making appointments, or if there is something particular to a list drawn from an electoral process. If the former, then the Court's opinion might have placed much greater restrictions on the front end of the selection process than many observers previously contemplated.

From the perspective of the Senate's function, a merit-based process that removes partisanship and patronage from the appointments process would also confer added legitimacy to the Senate as a body. Although not necessarily of the same magnitude or character as the democratic mandate afforded by an electoral process, a nonpartisan Senate composed of eminent Canadians appointed through a quasi-independent process arguably would mark a fundamental shift in the nature of the Senate's composition. It is conceivable that senators appointed via a nonpartisan process, and whom the public came to view with more respect by their not being beneficiaries of patronage, would recognize, and be emboldened by, the added perceived legitimacy such a context afforded. Although unlikely to transform the Senate into a body that would act in constant competition with the House of Commons, such a change nonetheless could lead to more frequent legislative activity in the form of amendments and even vetoes to bills coming up from the lower house. The Court's reference opinion leaves much doubt, however, about what degree of change in the Senate's function is sufficient to require a constitutional amendment under the general formula.

It is also unclear to what extent the prime minister may introduce new elements – even informal ones – into the process leading up to the final selection of senators that might bind his or her discretion. There is likely an important distinction to be made between an effort to establish formally a process in law (and thereby attempting to bind future prime ministers to a particular process) and informally constituting a committee or some new process of consultation before making an appointment. Or do these sorts of distinctions amount to constitutional hair-splitting? The notion that a prime minister can implement certain reforms, but only if he or she does so informally, speaks to the flexibility of our constitutional architecture, perhaps, or it might simply expose a fundamental logical inconsistency within the construction of the amending formula and the Supreme Court's interpretation of it. Is a prime minister free to attempt, informally, to establish a convention of appointing senators of a certain type to the Senate or by some particular process by which candidates' names are produced? The Court's opinion raises the question but does not answer it.

This question relates to another issue that is left unclear by the Court's opinion, and that is whether provinces are still free to run their own Senate elections. The reference asked if Parliament could pass legislation to run its own elections or "establish a framework" for provinces to consult their electors. Yet Alberta has long held Senate elections on its own initiative; indeed, a number of senators who won these contests were subsequently appointed to the upper chamber. The Court did not comment on this more informal (from the federal government's perspective) process, or on the legitimacy of these particular senators' standing in the Senate. From a constitutional perspective, it would be surprising if a province were somehow prohibited from canvassing its voters via plebiscite on any matter it wished. It is not clear if the prime minister is now prohibited from exercising the discretion to appoint someone who won one of these provincially administered contests.[22]

Term Limits

On term limits, the Court was asked the following:

1. In relation to each of the following proposed limits to the tenure of Senators, is it within the legislative authority of the Parliament of Canada, acting pursuant to section 44 of the *Constitution Act, 1982*, to make amendments to section 29 of the *Constitution Act, 1867* providing for
    (a) a fixed term of nine years for Senators, as set out in clause 5 of Bill C-7, the *Senate Reform Act*;
    (b) a fixed term of ten years or more for Senators;

(c) a fixed term of eight years or less for Senators;

(d) a fixed term of the life of two or three Parliaments for Senators;

(e) a renewable term for Senators, as set out in clause 2 of Bill S-4, *Constitution Act, 2006 (Senate tenure)*;

(f) limits to the terms for Senators appointed after October 14, 2008 as set out in subclause 4(1) of Bill C-7, the *Senate Reform Act*; and

(g) retrospective limits to the terms for Senators appointed before October 14, 2008?

On the question of term limits, the Court confronted arguably the most difficult issue of the reference. Unlike "the method of selecting senators," the specific issue of senatorial terms is not explicitly mentioned in Part V.[23] At issue with respect to term limits was whether Parliament could implement them unilaterally under section 44 or provincial consent under the general amending procedure was required. The justices concluded that, like consultative elections, term limits could be implemented only under the general amending formula. While noting that senatorial terms were not an issue encompassed by changes referred to in section 42(1)(b), the Court stated that provinces have an interest in any changes affecting the "fundamental nature and role" of the Senate.[24] Specifically, the justices wrote, "it does not follow that all changes to the Senate that fall outside of s.42 come within the scope of the unilateral amending procedure in s.44."[25]

The Court's approach to interpreting section 44 was guided by its understanding of the historical context surrounding that provision. In 1949, the British North America Act (No. 2) inserted section 91(1) into the BNA Act, giving Parliament broad new authority over constitutional amendments, with the exception of anything relating to provincial powers or rights, minority education, and languages. Until then, only a minimal set of changes to the original BNA Act of 1867 could be made domestically, as permitted through a handful of specific provisions. Parliament was authorized to make "housekeeping" changes to the Senate or House of Commons, such as increasing the number of MPs (under section 52), establishing and changing electoral districts (section 40), changing quorum in the Senate (section 35), and amending the privileges and immunities of MPs (section 18), while section 92(1) allowed provinces to make changes to provincial constitutions, so long as these did not affect the lieutenant-governor.[26]

The 1949 changes broadening the scope of federal amending authority were made without provincial consent. As Patrick Monahan and

Byron Shaw explain: "The federal position was that provincial consent was unnecessary because the new amending power was of concern to the federal government alone and could not be used to affect provincial powers. The provinces rejected this justification and claimed that section 91(1) could nonetheless operate to permit the federal government to enact amendments that would indirectly affect provincial interests in the federation."[27] In the *Senate Reform Reference*, the Court interpreted section 44 as effectively a replacement for this old provision, and determined that, despite the broad textual language of section 44, Parliament could effect only housekeeping changes to the Senate. Section 44 was thus regarded as a circumscribed exception to the general amending procedure.[28]

Any changes that might alter the Senate's function or role, or that have any implications for the provinces, require provincial consent. In the context of term limits, the justices stated:

> [T]he Senate's fundamental nature and role is that of a complementary legislative body of sober second thought. The current duration of senatorial terms is directly linked to this conception of the Senate. Senators are appointed roughly for the duration of their active professional lives. This security of tenure is intended to allow Senators to function with independence in conducting legislative review. This Court stated in the *Upper House Reference* that, "[a]t some point, a reduction of the term of office might impair the functioning of the Senate in providing what Sir John A. Macdonald described as 'the sober second thought in legislation'": p. 76. A significant change to senatorial tenure would thus affect the Senate's fundamental nature and role.[29]

It is notable that the Court acknowledged its statement in the 1980 *Upper House Reference*, where it held that the imposition of a mandatory retirement age "did not change the essential character of the Senate,"[30] and therefore could be regarded as a legitimate exercise of unilateral action by Parliament. Constitutional scholars who note that the procedures of Part V as they relate to the Senate were an attempt to "codify" the Court's opinion in the 1980 reference have also argued that it would be acceptable for Parliament to enact term limits of a certain length under section 44. Monahan and Shaw, for example, suggest: "The items specified in section 42 should be regarded as an exhaustive list of matters deemed fundamental or essential, as those terms were utilized in the Senate *Reference*. To hold that the unilateral federal power in section 44 is subject to a further limitation along the lines suggested would lead to needless uncertainty and ambiguity."[31]

Importantly, the Court explicitly refused to address the seemingly pertinent question of why a retirement age might fall under the category of "housekeeping," but the imposition of terms limits of *any* length or design does not. The justices wrote that "[i]t may be possible, as the Attorney General of Canada suggests, to devise a fixed term so lengthy that it provides a security of tenure which is functionally equivalent to that provided by life tenure. However, it is difficult to objectively identify the precise term duration that guarantees an equivalent degree of security of tenure."[32]

The Court's refusal to engage in a line-drawing exercise here is problematic to the extent that line-drawing is precisely what was being asked of it. The structure of the federal government's reference questions on term limits was clearly designed to encapsulate a range of alternatives. The questions posed to the Court provide a clear indication that guidance was sought as to whether certain types of term limits might be enacted under section 44 even if other types could not. By not addressing the question of whether a nonrenewable term limit long enough to avoid altering the basic function of the Senate or the role of senators is feasible, the Court sidestepped a contradiction and logical flaw in its approach to interpreting section 44. Presuming the validity of the Court's own interpretation of section 44's development, there is no reason to believe that Parliament is not theoretically free to lower the mandatory retirement age of senators to 70 or 65 unilaterally. However, it is not free, according to the Court, to enact a nonrenewable term limit of 15 years unilaterally. The idea that one of these changes would alter the fundamental features of the institution and the other would not is difficult to comprehend. By refusing to engage with this question, the Court not only failed to deliver a good standard by which some matters may fall under different procedures in Part V; it also arguably gutted section 44 in a way not reasonably contemplated.

The justices' refusal to distinguish between different types of term limits was also contrary to existing evidence that not all term limits would alter how the Senate functions. Fixed terms undoubtedly would run the risk of impairing the Senate's independence if they were renewable. Similarly, excessively short-term limits might make a Senate appointment a brief mid-career stint, something that might alter senators' approach to their role and skew their decision-making incentives. But there is little evidence that lengthy, nonrenewable terms would pose similar dangers. As Christopher Manfredi writes, in his expert submission for the reference, the "average age at which individuals have been appointed is 57, which means that, had the nine-year fixed term applied since 1867, the average senator would have left the Senate at age 66 and would not have expected a lengthy post-Senate career."[33] Moreover, the mean and median length of senatorial service since 1965 is 11.3 and 9.8 years, respectively.[34] The imposition of lengthy nonrenewable terms, be they 9, 12, or 15 years, would not constitute a departure from the Senate's existing reality, nor could it realistically be thought to alter the Senate's fundamental features or operation.

Senate Abolition

On the issue of abolishing the Senate, the Court was asked the following questions:

5. Can an amendment to the Constitution of Canada to abolish the Senate be accomplished by the general amending procedure set out in section 38 of the *Constitution Act, 1982*, by one of the following methods:
   (*a*) by inserting a separate provision stating that the Senate is to be abolished as of a certain date, as an amendment to the *Constitution Act, 1867* or as a separate provision that is outside of the *Constitution Acts, 1867 to 1982* but that is still part of the Constitution of Canada;
   (*b*) by amending or repealing some or all of the references to the Senate in the Constitution of Canada; or
   (*c*) by abolishing the powers of the Senate and eliminating the representation of provinces pursuant to paragraphs 42(1) (*b*) and (*c*) of the *Constitution Act, 1982*?
6. If the general amending procedure set out in section 38 of the *Constitution Act, 1982* is not sufficient to abolish the Senate, does the unanimous consent procedure set out in section 41 of the *Constitution Act, 1982* apply?

The question on abolition was perhaps the most straightforward in the reference for the Court, although a number of odd or erroneous arguments arose during political debate on the issue. For example, Premier Robert Ghiz of Prince Edward Island spoke out against Senate abolition because it would mean his province "would be down to one member of Parliament" as a result of the constitutional guarantee giving PEI the same number of MPs as it has senators.[35] The premier's fears were unfounded, however, because section 41(b) of the amending formula preserves the number of members in the House of Commons for each province such that they do not fall below their number of senators "at the time this Part comes into force." In other words, the abolition of the Senate would not reduce the number of MPs to which PEI is entitled barring a unanimous amendment that alters section 41(b).

With respect to Senate abolition, any change to the amending formula itself requires unanimity under section 41(e), and the Senate is referenced throughout Part V. The federal government attempted to argue that the Senate could be abolished under the general amending formula without amending the text of Part V, as references to the Senate in Part V would be viewed as "spent" provisions following any general amendment to do so. Notably, section 47 of Part V provides the Senate with a suspensive veto that requires the House of Commons to adopt a second resolution after 180 days if the Senate refuses to adopt an initial resolution to amend the Constitution under any of the procedures other than sections 44 or 45.[36] The federal government argued that, because the Senate could be overridden after 180 days under section 47, references to it in the amending formula were incidental to its abolition. It is worth noting that such logic could be flipped on its head: the fact that the Senate itself was granted the power to delay amendments for 180 days only underscores its relevance and the significance of its presence in Part V. The ratification of resolutions to amend the Constitution when provincial consent is required is a difficult process, and a 180-day delay could result in an intervening election in some provinces. During the ratification process for the Meech Lake Accord, the election of the Clyde Wells government resulted in Newfoundland and Labrador's revoking its assent to the Accord, which contributed to the failure of the constitutional package.[37] For this reason, the Senate's suspensive veto should be regarded as having substantive, in addition to symbolic, significance.

For its part, the Court concluded correctly that "Part V was drafted on the assumption that the federal Parliament would remain bicameral in nature, i.e. that there would continue to be both a lower legislative chamber and a complementary upper chamber. Removal of the upper chamber from our Constitution would alter the structure and functioning of Part V. Consequently, it requires the unanimous consent of Parliament and of all the provinces (s. 41(e))."[38] Despite this clarity, both the Conservatives and the New Democrats persist in the belief that the Senate can be left to die by neglect: Prime Minister Harper refused to make appointments to the upper chamber following the

Court's reference opinion, and the leader of the NDP, Thomas Mulcair, promised not to make appointments in the event he became prime minister. Harper's refusal to appoint generated a legal challenge on the basis that the Constitution compels appointments.[39] Section 32 of the Constitution Act, 1867, for example, states that "[w]hen a Vacancy happens in the Senate by Resignation, Death, or otherwise, the Governor General shall by Summons to a fit and qualified Person fill the Vacancy." In practice, the prime minister advises the governor general, who then makes the formal appointment. Although it is not clear that a court of law would be so bold as to interpret the Constitution as requiring timely appointments to the Senate, a long-term refusal to make appointments clearly would interfere with the sober second thought functioning of the upper house. Indeed, the Senate's function would suffer damage before the Senate was reduced to fewer than the 15 members needed for quorum; once the Senate's committee system and ability to engage in constructive debate became impaired due to the attrition of membership, a refusal to make appointments might be regarded as an unconstitutional attempt to change the essential features of the institution.

Implications of the *Senate Reform Reference*

The rationale employed by the Court in the *Senate Reform Reference* raises a number of issues with respect to Senate reform specifically and to future constitutional amendment generally. In the context of their reasoning regarding changes to the method of selecting senators, the justices' reliance on the amorphous notion of the constitutional architecture clouds the definable limits of the method of selection under section 42(1)(b). Although it would be unreasonable to expect the reference opinion to account for every hypothetical reform option, the Court should be counted on to provide clear guidelines about the scope of the relevant provisions in Part V. Instead, the reasoning the justices adopted adds to, rather than alleviates, the uncertainty over what other changes to the appointments process might be feasible without a formal constitutional amendment and provincial consent. This is not to argue that the Court reached an incorrect decision on whether consultative elections fall under the ambit of section 42(1)(b); nor is it to suggest that only a narrow, textual reading of the Constitution is the appropriate jurisprudential approach. However, the appeal to the Constitution's broader architecture introduces ambiguity where a focus on a contextual reading of 42(1)(b) would have sufficed.

By contrast, the Court's appeal to constitutional architecture not only led it to introduce problematic uncertainty into its discussion of the imposition of term limits, it also led the justices to an incorrect conclusion regarding Parliament's ability to enact changes unilaterally under section 44. The Court's explicit refusal to distinguish between the federal government's ability to enact a retirement age under section 44 and its logic that term limits, regardless of length, require the consent of the provinces under the general amending procedure lacks logical consistency and arguably erodes section 44 to a problematic degree. The justices' rationale also flies in the face of available evidence about the conceivable impact that lengthy, nonrenewable term limits would have on the Senate's function and essential features. The structure of the questions on term limits posed to the Court makes clear that the justices were being asked to examine whether some types of term limits might avoid implicating the general amending procedure even if others do. By sidestepping this question and by explicitly refusing to engage the issue of whether lengthy term limits might not alter the Senate's function, the Court effectively avoided dealing with the central issue at stake. The effect of this was to minimize section 44 in a manner not necessarily compatible with its historical context or even with the Court's stated rationale.

The Court's reasoning also might have the effect of producing unintended (or at least unanticipated) consequences, assuming its logic is employed consistently to other issues implicating the amending formula. One of the most obvious examples of unintended consequences emanates from the Court's opinion in the *Supreme Court Act Reference*. In that opinion, a majority of justices determined that the eligibility requirements for justices of the Supreme Court, as outlined in sections 5 and 6 of the Supreme Court Act, are entrenched in the Constitution. Any changes to the eligibility requirements thus require the unanimous approval of the provinces because they fall under section 41(d) of Part V as part of the "composition of the Supreme Court of Canada." Prior to the Court's decision, adding additional eligibility requirements under the Supreme Court Act, such as mandating bilingualism for Supreme Court appointees – a policy supported by the Liberal Party and New Democratic Party – was not thought to have required constitutional amendment. This renders any such changes extremely unlikely, as an amendment has never been successfully ratified under the Constitution's unanimity procedure.[40]

As it relates to the *Senate Reform Reference*, the Court's appeal to constitutional architecture and its general antipathy towards indirect

methods of amending the Constitution have obvious potential implications for other, even informal, changes to the senatorial appointments
process, as discussed above. Moreover, the Court's rationale might
have implications for statutes such as the Regional Veto Act. Following the 1995 Quebec secession referendum, the federal government
brought in the Regional Veto Act effectively to provide Quebec (and by
design Canada's other "regions") a veto over most major amendments.
The Act prohibits government ministers from proposing constitutional
resolutions unless consent is first obtained from Ontario, Quebec, British Columbia, at least two Atlantic provinces representing at least 50
per cent of the Atlantic populations, and at least two Prairie provinces
representing at least 50 per cent of the Prairie population (in effect also
giving Alberta its own veto). The Regional Veto Act effectively uses the
federal government's inherent veto under most of Part V's amending
procedures[41] to establish a system of regional vetoes for constitutional
amendment. The Act was passed to fulfil the government's commitment to Quebec federalists, but by giving Ontario, British Columbia,
and (in effect) Alberta a veto, it makes future constitutional reform –
including reform desired by Quebec federalists – considerably more
difficult.[42]

The Court's general rationale regarding Parliament's ability to implement changes to the Constitution without the consent of the provinces
would seem to apply to the Regional Veto Act, which in practice acts as a
unilateral amendment to Part V. From the perspective of the basic architecture of the Constitution, the law compels the federal government to
restrict the legitimate exercise of Part V, an indirect change to Part V
brought about without the consent of the provinces. Moreover, it goes
beyond a political decision by a government about whether to support
a resolution because it binds future governments in law. If Parliament is
not free to implement changes to the method of selecting senators or to
impose term limits without provincial consent, it would be inconsistent
with an approach to interpreting Part V to permit such disregard for
the basic constitutional architecture, which includes the foundational
agreement about the structure of the amending procedures in Part V.

From a broader perspective, the Court's approach to interpreting
the amending formula might also be evaluated on the basis of the balance between flexibility and rigidity that animates Part V's design. If
the Constitution represents the fundamental rules and structure for the
country's governing system, then the amending formula determines who
gets to write those rules. A good formula provides enough flexibility for

change to occur when it is needed or where there is sufficiently deep and broad consensus, but ensures enough rigidity so that fundamental changes can be accomplished only when consensus warrants. Debate during constitutional negotiations over the design of Part V recognized this tension.[43] The 1982 agreement resulted in a complex set of procedures designed to accommodate the need for consensus over fundamental change while ensuring the flexibility to prevent constitutional stasis. Judicial interpretation of these various procedures that expands the application of some over others risks imbalance, the result of which is either to lower the threshold for constitutional change to the point of disregarding the need for consensus or to raise it so high as to invite constitutional stasis.

On this score, the Court's *Senate Reform Reference* opinion is problematic for two reasons. First, as noted above, the justices minimized section 44, characterizing it as a very narrow exception to the general amending procedure. As I have argued, they did so without sufficiently addressing the logical consistency of their approach. Second, the Court's appeal to the basic structure or architecture of the Constitution ultimately obscures, rather than clarifies, the dividing line between the various amending procedures. This might have the effect of chilling future attempts at constitutional change or, at the very least, increasing contestation and future legal challenges to reform efforts. Greater clarity through more coherent guidelines about the scope of the various amending procedures would have reduced this uncertainty. In that respect, the *Senate Reform Reference* is a failure.

Notes

My thanks to Alexander Pless and anonymous reviewers for thoughtful comments on earlier versions of this chapter. A version of this chapter was previously published as Emmett Macfarlane, "Unsteady Architecture: Ambiguity, the Senate Reference, and the Future of Constitutional Amendment in Canada," *McGill Law Journal* 60, no. 4 (2015): 883–903.

1 *Reference re Supreme Court Act, ss.5 and 6*, 2014 SCC 21, [2014] 1 S.C.R. 433 [*Supreme Court Act Reference*].
2 *Reference re Senate Reform*, 2014 SCC 32, [2014] 1 S.C.R. [*Senate Reform Reference*].
3 The Court was also asked to address which amending procedure applied to the comparatively minor question of abolishing property requirements for senators.

4 The general procedure under section 38(1), reads as follows: "An amendment to the Constitution of Canada may be made by proclamation issued by the Governor General under the Great Seal of Canada where so authorized by (a) resolutions of the Senate and House of Commons; and (b) resolutions of the legislative assemblies of at least two-thirds of the provinces that have, in the aggregate, according to the then latest general census, at least fifty per cent of the population of all the provinces."

5 The unanimity procedure under section 41 reads as follows:

> An amendment to the Constitution of Canada in relation to the following matters may be made by proclamation issued by the Governor General under the Great Seal of Canada only where authorized by resolutions of the Senate and House of Commons and of the legislative assembly of each province:
>
> - (a) the office of the Queen, the Governor General and the Lieutenant Governor of a province;
> - (b) the right of a province to a number of members in the House of Commons not less than the number of Senators by which the province is entitled to be represented at the time this Part comes into force;
> - (c) subject to section 43, the use of the English or the French language;
> - (d) the composition of the Supreme Court of Canada; and
> - (e) an amendment to this Part.

6 Section 42(1) lists specific amendments to the Constitution that may be made only in accordance with subsection 38(1):

- (a) the principle of proportionate representation of the provinces in the House of Commons prescribed by the Constitution of Canada;
- (b) the powers of the Senate and the method of selecting Senators;
- (c) the number of members by which a province is entitled to be represented in the Senate and the residence qualifications of Senators;
- (d) subject to paragraph 41(d), the Supreme Court of Canada;
- (e) the extension of existing provinces into the territories; and
- (f) notwithstanding any other law or practice, the establishment of new provinces.

7 *Senate Reform Reference*, para. 25, citing *Reference re Secession of Quebec*, [1998] 2 S.C.R. 217, para. 32 [*Secession Reference*].

8 Ibid.

9 See *Secession Reference*, para. 50; *OPSEU v Ontario (Attorney General)*, [1987] 2 S.C.R. 2, 57.

10 *Senate Reform Reference*, para. 26.

11 Ibid., para. 62.

12 Ibid., para. 52.

13 Ibid., para. 57.

14 Ibid., para. 58.

15 Ibid., para. 59.
16 Paul Thomas, "Comparing the Lawmaking Roles of the Senate and the House of Commons," in *Protecting Canadian Democracy: The Senate You Never Knew*, ed. Serge Joyal (Montreal; Kingston, ON: McGill-Queen's University Press, 2003), 189; David E. Smith, *The Canadian Senate in Bicameral Perspective* (Toronto: University of Toronto Press, 2003).
17 Smith, *Canadian Senate*, 114.
18 Aaron Wherry, "Justin Trudeau's unilateral Senate reform." *Maclean's*, 29 January 2014, available online at http://www.macleans.ca/authors/aaron-wherry/justin-trudeaus-unilateral-senate-reform/.
19 In the interests of full disclosure, I was asked to advise the Liberal Party on the constitutionality of its proposals prior to the release of the Court's *Senate Reform Reference* opinion.
20 Ibid.
21 *Senate Reform Reference*, para. 65.
22 Plans by the New Brunswick government to hold Senate elections were described as being in "limbo" following the Court's decision; see Jacques Poitras, "David Alward's Senate reform plans in legal limbo," *CBC News*, 30 April 2014, available online at http://www.cbc.ca/news/canada/new-brunswick/david-alward-s-senate-reform-plans-in-legal-limbo-1.2625938.
23 Nonetheless, it was clear that an amendment would be required given that senatorial tenure is listed in section 29(2) of the Constitution Act, 1867, which states that "[a] Senator who is summoned to the Senate … shall … hold his place in the Senate until he attains the age of seventy-five years."
24 *Senate Reform Reference*, para. 78.
25 Ibid., para. 74.
26 Patrick J. Monahan and Byron Shaw, *Constitutional Law*, 4th ed. (Toronto: Irwin Law, 2013) 169–71.
27 Ibid., 171.
28 *Senate Reform Reference*, para. 75.
29 Ibid., para. 79, citing *Re: Authority of Parliament in relation to the Upper House*, [1980] 1 S.C.R. 54 [*Upper House Reference*].
30 *Upper House Reference*, para. 77.
31 Monahan and Shaw, *Constitutional Law*, 214.
32 *Senate Reform Reference*, para. 81.
33 Christopher P. Manfredi, "An Expert Opinion on the possible effects of Bill C-7," *AGC Record* 16, tab 105 (June 2013): 32.
34 Ibid., 34.
35 Teresa Wright, "Scrapping the Senate bad for P.E.I., local politicians argue," *Guardian* [Charlottetown] 28 May 2013, available online at

http://www.theguardian.pe.ca/News/Local/2013-05-28/article-3261747/
Scrapping-the-Senate-bad-for-P.E.I.,-local-politicians-argue/1.

36 Section 47 reads as follows: "47(1) An amendment to the Constitution of
Canada made by proclamation under section 38, 41, 42 or 43 may be made
without a resolution of the Senate authorizing the issue of the proclamation
if, within one hundred and eighty days after the adoption by the House of
Commons of a resolution authorizing its issue, the Senate has not adopted
such a resolution and if, at any time after the expiration of that period,
the House of Commons again adopts the resolution. (2) Any period when
Parliament is prorogued or dissolved shall not be counted in computing the
one hundred and eighty day period referred to in subsection (1)."

37 Peter H. Russell, *Constitutional Odyssey: Can Canadians Become a Sovereign
People?* (Toronto: University of Toronto Press, 2004), 142–8.

38 *Senate Reform Reference*, para. 106.

39 Joan Bryden, "Court asked to compel Senate appointments," Canadian
Press, 9 April 2015, available online at http://metronews.ca/news/
canada/1335989/court-asked-to-compel-senate-appointments-2/.

40 This might not have been an "unintended" feature of the Court's opinion –
it is in the Court's institutional interest to read section 41(d) as broadly as
possible and thereby to immunize it from a host of changes by Parliament.

41 It would not appear to apply to certain amendments under section 38 where
provinces can opt out, and presumably not to those that only require the
federal government acting alone; see Monahan and Shaw, *Constitutional
Law*, 217.

42 Ibid.

43 See Howard Leeson, *The Patriation Minutes* (Edmonton: University of Alberta,
Faculty of Law, Centre for Constitutional Studies, 2011); Barry L. Strayer,
Canada's Constitutional Revolution (Edmonton: University of Alberta Press,
2013); Russell, *Constitutional Odyssey*; Premiers' Conference, Ottawa, Ontario,
16 April 1981, in *Canada's Constitution Act 1982 & Amendments: A Documentary
History*, vol. 2, ed. Anne F. Bayefsky (Toronto: McGraw-Hill Ryerson, 1989),
804; James Ross Hurley, *Amending Canada's Constitution: History, Processes,
Problems and Prospects* (Ottawa: Canada Communication Group, 1996).

12 The Crown and Constitutional Amendment after the *Senate Reform* and *Supreme Court References*

PHILIPPE LAGASSÉ AND PATRICK BAUD

The Crown rests uncomfortably atop of Canada's constitutional architecture. Although the Crown continues to play several significant constitutional roles, the institution is increasingly called into question. Whether through legal challenges to oaths sworn to the Queen, commentators wanting an end to Canada's ties to the British royal family, or efforts to regulate the Crown's power to dissolve the legislatures, calls for the monarchy's reform or outright abolition are increasing.[1] Even those sympathetic towards the Crown can hardly deny its political vulnerability. Yet acting on these calls is much easier said than done. Doing so would require amending the Constitution using the complex and strict rules laid down in Part V of the Constitution Act, 1982.[2] Amendments to the Constitution in relation to the "office of the Queen, the Governor General and the Lieutenant of a province" are subject to the strictest amending procedure under paragraph 41(a) of the Act, which requires the unanimous consent of the Houses of Parliament and the provincial legislative assemblies. However narrowly this provision is read, it was evidently meant to provide Canada's constitutional monarchy with the highest degree of constitutional protection.[3]

Nonetheless, the Supreme Court of Canada's approach to Part V suggests that not all aspects of the Crown require unanimity to alter.[4] The general amending procedure in section 38 of the Act, which requires the consent of the Senate and House of Commons and at least seven of ten provincial legislative assemblies representing at least 50 per cent of the population of the provinces, might apply to constitutional amendments that affect the Crown in a way that engages the interests of the provinces, but leaves its "head of state" functions intact. Likewise, sections 44 and 45 of the Act allow Parliament and the provincial legislatures to make constitutional amendments involving the Crown that do not affect the other level of government's interests.

Drawing especially on the *Senate Reform Reference*, as well as earlier Judicial Committee of the Privy Council (JCPC) and Supreme Court judgments and court of appeal decisions, we examine which amending procedures likely apply to which sorts of changes to the Crown. We argue that unanimity is required for abolition of the monarchy, alterations to the principles governing royal succession, and changes to the Queen's role as "head of state" and the governor general's and lieutenant-governors' related roles and powers. The general amending procedure, we further posit, applies to executive powers of the Crown that affect provincial interests, particularly defence and foreign affairs prerogatives and judicial and senatorial appointments, as well as the royal recommendation. Unilateral federal and provincial procedures apply to changes to the Crown that do not affect the interests of the other level of government, such as the Crown's role as the legal personality of the executive and the first minister's control of ministerial appointments.

Amending the "Constitution of Canada"

In the *Senate Reform Reference*, the Supreme Court laid out a two-part test for constitutional amendments. The first step is to determine whether the contemplated change affects an element of the "Constitution of Canada." If so, the second step is to classify the contemplated change under one of the amending procedures. For the purposes of the test, the Court adopted a broad definition of the "Constitution of Canada": it includes not only the text, but also "[t]he assumptions that underlie the text and the manner in which the constitutional provisions are intended to interact with one another."[5] Together these elements form the "Constitution's architecture." Altering either the text or changing this broader architecture requires the use of the amending procedures outlined in Part V.[6]

According to the Supreme Court, the amending procedures must "be interpreted in a broad and purposive manner" that is attuned to both the general purpose of Part V and the specific purpose of each procedure.[7] The general purpose is "to foster dialogue between the federal government and the provinces on matters of constitutional change, and to protect Canada's constitutional *status quo* until such times as reforms are agreed upon."[8] This implies that most constitutional amendments cannot be made by a single federal or provincial legislature enacting what would otherwise be ordinary legislation. Instead, most constitutional amendments are to be made using the general procedure, which is "the general rule for amendments" and to which the other procedures are "exceptions."[9] The general procedure "reflects the principle that substantial provincial consent must be obtained for constitutional change that engages provincial interests."[10] Use of the general procedure is required for changes to the essential features of Canada's national institutions – the Senate, the House of Commons, the Supreme Court, and, as we argue in this chapter, the executive – as such changes engage provincial interests.[11]

The unanimity procedure, on the other hand, "'is justified by the need to give each of the partners of Canada's federal compromise a veto on those topics that are considered most essential to the survival of the state.'"[12] Unanimity is required to abolish the monarchy, the House of Commons, the Senate, and the Supreme Court.[13] It also applies to changes that affect certain fundamental features of these institutions, including the composition of the Supreme Court, the "Senate floor rule," which provides that no province can have fewer MPs than the number of senators it had in 1982, and, as we argue, the most significant aspects of the Crown's constitutional position.[14]

The unilateral federal and provincial amending procedures grant Parliament and the provincial legislatures "the ability to unilaterally amend certain aspects of the Constitution that relate to their own level of government, but which do not engage the interests of the other level of government."[15] This allows Parliament and the provincial legislatures to make changes to nonessential features of national and provincial institutions, including the composition of the House of Commons, property qualifications for senators, and likely aspects of the Crown's constitutional position that do not engage the other level of government's interests.[16]

As of the time of writing, the courts have not yet been called upon to apply the two-part test laid out in the *Senate Reform Reference* to a contemplated change affecting the Crown. Fortunately, the Supreme Court and lower courts have given indications of how they understand the Crown's place in Canada's constitutional order, and offered guidance as to which amending procedures might apply to which sorts of changes. The courts have tended to emphasize the Crown's position as head of state and its place in the legislatures, but to minimize its role as the executive power. This understanding of the Crown's constitutional status is likely to shape the manner in which the courts approach constitutional amendments affecting the Crown.

The Crown in the "Constitution of Canada"

In the *Senate Reform Reference*, the Supreme Court noted that the "basic structure of government" provided in the Constitution was meant to preserve "the British structure of a lower legislative chamber composed of elected representatives, an upper legislative chamber made up of elites appointed by the Crown, and the Crown as head of state."[17] The Court's reference to the Crown as "head of state" is significant, as it means that the Crown is not merely symbolic, but also the institution that is responsible for performing certain constitutional functions and given powers to fulfil them. Those functions and powers are allocated among the Queen, the governor general, and the lieutenant-governors. Given the close ties between the functions and powers and constitutional positions of the offices themselves, the Court likely would interpret paragraph 41(a) of the Constitution Act, 1982 as protecting not only the existence of these offices, but also their continued ability to fulfil their constitutional responsibilities.[18] Several lower courts, albeit in decisions handed down before the *Senate Reform Reference*, adopted such an interpretation of paragraph 41(a),[19] and the Supreme Court itself showed sympathy with this approach, although in *obiter*, in *Ontario (AG) v OPSEU.*[20]

Describing the Crown's constitutional role as "head of state" is equally significant for what it omits. Part III of the Constitution Act, 1867 vests executive power in the Queen, and provides for its exercise by her viceregal representatives acting on the advice of federal and provincial cabinets.[21] This means that, in addition to being the head of state, the Crown is formally the executive.[22] The Crown gives a legal personality to the executive, serves as the nominal source of government authority, and allows the executive powers of the Crown to be exercised by ministers.[23] Alongside its executive role, the Crown is also part of Parliament and the provincial legislatures.[24] In its legislative capacity, the Crown opens new legislative sessions with speeches from the throne, provides the royal recommendation for money votes, gives royal consent allowing for the debate of legislation affecting its interests, and grants Royal Assent that turns bills into law.[25] As David E. Smith argues, it is the Crown's everyday role in the executives and legislatures that makes the institution such a pervasive, if little appreciated, part of Canada's system of government.[26]

By describing the Crown as head of state, the Supreme Court implicitly differentiated the institution's head-of-state functions from its broader executive and legislative roles. This suggests that paragraph 41(a)'s ambit might not include certain of the Crown's executive and legislative aspects. Indeed, in *New Brunswick Broadcasting*, Justice Beverley McLachlin, as she then was, seemed to suggest that the Crown, represented by the governor general and lieutenant-governors, formed a distinct branch of government from the executive and legislative branches.[27] Justice John Sopinka made similar comments in *Reference re Canada Assistance Plan*.[28] Although McLachlin's and Sopinka's comments were made in the context of a discussion of parliamentary privilege and intergovernmental agreements, respectively, they could relatively easily be translated into the amendment context.

Such an approach would seem consistent with the intentions of the framers of Part V of the Constitution Act, 1982, since the general and unilateral procedures contemplated considerable reforms to the federal and provincial executives and legislatures without the unanimity required for changes to the offices of the Crown. For instance, although the governor general formally appoints senators under Part IV of the Constitution Act, 1867, it is clear that the general amending formula is sufficient to strip them of that power through an amendment to the "method of selecting Senators" by virtue of paragraph 42(1)(b) of the Constitution Act, 1982.[29]

Determining what aspects of the Crown fall under which amending procedure requires attending to "'the constitutional text itself, the historical context and previous judicial interpretations of constitutional meaning.'"[30] The Queen's position as head of state is clear in the Constitution Act, 1867 – particularly in the preamble, the first recital of which notes that the provinces "have expressed their Desire to be federally united into One Dominion *under the Crown* ... with a Constitution similar in Principle to that of the United Kingdom."[31] The Queen's role as head of state has been reaffirmed in recent rulings on the citizenship oath and the rules governing succession to the throne.[32]

Past JCPC and Supreme Court jurisprudence suggests that the "office of Lieutenant Governor" includes the functions in which and powers over which the lieutenant-governor exercises some degree of discretion.[33] In the *Quebec Senate Reference*, the Quebec Court of Appeal extended this logic to the governor general with regard to senatorial appointments.[34] According to this interpretation, which has been followed in other lower courts, the functions and powers over which the Crown exercises discretion form part of the respective offices of the Queen, the governor general, and lieutenant-governors.[35] Those over which the Crown has no discretion and are effectively exercised by ministers do not form part of their offices.[36]

Using a discretion-based framework, it is possible to classify which aspects of the Crown fall under which amending procedure:

- Unanimous amendments: Those functions and powers that involve an exercise of discretion by the Queen, the governor general or a lieutenant-governor are protected by paragraph 41(a), as are aspects of the Crown that are intimately tied to the institution's constitutional position as head of state.
- General procedure amendments: Those Crown functions and powers that involve ministerial, as opposed to viceregal, discretion do not enjoy the protection of paragraph 41(a). However, if these ministerial functions and powers affect provincial interests or significantly alter the nature of an institution, then the general amending procedure is required. The general procedure will be required for most changes, as "neither level of government acting alone can alter the fundamental nature and role of the institutions provided for in the Constitution."[37]
- Unilateral amendments: Federally, Parliament alone may amend those characteristics and authorities of the Crown that do not involve regal or viceregal discretion and do not affect provincial interests. At the provincial level, the provincial unilateral procedure applies so long as the Crown is not affected in a way that engages paragraph 41(a).[38]

The Crown as Head of State and the Unanimity Procedure

Given the Supreme Court's emphasis on the Crown's position as head of state in Canada's constitutional architecture, it seems likely that the reference to the "office of the Queen, Governor General and Lieutenant Governor of a province" in paragraph 41(a) of the Constitution Act, 1982 protects not only the existence of these offices, but also their "head-of-state" functions. As a result, changes to who holds these offices, how they are selected, how they can be removed, and to the powers over which office holders exercise discretion all require the consent of the Senate, the House of Commons, and the ten provincial legislative assemblies.

Symmetry with the British Crown

As we finalized this chapter, the Quebec Superior Court ruled on the constitutional validity of the Succession to the Throne Act, 2013. The case addressed two important questions: Is succession to the throne a matter of Canadian law? If so, is a change to the law of succession tantamount to a constitutional amendment to the "office of the Queen" under paragraph 41(a)? The Quebec Superior Court found that Canadian law does not include rules of royal succession. Instead, the Canadian Constitution includes a rule of recognition that ensures Canada and the United Kingdom share the same monarch, in accordance with the rule of succession laid out in UK law. This rule of recognition forms part of Canada's constitutional "tapestry" (in French, "*toile de fond.*") Hence, royal succession does not form part of Canadian law, but is a constitutional principle. The Court further found that Canada's assent to the UK Parliament's alterations of the law of succession for the United Kingdom did not engage paragraph 41(a) because succession does not form part of the office of the Queen.[39] What remains unclear, however, is whether the rule of recognition itself is protected by paragraph 41(a). It is difficult to conclude that this rule would not fall under the unanimous amending formula. For instance, if Parliament sought to replace the House of Windsor as Canada's royal family, paragraph 41(a) would probably be engaged. The same likely would be the case if Parliament sought to transform Canada's hereditary monarchy into an elective institution. Likewise, an effort to abolish the monarchy de facto by declaring the office of the Queen vacant or by refusing to recognize Queen Elizabeth II's successor would also require the unanimous consent of the federal and provincial legislative houses. Although the Quebec Superior Court left these issues unresolved, it appears unlikely that such a fundamental aspect of the Crown would not fall under paragraph 41(a).

Appointment and Removal of the Governor General and Lieutenant-Governors

The office of governor general is an appointed position. The governor general is appointed by the Queen on the advice of the prime minister.[40] Although the Queen is normally expected to accept the prime minister's advice on whom to appoint, she retains the discretion to reject the advice.[41] This discretion is necessary for the Queen to be able to fulfil her ultimate function as head of state: guarding against unconstitutional abuses of power when Parliament and the courts might be unable to do so.[42] Indeed, it is not hard to imagine situations in which the Queen might need to exercise such discretion. For instance, if the governor general were poised to refuse the prime minister's advice to dissolve Parliament, the prime minister might seek to have the governor general removed and a new, more amenable person named by the Queen.[43] In such a circumstance, the Queen would be justified in refusing to appoint the new governor general, since doing so would allow the prime minister to undermine the governor general's discretion over dissolution.

Since the Queen has discretion over the appointment of the governor general, a departure from this arrangement would require an amendment under paragraph 41(a). Also, holding elections to fill the office of governor general would require the unanimous consent of the federal and provincial legislatures, even if an attempt were made to do so indirectly, as the Supreme Court rejected in the *Senate Reform Reference* in relation to senatorial appointments.[44] It is possible that an amendment under the unanimity procedure would also be required to empower Parliament or a formal advisory committee to select the governor general.

Lieutenant-governors are appointed by the governor general in council, the governor general acting on the binding advice of the Queen's Privy Council for Canada – that is, effectively, the prime minister and the cabinet.[45] The governor general has no discretion over the appointment of lieutenant-governors, however, so it might be possible to reform the appointment procedure without an amendment that required unanimity, but likely not possible to make the office of lieutenant-governor an elected position, as this would transform the nature of the office so as to engage paragraph 41(a). The removal of lieutenant-governors, by contrast, might fall within the discretion of the governor general: section 59 of the Constitution Act, 1867 provides that lieutenant-governors serve "during the Pleasure of the Governor General," but specifies that they can be removed only for cause within their first five years in office, subject to notification of Parliament.[46] The governor general's discretion in this matter protects the Crown's representatives in the provinces from a federal government that might support unconstitutional behaviour on the part of a provincial government.

Appointment and Removal of First Ministers

The governor general and lieutenant-governors exercise discretion over the appointment and dismissal of first ministers,[47] which allows them to play their essential role in government formation: appointing first ministers who are expected to carry the confidence of the elected chamber of the legislature, and dismissing first ministers who have lost such confidence or otherwise cannot govern effectively, but who refuse to resign or request a dissolution.[48] The viceregal officers can also use their discretion to dismiss first ministers who act unconstitutionally or otherwise act in ways, such as being involved in criminal activity, that make them unsuited to head the government.[49]

Given the significance of the connection between the viceregal officers' constitutional responsibilities and the power to appoint and dismiss first ministers, removing this power would require an amendment under paragraph 41(a). In practical terms, this would mean that an effort to transfer the power to appoint and dismiss first ministers to the elected chamber of the legislature would require the unanimous consent of the Senate, the House of Commons, and the ten provincial legislative assemblies. Such an amendment would also be required for an indirect transfer of power in the form of a decision about who should be first minister by the legislature presented as a "recommendation" to the governor general and lieutenant-governor.[50] The same would be true of legislation that provided for the direct election of a first minister.[51]

Summoning, Proroguing, and Dissolving the Legislature

The governor general and lieutenant-governors dissolve Parliament and the provincial legislatures, respectively, on the advice of first ministers, but the viceregal officers have the discretion to refuse this advice,[52] to ensure that the legislature is given a proper opportunity to play its role after an election. A first minister might ask for dissolution too soon after an election or before the legislature has had a chance to meet and express its confidence (or lack thereof) in his or her ministry.[53] In such cases, the viceregal officer may refuse dissolution, dismiss the incumbent first minister or accept his or her resignation, and appoint a new first minister.

Such viceregal discretion over dissolution also ensures that an election is held if the legislature can no longer function.[54] If dissolution were made contingent on a supermajority vote in the elected legislature, as has been proposed in Canada and made law in the United Kingdom, the end of a legislative session could be determined by a relatively small number of members who are not entrusted with the legislature's confidence, as are first ministers.[55] Although it can be argued that such an arrangement is preferable to the current one, such a reform would affect the discretion of viceregal officers over dissolution, and thus require a unanimous constitutional amendment.[56]

It is less clear if a change to the power to summon and prorogue Parliament and the provincial legislatures would require unanimity.[57] Unlike the settled nature of the other powers we have discussed in this section, there is significant disagreement about whether the viceregal officers truly exercise discretion in granting a first minister's request to summon or prorogue an elected legislature, provided the government has not formally lost its confidence.[58] Any court facing a constitutional attempt to reform these powers would have to sort through conflicting views about where discretion on these matters lies.

If the governor general and lieutenant-governors retain such powers, which would allow them to refuse the advice of a first minister who was trying to avoid a possible vote of nonconfidence, it seems likely that curtailing them – by transferring them to the legislature, for example, as some have recommended – would require an amendment under paragraph 41(a).[59] If not, then an amendment under either the general procedure in the case of Parliament, to the degree that provincial interests can be said to be engaged, or the federal and provincial unilateral procedures, would suffice.

Royal Assent, Disallowance, and Reservation

Before a bill can become law, Royal Assent must be granted in the Queen's name by the governor general or one of his or her deputies. Royal Assent has not been refused in the United Kingdom since 1708, and it is very unlikely ever to be withheld in Canada. Nonetheless, section 55 of the Constitution Act, 1867 gives the governor general the discretion to withhold assent to a bill altogether or reserve it to allow the Queen-in-council to consider whether to assent to it. This provision reflects Canada's colonial past, in which the governor general was understood to be a representative of the British government and British ministers could block Canadian laws. Canada's legal independence has put an end to both these practices and led some to conclude that Royal Assent has become a nondiscretionary power.[60] If it remains subject to discretion, it would require an amendment under the unanimous consent procedure to change meaningfully. As we discuss below, however, even if it is nondiscretionary, unanimity might still be required to alter it.

The situation is slightly different when it comes to the lieutenant-governors. Section 90 of the Constitution Act, 1867 gives them the power to withhold assent and reserve bills for the governor-in-council's consideration, and the governor general the power to disallow provincial legislation within one year of its enactment. Lieutenant-governors have withheld assent, governors general have disallowed, and lieutenant-governors have reserved legislation on several occasions. There is disagreement as to whether they can still exercise these extraordinary powers or if a constitutional convention would prevent it.[61] But if, as Justice Gérard La Forest's comments in *Ontario Hydro v Ontario Labour Relations Board* suggest,[62] a court found that these powers can be exercised, it is likely their elimination or alteration would constitute a change to the "office of Lieutenant Governor," requiring a unanimous constitutional amendment.[63] This seems to have been the position the federal government and the provinces agreed to during the negotiations that led to the Charlottetown Accord, which was subject to unanimity on multiple grounds, and would have eliminated disallowance and reservation.[64]

Even if the viceregal officers no longer exercised discretion over whether to grant Royal Assent, it is likely that Royal Assent is subject to paragraph 41(a) for another reason: the Crown is the appropriate institution to grant assent in Canada's Constitution. Assent symbolizes the sanctioning of a new law by the Crown in its capacity as one of the three institutions that form Parliament and ultimately as the source of sovereign legislative power.[65] In theory, this means that the Crown can assess the merits of a bill without being caught up in the politics and partisanship of the legislative process. In practice, this is no longer the case. But the logic of having the Crown grant assent remains salient. The Queen is a part of Parliament and, through the lieutenant-governors, indirectly part of each provincial legislature. The House of Commons, the Senate, and provincial legislative assemblies are not above abusing their powers, so the act of granting assent, however symbolic, signals that a final check on excess exists within Parliament and the provincial legislatures.[66]

The Crown, the Political Executive, and General Procedure

Unlike the House of Commons, the Senate, and the Supreme Court, the Crown is not explicitly listed under section 42 of the Constitution Act, 1982, which requires that certain changes to these national institutions be made under the general amending procedure. Nonetheless, aspects of the Crown are liable to require this procedure – notably, those that surround the Crown as the executive power. Indeed, the executive has been recognized as a separate and distinct institution, one whose functions and powers engage provincial interests in meaningful ways.

Foreign Affairs and National Defence Prerogatives

Most of the powers that federal and provincial executives exercise in Canada are granted by statute. The executive, however, also draws on other sources of power – notably, the prerogative powers of the Crown, which belong to the Crown in its own right at common law. Ministers and civil servants exercise them by virtue of both the Crown's constitutional status as the formal executive and the constitutional conventions of responsible government. These prerogatives are the source of the power of the prime minister and cabinet to make appointments, conduct diplomacy, and deploy the armed forces. Courts in both the United Kingdom and Canada have found that prerogative powers can be limited, supplanted, or even abolished by statute, owing to the principle of parliamentary sovereignty over the Crown.[67] In Canada, this has been taken to mean that Parliament and the provincial legislatures have full control over the scope and indeed the very existence of prerogatives that fall within their legislative powers.[68] However, *obiter* in a series of Supreme Court decisions in recent decades suggest that a protected core of prerogative power may enjoy a degree of protection from both ordinary legislation and judicial remedies, and, by extension, likely cannot be affected without a constitutional amendment.

In the *Patriation Reference*, the majority held that, as a matter of constitutional convention, a substantial degree of provincial consent was required to amend the Constitution, and that the Constitution incorporated some prerogatives via sections 9 and 15 of the Constitution Act, 1867, which vest the Queen with executive power and the power of command-in-chief over the armed forces respectively.[69] A similar approach is taken in Australia towards the interpretation of equivalent provisions of its constitution.[70] In *Operation Dismantle*, which remains a leading case on the judicial review of the use of prerogative powers on Charter grounds, Justice Bertha Wilson seemed to take a similar view, acknowledging the connection asserted by the attorney general between defence and foreign affairs prerogatives at common law and section 15 powers.[71] In *New Brunswick Broadcasting* and the *Provincial Judges Reference*, the Supreme Court found, respectively, that parliamentary privilege and judicial independence are among the Constitution's fundamental principles.[72] In both judgments, the Court suggested that the separation of powers among the branches requires the protection of the powers and privileges that allow each branch to fulfil its constitutional responsibilities. This degree of protection suggests that each branch's fundamental powers and privileges cannot be displaced without a constitutional amendment.[73]

These two lines of reasoning arguably came together in *Khadr*, in which the Supreme Court noted that the foreign affairs prerogative is exercised by the executive, as it had "the constitutional responsibility ... to make decisions on matters of foreign affairs in the context of complex and ever-changing circumstances, taking into account Canada's broader national interests."[74] The foreign affairs prerogative, which belongs to the executive and thus the Crown under section 9 of the Constitution Act, 1867, is exercised by ministers in order to fulfil the executive's constitutional responsibilities. If this is the case, then aspects of the foreign affairs prerogative and related prerogatives that are vital to the executive's ability to fulfil its responsibilities, such as those related to the defence of Canada, require a constitutional amendment to alter materially.[75] This conclusion is consistent with the view expressed in several lower court decisions that the statutes on the Canadian military and foreign service regulate, but do not replace, prerogative powers.[76]

Since defence and diplomatic prerogatives are so closely identified with the federal government, it might seem that a unilateral amendment by Parliament is sufficient to alter them. After all, making the ratification of treaties conditional on parliamentary approval would leave unchanged the requirement for provinces to implement aspects of treaties that fall within their jurisdiction.[77] Likewise, it is hard to see what direct interest the provinces would have in whether the deployment of Canadian troops abroad requires parliamentary consent.[78] However, to take such a narrow view would be to give too little weight to the purpose of the amending procedures and to privilege form over substance.

The purpose of the procedures is "to foster dialogue between the federal government and the provinces on matters of constitutional change, and to protect Canada's constitutional *status quo* until such times as reforms are agreed upon."[79] The general procedure gives the provinces, in their capacity as parties to Confederation, the power to approve or reject proposed changes to the fundamental nature of Canada's national institutions.[80] The executive is undoubtedly one of those institutions, and the core discretion it enjoys over how to defend Canada and conduct its diplomacy seems fundamental to the executive's ability to fulfil its constitutional duties.[81] It is thus possible that an attempt to place meaningful limits on that discretion would require the use of the general amending procedure.

Judicial and Senatorial Appointments

The Constitution Act, 1867 vests in the governor general the power to appoint senators and superior court judges.[82] Both of these powers are exercised on the binding advice of the prime minister, and both engage provincial interests. Changes to the "method of selecting Senators" are expressly made subject to the general amending procedure by virtue of paragraph 42(1)(b) of the Constitution Act, 1982. It seems likely that significant changes to the method of selecting superior court judges, including making the executive's judicial appointments conditional on parliamentary approval or transferring the power to make such appointments to the provinces, would also require the use of the general procedure. More modest changes, such as the creation of a judicial appointments commission, would not seem to alter the appointment process so fundamentally as to require such an amendment. It is unclear whether such a commission could also be used for senatorial appointments without requiring constitutional amendment (see Emmett Macfarlane, in this volume).

Royal Recommendation

Any bill involving the spending of public money must receive the royal recommendation before it can become law.[83] Royal recommendations are granted on the Crown's behalf by ministers who decide when to grant or withhold it. Through royal recommendation, the executive is able to control nearly all government spending and determine the scope with which the legislature can shape government policy through statute. This allows the executive to exercise a minimum degree of control even in a minority Parliament. The royal recommendation is a key feature of the relationship between the executive and the legislature by forcing the executive to take responsibility for public spending.[84]

It is not obvious that the royal recommendation would require the general procedure to amend either at the federal level or in particular provinces. The two levels of government have no direct say in the passage of each other's money bills, and their influence on each other's policy choices is indirect and arises in specific areas of jurisdictional overlap.[85] Yet the royal recommendation is such an important feature of Canada's system of responsible government that eliminating or significantly weakening the practice likely would constitute a change to the "fundamental nature and role of the institutions provided for in the Constitution," which would trigger the general amending procedure, at least at the federal level of government.[86]

Residual Crown Aspects and Unilateral Procedures

There are residual aspects of the Crown that Parliament and the provincial legislatures could change using either the unilateral amending procedures in sections 44 and 45 of the Constitution Act, 1982, which allow for amendments to the "constitution of the province" and the "executive government of Canada," respectively, or their ordinary legislative powers drawn from the Constitution Act, 1867. The distinction between amendment and ordinary legislation is a significant one; as Justice John Major noted in *Eurig Estate (Re)*, provincial legislation that seeks unilaterally to amend the constitution of the province must "do so *expressly.*" The same logic presumably extends to the federal unilateral procedure, at least when it comes to changes to the constitutional text.[87]

The Crown as the Legal Personality of the Executive

Legally speaking the executive is the Queen in a legal capacity acting through her servants.[88] The Queen enjoys several legal privileges, and her personification of the executive ensures that the executive can benefit from them as well.[89] For example, the Queen's legal personality and Crown prerogatives are immune from statute unless it explicitly binds them.[90] As well, the sovereign is historically immune from civil and criminal proceedings, although this sovereign immunity has been gradually eroded through statutes that have opened up government to civil proceedings and public servants to criminal liability.[91]

For more than a century, British legal scholars and courts have sought to undermine the view that the executive is the Queen in her legal capacity.[92] The Law Reform Commission of Canada published a report in 1985 supportive of severing the link between Crown and state.[93] Such a move, whether at the federal or provincial level, perhaps as part of a broader effort to redefine the relationship between civil servants and the state or to further limit the Crown's legal privileges, could be carried out unilaterally so long as it preserved aspects of the Crown that fall under the unanimity or general amending procedures.

First Ministers' Appointment Power

Canada's system of government is routinely criticized for locating too much power in the hands of first ministers. At its root, this centralization reflects the first ministers' control over appointments made in the Crown's name.[94] First ministers appoint ministers, deputy ministers, ambassadors, and a number of other governor-in-council positions. To reduce first ministers' control over appointments and decentralize power in government, these appointments might be made on the advice of a public appointments commission or of Parliament, either as a whole or that of a particular house or committee.[95] Such reforms could be carried out largely through ordinary legislation, except for the appointment of ministers and parliamentary secretaries, which more likely fall within the scope of the "constitution of the province" and "executive government of Canada," respectively, requiring a unilateral constitutional amendment.[96]

Conclusion

Determining what aspects of the Crown fall under which amending procedure involves asking three questions. First, does the function or power in question include an exercise of discretion by the Queen, the governor general, or a lieutenant-governor? If so, then a unanimous constitutional amendment is required, as per paragraph 41(a). Second, does the function or power affect the Queen's status as head of state, including the principles that govern who holds the office of the Queen? If so, then unanimity is also needed to alter these principles. If, however, the answers to these first two questions is no, then a third question must be asked: do the functions or powers of the Crown affect provincial interests or the fundamental nature and role of the Crown as the executive power? If the answer is yes, then the general amending procedure applies. But if the answer is no, then the unilateral amending procedures apply.

The examples we have provided in this chapter when answering these questions are by no means exhaustive.[97] Among the issues we have not addressed are amendments to the oath of allegiance, the Queen's power to appoint additional senators upon the recommendation of the governor general, the Queen's power of command-in-chief over the armed forces, and the Crown's other prerogative powers, such as mercy, passports, the creation of First Nations reserves, and honours, and its common law powers, such as the ability to hold property, make contracts, and otherwise do anything that a natural person can do.[98] Similarly, we have not touched on other potential principles surrounding a change to the Crown's constitutional position, such as the potential convention to hold a national referendum before undertaking major constitutional alterations or the requirement to consult Aboriginal peoples (see Scholtz, in this volume), which would be particularly salient given their unique relationship with the Crown.[99] The functions and powers we have discussed in detail are merely those most likely to be targeted for reform.

In light of the *Senate Reform Reference*, moreover, it seems unlikely that the Supreme Court would be open to "informal" constitutional amendments to the Crown's head-of-state functions and powers (see Baker and Jarvis, in this volume). The most attractive of these informal reform options would be to amend the Crown's powers indirectly by binding the advice that first ministers or cabinets proffer the Queen, the governor general, or lieutenant-governors. Nearly all of the powers of the Crown we have discussed could be affected by this type of informal amendment. Yet it is probable that the Court would see this as an unacceptable effort to privilege "form over substance."[100] A fundamental feature of the Crown's constitutional role is that the Queen and her viceregal representatives almost always must act on the advice of the first minister and that they should always ensure there is a first minister in place to offer advice.[101]

Hence, although there is an evident desire to question the monarchy in Canada and an interest in curtailing the Crown's powers, particularly those exercised by the executive, the degree of political will required to make such a change and the difficulties it would involve suggest that the Crown is unlikely to be displaced in Canada's constitutional architecture in the near future. Certain reforms to the Crown could be undertaken unilaterally by Parliament and provincial legislative assemblies, but the monarch's position as head of state and holder of significant reserve powers regarding government formation and the life of parliaments are thoroughly entrenched in the Constitution of Canada.

Notes

1 *McAteer v Canada (AG)*, 2014 ONCA 578; Paul Heinbecker, "The monarchy hurts Canada's standing in the world. It's time to let go," *Globe and Mail*, 1 July 2014; Peter Aucoin, Mark D. Jarvis, and Lori Turnbull, *Democratizing the Constitution: Reforming Responsible Government* (Toronto: Emond Montgomery, 2011).

2 Constitution Act, 1982, being Schedule B to the Canada Act 1982 (UK), 1982, c 11.
3 Barbara Cameron, "The Office and Powers of the Governor General: Political Intention and Legal Interpretation," *Journal of Parliamentary and Political Law* 6 (2012): 87–106.
4 *Reference re Senate Reform*, 2014 SCC 32; *Reference re Supreme Court Act, ss 5 and 6*, 2014 SCC 21.
5 *Senate Reform Reference*, para. 25.
6 Ibid., para. 26.
7 Ibid., para. 25.
8 Ibid., para. 31.
9 Ibid., paras 34, 36.
10 Ibid., para. 34.
11 Ibid., paras 34, 37–8.
12 Ibid., para. 41, citing Benoît Pelletier, *La modification constitutionnelle au Canada* (Toronto: Carswell, 1996), 208.
13 Constitution Act, 1982, s 41(a)(d)(e); Pelletier, *Modification constitutionnelle*, 224–5; *Senate Reform Reference*, para. 97; *Supreme Court Reference*, para. 91.
14 Constitution Act, 1982, s 42(a)(b)(d); Pelletier, *Modification constitutionnelle*, 211–15; *Supreme Court Reference*, para. 91.
15 *Senate Reform Reference*, para. 48.
16 Constitution Act, 1982, ss 44–45; Pelletier, *Modification constitutionnelle*, 117–206.
17 *Senate Reform Reference*, para. 25.
18 Benoît Pelletier, "The Constitutional Requirements for the Royal Morganatic Marriage," *McGill Law Journal* 50, no. 2 (2005): 282.
19 *Roach v Canada (Secretary of State)*, 2007 CanLII 17373 (ONSC), para. 10; *Conacher v Canada (Prime Minister)*, 2009 FC 920, para. 53; *Motard c Canada (Procureure générale)*, 2016 QCCS 588, para. 138.
20 *Ontario (AG) v OPSEU*, [1987] 2 SCR 2, para. 108.
21 Constitution Act, 1867, ss 9–15.
22 David E. Smith, "The Crown and the Constitution: Sustaining Democracy?" in *The Evolving Canadian Crown*, ed. Jennifer Smith and D. Michael Jackson (Montreal; Kingston, ON: McGill-Queen's University Press, 2012), 60.
23 Peter Hogg, *Constitutional Law of Canada*, Student ed. (Toronto: Carswell, 2014), 1:20–2.
24 Constitution Act, 1867, ss 17, 69, 71, 88.
25 Ibid., ss 53–55, 90; Audrey O'Brien and Marc Bosc, *House of Commons Procedure and Practice*, 2nd ed. (Cowansville, QC: Éditions Yvon Blais), 367–72, 755–6.

26 David E. Smith, *The Invisible Crown: The First Principle of Canadian Government* (Toronto: University of Toronto Press, 1995), 62–133.

27 *New Brunswick Broadcasting Co v Nova Scotia (House of Assembly)*, [1993] 1 SCR 319, 389.

28 *Reference re Canada Assistance Plan* (BC), [1991] 2 SCR 525, 546–7.

29 *Senate Reform Reference*, paras 64–7.

30 *Senate Reform Reference*, para. 14.

31 Constitution Act, 1867; emphasis added.

32 *McAteer v Canada (AG)*, 2013 ONSC, para. 19, aff'd 2014 ONCA 578; *O'Donohue v Canada*, 2003 CanLII 41404 (ONSC).

33 *In re The Initiative and Referendum Act*, [1919] AC 935 (PC); *Ontario (AG) v OPSEU*, [1987] 2 SCR 2, para. 108; *Reference re Manitoba Language Rights*, [1992] 1 SCR, para. 135. See also *Crédit foncier franco-canadien v Ross*, [1937] 3 DLR 365 (ABSC(AD)), para. 15; *R ex rel Tolfree v Clark*, [1943] OR 501 (CA), paras 43–4.

34 *Projet de loi fédéral relatif au Sénat (Re)*, 2013 QCCA 1807, paras 51–61.

35 *Roach v Canada (Secretary of State)*, 2007 CanLII 17373 (ONSC), para. 10; *Conacher v Canada (Prime Minister)*, 2009 FC 920, para. 53; *Motard c Canada (Procureure générale)*, 2016 QCCS 588, para. 138. See also *R ex rel Brooks v Ulmer*, [1922] 19 Alta LR 12 (SC(AD)), paras 34–5; *Montplaisir v Québec (AG)*, [1997] RJQ 109 (CS); *R v Somers*, [1997] MJ No 57 (QB).

36 *Canada (Prime Minister) v Khadr*, 2010 SCC 3, paras 37, 39. See also *Black v Canada (Prime Minister)*, [2001] 54 OR (3d) 215 (CA), paras 31–2; *McAteer v Canada (AG)*, 2013 ONSC 5895, para. 19; *Hupacasath First Nation v Canada (AG)*, 2015 FCA 4, paras 32–5.

37 *Senate Reform Reference*, para. 48.

38 Constitution Act, 1982, s 45. Pelletier, *Modification constitutionnelle*, 146–8.

39 *Motard c Canada (Procureure générale)*, 2016 QCCS 588.

40 Andrew Heard, *Canadian Constitutional Conventions: The Marriage of Law and Politics*, 2nd ed. (Oxford: Oxford University Press, 2014), 35.

41 Vernon Bogdanor and Geoffrey Marshall, "Dismissing Governor-Generals," *Public Law* (1996): 205–13. Christopher McCreery, "Myth and Misunderstanding: The Origins and Meaning of the Letters Patent Constituting the Office of Governor General, 1947," in Smith and Jackson, *Evolving Canadian Crown*, 52–3.

42 Frank MacKinnon, *The Crown in Canada* (Calgary: Glenbow-Alberta Institute, 1976), 122–35.

43 Prime Minister Stephen Harper and his advisors reportedly considered taking such a course of action if the governor general had refused his request to prorogue Parliament in December 2008; see John Ibbitson,

"Stephen Harper pondered appeal to the Queen over prorogation," *Globe and Mail*, 30 September 2010.

44 *Senate Reform Reference*, para. 52.

45 Constitution Act, 1867, ss 13, 58.

46 Ibid., s 59. See also *Reference re the Power of the Governor General in Council to Disallow Provincial Legislation and the Power of Reservation of a Lieutenant Governor of a Province*, [1938] SCR 71, 77.

47 Heard, *Canadian Constitutional Conventions*, 47–60.

48 Ibid., 40–7.

49 British Columbia's lieutenant-governor David Lam claimed he would have dismissed Premier Bill Vander Zalm had the premier not agreed to resign when a conflict of interest came to light in 1991; see Ronald I. Cheffins, "The Royal Prerogative and the Office of Lieutenant Governor," *Canadian Parliamentary Review* 23, no. 1 (2000): 17.

50 *Senate Reform Reference*, para. 52.

51 Guy Tremblay, "La réforme des institutions démocratiques au Québec: commentaires en marge du rapport du Comité directeur," *Cahiers de droit* 44, no. 2 (2003): 207–35.

52 Heard, *Canadian Constitutional Conventions*, 60–70.

53 Smith, *Invisible Crown*, 58, 130.

54 The maximum duration of the House of Commons and provincial legislative assemblies is five years, although this can be extended by two-thirds majority "[i]n at time of real or apprehended war, invasion or insurrection" (Constitution Act, 1982, s 4).

55 Fixed-term Parliaments Act 2011 (UK), c 14, s 2.

56 *Conacher*, para. 53.

57 "The Governor General shall … summon and call together the House of Commons" (Constitution Act, 1867, s 38). Parliament and the provincial legislatures must sit "at least once every twelve months" (Constitution Act, 1982, s 5), placing a hard limit on the sort of advice the first minister can offer the governor general or lieutenant-governor about summoning and proroguing the legislature.

58 Peter H. Russell and Lorne Sossin, eds, *Parliamentary Democracy in Crisis* (Toronto: University of Toronto Press, 2009) 33; Nicholas A. Macdonald and James W.J. Bowden, "No Discretion: On Prorogation and the Governor General," *Canadian Parliamentary Review* 34, no. 1 (2011): 7–16.

59 See Aucoin, Jarvis, and Turnbull, *Democratizing the Constitution*, 217–27.

60 Heard, *Canadian Constitutional Conventions*, 72–3.

61 Ibid., 70–3.

62 *Ontario Hydro v Ontario Labour Relations Board*, [1993] 3 SCR 327, 371–3.

63 *In re The Initiative and Referendum Act; Manitoba Language Reference*, para. 135.

64 Government of Canada, *Charlottetown Accord – Draft Legal Text* (Ottawa: Privy Council Office, 1992).

65 Constitution Act, 1867, ss 17, 91; *Azevedo v Canada (Governor General)*, 2015 FC 91.

66 On the importance of seemingly anachronistic formal checks, see Dennis Baker, *Not Quite Supreme: The Courts and Coordinate Constitutional Interpretation* (Montreal; Kingston, ON: McGill-Queen's University Press, 2010).

67 Hogg, *Constitutional Law*, 1:20.

68 *Liquidators of the Maritime Bank of Canada v Receiver-General of New Brunswick*, [1892] AC 437.

69 *Re Resolution to amend the* Constitution, [1981] 1 SCR 753, 876.

70 George Winterton, *Parliament, the Executive and the Governor-General: A Constitutional Analysis* (Melbourne: Melbourne University Press, 1983), 48–52.

71 *Operation Dismantle v The Queen*, [1985] 1 SCR 441, para. 50.

72 *New Brunswick Broadcasting; Reference re Remuneration of Judges of the Provincial Court of Prince Edward Island; Reference re Independence and Impartiality of Judges of the Provincial Court of Prince Edward Island*, [1997] 3 SCR 3.

73 Dale Gibson, "Monitoring Arbitrary Government Authority: Charter Scrutiny of Legislative, Executive and Judicial Privilege," *Saskatchewan Law Review* 68 (1998): 297.

74 *Canada (Prime Minister) v Khadr*, 2010 SCC 3, paras 39–40.

75 For a comprehensive discussion of core prerogatives, see Irvin Studin, *The Strategic Constitution: Understanding Canadian Power in the World* (Vancouver: UBC Press, 2014), 29–54.

76 *Turp v Chrétien*, 2003 FCT 301; *Friends of the Earth v Canada (Governor in Council)*, 2008 FC 1183; *Turp v Canada (Justice)*, 2012 FC 893. See also Alexander Bolt, "Crown Prerogative Decisions to Deploy the Canadian Forces Internationally: A Fitting Mechanism for a Liberal Democracy," in *Canada and the Crown: Essays on Constitutional Monarchy*, ed. D. Michael Jackson and Philippe Lagassé, 219–36 (Montreal; Kingston, ON: McGill-Queen's University Press, 2013).

77 The UK House of Commons had a veto over treaty ratifications: Constitutional Reform Act 2010 (UK), c 25, Part 2. In the *Labour Conventions* case, the JCPC held that Parliament could not implement Canada's treaty obligations that fell under provincial jurisdiction: Canada *(AG) v Ontario (AG)*, [1937] AC 326.

78 The UK Parliament is considering formalizing a constitutional convention that requires the approval of the House of Commons for overseas military deployments: UK, HC, "Parliament's Role in Conflict Decisions: A Way Forward," Cm 892 in *Sessional Papers* (2013–14).

79 *Senate Reform Reference*, para. 31.

80 Ibid., para. 48.

81 Studin, *Strategic Constitution*; Philippe Lagassé, "The Crown's Powers of Command-in-Chief: Interpreting Section 15 of the *Constitution Act, 1867*," *Review of Constitutional Studies* 18, no. 2 (2013): 189–220.

82 Constitution Act, 1867, ss 24, 96.

83 Ibid., ss 54, 90.

84 Baker, *Not Quite Supreme*, 61–2.

85 John Mark Keyes, "The Legislative Process and Judicial Review: Royal Functions and Their Justiciability," in *The Crown and Parliament in Canada*, ed. Michel Bédard and Philippe Lagassé, 61–93 (Cowansville, QC: Éditions Yvon Blais, 2015).

86 Smith, *Invisible Crown*, 66, 82.

87 *Eurig Estate (Re)*, [1998] 2 SCR 565, para. 35. See also Warren J. Newman, "Defining the 'Constitution of Canada' since 1982: The Scope of the Legislative Powers of Constitutional Amendment under Sections 44 and 45 of the *Constitution Act, 1982*," *Supreme Court Law Review* (2d) 22 (2003): 423.

88 Paul Lordon, *Crown Law* (Toronto: Butterworths, 1991), chap. 1.

89 See Peter W. Hogg, Patrick J. Monahan, and Wake K. Wright, *Liability of the Crown*, 4th ed. (Toronto: Carswell, 2011).

90 Interpretation Act, RSC 1985, c I-21, s 17.

91 Crown Liability and Proceedings Act, RSC 1985, c C-50.

92 Janet McLean, *Searching for the State in British Legal Thought: Competing Conceptions of the Public Sphere* (Cambridge: Cambridge University Press, 2012).

93 Law Reform Commission of Canada, *The Legal Status of the Federal Administration* (Ottawa: Law Reform Commission of Canada, 1985).

94 Smith, *Invisible Crown*, 30.

95 Aucoin, Jarvis, and Turnbull, *Democratizing the Constitution*.

96 *Guergis v Novak*, 2012 ONSC 4579, para. 13; *League for Human Rights of B'Nai Brith Canada v Odynsky*, 2010 FCA 307, paras 77–8.

97 For a discussion of other issues surrounding paragraph 41(a), see Philippe Lagassé and Patrick Baud, "The Crown and Constitutional Amendment in Canada," in Bédard and Lagassé, *Crown and Parliament in Canada*, 203–40.

98 Constitution Act, 1867, ss 15, 26, 128.

99 Constitution Act, 1982, s 35.1; Patrick J. Monahan and Byron Shaw, *Constitutional Law*, 4th ed. (Toronto: Irwin Law, 2013), 197–8, 516–17.

100 *Senate Reform Reference*, paras 52, 106.
101 Warren J. Newman, "Of Dissolution, Prorogation, and Constitutional Law, Principle and Convention: Maintaining Fundamental Distinctions during a Parliamentary Crisis," *National Journal of Constitutional Law* 27 (2010): 217–29.

13 "The Most Radical Amendment of All": The Power to Secede and the *Secession Reference*

KATE PUDDISTER

The Canadian Constitution is silent on the issue of secession. In both the Constitution Act 1867 and Constitution Act 1982, there is no mention of the power to secede nor is there any guidance on how to amend the Constitution in the event of secession. This should be unsurprising, as constitutions are crafted with the purpose of nation-building and tend not to contemplate a country's breaking up. Yet simply because something is not mentioned in the constitutional text does not preclude the growth of constitutional interpretation to address novel or unmentioned issues.[1] Regardless of the constitutional silence on secession, the possible secession of a province – specifically Quebec – is a reality of Canadian politics. Indeed, Quebec has administered two referendums on some form of separation from Canada, and the Supreme Court of Canada has pronounced on the domestic and international legal parameters concerning secession in the *Secession Reference*.

Although the Supreme Court's *Secession* decision was generally well received by the parties to the dispute, much remains uncertain regarding the specific mechanics and amending formula needed for a province to secede from the federation. Indeed, in the *Secession Reference*, the Court made no specific mention of the Part V amending formula, and did not explain which specific formula would apply in light of a clear vote for secession by the people of Quebec. The guidance the Court offered in the reference was limited due to the specific questions referred to it, the abstract nature of the case, and the lack of analysis of Part V. However, when assessing some of the constitutional changes secession would require in light of the requirements of constitutional amendment in Part V and recent Supreme Court decisions that consider constitutional amendment, it is possible to deduce how secession could be addressed within the confines of the Canadian Constitution.

Any discussion of secession and the place of Quebec within the constitutional framework must begin by acknowledging the thorny relationship between Quebec and constitutional amendment. As such, I begin with a brief overview of Quebec's role in previous attempts at constitutional reform and its connection to the secessionist movement. I then turn to the *Secession Reference*, examine the guidance offered by the Supreme Court, and investigate the implications of this case for secession. Finally, in light of the preceding discussion, I conclude with an analysis of how secession could be constitutionally permissible through amendment.

Secession

Secession is the separation of a portion of an existing independent state as a means to form a new state. In most circumstances, the existing state will oppose secession as an affront to its goals, territorial integrity, and existing constitutional order. In a federal state, secession requires the termination of the federal or national institutions within the seceding territory. Secession has significant implications for existing relationships within the federation and with other international actors and organizations.[2] Although constitutions that allow for secession are rare, no constitution provides for unilateral secession.[3] This prohibition on unilateral declarations of independence (UDI) means that any unit that wishes to secede cannot determine its independence in isolation from the existing state.

The threat of provincial secession has been a prevalent and recurring force in Canadian politics. Indeed, almost immediately after the adoption of the British North America Act, 1867, provinces questioned the utility of federalism and demanded to secede from the newly created Canadian federation. Within the first year of confederation, Nova Scotia petitioned the Imperial Parliament in the United Kingdom for amendment to the BNA Act to allow for its withdrawal from the federation. Westminster denied this request, and with no possibility for repeal or amendment of the BNA Act, Nova Scotia's secessionist movement slowly faded away.[4]

The real threat of secession in modern Canadian politics has come from Quebec, which has held two referendums on the issue of sovereignty and independence. The first, held in 1980, centred on "sovereignty association," a supposed middle ground between Quebec's complete separation from Canada and its continued place within the federation. The second referendum, in 1995, struck a more radical tone, and concerned Quebec's unilateral secession through the adoption of Bill 1, An Act respecting the future of Quebec, by the Quebec National Assembly (a form of UDI). Both these referendums were unsuccessful, but the 1995 vote was incredibly close, with only 50.58 per cent voting against secession. This close brush with secession prompted the 1998 reference, which asked the Supreme Court to explain the legal and constitutional obligations concerning a UDI. Most parties in the reference agreed that constitutional amendment would be required to affect Quebec's secession.

Before examining the Supreme Court's decision in the *Secession Reference* and its impact on constitutional amendment, it is important first to investigate the historical relationship between Quebec and constitutional amendment so as to have a full understanding of the many variables involved. As I detail below, Quebec was a central force in the push to adopt a domestic amending formula. Although Quebec initially agreed to an amending formula, the final agreement on the Constitution Act, 1982 (including the Part V amending formula) was ultimately reached without the support of Quebec. Leaving Quebec out of the constitutional agreement not only provided fuel for secession; it influenced the movement towards unilateral secession, rather than negotiations between Quebec and the rest of Canada. The relationships between constitutional amending formulas, the failure to accommodate Quebec, and the threat of Quebec secession are intertwined and mutually dependent.

Quebec and Amending Formulas

Quebec has always been a central player in negotiations over constitutional amendment. Prior to 1982, the province was instrumental in bringing together the partners in Canadian federalism to negotiate an amending formula. The position of several Quebec leaders, beginning with Premier Louis-Alexandre Taschereau in the late 1920s, was to approach constitutional amendment through the lens of compact theory, which envisions Confederation as an agreement between independent, sovereign provinces, meaning no amendment can be undertaken without provincial agreement. Although compact theory has been largely dismissed,[5] it was a central part of Quebec's position on constitutional amendment until at least 1950, and has reappeared in the province's positioning through various attempts at amendment.[6] According to Quebec's interpretation of compact theory, as a founding party of Confederation the province is entitled to a veto on constitutional amendment.[7]

The Quebec veto is a recurring theme in the province's approach to constitutional negotiations. Two prior (and failed) attempts at securing a constitutional amending formula – the Fulton-Favreau Formula and the Victoria Charter – would have given Quebec a veto over constitutional amendments (see Verrelli, in this volume). Initially, Quebec signalled its support for the Fulton-Favreau Formula and its accommodation of compact theory. Fulton-Favreau's principle of unanimity for amendments concerning the use of English or French would have served to protect Quebec's interests and the preservation of the French language and culture. Quebec ultimately felt, however, that the Fulton-Favreau Formula was not in its interest, for two central reasons. First, a simple defensive veto would not have protected Quebec's unique interests, satisfied the Quebec government's mantra of *maîtres chez nous* following the Quiet Revolution, or further Quebec's desire to expand provincial jurisdiction: since Quebec's approach to constitutional negotiations was to assume control over the central functions of the state in a way that would make the province distinct from all others, Quebec was not satisfied with the status quo of the provincial powers at Confederation.[8] Instead, Fulton-Favreau served to treat all provinces as equals through its unanimity requirements that essentially provided each province with a veto. The second reason Quebec opposed the Fulton-Favreau Formula was because its unanimity requirements would have meant that constitutional change would be extremely difficult at best.[9] Without the support of Quebec, Fulton-Favreau failed.

The Victoria Charter of 1971 suffered a similar fate. Although Fulton-Favreau emphasized some aspects of compact theory, Quebec rejected it for its equal treatment of all provinces. The Victoria Charter, on the other hand, served to recognize and protect the role of Quebec as a founding nation and the guardian of French culture, which gained the initial support of Premier Robert Bourassa. The amending formula agreed to in Victoria provided Ontario and Quebec each with a veto over constitutional change, while denying it to all other provinces. It did not, however, provide an expansion of provincial powers – one of Quebec's most central concerns and demands. Ultimately, after conferring with his cabinet and an outpouring of criticism from several provincial unions, Bourassa rejected the Victoria Charter.

Beyond the failure to adopt a domestic constitutional amending formula, the Fulton-Favreau and the Victoria Charter demonstrate the important position of Quebec in constitutional negotiations. The failure to secure the Quebec's support was enough to cause both attempts to collapse, as those involved in the negotiations understood that a legitimate agreement could not go forward without it[10] – indeed, the unravelling of the two agreements gave the impression that it had become political convention to obtain Quebec's support for constitutional change.[11] This understanding of Quebec's special role in such negotiations and the failure to accommodate the province contributed to the growth of secessionist forces in Quebec – propelling the province towards the 1980 referendum.

The election of the Parti Québécois in 1976 made the prospect of Quebec sovereignty a reality, threatening the stability of Canadian federalism. The sovereignty movement served to push the Constitution and the search for an amending formula back into the public debate. Quebec and its political leaders demanded change to the existing constitutional framework. Recognizing this during the final days before the referendum vote, speaking at a "no" rally, Prime Minister Pierre Trudeau promised that a vote against Quebec sovereignty would ensure the return to constitutional negotiations and a renewal of the Constitution. With the victory of the "no" side, executive-level negotiations on the Constitution resumed, but provincial support diminished over time.

Trudeau pushed forward with his constitutional project, and attempted to secure an agreement without the consent of the provinces, a unilateral move that was challenged in the *Patriation Reference*.[12] The Supreme Court held that the participation of the provinces was conventionally (but not legally) required, and that the consent of Quebec was not required for the project to go forward. Once again, Quebec, central to the drive towards constitutional negotiation, was left unsatisfied and absent from the agreement reached by the rest of Canada. Unlike previous attempts, however, this episode was different. Quebec's lack of support for the 1980 constitutional package failed to block constitutional change, violating what seemed to be an accepted constitutional convention. Instead, the patriation of the Constitution Act, 1982 was completed without Quebec and against the clear opposition of the Quebec National Assembly.[13]

In signifying its objection to patriation without its consent, Quebec initiated a reference case to ask the Supreme Court of Canada to intervene and to recognize and protect the province's historical right to veto constitutional change.[14] The *Quebec Veto Reference* asked the Court to recognize the distinct status of Quebec with respect to the two founding cultures and languages of Canada.[15] The province based its argument on the fact that, throughout Canadian history, Quebec consistently had claimed a veto, based on its unique position as one of the founding parties to Confederation, a nod to compact theory. Quebec argued that, due to its historical practice of having a veto, a constitutional amendment could not be completed without Quebec's agreement.

The Supreme Court, however, was not persuaded by Quebec's arguments; instead, a unanimous Court dealt a strong rejection of the idea of a Quebec veto. The Court explained that it was not presented with any evidence that explicitly recognized a Quebec veto by either provincial or federal authorities. Finding a lack of concrete evidence demonstrating a convention of a Quebec veto, the Court wrote: "We know of no example of a convention being born while remaining completely unspoken, and none was cited to us."[16] Through this reference case, the Court shut the door on any notion of a veto for Quebec, profoundly altering the province's position in constitutional negotiations and its efforts to protect the distinct society of Quebec.

Following the strong rejection of a conventional veto in the *Quebec Veto Reference*, the alienation of the province from constitutional negotiations became an important force in Quebec politics, which ultimately would help contribute to the second referendum on Quebec sovereignty.[17] With the National Assembly under the control of the Parti Québécois and Premier Jacques Parizeau, the Quebec government introduced An Act Respecting the Sovereignty of Quebec (Draft Bill), which outlined the steps that would be followed to provide for the secession of Quebec from Canada, with the final objective creating a "sovereign country."[18] Although the Bill included the consultation of the people of Quebec through a referendum, there was no mention of constitutional negotiations with the rest of Canada, making the declaration unilateral. As Quebec went forward with a referendum in the fall of 1995, the battle over a unilateral declaration of independence without a constitutional amendment was under way in Canadian courts.

The *Secession Reference*

Following the tabling of the Draft Bill, Guy Bertrand, a Quebec lawyer (and founding member of the Parti Québécois), sought a declaratory judgment at the Superior Court of Quebec challenging the constitutionality of the Bill and the unilateral path to secession. Bertrand argued that the separation of Quebec from Canada was both possible and necessary under the Part V amending formula, and that "Quebec independence would be the 'amendment of all amendments.'"[19] Although the Superior Court agreed with Bertrand that Quebec sovereignty is subject to the amending formula in Part V, the Court would not grant an injunction against the referendum.[20] As this matter was being dealt with in the Quebec courts, Premier Parizeau introduced Bill 1, An Act Respecting the Future of Quebec, which explicitly provided for a unilateral declaration of sovereignty by the Quebec National Assembly and expanded on the text provided in the Draft Bill.[21] After the narrow loss by the pro-sovereignty side in the 1995 referendum, it was clear that clarification regarding the legal parameters of secession was needed, and the federal government responded with a reference to the Supreme Court of Canada.

Through section 53 of the Supreme Court of Canada Act, the Governor in Council – in practice, the federal cabinet – referred the following questions to the Supreme Court:

1. Under the Constitution of Canada, can the National Assembly, legislature or government of Quebec effect the secession of Quebec from Canada unilaterally?
2. Does international law give the National Assembly, legislature or government of Quebec the right to effect the secession of Quebec from Canada unilaterally? In this regard, is there a right to self-determination under international law that would give the National Assembly, legislature or government of Quebec the right to effect the secession of Quebec from Canada unilaterally?
3. In the event of a conflict between domestic and international law on the right of the National Assembly, legislature or government of Quebec to effect the secession of Quebec from Canada unilaterally, which would take precedence in Canada?[22]

The questions referred to the Court largely centred on the UDI made by the government of Quebec through Bill 1. Question 1 asks the Court to explain the implications of domestic Canadian law for secession. It is important to note that the question does not ask the Court to explain which specific amending formula in Part V would apply in secession negotiations. Instead, Question 1 is concerned only with *unilateral* secession. Questions 2 and 3 concern the interpretation of international law on secession and its compatibility with domestic Canadian law.

For the sake of brevity, my discussion will focus on Question 1 and the route to secession under the Canadian Constitution.[23] As I substantiate below in examining the Supreme Court's opinion in the *Secession Reference*, the Court's limited discussion of amending formulas reflects the arguments made by the attorney general of Canada and the specific limitation to unilateralism in Question 1.

The Supreme Court delivered its opinion in the *Secession Reference* late in the summer of 1998, almost two full years after the referral of the questions by the attorney general. As to be expected, the decision received a great deal of media attention. For example, in an extremely rare occurrence, the day after the decision was released all nine justices provided interviews to the *Globe and Mail* detailing their motivations and considerations behind the ruling, a clear indication of the significance of the *Secession Reference*.[24] In another demonstration of the highly contentious and important nature of the reference, the Court issued an anonymous and unanimous *per curiam* decision, showing the importance the Court attached to speaking not only with one voice, but also with the legitimacy of the Court as an institution, rather than as the justices that then filled the bench.[25]

In the *Secession Reference*, the Court found that the Canadian Constitution is guided by four principles: federalism, democracy, constitutionalism and the rule of law, and respect for minority rights, which serve to "inform and sustain the constitutional text: they are the vital unstated assumptions upon which the text is based."[26] The Court explained that one single principle cannot serve to trump the others and that all four principles are understood to be interrelated and equally as important. When dealing with secession, the actions of all parties involved must be limited and guided by these four principles working in conjunction with one another. For the purposes of Question 1 specifically and in the context of constitutional amendment, the principles of federalism and constitutionalism and the rule of law are central. Federalism infers that provincial and central governments have a legitimate and important role to play in the collective governance of the federation as a whole, and must also protect the diversity and priorities unique to individual jurisdictions. The principle of constitutionalism and the rule of law requires that the decisions and actions taken in the collective governance of the Canadian federation must be done within the constraints of the law and Constitution, and the Constitution could not be circumvented through the demonstration of a majority vote in a referendum or the simple declaration of a legislature.[27]

In answering Question 1, the Court found that, regardless of the lack of a reference to secession in the amending formula, in the Canadian legal and constitutional framework secession requires a constitutional amendment: "secession would purport to alter the governance of Canadian territory in a manner which undoubtedly is inconsistent with our current constitutional arrangements. The fact that those changes would be profound ... does not negate their nature as amendments to the Constitution of Canada."[28] The Court made it clear that simply because the Constitution is silent on secession does not mean that the secession of a province is outside the reach of the Constitution. Secession cannot be contemplated or achieved in ignorance of the Constitution. Linking the Court's reasoning to the actions of the Quebec government, it is clear that the UDI through Bill 1 did not consider the Constitution and stood in violation of this reasoning.

Turning to the specific issue of unilateral secession, the Court addressed the pro-sovereignty argument that, following a clear majority vote for secession on a clear question, the federal and provincial governments would be forced to participate in negotiations and determine the logistical requirements of secession. After considering the four previously mentioned principles of the Constitution – in particular, federalism and the rule of law – the Court rejected this argument.[29] The Court also rejected the reverse argument – that the provinces and the federal government would not be obligated to negotiate with Quebec following a clear vote for secession, explaining, "[n]egotiations would be necessary to address the interests of the federal government, of Quebec and the other provinces, and other participants, as well as the rights of all Canadians both within and outside Quebec."[30] Without prioritizing one constitutional principle over another, in the event of a clear expression of self-determination by the people of Quebec, the government of Quebec, the government of Canada, and all provincial governments would be constitutionally obligated to negotiate the terms of secession. The Court stated that this would be a political process, and that "[t]he Court has no supervisory role over the political aspects of constitutional negotiations."[31] Based on this reasoning, the unilateral secession of Quebec through the Quebec legislature would be illegal and an affront to the rule of law and the Constitution.[32]

The *Secession Reference* made it clear that unilateral secession is both unconstitutional and illegal, but it did not explain how constitutional secession could be achieved. Indeed, in the Court's lengthy decision, there is no discussion of amending formulas or clarification on which specific formula would apply to secession. Although the Court came under fire for its lack of discussion of Part V,[33] its absence does not reflect the Court's avoidance of the discussion but the limitation of reference cases in general and the specific arguments made by the attorney general of Canada.

Most Canadian reference cases are examples of abstract review. Since a reference is initiated simply through the referral of questions from a government to a provincial appellate court or to the Supreme Court of Canada, there is often no live legal dispute. Unlike routine or concrete review, a reference case often contains no real facts for the court to sort out, and technically there is only one party to the dispute: the referring government.[34] Without facts and a concrete dispute, the questions referred to the courts in reference cases become the central conduit for the decision and provide framework for legal and constitutional analysis. When the questions referred are vague or do not address all aspects of the constitutional controversy under dispute, the court's decision will likely be imprecise or limited.[35] As a result, the questions asked will have a determinative effect on the court's reasoning, and courts are often unwilling to address issues that are external to the specific questions referred.

In the context of Question 1 in the *Secession Reference*, the Supreme Court was only asked if unilateral secession was permissible, not to consider how nonunilateral secession could be completed through the Constitution and its amending formula. Although it certainly would have been helpful had the Court outlined which amending formula would apply to the various constitutional changes required by secession, it was not asked specifically to provide such clarification. Indeed, the Court explained that it was limited by the questions referred: "It will be noted that Question 1 does not ask how secession could be achieved in a constitutional manner, but addresses one form of secession only, namely unilateral secession."[36]

This focus on unilateral secession came at the expense of addressing secession through constitutional amendment, and reflected the arguments made by the appellant, the attorney general of Canada. The attorney general's factum explains at length the incompatibility between unilateralism and the Constitution based on the principle of federalism and the rule of law. In an argument supported by other government interveners, the attorney general explained that the only unilateral amending formula provided to provinces, section 45 of Part V of the Constitution Act, 1982, does not apply to secession.[37]

The attorney general further argued that, because Quebec sought unilateral secession, the Court should limit its analysis to the only amending formula that allows for unilateralism: section 45. The attorney general then suggested that the changes required by secession – such as the termination of the federal Parliament's legislative jurisdiction over the territory of Quebec – would require fundamental changes to the Canadian constitutional order that could not be achieved through an amending formula designed for changes to a province alone.[38] Finally, the attorney general urged the Court to limit analysis to the provincial unilateral amending power, as any other formula would require the participation of the federal government and/or other provinces. Further, without the participation of all of these parties in the case, any discussion beyond this unilateral formula would be inappropriate: "Without the participation of many of the provinces, it would not be appropriate for this Court to address issues that are outside the express terms of the reference questions. In particular, if this Court were to embark on a broader examination of other issues relating to the constitutional amending procedures, it would be deprived of the views of many provinces on matters that affect them directly."[39]

The attorney general concluded its arguments on Question 1 by urging the Court not to wade into the debate over which constitutional provisions would be affected by secession.[40] Unfortunately, in the *Secession Reference*, the Court complied with this argument, thereby sacrificing a clear elucidation of the specific constitutional changes and amending formula required by secession.

Some scholars speculate, however, when considering the historical relationship between Quebec and amending formulas, that the Court's lack of textual focus was sympathetic to this history. Sujit Choudhry and Robert Howse, for example, argue that the Court understood that, for the *Secession Reference* to be accepted in Quebec, particularly in the pro-sovereignty camp, the decision had to be sensitive to the rejection of the Constitution and the grievance over amending formulas in the province.[41] Therefore, the Court was well aware that "reliance on the text would have accentuated normative dissensus."[42] Instead, the Court focused on general underlying constitutional principles such as federalism and the rule of law that could easy be supported by both sides in the secession debate. This reluctance to rely on a specific textual argument and the limitations imposed by the structure of the reference itself resulted in a Supreme Court ruling on secession that provided very little in terms of a legal roadmap to dealing with secession within the confines of the Constitution.

The Constitutionality of Secession

Although the Supreme Court failed to provide a detailed roadmap of the application of Part V to secession, it is possible to examine some of the major changes secession would require and to analyse which amending formula likely would apply. That being said, the Court did make two important clarifications in the *Secession Reference*: first, that secession is constitutionally possible but must be done through a constitutional amendment; and, second, that the unilateral amending formulas, both federal (section 44) and provincial (section 45), cannot be applied to the secession of a province. Secession would lead to changes to the structures of Canadian governance (including both representation in elected bodies and the composition of the Supreme Court), relations with the international community, territorial boundaries, citizenship, and immigration that clearly could not be undertaken by amending a provincial constitution under section 45. Similarly, such changes to the essential characteristics of the Canadian federation would be well beyond the unilateral powers of the federal government that section 44 provides. Considering the number and expansive nature of changes secession would require in light of the constitutional principle of federalism articulated by the Court, secession clearly would also be beyond the reach of the amending formula in the some-but-not-all-provinces amending formula in section 43.[43] As a result, the central debate occurs on the application of either section 41 (the unanimity of all provincial legislative assemblies and the federal Parliament) or the general amending formula (the 7/50 arrangement) found in section 38.

Scholars who argue for the application of section 38[44] ground their claims in the fact that there is no specific mention of secession in the Constitution and, as a general amending procedure, the purpose of section 38 is to address issues not addressed by other amending formulas. The main advocate of this position, constitutional scholar Peter Hogg, is certainly correct in that the act of secession itself is not provided for in the Constitution, seemingly leading to the use of the 7/50 amending formula (section 38). An exclusive focus on the lack of a secession provision, however, is narrow and problematic considering the numerous constitutional changes secession would require. Using an amending formula that does not give a role to all members of the

Canadian federation – as in the majority requirements of section 38 – poses a practical and theoretical dilemma for secession negotiations. Relying on the 7/50 or majority amending formula could result in a situation where Quebec (or any other province desiring secession) could be outnumbered or overruled by other provinces and the federal government. On the other hand, using the section 41 unanimity formula means that each party would have equitable power in negotiations.

Furthermore, arguments in support of applying section 38 to secession are tenuous following the Supreme Court's clarification of the purpose of the section 41 formula in the *Senate Reform Reference*. In that reference, the Court explained that, when dealing with matters essential to the functioning and survival of the Canadian state (such as the abolition of the Senate), section 41 must be engaged, as it is the only amending formula that provides all parties to Canadian federalism a role and a veto in the negotiations.[45] According to this reasoning, the unanimity requirement of section 41 also would apply to secession because the secession of a province undoubtedly would alter the fundamental characteristics of the Canadian Constitution, thereby requiring that all partners of Canadian federalism have a role to play in the process. If the abolition of the Senate requires unanimity, it is quite convincing that the abolition of a province from the Canadian federation would also require the high standard of unanimity.

The secession of Quebec would involve the repeal of several constitutional provisions that make explicit reference to the province and it ultimately would result in the transfer of legislative authority from the Parliament of Canada to the National Assembly of Quebec.[46] Secession would require the elimination of the office of lieutenant-governor in Quebec, amendments to the provision of the French and English languages in Quebec (affecting section 23 of the Charter), and have repercussions for the Supreme Court Act. Although these are just some of the specific amendments secession would necessitate, their amendment is listed under section 41, and therefore subject to the unanimity formula.

Legal scholar Patrick Monahan shares the position that section 41, unanimity, would apply to secession. Monahan argues that amending formulas must be viewed as cumulative, not disjunctive. In other words, once it became clear that secession would require the amendment of items specifically mentioned in subsections of section 41 – namely, changes to official languages, the Supreme Court, and the lieutenant-governor – section 41 would be engaged automatically. The entirety of the amendments required by the secession of a province would have to satisfy section 41 requirements, and could not be viewed in isolation from one another.[47]

The secession of Quebec would necessitate the transfer of many legislative powers from Parliament to the National Assembly; it would also require amendments of several federally enacted statutes. On the Supreme Court, for example, secession would require amendments to provisions of the Supreme Court Act that require the appointment of three jurists from Quebec to protect the interpretation of civil law, which would no longer be necessary. As the Supreme Court Act is not included in section 52(2) of the Constitution Act, 1982, which defines the "Constitution of Canada," some commentators argue that amendments to the Supreme Court and the Supreme Court Act are not subject to Part V.[48] However, the composition of the Supreme Court is explicitly listed under section 41(d) of the Part V amending formula, and thus its amendment requires the unanimous consent of Parliament and all provinces. Furthermore, the Court's ruling in the *Supreme Court Act Reference* (generally referred to as the *Nadon Reference*) made it clear that the composition of the Supreme Court – specifically the provision relating to civil law jurists, is constitutionally protected.[49]

As Crandall explains (in this volume), the *Nadon Reference* clarified that amendments concerning the composition of the Supreme Court – specifically, the eligibility of judges from Quebec – are possible only through section 41(d). In this reference, the Court was asked to rule on the constitutionality of the federal government's unilateral amendment of the Supreme Court Act to provide for the appointment of Justice Marc Nadon to the Court without following the required constitutional amendment procedures. The Court made it explicit that, although it is not listed in the confines of the Constitution, the Supreme Court is constitutionally protected, and any change in its composition – such as the secession of Quebec – would require a constitutional amendment under section 41.[50] If amending formulas should be interpreted in a cumulative manner, then activating the section 41 formula to eliminate the requirement for civil law jurists on the Supreme Court would require that all other secession-related amendments, at least those concerning the Court, also be subject to section 41.

It is important to note that, even though the Supreme Court is *not* listed in the Constitution, the Court did not apply section 38, the general amending formula. The Court's reasoning in *Nadon* thus serves to undermine the argument that the general amending formula applies to issues not specifically listed in the Constitution – such as the Supreme

Court or secession. Section 38 is not simply a catch-all amending formula to address novel issues or matters outside the constitutional text.

The interpretation that section 41 would apply to secession is further supported by the Supreme Court's most significant clarification of Part V amending formulas to date in the *Senate Reform Reference*. In this reference, the Court explained that the individual elements of the Constitution are not insular; instead, the provisions and principles of the Constitution are linked with one another and should be interpreted in conjunction with one another.[51] In other words, addressing which amending formula should apply to secession must be done in light of all the changes secession would require, and with respect for the specific requirements of the formula. An understanding of the interdependent nature of the Constitution requires that amending formulas be viewed in a cumulative, rather than insular, fashion. Although some of the changes required by secession could be achieved through the general amending formula (section 38), this does not negate the changes that are listed under the section 41 formula. Following the Court's interpretation in the *Senate Reform Reference* that secession would require changes to specific institutions that are explicitly listed as requiring the section 41 formula, *all* secession amendments must be addressed in light of the section 41 formula.

Moving from the specific example of the Supreme Court Act to the general principles of the Constitution the Supreme Court provided in the *Secession Reference*, it becomes clear that, even after a clear majority vote, secession could not be completed by ignoring the central principles of the Constitution. As the Court explained in the *Senate Reform Reference*, the Constitution must be interpreted with respect to its "architecture," not simply through analysis of the text. A respect for constitutional architecture requires a constitutional interpretation that is not merely narrow and technical, but has an understanding of the spirit, ideas, and meaning behind the text. Applying this reasoning to secession, the Part V amending formula must be read with an understanding of constitutional principles provided in the *Secession Reference*: federalism, democracy, constitutionalism and the rule of law, and respect for minorities.

Some sovereigntists argue that a clear demonstration of a democratic majority vote in support of secession would be enough to allow Quebec to leave the federation, but the Supreme Court has strongly rejected this position. The Court acknowledges that such a vote would impose obligations both on the other provinces and on the federal government, but

it would not overrule other constitutional principles.[52] For any secession process to be both legitimate and constitutional, it must ensure
that four constitutional principles are followed:

- democracy: a clear majority of the people in the province wishing to
  secede must support this goal after answering a clear question;
- federalism: all parties have an obligation to negotiate; secession
  negotiations must address the interests of the seceding province, the
  remaining provinces, and the federal government, not done in isolation from the other partners of Canadian federalism;
- constitutionalism and the rule of law: both the negotiations and the
  effects of the secession of a province must be pursuant to the Constitution and require the negotiation of a constitutional amendment; and
- minority rights: the rights of all Canadians both within the seceding
  province and elsewhere must be protected; the democratic majority
  must respect and protect the rights of minority groups (although the
  Court explained the need to protect the rights of Aboriginal Canadians
  specifically, it unfortunately provided no specific guidance on their
  role within secession negotiations – see Scholtz, in this volume).

Conclusion

The Canadian Constitution and amending formulas make no mention of
secession. The Supreme Court has provided little in the way of specific
details on how the secession of a province could take shape in Canada.
Therefore, it was the central aim in this chapter to provide an overview
of the considerations that would inform secession negotiations with
respect to Quebec and its unique history with both the Constitution in
general and amending formulas in particular. I have sought to provide
guidance on how the amending formulas could apply to some of the
changes secession would require, but I have focused on the process,
rather than the outcome, of secession. To be sure, the results of any
secession negotiations would be key to the subsequent functioning of
Canadian federalism, but those results would depend upon and ultimately be shaped by the process of constitutional amendment.[53]

The Supreme Court's decision in the *Secession Reference* could be criticized for its lack of a clear legal roadmap for secession. Such criticism,
however, ignores the constraints placed on the Court by the questions
asked in the reference and by the structure of the reference procedure
itself. Unquestionably, if a significant movement towards secession

were to manifest itself, the Supreme Court would be implicated in helping to navigate the specific legalities of negotiation. The Court's involvement, however, would not negate the role of political actors, who would have to negotiate in good faith and in accordance with the guiding constitutional principles offered by the Court. Although the specific mechanics of amending the Constitution to allow for secession remain uncertain, the separation of a province would alter the very foundation of the Canadian state, with significant repercussions in both domestic and international relations, making secession the "most radical amendment of all."

Notes

1 *Reference re: Secession of Quebec* [1998] 2 S.C.R. 217 [*Secession Reference*]; *Edwards v Canada (Attorney General)* [1930] A.C. 124.
2 *Secession Reference*, factum of the attorney general of Canada, paras 80–1.
3 Patrick J. Monahan and Michael J. Bryant with Nancy C. Coté, "Coming to Terms with Plan B: Ten Principles Governing Secession," *C.D. Howe Institute Commentary* 83 (Toronto: C.D. Howe Institute, June 1996).
4 George Rawlyk, "The Historical Framework of the Maritimes and the Problems of Confederation," in *Essential Readings in Canadian Constitutional Politics*, ed. Christian Leuprecht and Peter H. Russell, 87–95 (Toronto: University of Toronto Press, 2011).
5 The compact theory of Confederation is often dismissed for several reasons. First, it overlooks that, at the time of Confederation, provinces were not fully sovereign and changes to the BNA Act could be made only through the UK Parliament. Second, this understanding of Confederation provides no role for Canada's founding Indigenous groups. Finally, even the meaning of compact theory is contested: in some iterations, it refers to an agreement between the founding provinces; in others, it refers to the agreement between the French- and English-speaking peoples. See Filippo Sabetti, "The Historical Context of Constitutional Change in Canada," *Law and Contemporary Problems* 45, no. 4 (1982): 11–32; Peter H. Russell, *Constitutional Odyssey: Can Canadians Become a Sovereign People?* 3rd ed. (Toronto: University of Toronto Press, 2004).
6 Peter C. Oliver, "Quebec and the Amending Formula: Protection, Promotion and Federalism," in *Accommodating Cultural Diversity*, ed. Stephen Tierney, 167–97 (Abingdon, UK: Ashgate, 2007).
7 Russell, *Constitutional Odyssey*, 17.

8 Ibid., 73.
9 Oliver, "Quebec and the Amending Formula," 173.
10 Peter W. Hogg, *Constitutional Law of Canada*, Student ed. (Toronto: Carswell, 2012), 4–7.
11 Russell, *Constitutional Odyssey*, 91.
12 *Reference re Constitution of Canada* [1981] 1 S.C.R. 753.
13 Quebec, National Assembly, Decree No. 3214–81 of the Government of Quebec, 25 November 1981.
14 Nathalie Des Rosiers, "From Quebec Veto to Quebec Secession: The Evolution of the Supreme Court of Canada on Quebec-Canada Disputes," *Canadian Journal of Law and Jurisprudence* 13, no. 2 (2000): 171.
15 *Reference re: Objection by Quebec to a Resolution to Amend the Constitution* [1982] 2 S.C.R. 793, factum of the attorney general of Quebec, 8 [translated by the Supreme Court].
16 Ibid., para. 96.
17 Peter H. Russell, "The Patriation and Quebec Veto References: The Supreme Court Wrestles with the Political Part of the Constitution," *Supreme Court Law Review* 54 (2d) (2011): 69–76.
18 *Secession Reference*, factum of the attorney general of Canada.
19 Guy Bertrand and Angéline Fournier, *Enough Is Enough: An Attorney's Struggle for Democracy in Quebec* (Toronto: ECW Press, 1996).
20 Declaratory judgment of Justice Robert Lesage in *Bertrand v Bégin* (8 September 1995) Quebec 200–05–002117–955 (Sup. Ct.), as quoted in *Secession Reference*, factum of the attorney general of Canada.
21 Quebec, National Assembly, *Journal des débats*, vol. 34–70 (7 September 1995), 4707.
22 Order in Council P.C. 1996–1497, vol. 1, 1, 30 September 1996.
23 For a discussion of the *Secession Reference* from the perspective of international law, see Karen Knop, *Diversity and Self-Determination in International Law* (Cambridge: Cambridge University Press, 2004); William A. Schabas, "Twenty-five Years of Public International Law at the Supreme Court of Canada," *Canadian Bar Review* 79, no. 2 (2000): 174–95; Gibran Van Ert, "Nationality, State Succession, and the Right of Option: The Case of Quebec," *Canadian Yearbook of International Law* 36 (1998): 151–80.
24 Sean Fine, "Behind the scenes as history was made," *Globe and Mail*, 21 August 1998, A1.
25 Claire L'Heureux-Dube, "The Dissenting Opinion: Voice of the Future?" *Osgoode Hall Law Journal* 38, no. 3 (2000): 495–517.
26 *Secession Reference*, para. 49.
27 Ibid, para. 75.

28 Ibid., para. 84.

29 Ibid., para. 91.

30 Ibid., para. 92.

31 Ibid., para. 100.

32 Ibid., para. 105.

33 See, for example, Donna Greschner, "The Quebec Secession Reference: Goodbye to Part V," *Constitutional Forum* 10, no. 1 (1998): 19–25.

34 For more on abstract review in general, see Alec Stone Sweet, *Governing with Judges: Constitutional Politics in Europe* (New York: Oxford University Press, 2000).

35 Hogg, *Constitutional Law of Canada*, 8–20, 8–21.

36 *Secession Reference*, para. 105.

37 Ibid., factum of the attorney general of Canada, para. 98; factum of the attorney general of Manitoba, para. 67; factum of the attorney general of Saskatchewan, para. 49.

38 Ibid., factum of the attorney general of Canada, para. 110.

39 Ibid., para. 118.

40 Ibid., para. 119.

41 Sujit Choudhry and Robert Howse, "Constitutional Theory and the Quebec Secession Reference," *Canadian Journal of Law and Jurisprudence* 13, no. 2 (2000): 143–69.

42 Ibid., 150.

43 This position is supported by several scholars; see, for example, Hogg, *Constitutional Law of Canada*, 5–39; and Patrick J. Monahan, "The Law and Politics of Quebec Secession," *Osgoode Hall Law Journal* 33, no. 1 (1995): 1.

44 See Hogg, *Constitutional Law of Canada*, 5–40; José Woehrling, "Les aspects juridiques d'une éventuelle sécession du Québec," *Canadian Bar Review* 74, no. 2 (1995): 293, 310–13.

45 *Reference re: Senate Reform* [2014] 1 S.C.R. 704, para. 41.

46 Bertrand and Fournier, *Enough Is Enough*, 68.

47 Monahan, "Law and Politics of Quebec Secession," 9.

48 See ibid. for an overview of these arguments.

49 *Reference re Supreme Court Act, ss. 5 and 6* [2014] 1 S.C.R. 433.

50 Ibid., para. 75.

51 *Reference re: Senate Reform* [2014] 1 S.C.R. 704, para. 26.

52 *Secession Reference*, paras 90–3.

53 Robert A. Young, *The Struggle for Quebec: From Referendum to Referendum?* Montreal; Kingston, ON: McGill-Queen's University Press, 1999), 4.

Conclusion
The Future of Canadian Constitutional Amendment

EMMETT MACFARLANE

The question of whether Canada suffers from a constitutional stasis was an open one well before the Supreme Court's two opinions in the *Senate Reform* and *Supreme Court Act References*. The very fact that the Court had not engaged with Part V of the Constitution Act, 1982 in any comprehensive way prior to 2014 might itself reflect a general inability or antipathy to engage in major constitutional change among Canada's political class. The two failed efforts at major constitutional reform post-1982 – the Meech Lake and Charlottetown accords – made it clear that the threshold for significant constitutional change was high indeed. According to Janet Ajzenstat, "the long debate on constitutional reform – our constitutional odyssey, to use Peter Russell's excellent term – uncovered an uncomfortable fact: Canadians have no shared sense of history; there is no consensus about cultural identity."[1] There is little doubt that Canadian diversity and regionalism, expressed through federalism in the country's constitutional design generally and in the amending formula specifically, can act as a barrier to achieving high enough levels of support for unanimous consent, or even the consent of two-thirds of the provinces representing 50 per cent of the population, for significant constitutional change. The decades-long debate to secure a domestic amending formula is also a testament to this fact.

Yet attention paid to Meech and Charlottetown in some ways obscures, rather than clarifies, any assessment of the flexibility or rigidity of the amending formula. Those reform proposals were so expansive – and certain elements so controversial – that perhaps the lack of consensus on them simply reflected an honest rejection of their substantive content by elected representatives (or, in Charlottetown's case, the people) rather than proof of an unjustifiably high threshold demanded by the amending formula. It is possible that Canadians have permitted their justifiable constitutional fatigue, spurred by consecutive decades of sweeping intergovernmental negotiations over major reform from the 1960s to the 1990s, to blind us to the prospects of narrower, yet still significant, constitutional changes.

Only in recent years, then, spurred by issues such as Senate reform and controversies over royal succession and a failed Supreme Court appointment, have we seriously visited the amending formula's capacity to accommodate changes of a more specific nature. The contributions in this volume have explored constitutional amendment from the perspective of the formula's specific provisions as well as the Court's recent jurisprudence and other contemporary issues to examine the rigidity or flexibility of constitutional change, the politics of inclusion and exclusion, and the legal and institutional relationships that surround the amendment process. In this chapter, I examine areas of clarity, disagreement, and uncertainty surrounding the future of constitutional amendment in Canada. Despite some flexibility for future constitutional change in specific contexts, the Court's 2014 reference opinions are likely to exacerbate the difficulty of achieving support for major constitutional amendment, to the extent that the Court has contributed to a chilling effect, at least in the short to medium term, on attempts to amend, formally and informally, the Canadian Constitution. I conclude, however, by briefly explaining why this need not be the case.

A Constitutional Stasis?

The procedures that comprise the amending formula in Part V of the Constitution Act, 1982, are structured in a way to ensure flexibility where warranted, while demanding a high level of consensus (and, for specific matters, unanimity) for major changes affecting the country as a whole. The analyses in this volume suggest that, although there are serious questions about the Supreme Court's interpretation of Part V and about whether the balance between these various procedures is ideal, the basic structure of the formula has the potential to work as intended. Several contributors point to key areas of flexibility in the amending formula, particularly via the bilateral procedure in section 43, the unilateral procedure of section 44, and through reform to provincial constitutions via section 45.

A number of modest but important changes have been implemented via the bilateral procedure, as I note in the introductory chapter. In Chapter 7, Dwight Newman argues that there are greater prospects for section 43, including in the areas of the modern treaty context – although it is perhaps unclear if the creation of modern treaties counts as a formal amendment to the Constitution itself – and Charter rights. As Adam Dodek notes in Chapter 2, the Court provided some clarity in emphasizing that the general procedure is regarded as the default entry point to the amending formula. Thus, matters that directly affect nonconsenting provinces or the federation writ large are also proscribed from using the bilateral procedure. Yet it is not necessarily obvious where those limits might be. The potential for province-specific Charter rights, for example, has not received much academic attention.[2] The special provisions for New Brunswick in the Charter's official-languages section provide an obvious precedent for unique rights provisions relating to specific provinces, and attest to the basic legality of using the bilateral procedure to add new rights generally. But could certain types of rights have implications for other provinces or the federation as a whole? The introduction of specific rights for particular provinces – such as property rights, as Newman discusses – would certainly contribute to asymmetry, too much of which arguably could vitiate one of the central goals of the Charter itself, which was to foster national unity through a symbol of shared values.[3] Property rights might have implications for national or interprovincial projects (the building of oil pipelines, for example). It is not clear that this fact alone would make the entrenchment of province-specific property rights subject to the general amending procedure, but the federal government might be opposed to including new Charter rights on such a substantive basis. There might also be a desire to prevent the proliferation of province-specific Charter rights from a normative or political perspective but, as noted, nothing in Part V appears to prevent it.

It is here that the role of Parliament as an *institution of federalism* is often overlooked. Parliament is justified in protecting the national interest, and that might include preventing new asymmetries in the Charter – something some critics might regard as analogous to its balkanization. Thus, although there might be considerable legal flexibility for bilateral amendments to the Charter, Newman is right to point out that there are also potential political constraints. Similarly, more significant changes to the Charter – such as the insertion of a new interpretative provision (say, a distinct society clause for Quebec) – would, in my view, introduce fundamental asymmetry into the interpretation of rights that certainly would implicate the federation as a whole. Any such changes that do so must be brought forward under the general amending procedure.

The dividing line here is much the same with respect to section 45 and the provinces' ability to enact unilateral changes to their own constitutions. As Emmanuelle Richez explores in Chapter 8, provinces have considerable authority to effect institutional changes in areas such as electoral reform or those relating to the executive, as these do not impact the other provinces or the federation generally. Yet, as she explains, the ability of provinces to introduce asymmetry in the areas of cultural identity or citizenship is significantly constrained.

If Canada suffers from a general constitutional stasis, these analyses of the bilateral and provincial constitutional amending procedures suggest this stasis is by no means absolute. Further, under sections 43 and 45, there appears to be some (less than perfect) clarity regarding when specific changes to the Constitution are possible. The lines become especially blurred, however, in relation to Parliament's ability to effect unilateral changes under section 44. There is some disagreement among the contributors to this volume over how optimistic we should be about whether certain changes are possible, particularly regarding reform via "informal" or quasi-constitutional amendments. In Chapter 5, Warren Newman expresses some optimism about the potential enactment of statutes of an "organic nature" to provide great flexibility for Parliament, particularly if they enhanced entrenched features or values. Rainer Knopff's analysis of the regional veto and fixed-election-date legislation in Chapter 6 suggests that such laws have been defended or upheld as valid to the extent that they are not formally binding, something that he points out did not save the government's consultative senate elections proposal in the *Senate Reform Reference*. Dennis Baker and Mark Jarvis argue in Chapter 9 that a "chilling effect" might result from the Supreme Court's reasoning, which accords with my own view in Chapter 11 that the Court has further diminished the role of section 44.

In part, the source of this disagreement might stem from the fact that not all statutory or informal amendments are of the same kind. Newman points to the Official Languages Act and the Multiculturalism Act as examples of organic legislation, and he is undoubtedly correct to note that these sorts of changes should be described as being of a constitutional character, rather than necessarily of a constitutional nature. Both official-languages policy and Canada's multicultural heritage receive recognition in the Constitution's text, and although the statutes Newman points to provide specific policy measures designed to protect and promote them, they neither constitute changes to the Constitution itself nor depart from any of its specific measures. By contrast, certain statutes, such as the regional veto law, arguably do more than supplement existing values via policy. The regional veto legislation provides an express limit, for government ministers at least, on the introduction of resolutions relating to Part V that differs from the express requirements of Part V itself. The law prevents a minister from proposing an amendment unless it has secured the support of a majority of the population of Ontario, Quebec, British Columbia, the Prairie provinces, and the Atlantic provinces. Although not an explicit change to Part V itself – which would require a formal amendment under section 41's unanimity procedure – the regional veto law essentially adds an additional procedural hoop as part of the general amending procedure. In the *Senate Reform Reference*, the Court frowned upon this sort of indirect amendment to the Constitution, both in the context of Senate abolition and with respect to the proposed consultative elections. The Court's reasoning arguably calls into question the constitutionality of the regional veto act, which indirectly alters Part V itself, and similar types of statutes. When it comes to unilateral amendments under section 44 or informal changes generally, the prospects for future flexibility are far from clear.

Judicial Interpretation

Two elements of the Court's approach to Part V have obvious implications for the flexibility or rigidity of the Constitution. The first, as Dodek notes, relates to identifying what counts as part of the Constitution. The decision by the Court to entrench certain aspects of the Supreme Court Act – specifically, the eligibility criteria – was controversial. In Chapter 3 Carissima Mathen writes that this effectively renders the prospect of inserting new requirements, such as mandatory bilingualism or designating a seat on the Court for an Indigenous judge, a nonstarter. Mathen also questions whether the Court's appellate jurisdiction is now frozen, something she rightly argues is a worrisome prospect. Baker and Jarvis, along similar lines, wonder whether the regional veto law is itself now similarly entrenched. Of serious concern is that relatively minor institutional changes might now be subject to the onerous demands of the general or unanimous amending procedures. Indeed, in some instances, such as with respect to a potential bilingualism requirement for Supreme Court justices, this raised threshold might be an unintended consequence that flows from the Court's logic. Prior to the reference opinion few, if any, commentators thought a mandatory bilingualism rule would require a formal constitutional amendment.

Not all contributors to this volume agree that this problem is so clear-cut. In Chapter 10 Erin Crandall writes that the Court's reasoning in the *Supreme Court Act Reference* regarding constitutionalizing certain elements of the statute might not track directly from specific provisions, but instead might arise from practice. To the extent that the Court has operated as a bilingual institution, then, there might be room for Parliament to implement statutory changes to the eligibility requirements without the need for a formal amendment. In Chapter 11 I argue that it would be difficult for the Court to thread the logical needle of permitting the addition of new eligibility requirements while not allowing other types of changes to them; if the eligibility criteria for judges under the act fall under the "composition of the Supreme Court" in section 41(d), then drawing such distinctions becomes difficult from the perspective of maintaining fidelity to the text. Even permitting such a change on the basis of practice is problematic to the extent that, *in practice*, unilingual justices have been appointed to the Court throughout its history. Nonetheless, Crandall's suggestion that changes in line with existing practices might open the door to unilateral amendment on specific matters is consistent with Newman's view that statutory changes that enhance existing values, rather than depart from them, are more feasible.

This issue is illustrative of the second aspect of the Court's approach to Part V, which is its relative focus beyond the text in favour of context and the nebulous constitutional architecture concept. As Baker and Jarvis note, the "meta-rule" adopted by the justices when assessing whether section 44 applies appears to hinge on whether the Court views a particular change to be "housekeeping," as opposed to a "fundamental" change to some essential feature of the Constitution, an approach which the authors warn could collapse into deciding whether a particular change is desirable or not.[4] Despite the justices' firm denial that the desirability of amendments is a question for the Court, their own analysis in the *Senate Reform Reference* hinges so much on their articulation of the principles underlying the constitutional architecture and the role of the Senate that any change that departs from that understanding, even if minor, is regarded as incompatible with unilateral or informal amendment.

It is for this reason that an overly broad appeal to the contextual principles animating the Constitution can muddy any analysis of Part V. Appealing to certain values as consistent or inconsistent with the constitutional architecture might, in some contexts, belie the fact that competing values inhabit it. For example, suppose Parliament were deemed empowered to insert a new mandatory bilingualism rule unilaterally into the Supreme Court's eligibility criteria, on the basis that bilingualism is already a fundamental feature of the Court's operations – and despite the Court's opinion regarding changes to the eligibility rules for Quebec judges in the reference. Such a change would enhance an existing constitutional value, but it would do so at the expense of other realities. In this example, the Court's regional composition might also be regarded as an entrenched value, and a mandatory bilingualism rule might advantage certain provinces at the expense of others given the impact such a rule might have on the pool of potential regional candidates for appointment.

The justices' historical analysis of the position of the Court itself as part of the constitutional architecture in the *Supreme Court Act Reference* is particularly adventurous.[5] The justices asserted that the Court evolved "into an institution whose continued existence and function engaged the interests of both Parliament and the provinces" *before* 1982, and that the Constitution Act, 1982 merely "confirmed" its status as an institution whose essential features formed part of the Constitution.[6] Recall that, prior to 2014, a major debate among legal scholars was whether the Court itself was part of the Constitution *despite* the references to it in Part V. James Ross Hurley, writing in 1996, noted that it was not clear "whether the current composition of the Supreme Court of Canada is protected by the unanimity rule or whether this procedure applies only to the amendment of whatever composition of the Supreme Court is eventually entrenched in the Constitution."[7] I can find no authority prior to the Court's recent reference opinion that suggests the Court was itself constitutionally entrenched before 1982. The justices' analysis here is a fundamental departure from the constitutional text and its explicit recognition of Parliament's authority under section 101 over the establishment and maintenance of a general court of appeal.

Another important impact of the Court's contextual approach is that it results in a lack of clarity over when informal changes to certain political processes require formal amendment. A number of contributors to this volume raise concerns about potential changes to the Senate appointments process. The proposal by Justin Trudeau, then leader of the federal Liberals, to make Senate appointments nonpartisan and independent is cast in doubt to the extent that such procedural changes might be regarded as binding on future prime ministers. The Court placed a lot of emphasis on the fact that consultative elections are likely to be binding in practice, even if not formally. The justices stated that the democratic mandate explicitly sought through such reforms would make it unlikely that future prime ministers would refuse to appoint the winners of such elections. It is unclear how much of the Court's reasoning hinged on the nature of the democratic mandate sought by consultative elections specifically. Would other types of changes to the process that might create new norms surrounding the prime minister's selections – such as having names proposed by an independent advisory body – also be regarded as indirectly binding? If so, even modest procedural changes might require formal amendment. Another relevant distinction might be whether such changes are formalized, such as being brought in by statute, or simply established on an ad hoc basis by the sitting prime minister. Where the former might be regarded as an attempt to bind the hands of future prime ministers, the latter could be viewed as a legitimate part of the current prime minister's discretion over how he or she conducts the selection process. (I believe this distinction to be important; in the interests of full disclosure, I provided nonpartisan advice to the Liberal Party of Canada on its Senate proposals along these lines.)

If one thing is clear from the contributions to this volume, it is that the Court itself is a major player in constitutional amendment. This extends well beyond its role in constitutional interpretation of Part V, where the impact of its recent jurisprudence on the breadth of the amending formula's various procedures is significant. Having helped to shape the events leading to entrenchment of a domestic amending formula, particularly with its opinion in the *Patriation Reference*, the Court has now begun to develop guidelines around the use of the amending procedures. Much like with judicial interpretation of the Charter or other aspects of the Constitution, the politics of the judicial role is also relevant in the context of the amending formula. Much of the political science literature, to varying degrees, envisions judicial behaviour as premised on the ideological or strategically based policy preferences of individual justices.[8] It is easy to see how similar political and strategic implications might be relevant with respect to the Court's approach to Part V. For example, the strategic incentive for the justices to entrench key aspects of their own institution is obvious: why not make it more difficult for the government of the day to institute changes under the Supreme Court Act?

Even more significant is the extent to which judicial interpretation effectively can amount to judicial amendment of the Constitution. Admittedly, the line between judicial interpretation and judicial amendment is tricky to identify, but a strong case can be made that every time the Court has decided to entrench some aspect of what it identified as falling within the constitutional architecture or a provision of a statute that, until that point, had been regarded as ordinary legislation, it has amended the Constitution itself. Even beyond the context of interpreting Part V, the Court, by virtue of its power of interpretation, perhaps has a stronger hand than any other actor in the Canadian political system to amend the Constitution. One example from the legal scholarship on the Charter illustrates how this could work. Progressive scholars have long argued in favour of the Court's reading positive economic and social rights into section 7 of the Charter,[9] something the Charter's drafters certainly did not intend and that the Court has so far largely resisted.[10] Further, there is at least some evidence of a prior political consensus that a formal amendment would be required to insert such positive rights in the Constitution, as a social charter was notably part of the failed Charlottetown Accord package. At that time, the Charter was obviously regarded as not containing positive economic rights, and an amendment was viewed as necessary to effect change. Any decision by the Court to open the door to positive economic rights under section 7 could be regarded as an amendment to the Constitution, rather than ordinary constitutional interpretation.[11] Notably, the Court left the door open to such an interpretation in its 2002 *Gosselin* decision, citing the "living tree metaphor" to justify the possibility.[12] The living tree metaphor is viewed as ensuring that existing rights can be applied to new circumstances and to prevent such rights from being frozen in time. It seems an extreme version of the living tree, however, to permit the addition of entirely new rights. In leaving open the possibility, the Court effectively granted itself the power of unilateral amendment, despite the requirement under Part V that any such additions to the Charter be brought in under the general amending procedure.

Even aside from the potential for judicial amendment of the Constitution, the Court's interpretative authority by itself leaves the justices with significant power to affect the future of constitutional change in Canada. As the contributions to this volume make clear, the Court's contextual approach in many ways has added to the complexity to an already multifaceted formula. Yet in some areas its approach appears instructive, as Philippe Lagassé and Patrick Baud explore in relation to changes affecting the Crown in Chapter 12. In other areas the Court has introduced ambiguity into the feasibility of certain changes, such as with respect to the senatorial selection process or reform of the Court itself. On balance, the Court's approach has also raised the threshold for certain changes by minimizing the scope for unilateral changes under section 44. I and some of the other contributors to this volume are critical of this outcome, but, as I explore briefly in the next section, there is a normative desirability to the sort of broader inclusivity the Court has guaranteed, at least from the perspective of the provinces.

Inclusivity and the Amending Formula

The amending formula privileges Parliament and the provincial legislatures as the primary actors capable of implementing constitutional change. The Court's recent jurisprudence on Part V was a victory for champions of the federal principle, as Mathen explores in depth in Chapter 3. Substantial provincial consent under the general amending procedure is required for any changes that affect provincial interests, as is unanimity for matters falling under section 41. The Court's two 2014 reference opinions made clear that this extends to any changes affecting the essential features of the Senate or the Supreme Court. The Court's approach also emphasized that constitutional change is not just limited to amendments to discrete provisions of the constitutional text, but includes any changes implicating the broader constitutional architecture, which the Court might deem to include ordinary statutes (or parts thereof), as it did with the eligibility requirements of the Supreme Court Act. At the very least, fundamental changes (as opposed to matters of housekeeping) to federal institutions require provincial consent. As a general principle, and regardless of the debate over whether the Court has articulated a good approach to distinguishing between housekeeping versus fundamental changes, this rule is very much in keeping with the intent and spirit of the design of Part V.

One aspect of the inclusivity of Part V that warrants attention is whether its focus on legislative assent is sufficient to ensure amendments receive popular support. It is worth noting that a referendum procedure was included in draft versions of the amending formula during negotiations in 1981 and as part of the plan Prime Minister Pierre Trudeau sought to take to the UK Parliament unilaterally for patriation.[13] Further, some commentators have argued that, since Charlottetown, a referendum has been regarded as a requirement for future constitutional change, and any "Meech-like attempt at reform through pure executive federalism is now unthinkable."[14] It would go too far to suggest that the Charlottetown process established a convention requiring popular consent for constitutional amendment. Nonetheless, as Knopff examines in Chapter 6, both British Columbia and Alberta have passed legislation mandating referendums on proposed constitutional changes before they are brought to the provincial legislature for ratification. Like the federal regional veto law, it is not clear, Knopff points out, whether such legislation represents an unconstitutional attempt to alter Part V itself indirectly. Nevertheless, it is significant that at least two provinces view seeking an explicit popular mandate to be a necessary step of any amending process.

Whether or not direct popular input is normatively desirable, some commentators have viewed the Charlottetown process as instructive. For example, Michael Stein notes that, although some viewed the Charlottetown referendum as a cynical ploy by politicians of the day, the campaign itself provided legitimate public education about the substance of the Accord, and the vote ultimately expressed a clear indication of public sentiment on its merits.[15] Where rules limit the activity of special interests, where there is sufficient time for the public to learn about any constitutional proposals, and where yes and no sides both are organized effectively, providing for popular input into constitutional changes might enhance the overall legitimacy of the amending process.

Another key debate about the inclusivity of the amending procedure is whether Canada's Indigenous population has a special claim to involvement or consent to proposals. As Christa Scholtz examines in Chapter 4, section 35 of the Constitution Act, 1982 commits the federal and provincial governments to a "principle" of consultation regarding any proposed changes affecting Aboriginal interests – specifically, those pertaining to sections 25 and 35 of the 1982 Act and section 91(24) of the Constitution Act, 1867. Part V makes no mention of Indigenous interests in constitutional amendment, and the principle in section 35 does not make Indigenous consent a legal requirement for any changes, even those directly affecting Indigenous interests. As Scholtz's analysis suggests, it is not clear whether this principle rises to the level of a legal duty to consult. Yet it is clear, in my view, that a political duty to consult with Canada's Indigenous people's would go some way towards increasing the legitimacy of any future constitutional amendments – and, for some Indigenous peoples, of the Canadian Constitution in general. Despite the explicit constitutional recognition of Aboriginal and treaty rights in 1982, Canada's Indigenous peoples for too long have been left on the sidelines of constitutional debate, as represented both by the failed Meech Lake Accord process and the federal government's refusal to consider seriously constitutional changes recommended in the report of the Royal Commission on Aboriginal Peoples.[16] A meaningful process of consultation – particularly on, though not necessarily limited to, changes directly affecting Indigenous interests – is an unquestionable prerequisite for the legitimacy of future amendments.

Conclusion: Thoughts on a Way Forward

This volume has explored the law and politics of Part V of the Constitution Act, 1982. Amending the Constitution should not be easy. The Constitution represents the country's foundational law, and provides a permanence to society's most deeply held values. Yet if certain aspects of the Constitution are too difficult or impossible to change, even in the face of deep and broad consensus over the need to reform nineteenth-century institutions to fit twenty-first-century needs, then a constitutional paralysis can pose significant dangers for the democratic vitality and legitimacy of the governing system as a whole. The status of the Senate is but one recent and prominent example. Canadians overwhelmingly oppose the current status quo,[17] yet the prospects for meaningful Senate reform remain slim.[18] Many of the contributors to this volume have raised concerns about and provided criticism of the amending formula and the Supreme Court's recent jurisprudence pertaining to it along these lines. Despite these concerns, however, none of the authors suggests that Canadian governments ought to abandon all hope in the face of perceived constitutional paralysis. This book provides a comprehensive, but not exhaustive, examination of Canadian constitutional amendment, and the conclusions reached in its various chapters, we hope, will provide some guidance to the country's political and judicial actors. By way of conclusion, I offer some thoughts on how to go forward from here.

First despite the perception among some commentators (myself included) that the amending formula as a whole is imperfect or that the Court has failed to provide a clear or balanced interpretation of its various provisions, Canada's various governments and legislatures still have the option of demonstrating the political will and statecraft to implement fundamental changes to the Constitution. A key strategy should be to engage in focused efforts at meaningful, specific changes, rather than sweeping packages of reform, as scholars have suggested elsewhere.[19] Any province or the federal government can initiate a proposal by passing a resolution in its legislature. There is no reason to fear (or relent to) demands that constitutional negotiations be expanded to include other issues or that *quid pro quo* resolutions be put into place. Canadians should be able to expect affirmative or negative support from their provincial legislature or Parliament on specific issues. Governments also have obvious avenues for implementing changes of more narrow or specific types by virtue of the unilateral and bilateral amending procedures in sections 43, 44, and 45. These procedures alone make it emphatically clear that significant areas of constitutional concern are not frozen in time. The bilateral procedure might be particularly fruitful for future reform efforts.

Second, politicians need to take the Constitution seriously. There is much room for improvement in the knowledge (or lack thereof) elected representatives demonstrate when discussing or raising specific proposals. The position adopted by both the federal Conservatives and the New Democratic Party that the Senate can be left to die by neglect by having the prime minister simply refuse to make new appointments to the upper chamber is a significant failure in this regard. Whatever the fate of the ongoing legal challenge that the prime minister is compelled to make regular appointments to the Senate,[20] politicians need to reflect on their constitutional responsibilities and avoid political gamesmanship that flies in the face of principled practice.

Third, elected representatives should take care to ensure that inclusive practices surround reform proposals. The duty to consult Indigenous peoples on constitutional amendment might not be a binding legal principle, but it should be regarded as implicating the honour of the Crown as binding political practice. The federal government, through the regional veto act, and a number of provinces, through statutes requiring referendums, have implemented formal mechanisms for broader forms of approval, but there are also informal methods of guaranteeing more inclusive politics surrounding constitutional proposals. These might include political parties ensuring that they include major reform proposals in their election platforms, that the proposals receive debate during campaigns, that sufficient public and transparent consultations are held in legislative committees, town halls, or other democratic assemblies, and that robust political debate takes place more generally.

Finally, the Supreme Court needs to provide a more refined, less amorphous approach to interpreting Part V. At some point the Court likely will be confronted with reform attempts that places under tension the approach and rationale the justices employed in the recent Part V references. Such a case might come following an attempt by Parliament to pass a bill imposing a bilingualism requirement on future Supreme Court justices, some informal change to the Senate selection process, or some other issue not yet on the political agenda. The Court needs to be willing to clarify, revise, or even reverse its general rationale if obvious contradictions emerge in its jurisprudence surrounding Part V.

Even more significantly, elected representatives must not allow the potential uncertainty that has emerged in specific areas following the recent references to prevent them from pursuing reform when they believe it is necessary. To a great degree, any constitutional paralysis that Canada ultimately suffers will be the result of the lack of political will to negotiate, compromise, or cooperate. The most basic meaning of the amending formula is the recognition that the Constitution is never a finished product.

Notes

1 Janet Ajzenstat, *The Canadian Founding: John Locke and Parliament* (Montreal; Kingston, ON: McGill-Queen's University Press, 2007), 12–13.

2 Although scholars have examined the tensions between federalism and the Charter and have debated the extent to which the Charter is a centralizing force or whether there is a "federalist sensitivity" to judicial interpretations of rights. See Alan C. Cairns, *Charter versus Federalism: The Dilemmas of Constitutional Reform* (Montreal; Kingston, ON: McGill-Queen's University Press, 1991); Janet Hiebert, "The Charter and Federalism: Revisiting the Nation-Building Thesis," in *Canada: The State of the Federation 1994*, ed. Douglas M. Brown and Janet Hiebert, 153–78 (Kingston, ON: Queen's University, Institute of Intergovernmental Relations, 1994); James B. Kelly, "Reconciling Rights and Federalism during Review of the Charter of Rights and Freedoms: The Supreme Court of Canada and the Centralization Thesis, 1982 to 1999," *Canadian Journal of Political Science* 34, no. 2 (2001): 321–55; F.L. Morton, "The Effect of the Charter of Rights on Canadian Federalism," *Publius: The Journal of Federalism* 25, no. 3 (1995): 173–88; Jeremy A. Clarke, "Beyond the Democratic Dialogue, and Towards a Federalist One: Provincial Arguments and Supreme Court Responses in Charter Litigation," *Canadian Journal of Political Science* 39, no. 2 (2006): 293–314.

3 Peter H. Russell, "The Political Purposes of the Canadian Charter of Rights and Freedoms," *Canadian Bar Review* 61 (1983): 30–54.

4 Baker and Jarvis note the Court explicitly denied this was what it was doing; see: *Reference re Senate Reform*, 2014 SCC 32, para. 4.

5 *Reference re Supreme Court Act, ss. 5 and 6*, SCC 21, [2014] 1 S.C.R. 433, paras 76–87.
6 Ibid., para. 76.
7 James Ross Hurley, *Amending Canada's Constitution: History, Processes, Problems and Prospects* (Ottawa: Canada Communication Group, 1996), 76.
8 See C.L. Ostberg and Matthew Wetstein, *Attitudinal Decision Making in the Supreme Court of Canada* (Vancouver: UBC Press, 2007); Christopher P. Manfredi, "Strategic Behavior and the Canadian Charter of Rights and Freedoms," in *The Myth of the Sacred: The Charter, the Courts and the Politics of the Constitution in Canada*, ed. Patrick James, Donald E. Abelson, and Michael Lusztig, 143–70 (Montreal; Kingston, ON: McGill-Queen's University Press, 2002); and Emmett Macfarlane, *Governing from the Bench: The Supreme Court of Canada and the Judicial Role* (Vancouver: UBC Press, 2013).
9 See, for example, Martha Jackman, "The Protection of Welfare Rights under the Charter," *Ottawa Law Review* 20, no. 2 (1988): 257–329; and Margot Young, "Section 7 and the Politics of Social Justice," *University of British Columbia Law Review* 38 (2005): 539–60.
10 *Gosselin v Quebec (Attorney General)*, [2002] 4 S.C.R. 429, 2002 SCC 84.
11 For more on this topic, see Emmett Macfarlane, "The Dilemma of Positive Rights: Access to Health Care and the Canadian Charter of Rights and Freedoms," *Journal of Canadian Studies* 48, no. 33 (2014): 49–78.
12 *Gosselin*, para. 82.
13 "Proposed Resolution for a Joint Address to Her Majesty The Queen Respecting the Constitution of Canada, as Amended by the Committee (moved in the House February 17, 1981)," in *Canada's Constitution Act 1982 & Amendments: A Documentary History*, vol. 2, ed. Anne F. Bayefsky (Toronto: McGraw-Hill Ryerson, 1989).
14 Patrick James, *Constitutional Politics in Canada after the Charter: Liberalism, Communitarianism, and Systemism* (Vancouver: UBC Press, 2010), 101.
15 Michael B. Stein, "Improving the Process of Constitutional Reform in Canada: Lessons from the Meech Lake and Charlottetown Constitutional Rounds," *Canadian Journal of Political Science* 30, no. 2 (1997): 328–9.
16 Among these recommendations were a new Royal Proclamation and recognition of an Aboriginal order of government. See Canada, Royal Commission on Aboriginal Peoples, *Report* (Ottawa: Indian and Northern Affairs Canada, 1996).
17 Joseph Brean, "Majority of Canadians support either abolished or reformed Senate: poll," *National Post*, 7 April 2015; available online at http://news.nationalpost.com/news/canada/canadian-politics/majority-of-canadians-support-either-abolished-or-reformed-senate-poll, accessed 10 May 2015.

18 In part this is due to disagreement over whether the institution should be reformed or abolished entirely.

19 Peter Aucoin, Mark D. Jarvis, and Lori Turnbull, *Democratizing the Constitution: Reforming Responsible Government* (Toronto: Emond Montgomery, 2011), 226.

20 Joan Bryden, "Court asked to compel Senate appointments," *Canadian Press*, 9 April 2015; available online at http://www.metronews.ca/news/canada/2015/04/09/court-asked-to-compel-senate-appointments-2.html, accessed 28 April 2015.

Appendix

PART V of the Constitution Act, 1982

PROCEDURE FOR AMENDING THE CONSTITUTION OF CANADA

General procedure for amending the Constitution of Canada

38. (1) An amendment to the Constitution of Canada may be made by proclamation issued by the Governor General under the Great Seal of Canada where so authorized by

(*a*) resolutions of the Senate and House of Commons; and

(*b*) resolutions of the legislative assemblies of at least two-thirds of the provinces that have, in the aggregate, according to the then latest general census, at least fifty per cent of the population of all the provinces.

MAJORITY OF MEMBERS

(2) An amendment made under subsection (1) that derogates from the legislative powers, the proprietary rights or any other rights or privileges of the legislature or government of a province shall require a resolution supported by a majority of the members of each of the Senate, the House of Commons and the legislative assemblies required under subsection (1).

EXPRESSION OF DISSENT

(3) An amendment referred to in subsection (2) shall not have effect in a province the legislative assembly of which has expressed its dissent thereto by resolution supported by a majority of its members prior to the

issue of the proclamation to which the amendment relates unless that legislative assembly, subsequently, by resolution supported by a majority of its members, revokes its dissent and authorizes the amendment.

REVOCATION OF DISSENT
(4) A resolution of dissent made for the purposes of subsection (3) may be revoked at any time before or after the issue of the proclamation to which it relates.

Restriction on proclamation

39. (1) A proclamation shall not be issued under subsection 38(1) before the expiration of one year from the adoption of the resolution initiating the amendment procedure thereunder, unless the legislative assembly of each province has previously adopted a resolution of assent or dissent.

IDEM
(2) A proclamation shall not be issued under subsection 38(1) after the expiration of three years from the adoption of the resolution initiating the amendment procedure thereunder.

Compensation

40. Where an amendment is made under subsection 38(1) that transfers provincial legislative powers relating to education or other cultural matters from provincial legislatures to Parliament, Canada shall provide reasonable compensation to any province to which the amendment does not apply.

Amendment by unanimous consent

41. An amendment to the Constitution of Canada in relation to the following matters may be made by proclamation issued by the Governor General under the Great Seal of Canada only where authorized by resolutions of the Senate and House of Commons and of the legislative assembly of each province:

> (a) the office of the Queen, the Governor General and the Lieutenant Governor of a province;
> (b) the right of a province to a number of members in the House of Commons not less than the number of Senators by which the

province is entitled to be represented at the time this Part comes
into force;

(c) subject to section 43, the use of the English or the French
language;

(d) the composition of the Supreme Court of Canada; and

(e) an amendment to this Part.

Amendment by general procedure

42. (1) An amendment to the Constitution of Canada in relation
to the following matters may be made only in accordance with
subsection 38(1):

(a) the principle of proportionate representation of the provinces
in the House of Commons prescribed by the Constitution of
Canada;

(b) the powers of the Senate and the method of selecting Senators;

(c) the number of members by which a province is entitled to be
represented in the Senate and the residence qualifications of
Senators;

(d) subject to paragraph 41(d), the Supreme Court of Canada;

(e) the extension of existing provinces into the territories; and

(f) notwithstanding any other law or practice, the establishment of
new provinces.

EXCEPTION
(2) Subsections 38(2) to (4) do not apply in respect of amendments in
relation to matters referred to in subsection (1).

Amendment of provisions relating to some but not all provinces

43. An amendment to the Constitution of Canada in relation to any
provision that applies to one or more, but not all, provinces, including

(a) any alteration to boundaries between provinces, and

(b) any amendment to any provision that relates to the use of the
English or the French language within a province,

may be made by proclamation issued by the Governor General under
the Great Seal of Canada only where so authorized by resolutions of the

Senate and House of Commons and of the legislative assembly of each province to which the amendment applies.

Amendments by Parliament

44. Subject to sections 41 and 42, Parliament may exclusively make laws amending the Constitution of Canada in relation to the executive government of Canada or the Senate and House of Commons.

Amendments by provincial legislatures

45. Subject to section 41, the legislature of each province may exclusively make laws amending the constitution of the province.

Initiation of amendment procedures

46. (1) The procedures for amendment under sections 38, 41, 42 and 43 may be initiated either by the Senate or the House of Commons or by the legislative assembly of a province.

REVOCATION OF AUTHORIZATION
(2) A resolution of assent made for the purposes of this Part may be revoked at any time before the issue of a proclamation authorized by it.

Amendments without Senate resolution

47. (1) An amendment to the Constitution of Canada made by proclamation under section 38, 41, 42 or 43 may be made without a resolution of the Senate authorizing the issue of the proclamation if, within one hundred and eighty days after the adoption by the House of Commons of a resolution authorizing its issue, the Senate has not adopted such a resolution and if, at any time after the expiration of that period, the House of Commons again adopts the resolution.

COMPUTATION OF PERIOD
(2) Any period when Parliament is prorogued or dissolved shall not be counted in computing the one hundred and eighty day period referred to in subsection (1).

Advice to issue proclamation

48. The Queen's Privy Council for Canada shall advise the Governor General to issue a proclamation under this Part forthwith on the adoption of the resolutions required for an amendment made by proclamation under this Part.

Constitutional conference

49. A constitutional conference composed of the Prime Minister of Canada and the first ministers of the provinces shall be convened by the Prime Minister of Canada within fifteen years after this Part comes into force to review the provisions of this Part.

Selected Bibliography

Ackerman, Bruce. *We the People: Foundations*. Cambridge, MA: Harvard University Press, 1991.

Ackerman, Bruce. *We the People: Transformations*. Cambridge, MA: Harvard University Press, 1998.

Ajzenstat, Janet. *The Canadian Founding*. Montreal; Kingston, ON: McGill-Queen's University Press, 2007.

Albert, Richard. "Constitutional Amendment by Constitutional Desuetude." *American Journal of Comparative Law* 62 (2014): 641–86.

Albert, Richard. "Constructive Unamendability in Canada and the United States." *Supreme Court Law Review* (2d) 67 (2014): 181–219.

Albert, Richard. "The Difficulty of Constitutional Amendment in Canada." *Alberta Law Review* 53, no. 1 (2015): 85–114.

Alexander, Larry, and Frederick Schauer. "On Extrajudicial Constitutional Interpretation." *Harvard Law Review* 110, no. 7 (1997): 1359–87.

Aucoin, Peter, Mark D. Jarvis, and Lori Turnbull. *Democratizing the Constitution: Reforming Responsible Government*. Toronto: Emond Montgomery, 2011.

Aucoin, Peter, and Lori Turnbull. "The Democratic Deficit: Paul Martin and Parliamentary Reform." *Canadian Public Administration* 46, no. 4 (2003): 427–49.

Aucoin, Peter, and Lori Turnbull. "Removing the Virtual Right of First Ministers to Demand Dissolution." *Canadian Parliamentary Review* 27, no. 2 (2004): 16–19.

Baier, Gerald. "Canada: Federal and Subnational Constitutional Practices." In *Constitutional Dynamics in Federal Systems: Sub-national Perspectives*, edited by Michael Burgess and G. Alan Tarr, 174–92. Montreal; Kingston, ON: McGill-Queen's University Press, 2012.

Baker, Dennis R. *Not Quite Supreme: The Courts and Coordinate Constitutional Interpretation*. Montreal; Kingston, ON: McGill-Queen's University Press, 2010.

Bertrand, Guy, and Angéline Fournier. *Enough Is Enough: An Attorney's Struggle for Democracy in Quebec*. Toronto: ECW Press, 1996.

Bolt, Alexander. "Crown Prerogative Decisions to Deploy the Canadian Forces Internationally: A Fitting Mechanism for a Liberal Democracy." In *Canada and the Crown: Essays on Constitutional Monarchy*, edited by D. Michael Jackson and Philippe Lagassé, 219–36. Montreal; Kingston, ON: McGill-Queen's University Press, 2013.

Braën, André. "Les recours en matière de droits linguistiques." In *Les droits linguistiques au Canada*, edited by Michel Bastarache et al. Cowansville, QC: Éditions Yvon Blais, 1986.

Brock, Kathy. "Diversity within Unity: Constitutional Amendments under Section 43." *Canadian Parliamentary Review* 20, no. 1 (1997): 23–7.

Brun, Henri, Guy Tremblay, and Eugénie Brouillet. *Droit constitutionnel*, 5th ed. Cowansville, QC: Éditions Yvon Blais, 2008.

Burgess, Michael, and G. Alan Tarr. "Introduction: Subnational Constitutionalism and Constitutional Development." In *Constitutional Dynamics in Federal Systems: Sub-national Perspectives*, edited by Michael Burgess and G. Alan Tarr, 3–40. Montreal; Kingston, ON: McGill-Queen's University Press, 2012.

Cairns, Alan. "The Quebec Secession Reference: The Constitutional Obligation to Negotiate." *Constitutional Forum* 10, no. 1 (1998): 26–30.

Cairns, Alan. *Charter versus Federalism: The Dilemmas of Constitutional Reform*. Montreal; Kingston, ON: McGill-Queen's University Press, 1991.

Cameron, Barbara. "The Office and Powers of the Governor General: Political Intention and Legal Interpretation." *Journal of Parliamentary and Political Law* 6 (2012): 87–105.

Cameron, David R., and Jacqueline D. Krikorian. "Recognizing Quebec in the Constitution: Using the Bilateral Constitutional Amendment Process." *University of Toronto Law Journal* 58, no. 4 (2008): 389–420.

Carter, Mark. "An Analysis of the 'No Hierarchy of Constitutional Rights' Doctrine." *Review of Constitutional Studies* 12, no. 1 (2007): 19–51.

Chambers, Simone. "Contract or Conversation? Theoretical Lessons from the Canadian Constitutional Crisis." *Politics & Society* 26, no. 1 (1998): 143–72.

Cheffins, Ronald I. "The Constitution Act, 1982 and the Amending Formula: Political and Legal Implications." *Supreme Court Law Review* 4 (1982): 43.

Cheffins, Ronald I. "The Royal Prerogative and the Office of Lieutenant Governor." *Canadian Parliamentary Review* 23, no. 1 (2000): 14–19.

Choudhry, Sujit, and Robert Howse. "Constitutional Theory and the Quebec Secession Reference." *Canadian Journal of Law and Jurisprudence* 13, no. 2 (2000): 143–69.

Cotler, Irwin. "The Supreme Court Appointment Process: Chronology, Context, and Reform." *University of New Brunswick Law Journal* 58 (2008): 131–46.

Crandall, Erin. "Intergovernmental Relations and the Supreme Court of Canada: The Changing Place of the Provinces in Judicial Selection Reform." In *The Democratic Dilemma: Reforming Canada's Supreme Court*, edited by Nadia Verrelli, 71–85. Montreal; Kingston, ON: McGill-Queen's University Press, 2013.

Dawson, R. MacGregor. *The Government of Canada*, 4th ed. Toronto: University of Toronto Press, 1967.

Des Rosiers, Nathalie. "From Quebec Veto to Quebec Secession: The Evolution of the Supreme Court of Canada on Quebec-Canada Disputes." *Canadian Journal of Law and Jurisprudence* 13, no. 2 (2000): 171–83.

Dodek, Adam. "Courting Constitutional Danger: Constitutional Conventions and the Legacy of the Patriation Reference." *Supreme Court Law Review* (2d) (2011): 117–42.

Fox-Decent, Evan. *Sovereignty's Promise: The State as Fiduciary*. Oxford: Oxford University Press, 2011.

Friedman, Barry. "Mediated Popular Constitutionalism." *Michigan Law Review* 101, no. 8 (2003): 2596–636.

Gérin-Lajoie, Paul. *Constitutional Amendment in Canada*, vol. 3. Toronto: University of Toronto Press, 1950.

Gerken, Heather K. "The Hydraulics of Constitutional Reform: A Skeptical Response to Our Undemocratic Constitution." *Drake Law Review* 55, no. 4 (2007): 925–52.

Gibson, Dale. "Founding Fathers-in-Law: Judicial Amendment of the Canadian Constitution." *Law and Contemporary Problems* 55, no. 1 (1992): 261–84.

Gibson, Dale. "Monitoring Arbitrary Government Authority: Charter Scrutiny of Legislative, Executive and Judicial Privilege." *Saskatchewan Law Review* 61, no. 2 (1998): 297–321.

Goldsworthy, Jeffrey. "Unwritten Constitutional Principles." In *Expounding the Constitution*, edited by Grant Huscroft, 277–312. New York: Cambridge University Press, 2008.

Hawkins, Robert E. "Constitutional Workarounds: Senate Reform and Other Examples." *Canadian Bar Review* 89, no. 3 (2010): 513–43.

Heard, Andrew. *Canadian Constitutional Conventions: The Marriage of Law and Politics*, 2nd ed. Oxford: Oxford University Press, 2014.

Heard, Andrew. "Conacher Missed the Mark on Constitutional Conventions and Fixed Election Dates." *Constitutional Forum* 19, no. 1 (2010): 21–32.

Hogg, Peter W. *Constitutional Law of Canada*, Student ed. Toronto: Carswell, 2014.

Hogg, Peter W. *Meech Lake Constitutional Accord Annotated*. Scarborough, ON: Carswell, 1988.

Hogg, Peter W. "Succession to the Throne." *National Journal of Constitutional Law* 33, no. 1 (2014): 83–95.

Hogg, Peter W., Patrick J. Monahan, and Wade K. Wright. *Liability of the Crown*, 4th ed. Toronto: Carswell, 2011.

Hurley, James Ross. *Amending Canada's Constitution: History, Processes, Problems and Prospects*. Ottawa: Minister of Supply and Services Canada, 1996.

Isaac, Thomas. *Aboriginal Law: Commentary and Analysis*. Saskatoon: Purich, 2012.

James, Patrick. *Constitutional Politics in Canada after the Charter: Liberalism, Communitarianism, and Systemism*. Vancouver: UBC Press, 2010.

Jennings, Ivor. *The Law and the Constitution*. London: University of London Press, 1959.

Kelly, Paul. *November 1975*. Crows Nest, Australia: Allen & Unwin, 1995.

Keyes, John Mark. "The Legislative Process and Judicial Review: Royal Functions and Their Justiciability." In *The Crown and Parliament in Canada*, edited by Michel Bédard and Philippe Lagassé, 61–93. Cowansville, QC: Éditions Yvon Blais, 2015.

Knopff, Rainer. "Legal Theory and the 'Patriation' Debate." *Queen's Law Journal* 7, no. 1 (1981): 41–65.

Kramer, Larry D. *The People Themselves: Popular Constitutionalism and Judicial Review*. Oxford: Oxford University Press, 2004.

Lagassé, Philippe. "The Crown's Powers of Command-in-Chief: Interpreting Section 15 of the Constitution, 1867." *Review of Constitutional Studies* 18, no. 2 (2013): 189–220.

Lagassé, Philippe, and Patrick Baud. "The Crown and Constitutional Amendment in Canada." In *The Crown and Parliament in Canada*, edited by Michel Bédard and Philippe Lagassé, 203–40. Cowansville, QC: Éditions Yvon Blais, 2015.

Lagassé, Philippe, and James W.J. Bowden. "Royal Succession and the Canadian Crown as Corporation Sole: A Critique of Canada's Succession to the Throne Act, 2013." *Constitutional Forum* 23, no. 1 (2014): 17–26.

Lederman, William R. "Constitutional Procedure for the Reform of the Supreme Court of Canada." *Cahiers de droit* 26, no. 1 (1985): 195–204.

Leeson, Howard A. *The Patriation Minutes*. Edmonton: University of Alberta, Faculty of Law, Centre for Constitutional Studies, 2011.

LeSelva, Samuel V. *The Moral Foundations of Canadian Federalism: Paradoxes, Achievements, and Tragedies of Nationhood*. Montreal; Kingston, ON: McGill-Queen's University Press, 1996.

Levinson, Sanford. "How Many Times Has the United States Constitution Been Amended? (A) <26; (B) 26; (C) 27; (D) >27: Accounting for Constitutional Change." In *Responding to Imperfection: The Theory and Practice of Constitutional Amendment*, edited by Sanford Levinson, 13–36. Princeton, NJ: Princeton University Press, 1995.

Levy, Gary. "A Crisis not Made in a Day." In *Parliamentary Democracy in Crisis*, edited by Peter H. Russell and Lorne Sossin, 19–30. Toronto: University of Toronto Press, 2009.

L'Heureux-Dube, Claire. "The Dissenting Opinion: Voice of the Future?" *Osgoode Hall Law Journal* 38, no. 3 (2000): 495–517.

Lordon, Paul. *Crown Law*. Toronto: Butterworths, 1991.

Lusztig, Michael, "Constitutional Paralysis: Why Canadian Constitutional Initiatives Are Doomed to Fail." *Canadian Journal of Political Science* 27, no. 4 (1994): 747–71.

Macdonald, Nicholas A., and James W.J. Bowden. "No Discretion: On Prorogation and the Governor General." *Canadian Parliamentary Review* 34, no. 1 (2011): 7–16.

Macfarlane, Emmett. *Governing from the Bench: The Supreme Court of Canada and the Judicial Role*. Vancouver: UBC Press, 2013.

Macfarlane, Emmett. "Unsteady Architecture: Ambiguity, the Senate Reference, and the Future of Constitutional Amendment in Canada." *McGill Law Journal* 60, no. 4 (2015): 883–903.

MacKinnon, Frank. *The Crown in Canada*. Calgary: Glenbow-Alberta Institute, 1976.

Manfredi, Christopher P. "Strategic Behaviour and the Canadian Charter of Rights and Freedoms." In *The Myth of the Sacred: The Charter, the Courts, and the Politics of the Constitution in Canada*, edited by P. James, D. Abelson, and Michael Lusztig, 147–70. Montreal; Kingston, ON: McGill-Queen's University Press, 2002.

Manfredi, Christopher P., and Michael Lusztig. "Why Do Formal Amendments Fail?: An Institutional Design Analysis." *World Politics* 50, no. 3 (1999): 377–400.

Mathen, Carissima. "Constitutional Dialogue in Canada and the United States." *National Journal of Constitutional Law* 14, no. 3 (2003): 403–67.

Mathen, Carissima. "Dialogue Theory, Judicial Review, and Judicial Supremacy: A Comment on 'Charter Dialogue Revisited.'" *Osgoode Hall Law Journal* 45, no. 1 (2007): 125–46.

Mathen, Carissima. "'The question calls for an answer, and I propose to answer it': The Patriation Reference as Constitutional Method." *Supreme Court Law Review* (2d) 54 (2011): 143–66.

McCreery, Christopher. "Myth and Misunderstanding: The Origins and Meaning of the Letters Patent Constituting the Office of Governor General, 1947."

In *The Evolving Canadian Crown*, edited by Jennifer Smith and D. Michael Jackson, 31–54. Montreal; Kingston, ON: McGill-Queen's University Press, 2012.

McLean, Janet. *Searching for the State in British Legal Thought: Competing Conceptions of the Public Sphere*. Cambridge: Cambridge University Press, 2012.

Meekison, J. Peter. "The Amending Formula." *Queen's Law Journal* 8, nos. 1–2 (1982): 99–122.

Meekison, J. Peter. "Introduction." In *Constitutional Patriation: The Lougheed-Lévesque Correspondence*. Kingston, ON: Queen's University, Institute of Intergovernmental Relations, 1999.

Miller, Bradley W. "Origin Myth: The Persons Case, the Living Tree, and the New Originalism." In *The Challenge of Originalism*, edited by Grant Huscroft and Bradley Miller, 120–44. Cambridge: Cambridge University Press, 2011.

Monahan, Patrick. *Constitutional Law*, 2nd ed. Toronto: Irwin Law, 2002.

Monahan, Patrick. "The Law and Politics of Quebec Secession." *Osgoode Hall Law Journal* 33, no. 1 (1995): 1–33.

Monahan, Patrick, Michael J. Bryant, and Nancy C. Cote. "Coming to Terms with Plan B: Ten Principles Governing Secession." *C.D. Howe Institute Commentary* 83. Toronto: C.D. Howe Institute, June 1996.

Monahan, Patrick, and Byron Shaw. *Constitutional Law*, 4th ed. Toronto: Irwin Law, 2013.

Morin, Jacques-Yvan. "Une constitution nouvelle pour le Québec: le pourquoi, le contenu et le comment." *Revue québécoise de droit constitutionnel* 2 (2008): 5–15.

Morin, Jacques-Yvan, and José Woehrling. *Les constitutions du Canada et du Québec (du régime français à nos jours)*, 2nd ed., vol. 1. Montreal: Thémis, 1994.

Newman, Dwight. "The Bilateral Amending Formula as a Mechanism for the Entrenchment of Property Rights." *Constitutional Forum* 21, no. 2 (2013): 17–22.

Newman, Dwight. *Revisiting the Duty to Consult Aboriginal Peoples*. Saskatoon: Purich, 2014.

Newman, Dwight, and Lorelle Binnion. "The Exclusion of Property Rights from the *Charter*: Correcting the Historical Record." *Alberta Law Review* 52, no. 3 (2015): 543–66.

Newman, Warren J. "The Constitutional Status of the Supreme Court of Canada." *Supreme Court Law Review* (2d) (2009): 429–43.

Newman, Warren J. "Defining the 'Constitution of Canada' since 1982: The Scope of the Legislative Powers of Constitutional Amendment under Sections 44 and 45 of the *Constitution Act, 1982*." *Supreme Court Law Review* (2d) 22 (2003): 423–98.

Newman, Warren J. "'Grand Entrance Hall,' Back Door or Foundation Stone? The Role of Constitutional Principles in Constructing and Applying the Constitution of Canada." *Supreme Court Law Review* (2d) 14 (2001): 197–234.

Newman, Warren J. "Living with the Amending Procedures: Prospects for Future Constitutional Reform in Canada." In *A Living Tree: The Legacy of 1982 in Canada's Political Evolution*, edited by Graeme Mitchell et al., 747–80. Markham, ON: LexisNexis Canada, 2007.

Newman, Warren J. "Living with the Amending Procedures: Prospects for Future Constitutional Reform in Canada." *Supreme Court Law Review* (2d) 37 (2007): 383–416.

Newman, Warren J. "Of Dissolution, Prorogation, and Constitutional Law, Principle and Convention: Maintaining Fundamental Distinctions during a Parliamentary Crisis." *National Journal of Constitutional Law* 27 (2009): 217–29.

Newman, Warren J. "The Official Languages Act and the Constitutional and Legislative Recognition of Language Rights in Canada." In *Language and Governance*, edited by Colin Williams, 196–234. Cardiff: University of Wales Press, 2007.

Newman, Warren J. "Parliamentary Privilege, the Constitution and the Courts." *Ottawa Law Review* 39, no. 3 (2008): 573–609.

Newman, Warren J. "Putting One's Faith in a Higher Power: Supreme Law, the Senate Reform Reference, Legislative Authority and the Amending Procedures." *National Journal of Constitutional Law* 34, no. 2 (2015): 99–120.

Newman, Warren J. *The Quebec Secession Reference – The Rule of Law and the Position of the Attorney General of Canada*. Toronto: York University, Centre for Public Law and Public Policy, 1999.

O'Brien, Audrey, and Marc Bosc. *House of Commons Procedure and Practice*, 2nd ed. Cowansville, QC: Éditions Yvon Blais, 2009.

Oliver, Peter. "Canada, Quebec, and Constitutional Amendment." *University of Toronto Law Journal* 49, no. 4 (1999): 519–610.

Oliver, Peter. "Quebec and the Amending Formula: Protection, Promotion and Federalism." In *Accommodating Cultural Diversity*, edited by Stephen Tierney, 167–97. Abingdon, UK: Ashgate, 2007.

Pelletier, Benoît. "The Constitutional Requirements for Royal Morganatic Marriage." *McGill Law Journal* 50, no. 2 (2005): 265–84.

Pelletier, Benoît. "Les modalités de la modification de la constitution du Canada." *Revue juridique Themis* 33, no. 1 (1999): 1–58.

Pelletier, Benoît. *La modification constitutionnelle au Canada*. Scarborough, ON: Carswell, 1996.

Piersig, Elsa. "No Confidence in Non-Confidence Votes: Would the New Zealand Confidence Protocol or Constructive Non-Confidence Restore the Canadian Confidence Convention?" MA thesis, University of Calgary, 2014.

Plaxton, Michael, and Carissima Mathen. "Purposive Interpretation, Quebec and the Supreme Court Act." *Constitutional Forum* 22, no. 3 (2013): 15–25.

"Premiers' Conference, Ottawa, Ontario, April 16, 1981." In *Canada's Constitution Act 1982 & Amendments: A Documentary History*, vol. 2, edited by Anne F. Bayefsky. Toronto: McGraw-Hill Ryerson, 1989.

Rawlyk, George. "The Historical Framework of the Maritimes and the Problems of Confederation." In *Essential Readings in Canadian Constitutional Politics*, edited by Christian Leuprecht and Peter H. Russell, 87–95. Toronto: University of Toronto Press, 2011.

Régimbald, Guy, and Dwight Newman. *The Law of the Canadian Constitution*. Markham, ON: LexisNexis Canada, 2013.

Russell, Peter H. "Bold Statecraft, Questionable Jurisprudence." In *And No One Cheered: Federalism, Democracy and the Constitution Act*, edited by Keith G. Banting and Richard Simeon, 210–38. Toronto: Methuen, 1983.

Russell, Peter H. *Constitutional Odyssey: Can Canadians Become a Sovereign People?* 3rd ed. Toronto: University of Toronto Press, 2004.

Russell, Peter H. "Learning to Live with Minority Parliaments." In *Parliamentary Democracy in Crisis*, edited by Peter H. Russell and Lorne Sossin, 138–41. Toronto: University of Toronto Press, 2009.

Russell, Peter H. "The Patriation and Quebec Veto References: The Supreme Court Wrestles with the Political Part of the Constitution." *Supreme Court Law Review* (2d) 54 (2011): 69–76.

Russell, Peter H. "The Political Purposes of the Canadian Charter of Rights and Freedoms." *Canadian Bar Review* 61 (1983): 30–54.

Russell, Peter H. *Two Cheers for Minority Government: The Evolution of Canadian Parliamentary Democracy*. Toronto: Emond Montgomery, 2008.

Russell, Peter H., and Lorne Sossin, eds. *Parliamentary Democracy in Crisis*. Toronto: University of Toronto Press, 2009.

Sanders, Douglas E. "The Indian Lobby." In *And No One Cheered: Federalism, Democracy, and the Constitution Act*, edited by Keith G. Banting and Richard Simeon, 311–32. Toronto: Methuen, 1983.

Schwartz, Bryan. *First Principles, Second Thoughts*. Montreal: Institute for Research on Public Policy, 1986.

Scott, Stephen A. "The Canadian Constitutional Amendment Process." *Law and Contemporary Problems* 45, no. 4 (1982): 249–81.

Scott, Stephen A. "Pussycat, Pussycat or Patriation and New Constitutional Amendment Processes." *University of Western Ontario Law Review* 20 (1982): 247–306.

Sharman, Campbell. "The Strange Case of a Provincial Constitution: The British Columbia Constitutional Act." *Canadian Journal of Political Science* 17, no. 1 (1984): 87–108.

Smith, David E. *The Canadian Senate in Bicameral Perspective*. Toronto: University of Toronto Press, 2003.

Smith, David E. *Federalism and the Constitution of Canada*. Toronto: University of Toronto Press, 2010.

Smith, David E. "The Crown and the Constitution: Sustaining Democracy?" In *The Evolving Canadian Crown*, edited by Jennifer Smith and D. Michael Jackson. Montreal; Kingston, ON: McGill-Queen's University Press, 2012.

Smith, David E. *The Invisible Crown: The First Principle of Canadian Government*, 2nd ed. Toronto: University of Toronto Press, 2013.

Sneiderman, David. "Dual(ling) Charters: The Harmonics of Rights in Canada and Quebec." *Ottawa Law Review* 24, no. 1 (1992): 235–63.

Snell, James G., and Vaughan Frederick. *The Supreme Court of Canada: History of the Institution*. Toronto: University of Toronto Press, 1985.

St-Hilaire, Maxime. "The Codification of Human Rights in Canada." *Revue de Droit, Université de Sherbrooke* 42 (2012): 505–69.

Stein, Michael B. "Improving the Process of Constitutional Reform in Canada: Lessons from the Meech Lake and Charlottetown Constitutional Rounds." *Canadian Journal of Political Science* 30, no. 2 (1997): 307–38.

Strayer, Barry L. *Canada's Constitutional Revolution*. Edmonton: University of Alberta Press, 2013.

Studin, Irvin. *The Strategic Constitution: Understanding Canadian Power in the World*. Vancouver: UBC Press, 2014.

Swinton, Katherine. "Amending the Canadian Constitution: Lessons from Meech Lake." *University of Toronto Law Journal* 42, no. 2 (1992): 139–69.

Thomas, Paul. "Comparing the Lawmaking Roles of the Senate and the House of Commons." In *Protecting Canadian Democracy: The Senate You Never Knew*, edited by Serge Joyal, 189–228. Montreal; Kingston, ON: McGill-Queen's University Press, 2003.

Tremblay, Guy. "La portée élargie de la procédure bilatérale de modification de la constitution." *Revue générale de droit* 41, no. 2 (2011): 417–49.

Tribe, Laurence H. *American Constitutional Law*, 2nd ed. New York: Foundation Press, 1988.

Turp, Daniel. "La constitution québécoise: une perspective historique." *Revue québécoise de droit constitutionnel* 2 (2008): 16–71.

Tushnet, Mark. *Taking the Constitution Away from the Courts*. Princeton, NJ: Princeton University Press, 1999.

Walters, Mark D. "Written Constitutions and Unwritten Constitutionalism." In *Expounding the Constitution: Essays in Constitutional Theory*, edited by Grant Huscroft, 245–76. New York: Cambridge University Press, 2008.

Webber, Jeremy. *Reimagining Canada: Language, Culture, Community, and the Canadian Constitution*. Montreal; Kingston, ON: McGill-Queen's University Press, 1994.

Whyte, John D. "Senate Reform: What Does the Constitution Say?" In *The Democratic Dilemma: Reforming the Canadian Senate*, edited by Jennifer Smith, 97–109. Montreal; Kingston, ON: McGill-Queen's University Press, 2009.

Wiktor, Christian L., and Guy Tremblay, eds. *Constitutions of Canada: Federal and Provincial*. Dobbs Ferry, NY: Oceana, 1987.

Winterton, George. *Parliament, the Executive and the Governor-General: A Constitutional Analysis*. Melbourne: Melbourne University Press, 1983.

Wiseman, Nelson. "Clarifying Provincial Constitutions." *National Journal of Constitutional Law* 6 (1996): 269–94.

Wiseman, Nelson. "In Search of a Quebec Constitution." *Revue québécoise de droit constitutionnel* 2 (2008): 130–149.

Young, Robert A. *The Struggle for Quebec: From Referendum to Referendum?* Montreal; Kingston, ON: McGill-Queen's University Press, 1999.

Contributors

Dennis Baker, Associate Professor, Department of Political Science, University of Guelph.

Patrick Baud, BCL/LLB student, McGill University.

Erin Crandall, Assistant Professor, Department of Politics, Acadia University.

Adam Dodek, Associate Professor, Faculty of Law, University of Ottawa.

Mark D. Jarvis, Doctoral Candidate, School of Public Administration, University of Victoria.

Rainer Knopff, Professor, Department of Political Science, University of Calgary.

Philippe Lagassé, Associate Professor and Barton Chair in International Affairs, Norman Paterson School of International Affairs, Carleton University.

Emmett Macfarlane, Assistant Professor, Department of Political Science, University of Waterloo.

Carissima Mathen, Associate Professor, Faculty of Law, University of Ottawa.

Dwight Newman, Professor and Canada Research Chair, College of Law, University of Saskatchewan.

Warren J. Newman, Senior General Counsel, Constitutional, Administrative & International Law Section, Department of Justice, Canada.

Kate Puddister, Assistant Professor, Department of Political Science, University of Guelph.

Emmanuelle Richez, Assistant Professor, Department of Political Science, University of Windsor.

Christa Scholtz, Associate Professor, Department of Political Science, McGill University.

Nadia Verrelli, Assistant Professor, Department of Political Science, Laurentian University.

Index